THE CYNIC EPISTLES

SBL

Society of Biblical Literature

Sources for Biblical Study

Wayne A. Meeks
Editor

Number 12
THE CYNIC EPISTLES

THE CYNIC EPISTLES

A Study Edition

Edited by
Abraham J. Malherbe

Translated by
Benjamin Fiore, S. J.
Ronald F. Hock
Anne M. McGuire
Stanley K. Stowers
David R. Worley

Society of Biblical Literature
Atlanta

THE CYNIC EPISTLES
A Study Edition

Edited by
Abraham J. Malherbe

Library of Congress Cataloging-in-Publication Data

Main entry under title:

The Cynic epistles.

> (Sources for Biblical Study ; v. 12)
> Greek and English.
> Includes bibliographical references and index.
> CONTENTS: The epistles of Anarcharsis.—The epistles of Crates.—The epistles of Diogenes.—The epistles of Heraclitus.—The epistles of Socrates and the Socratics.
> 1. Cynicism—Collected works. I. Malherbe, Abraham J. II. Series.

B508.C93   183'.4   77-21619
ISBN 0-89130-151-8

Printed in the United States of America
on acid-free paper

∞

TABLE OF CONTENTS

ACKNOWLEDGMENTS

We wish to extend our thanks to the Akademie Verlag for permission to use the texts of the letters of Anacharsis and of Socrates and the Socratics, and to La Nuova Italia Editrice for permission to use the text of the letters of Heraclitus. We are grateful to Professor Wayne A. Meeks for including this collection in the Sources for Biblical Study series, and to Professor Robert W. Funk and his efficient staff at Scholars Press for producing the volume. A special word of thanks is due Joann Burnich of Scholars Press for her considerable contribution in preparing the manuscript for printing.

INTRODUCTION

There exists no collection of Cynic texts on the scope of those of the Stoics and Epicureans.[1] Editions of a few individual authors are available, for example, of Antisthenes[2] and Teles,[3] but the fragments of others, such as Crates, Demetrius and Oenomaus of Gadara, have not been collected and published in an easily usable form.[4] The editions that do exist are not readily available, and important texts have not been translated into English. The result is that Cynicism is most frequently studied on the basis of Musonius Rufus,[5] Epictetus,[6] and Dio Chrysostom,[7] whose works are easily accessible in modern translation, but whose views are heavily Stoicized. They do, however, preserve Cynic traditions, as does Lucian,[8] whose burlesques unfortunately provide a view of Cynicism shared by the ancient public and many modern writers. The Cynic material in Diogenes Laertius[9] is mostly anecdotal, and Julian's writings[10] on the Cynics come from a much later period and have a strong apologetic bias which requires that they be used with great care as sources for Cynicism.

The importance of Stoicism and Cynicism for the study of Christian origins has long been recognized.[11] Johannes Weiss's insistence that the student of the New Testament should know Seneca, Epictetus, Lucian, Musonius and Marcus Aurelius intimately, and that the New Testament should be read with von Arnim's collection of Stoic texts at hand,[12] reflected the general interest in the moral philosophers around the turn of the century. During that period the first work was done on those literary forms found in the New Testament which were thought to have been derived from Stoicism and Cynicism, viz. the diatribe, the *Haustafel*, the catalogues of virtues and vices, and interest was shown in the ideal philosopher as in some way a counterpart of the Christian apostle. It was primarily the Stoic

sources cited by Weiss that were brought into the discussion, and contemporary scholars still largely depend on
them for their understanding of what is "Cynic-Stoic," a
hyphenation that has contributed to obscurity about what
is Cynic and what is Stoic. Little awareness is shown of
the differences, not only between Stoics and Cynics, but
among Cynics themselves. It is ironic that scholars who
are at pains to sketch in great detail the diversity of
early Christianity, should be content to be highly selec-
tive in the sources they use, and to homogenize these
sources when they delineate the cultural and religious
context which they consider important for making that diversity intelligible. Thus Walter Schmithals, for example,
although aware of the sources which give an impression of
the diversity of religious emissaries in Hellenism, arbi-
trarily selects Epictetus's presentation of the "Cynic-
Stoic sage" as the preeminent source, and confidently
asserts that in addition to it "it is not rewarding to
consider other sources."[13] What is stated explicitly by
Schmithals is assumed by others.[14] Greater precision is
required if we are to gain a realistic picture of the
philosophical and religious context of early Christianity,
and for that a better understanding of Cynicism in the
early Empire is necessary.

A valuable but neglected source for the history of
Cynicism is the Cynic letters. Most of these letters come
from the Augustan age and purport to have been written by
such ancient worthies of the sect as Antisthenes, Diogenes
and Crates and by such non-Cynics as Anacharsis, Heraclitus, Hippocrates and Socrates and his followers, all of
whom are represented as advancing Cynic views. The value
of these letters lies in the fact that they are Cynic
writings which provide evidence of Cynicism at the time
when it was experiencing a reawakening. While a rhetorical
interest can be discerned in some of the letters, they are
much more than rhetorical school exercises, as has sometimes been thought. That some were peculiarly suited to

propaganda would seem to be clear. Others reflect the
diversity which existed within Cynicism, and reveal the
issues which were subjects of discussion and debate within
the school. The picture of Cynicism that emerges from the
letters is of a rich diversity that compels us to be more
circumspect in using the Stoic writers as authorities on
Cynicism.

One reason for the neglect of the Cynic letters has
been that they have not been readily available. The most
convenient collection of the texts, with a Latin translation, is still that of Richard Hercher, *Epistolographi
Graeci* (Paris, 1873), reprinted in 1965. With the exception of the letters attributed to Heraclitus, no English
translations of the collections have been published. The
modest aim of the present volume is to introduce the letters to a larger audience with the hope of stimulating
research in the field. The letters included in this
volume represent the main body, but not all, of the Cynic
letters. Some of the letters attributed to Hippocrates
could, for example, have been included, but what has been
included is representative and should serve adequately as
an introduction to the material.

The volume makes no pretensions to being a critical
edition. The best recent text has in each case been
printed, but without a textual apparatus. To have included an apparatus would have made the manuscript unnecessarily complicated for the purpose the contributors
had in mind. Serious students will want to consult the
critical editions whose texts are reprinted here.

The translators are aware of the inadequacy of their
efforts for which the corrupt condition of the text and at
times difficult or unintelligible Greek are partly responsible. Except for Attridge's translation of the epistles
of Heraclitus, which appeared after Worley's had been
completed, these are the only available English translations of the various collections. Should the translators'
attempt evoke more accurate and felicitous renderings than

those presented here, one of their goals will have been
reached.

The introductions have been kept brief. Their aim
has been to inform readers of the main issues touching the
letters without unnecessarily intruding personal views.
When bibliographical information is readily available
elsewhere it has not been repeated here. Again, the
serious student is urged to consult the sources on which
this volume is based. Hock is responsible for the introduction to the letters of Crates; Malherbe wrote the rest
and compiled the indices.

Notes

[1]The collection of fragments by F. W. A. Mullach,
Fragmenta philosophorum graecorum I (Paris, 1881) 261-395,
although the most extensive available, does not claim to
be complete.

[2]*Antisthenis fragmenta* (ed. by F. D. Caizzi; Milan,
1966).

[3]*Teletis reliquiae* (ed. by O. Hense; Tübingen,
1909); *Teles (The Cynic Teacher)* (ed. and trans. by Edward
O'Neil; Missoula, Montana, 1977).

[4]Some of the fragments attributed to Crates and
Oenomaus are included in Mullach's collection, and the
fragments of Crates are collected in *Poetarum graecorum
fragmenta* III.1: *Poetarum philosophorum fragmenta* (ed. by
H. Diels; Berlin, 1901) 207-23.

[5]*C. Musonii Rufi: Reliquiae* (ed. by O. Hense; Leipzig, 1905). A useful edition consisting of introduction,
Hense's text, and English translation, is that by Cora E.
Lutz, *Musonius Rufus: "The Roman Socrates"* (Yale Classical Studies 10; New Haven, 1947).

[6]*Epicteti dissertationes ab Arriani digestae* (ed. by
H. Schenkl; 2nd edition; Leipzig, 1916). Uncritical text
with English translation available in the Loeb Classical
Library.

[7]*Dionis Prusaensis quem vocant Chrysostomum quae
exstant* (ed. by H. von Arnim; Berlin, 1893-96). Uncritical text with English translation available in the Loeb
Classical Library.

[8]*Luciani Samosatensis opera* (ed. by C. Jacobitz;
Leipzig, 1896). Uncritical text with English translation
available in the Loeb Classical Library.

[9]*Diogenis Laertii: Vitae philosophorum* (ed. by H. S. Long; Oxford Classical Texts; Oxford, 1964). Uncritical text with English translation available in the Loeb Classical Library.

[10]*L'Empereur Julien: Ouevres complètes* (ed. by J. Bidez, G. Rochefort and C. Lacombrade; Collection des Universités de France; Paris, 1932-64). Uncritical text with English translation available in the Loeb Classical Library.

[11]See Abraham J. Malherbe, "Hellenistic Moralists and the New Testament," in *Aufstieg und Niedergang der römischen Welt* III (ed. by H. Temporini; Berlin, 1977).

[12]J. Weiss, *Die Aufgaben der neutestamentlichen Wissenschaft in der Gegenwart* (Göttingen, 1908) 4, 11, 55.

[13]W. Schmithals, *The Office of Apostle in the Early Church* (Nashville, 1969) 111.

[14]D. Georgi, *Die Gegner des Paulus im 2. Korintherbrief. Studien zur religiösen Propaganda in der Spätantike* (Neukirchen/Vluyn, 1964) 32ff., 110f., 187ff., 193ff. is a prime example of homogenization.

1. The Epistles of Anacharsis

Anacharsis, a Scythian prince, visited Greece in the early sixth century B.C. in a quest for wisdom. As a type of the "noble savage" he captured the imagination of the Greeks, and was alternatively viewed as a lover of all things Greek and a despiser of all the Greeks except the Spartans. The latter view came to prevail.

The ten letters attributed to Anacharsis are certainly spurious. It has traditionally been thought that in their present form they date from the early Empire[1] or, since Cicero, *Tusc.* 5, 90 (written in 45 B.C.) translates *Ep.* 5, from early in the first century B.C., which would make them, together with some of the letters attributed to Hippocrates and Diogenes, the earliest extant Cynic letters.[2] U. von Wilamowitz-Moellendorff, also arguing on the basis of Cicero's acquaintance with *Ep.* 5, was led to the third century B.C. as the date of composition of that letter.[3] Recently F. H. Reuters has contended that all the letters, with the exception of *Ep.* 10, which was written by a different author, were written in the third century B.C.[4]

Reuters's determination of the letters' date depends on their language and style. He finds *Epp.* 1-9 to be written in Koine rather than Attic, and identifies many words used in them that do not appear before the third century B.C. On the other hand, there are no traces of Atticism in these letters. They must therefore have been written before the second century B.C., when Atticism arose as a reaction to Asianism. Of particular importance to Reuters is the use of σολοικίζειν in *Ep.* 1 with the meaning of inarticulate speech rather than grammatically incorrect speech. The word is not found with that meaning after 250 B.C., which is then taken to be the *terminus ante quem* for the first nine letters. Reuters thus decides on 300-250 B.C. as their probable date.

The letters are generally regarded as showing Cynic tendencies. The Cynics, who criticized culture and

civilization, made Anacharsis, who was uncultured by Greek
standards, a preacher of their own doctrines. If these
letters are indeed from the third century B.C., they would
be a valuable witness to the existence of Cynicism at the
time, in contradiction to the theory that it had died out
by then only to revive again in the early Empire.[5] They
would be parallel sources to those letters attributed to
Diogenes which circulated around 200 B.C., but which have
not been preserved.[6]

Ep. 10 is transmitted by Diogenes Laertius (1.105),
who knows only this letter. From the manuscript tradition
also it is clear that this letter circulated separately.
Furthermore, its language, an attempt at Ionic, shows
that an author different from that of the first nine wrote
it. It is untouched by the Koine, and Reuters with some
hesitancy dates it in the fifth or fourth century B.C. He
is inclined to think that it also is Cynic.

Notes

[1]W. Schmid, "Anacharsis," *Pauly-Wissowa Realencyklopädie* I (1894) 2017-18; G. A. Gerhard, *Phoinix von Kolophon*
(Berlin/Leipzig, 1909) 99, 172.

[2]J. Sykutris, "Epistolographie," *Pauly-Wissowa Realencyklopädie*, Supp. 5 (1931) 210f.; cf. O. Gigon, "Kynikerbriefe," *Lexikon der Alten Welt* (Zurich/Stuttgart, 1965)
1658f.

[3]U. von Wilamowitz-Moellendorff, *Commentariolum grammaticum* III (Göttingen, 1889) 28f.

[4]F. H. Reuters, *De Anacharsidis epistulis* (Inaugural
dissertation; Bonn, 1957) and *Die Briefe des Anacharsis*
(Schriften und Quellen der Alten Welt 14; Berlin, 1963).

[5]For the theory that Cynicism had died out, see J. F.
Marcks, *Symbola critica ad epistolographos Graecos* (Dis-
sertation; Bonn, 1883) 13f.; E. Zeller, *Die Philosophie
der Griechen* II.1 (6th ed.; Leipzig, 1922) 286ff.; M.
Pohlenz, *Die Stoa* I (2nd ed.; Göttingen, 1959) 170f. In
opposition to the theory, see R. Helm, "Kynismus," *Pauly-
Wissowa Realencyklopädie* XII (1924) 5; D. R. Dudley, *A
History of Cynicism* (London, 1937) 117ff., 187f.; A. J.
Malherbe, "Cynicism," *Interpreter's Dictionary of the
Bible*, Supp. (1976) 201-203.

[6]Cf. W. Capelle, *De cynicorum epistulis* (Dissertation; Göttingen, 1896) 58; Gerhard, *Phoinix*, 171f.

Bibliography

Text and Translation

Reuters, F. H. *De Anacharsidis epistulis*. Inaugural dissertation, Bonn, 1957. Critical edition with full textual apparatus; extensive treatment of the textual tradition and printed editions (with Latin translations); full commentary.

_____. *Die Briefe des Anacharsis*. Schriften und Quellen der Alten Welt 14. Berlin, 1963. Based on his dissertation; introduction, critical text, German translation, brief commentary; text printed in this volume is used by permission of Akademie Verlag.

For criticism of Reuters's text and translation, see the review by E. Heitsch in *Gnomon* 36 (1964) 144-46.

Studies

Tollens, F. J. P. *Quaestiones Anacharsideae*. Dissertation, Leiden, 1843.

Westermann, A. *Commentationum criticarum in scriptores graecos* III. Leipzig, 1851. Pp. 6ff.

Hercher, R. "Zu griechischen Prosaikern." *Hermes* 6 (1872) 55-67.

von Wilamowitz-Moellendorff, U. *Commentariolum grammaticum* III. Göttingen, 1889. Pp. 28f.

Heinze, R. "Anacharsis." *Philologus* 50 (1891) 458-68.

Schafstaedt, H. *De Diogenis epistulis*. Dissertation, Göttingen, 1892.

Norden, E. "Zu den Briefen des Heraklit und der Kyniker." *Jahrbücher für classische Philologie*. Supp. 19 (1893) 386ff.

Schmid, W. "Anacharsis." *Pauly-Wissowa Realencyklopädie* I (1894) 2017-18.

Praechter, K. "Die Berner Handschrift der Anacharsisbriefe." *Philologus* 58 (1899) 252-57.

Geffcken, J. *Kynika und Verwandtes*. Heidelberg, 1909.

Gerhard, G. A. *Phoinix von Kolophon*. Leipzig/Berlin,
    1909. Pp. 99, 172.

Minns, Ellis H. *Scythians and Greeks*. Cambridge, 1913.

von der Mühll, P. In *Festgabe Hugo Blümner*. Zurich,
    1914. Pp. 432f.

Praechter, K. "Der fünfte Anacharsisbrief." *Hermes* 56
    (1921) 422-31.

Ueberweg, F. and Praechter, K. *Philosophie des Altertums*.
    Berlin, 1926. Pp. 160, 504.

Sykutris, J. "Epistolographie." *Pauly-Wissowa Realency-
    klopädie*, Supp. 5 (1931) 210f.

Gigon, O. "Kynikerbriefe." *Lexikon der Alten Welt*.
    Zurich/Stuttgart, 1965. Pp. 1658f.

Muehl, M. "Der 2. und 9. Anacharsisbrief und Isokrates."
    L'Antiquité Classique 40 (1971) 111-20.

Attridge, H. W. *First Century Cynicism in the Epistles of
    Heraclitus*. Harvard Theological Studies 29.
    Missoula, Montana, 1976. Pp. 41ff.

2. The Epistles of Crates

Diogenes Laertius (6.98) reports in the third century A.D. that there existed a collection of letters written by Crates of Thebes (*flor*. fourth-third century B.C.),
a pupil of Diogenes and a Cynic philosopher of considerable influence.[1] That this collection, distinguished for
its philosophical content as well as for its literary
style, is not the same as that collection of thirty-six
letters attributed to Crates and included in this volume,
has long been recognized.[2]

Given the pseudonymous character of the extant letters, the questions of their authorship and dating have
been answered on the basis of the variety of similarities
between the letters attributed to Crates and those to
Diogenes. The similarities between Crates, *Ep*. 6 and
Diogenes, *Ep*. 30.2, and between Crates, *Ep*. 8 and Diogenes,
Ep. 9, were the first to be observed.[3] Later, more were
noted,[4] and finally only Crates, *Epp*. 24 and 25 could not
be related, either in language or content, to one or more
of the letters of Diogenes.[5]

At first, the explanation of these similarities was
that the same author had written both collections of letters,[6] but later scholars, equally aware of differences
between the collections, such as the opposing views regarding Odysseus in Crates, *Ep*. 19 and Diogenes, *Epp*. 7
and 34, rejected this explanation,[7] and proposed instead
a theory of literary dependence and specifically a dependence of the Crates letters on the Diogenes letters. With
this explanation, moreover, the question of dating is par-
tially resolved: the Crates letters are later than the
Diogenes letters,[8] which means that the Crates letters are
to be dated at the earliest in the first or second century
A.D.

Furthermore, even within the Crates letters many differences between individual letters were observed, which
has complicated the question regarding authorship. Crates,
Ep. 35, regarded as more Stoic than Cynic, was the first

letter to be separated from the others,[9] and a variety of
views were detected in those letters dealing with begging.[10]
Conversely, Capelle found *Epp.* 27 and 32 too similar in
theme and treatment to *Epp.* 26 and 30, respectively, to
have been written by the same author, and suggested that
the former were rhetorical exercises based on the latter.[11]
Consequently, he counted three authors: one for *Epp.* 1-26,
28, (29?), 30, 31, 33, (34?) and (36?); a second for *Epp.*
27 and 32; and a third for *Ep.* 35.[12] Olivieri's count is
higher, perhaps a half dozen authors.[13] All the letters
of Crates are paraenetic, except for *Epp.* 20 and 34, which
are narrative, and *Epp.* 7, 24, and 25, which are invective.[14]

While these conclusions are generally accepted, the
investigation needs to move beyond the question of the
literary relationship between the letters of Diogenes and
Crates. Many of the similarities between the letters in
the two collections are striking and significant, but many
others are not. The method of source criticism should be
supplemented by a *traditionsgeschichtliche* study of these
letters and other Cynic writings.[15] Such a study may further clarify matters regarding authorship and date, and
will certainly contribute to a better understanding of the
letters.

Notes

[1]Cf. Diog. Laert. 6.85-98, and see J. Stenzel,
"Krates," *Pauly-Wissowa Realencyklopädie* XI (1922) 1625-
31; D. R. Dudley, *A History of Cynicism* (London, 1937)
42ff.; R. Hoistad, *Cynic Hero and Cynic King* (Uppsala,
1948) 126ff.

[2]M. Boissonade, "Notice des lettres de Crates le
Cynique contenus dans le manuscrit 483 du Vatican,"
*Notices et Extraits des Manuscrits de la Bibliothèque du
Roi* XI/2 (1827) 1f., 5, and all scholars since.

[3]Ibid., 14; J. F. Marcks, *Symbola critica ad epistolographos Graecos* (Dissertation; Bonn, 1883) 17.

[4]W. Capelle, *De cynicorum epistulis* (Dissertation;
Göttingen, 1896) 53f.

[5]A. Olivieri, "Le epistole del Pseudo-Cratete,"
Rivista di filologia 27 (1899) 406-21.

[6]Boissonade, "Notice des lettres de Crates," 14.

[7]See Capelle, *De cynicorum epistulis*, 53; E. Norden,
"Beiträge zur Geschichte der griechischen Philosophie,"
Jahrbücher für classische Philologie, Supp. 19 (1893)
393ff.

[8]Crates, *Ep.* 8 answers Diogenes, *Ep.* 9; either
Crates, *Ep.* 6 knew Diogenes, *Ep.* 30 (37), or both reflect
a late vocabulary; Crates, *Epp.* 20 and 21 appear to have
known Diogenes, *Epp.* 6 and 12 respectively.

[9]Marcks, *Symbola critica*, 17-21; Capelle, *De
cynicorum epistulis*, 49; Olivieri, "Pseudo-Cratete," 411.

[10]Olivieri, "Pseudo-Cratete," 417, 421. *Epp.* 2, 17,
22, 26, and 27 deal with begging, on which see Ronald F.
Hock, *The Working Apostle: An Examination of Paul's Means
of Livelihood* (Yale Ph.D. dissertation; New Haven, 1974).

[11]Capelle, *De cynicorum epistulis*, 50f.

[12]Ibid., 49-51.

[13]Olivieri, "Pseudo-Cratete," 421.

[14]Capelle, *De cynicorum epistulis*, 49.

[15]For the method applied to a Cynic tradition, see
Ronald F. Hock, "Simon the Shoemaker as an Ideal Cynic,"
Greek, Roman, and Byzantine Studies 17 (1976) 41-53.

Bibliography

Boissonade, M. "Notice des lettres de Crates le Cynique
    contenus dans le manuscrit 483 du Vatican." *Notices
    et Extraits des Manuscrits de la Bibliothèque du Roi*
    XI/2 (1827) 1-46. Introduction, text, French trans-
    lation and brief commentary.

Hercher, R. *Epistolographi Graeci*. Paris, 1873. The
    most recent critical text with Latin translation;
    text is printed in the present volume.

Studies

Marcks, J. F. *Symbola critica ad epistolographos Graecos*.
    Dissertation, Bonn, 1883. Pp. 17-20.

Dümmler, F. *Akademika*. Giessen, 1889. Pp. 209f.

Nauck, A. "Analecta critica." *Hermes* 24 (1889) 447-72.

Susemihl, F. *Geschichte der griechischen Litteratur in der Alexandrinerzeit*. Leipzig, 1891. I, 29f., 43f.; II, 600.

Norden, E. "Beiträge zur Geschichte der griechischen Philosophie." *Jahrbücher für classische Philologie*. Supp. 19 (1893) 393ff.

Capelle, W. *De cynicorum epistulis*. Dissertation, Göttingen, 1896. Esp. pp. 49-62.

Olivieri, A. "Le epistole del Pseudo-Cratete." *Rivista di filologia* 27 (1899) 406-21.

Helm, R. *Lucian und Menipp*. Leipzig/Berlin, 1906. Pp. 241, 243, and passim.

Gerhard, G. A. *Phoinix von Kolophon*. Leipzig/Berlin, 1909. Pp. 128, 142, 166, and passim.

Shorey, P. "Emendation of Crates, *Epist*. XIX." *Classical Philology* 4 (1909) 323.

Gerhard, G. A. "Zur Legende vom Kyniker Diogenes." *Archiv für Religionswissenschaft* 15 (1912) 388-408.

Gomperz, T. *Griechische Denker*. 4th edition. Berlin/ Leipzig, 1925. Esp. II, 546.

Ueberweg, F. and Praechter, K. *Philosophie des Altertums*. Berlin, 1926. Pp. 160, 504f., 64*.

Dudley, D. R. *A History of Cynicism*. London, 1937. Pp. 123f.

Pianko, G. "Kratos z Teb, cynik i parodysta." *Meander* 9 (1954) 203-29.

Gigon, O. "Kynikerbriefe." *Lexikon der Alten Welt*. Zurich/Stuttgart, 1965. Pp. 1658f.

Caizzi, F. C. *Antisthenis Fragmenta*. Milan, 1966. Passim.

Dörrie, H. "Krates." *Der kleine Pauly* III (1969) 327f.

Criscuolo, U. "Cratete di Tebe e la tradizione cinica." *Maia* 22 (1970) 360-67.

Hock, Ronald F. *The Working Apostle: An Examination of Paul's Means of Livelihood*. Yale Ph.D. dissertation, New Haven, 1974.

3. The Epistles of Diogenes

Epictetus (4.1.29-31, 156) and Julian (7.212D) refer
to letters written by Diogenes of Sinope (4th century
B.C.), and Diogenes Laertius (6.80) gives a catalogue of
Diogenes' letters which Sotion (ca. 200 B.C.) had regarded
as genuine. The letters they refer to were part of a
pseudepigraphic literature ascribed to Diogenes that ex-
erted great influence in the period between Teles and
Philo, but those letters are no longer extant.[1] The fifty-
one letters included in this volume come from a later
period.

Boissonade demonstrated that these letters were not
written by Diogenes, and he has been followed in this
judgment by all scholars since.[2] Marcks further showed,
on the basis of historical references in them, that *Ep.* 31
must have been written a long time after 200 B.C., and *Ep.*
19 shortly after 28 B.C.[3] Research since then has primarily been concerned with identifying individual letters
or groups of letters which seem to belong together.

Capelle was the first to provide extensive evidence
that all the letters were not written by the same author.[4]
He made his determination primarily on the basis of three
criteria: style, content, and *Tendenz*. Some letters, for
example, are written in a rhetorical style, while others
are not, only some contain epistolary greetings, while
some are hortatory and others invective. As to subject
matter, some are anecdotal and others not. When letters
are similar in subject or content, he assigned them to
different authors, e.g. *Epp.* 40 and 29, 7 and 34, 6 and 13.
Conversely, when they betray different philosophical tendencies or contradict each other, they were assigned to
different authors, e.g. *Epp.* 25 and 39, 7 and 30, 45 and 5.
Using such criteria, Capelle identified the following
groups:

  1. *Epp.* 8, 30, 31, 33, 35-38 are related to one another
     by their anecdotal matter and non-rhetorical style,
     which suggests that they were written by the same

author. The same author perhaps also wrote *Epp.* 3,
9-12, (26), 44, 47, (34). Accepting Marcks's date
for *Ep.* 31, Capelle dates it, and thus the other letters in the group, to the first century B.C.

2. *Epp.* 1, 2, 4-7 come from another author.

3. *Epp.* 13-18, 20, (21), 22-25, 27, 32, 41-43, 46, 48-51
   were written by a third author. *Ep.* 16 alone was
   known to Diogenes Laertius (6.23), and probably to
   his source, so it and the rest of its group should be
   dated no later than the end of the second century or
   the beginning of the third century A.D.[5]

4. *Epp.* 19, 28, 29, 39, 40, (43, 45) were written by
   different individuals over a long period of time.
   Thus, again accepting Marcks's judgment, *Ep.* 19 was
   written shortly after 28 B.C., while others of the
   group may be as late as the fourth century, for example, *Ep.* 39, which is heavily influenced by Plato-
   nism, probably at a time when Cynicism was losing its
   popularity.

With some exceptions,[6] the letters were not written as
rhetorical exercises, but as Cynic propaganda.

Kurt von Fritz was skeptical of the possibility to
determine authorship on the basis of the contents of the
letters, and argued that the form of the letters was more
decisive.[7] By form he did not understand epistolary form,
properly speaking, but rather drew attention to other
characteristics of the letters. He concentrated on *Epp.*
28-40, which are distinguished from the others by their
length, and which for the greater part also seem to belong
together. Von Fritz identified a strong Socratic element
in these letters. *Epp.* 31, 33, 35-39 contain long dialogues in which Diogenes uses a Socratic method of questioning which is absent from the anecdotes in Diogenes
Laertius. Socratic influence in language and style (irony)
can also be detected. The letters place Diogenes in Olympia; he thus appears as a wandering Cynic, a figure we
come to know under the Empire. *Ep.* 29, which appears to

be cited by *Ep*. 40, is especially important to von Fritz.
It bears a strong similarity to Socrates, *Ep*. 12,[8] which
was part of an epistolary novel consisting of Socrates,
Epp. 8, 9, 12, 13.[9] *Ep*. 29 uses this epistolary novel
which must have belonged to a larger collection of Socratic letters, whose purpose was to present the Socratics as
in contact with each other. *Ep*. 29 could not have belonged to this collection, since it is too similar to
Socrates, *Ep*. 12, and does not belong to the Socratic
circle. But the contact that it does have with this Socratic literature is further evidence to von Fritz of the
influence of the latter on it. As to its content, *Ep*. 39
is the most Socratic of all the letters. It sounds like a
short paraphrase of the *Phaedo*, and has nothing to do with
the Cynicism of Diogenes. Thus, in *Epp*. 29-40 one sees a
kind of "Unterhaltungsliteratur" which is more concerned
with the writings of the Socratics than is usually thought.

      Von Fritz was able to identify Socratic elements in
all the letters of his group with the exception of *Ep*. 28,
which he apparently felt obliged to include in the group
because of its length. As he had in the case of Heraclitus (*Epp*. 4, 7 and 9), Jacob Bernays had assigned this
letter as well to a Christian, or most likely, a Jewish
author, and drawn attention to the parallels between it
and Heraclitus, *Ep*. 7.[10] Despite the fact that Bernays's
views had been refuted,[11] von Fritz remained uncertain on
the point, and maintained that the vocabulary of the letter shows that it was written in an "Oriental-Christian"
atmosphere which is also reflected in *Ep*. 45.[12]

      Attempts have also been made to separate the letters
into different groups on the basis of the textual tradition. Thus Gercke surmised that there may have been four
groups consisting of *Epp*. 1-17, 18-29, 30-40, and 41-51.[13]
Most recently, Victor Emeljanow has returned to the textual tradition to identify more than one author.[14] He is
not satisfied with the attempts to group the letters according to thought patterns or types in order to identify

the writers, yet, modifying von Fritz's results, does con-
clude that *Epp*. 30-40 show an awareness of Socratic dialogue, a preference for Socratic idiom, a late-Hellenistic
vocabulary, and a view of Diogenes as a wandering preacher,
features that set them apart from the other letters. In
addition, *Epp*. 1-29 show some characteristics that set
them apart: they are simpler in statement, shorter, less
explanatory, and have a different characterization from
those that follow.[15]

These findings are confirmed for Emeljanow by the
textual tradition, which reveals at least two, and possibly three strands. There was in existence an early collection, consisting of *Epp*. 1-29. Some manuscripts contain
only these letters. The collection dated from the first
century B.C. or even earlier. That Diogenes Laertius cites
Ep. 16, and that many of the anecdotes he records form the
core of a large number of these letters, are taken to be
significant. A second collection, consisting of *Epp*. 30-
40, was composed around the second century A.D. by a
writer who had the first collection in mind, but published
his own separately. A third collection, consisting of *Epp*.
41-51, could possibly have existed. In a sense the letters of this collection hark back to the earlier letters,
but their harsher tone and the absence of any anecdotal
origin of the letters suggest a third collection. That
there appear to be duplications in *Epp*. 29, 40:7 and 34
further suggest that there was more than one author.

The letters have been regarded as the work of three
or four untalented rhetoricians who were content, for the
most part, to reproduce or develop the themes of the Stoic
diatribe as school exercises,[16] and this has led to their
neglect. It is much more likely, however, that they were
composed as Cynic propaganda, to justify the Cynic *modus
vivendi*, and perhaps to offset the picture of Cynics we
find in such authors as Lucian.[17] The value of the letters lie, not only in the way they create an epistolary
literature out of anecdotal material,[18] but in their

witness to the development and diversity of Cynicism, and
to its relationship to other philosophical schools, especially Stoicism.[19]

Notes

[1]Cf. W. Capelle, *De cynicorum epistulis* (Dissertation; Göttingen, 1896) 58; G. A. Gerhard, *Phoinix von
Kolophon* (Leipzig/Berlin, 1909) 171f.

[2]Fr. Boissonade, "Notices des lettres inédits de
Diogène le Cynique," *Notes et extraits des MSS. de la
Bibliothèque Nationale* X (Paris, 1818). K. von Fritz,
"Quellenuntersuchungen zu Leben und Philosophie des
Diogenes von Sinope," *Philologus*, Supp. 18 (1926) 70f.,
thinks that only *Ep.* 10 may provide us with information
about Diogenes.

[3]J. F. Marcks, *Symbola critica ad epistolographos
Graecos* (Dissertation; Bonn, 1883) 14f.

[4]Capelle, *De cynicorum epistulis*.

[5]Von Fritz, "Quellenuntersuchungen," 64, rejects the
use of Diog. Laert. 6.23 in determining the date on the
grounds that one is dealing with unknown quantities.

[6]Capelle, *De cynicorum epistulis*, 17.

[7]Von Fritz, "Quellenuntersuchungen," 63-71.

[8]Already pointed to by Capelle, *De cynicorum epistulis*, 9.

[9]For an insistence that only the letters attributed
to Chion can justly be called a "Briefroman," see I.
Düring, *Chion of Heraclea. A Novel in Letters*. Acta Uni-
versitatis Gotoburgensis (Göteborgs högskolas årsskrift
57/5; Göteborg, 1951) 18f., 23ff.

[10]Jacob Bernays, *Lucian und die Kyniker* (Berlin, 1879)
96-98.

[11]Especially by E. Norden, "Beiträge zur Geschichte
der griechischen Philosophie," *Jahrbücher für classische
Philologie*, Supp. 19 (1893) 392ff. Cf. Capelle, *De cyni-
corum epistulis*, 25ff.; Gerhard, *Phoinix*, 172ff.; W.
Schmid-O. Stählin, *Geschichte der griechischen Literatur*
II.1 (6th edition; Munich, 1920) 624f.

[12]He rejects (von Fritz, "Quellenuntersuchungen," 80,
note 169) the theory of C. Hahn, *De Dionis Chrysostomi
orationibus VI, VIII, IX, X* (Dissertation; Giessen, 1896),
that this letter and Dio, *Or.* VI go back to the same source.

[13]A. Gercke, "Handschriftliche Ordnung der Diogenesbriefe," an excursus to his "Seneca-Studien," *Jahrbücher
für classische Philologie*, Supp. 22 (1896) 85f.; cf. von
Fritz, "Quellenuntersuchungen," 64, 70.

[14]Victor E. Emeljanow, *The Letters of Diogenes* (Ph.D.
dissertation; Stanford University, 1967; Ann Arbor, MI:
University Microfilms, 1974) 3-6.

[15]For example, whereas *Epp.* 1-29 are opposed to
ἡδονή, *Epp.* 30-40 hold out the possibility that the philosopher's ἀσκήματα may turn into ἡδονή.

[16]Thus A. Oltramare, *Les origines de la diatribe
romaine* (Lausanne, 1926) 21.

[17]Emeljanow, *Letters of Diogenes*, 20, 22; cf. Bernays,
Lucian, 96-98; Norden, "Beiträge zur Geschichte," 393f.;
F. Ueberweg-K. Praechter, *Philosophie des Altertums*
(Berlin, 1926) 504.

[18]Emeljanow's work is especially valuable in this
regard.

[19]To say that the biggest contribution of the letters
is to "bring together several disparate strands...and to
weld them into a single coherent philosophical viewpoint"
(Emeljanow, *Letters of Diogenes*, iii) is an overstatement.
Despite his negative evaluation of the letters, Oltramare
shows an awareness of the philosophical tendencies in
them. In one place, *Epp.* 12, 35 and 37 are said to betray
a Stoic tendency and the others to incline toward hedonism
(ibid., 21, note 5), while elsewhere the letters are
cited as evidence of a violent reaction to Cynic hedonism
and a return to Cynicism's ascetic origins (ibid., 40f.).
For the hedonism that he has in mind, see G. A. Gerhard,
"Zur Legende vom Kyniker Diogenes," *Archiv für Religionswissenschaft* 15 (1912) 388-408.

Bibliography

Text and Translation

Hercher, R. *Epistolographi Graeci*. Paris, 1873. The
    most recent critical text with Latin translation;
    text is printed in this volume.

Emeljanow, Victor E. *The Letters of Diogenes*. Ph.D.
    dissertation, Stanford University, 1967 (Ann Arbor,
    MI: University Microfilms, 1974). Does not establish
    a text, but attempts to clarify the textual tradition;
    offers emendations of numerous passages; extensive
    commentary on the letters; to be consulted for bib-
    liography and early editions of the letters; to be

added to his bibliography of editions of the letters:
E. Lubinus, *Epistolae Hippocratis, Democriti, Hera-
cliti, Diogenis nunc primum editae Graece simul ac
Latine* (Heidelberg, 1601).

Savage, John. *A Select Collection of Letters of the
Antients*. London, 1703. Pp. 421-36. English
paraphrases of parts of some of the letters (*Epp*. 1,
28, 30, 31, 33, 38, 40).

Studies

See the bibliography in Emeljanow, to which the
following should be added:

Bernays, J. *Lucian und die Kyniker*. Berlin, 1879. Pp.
96ff.

Weber, E. *De Dione Chrysostomo Cynicorum sectatore*.
Leipziger Studien zur classischen Philologie 10.
Leipzig, 1887. Pp. 135 and passim.

Dümmler, F. *Akademika*. Giessen, 1889. Pp. 242f.

Susemihl, F. *Geschichte der griechischen Litteratur in der
Alexandrinerzeit* II. Leipzig, 1891. P. 600.

Norden, E. "Beiträge zur Geschichte der griechischen
Philosophie." *Jahrbücher für classische Philologie*,
Supp. 19 (1893) 392ff.

Gercke, A. "Handschriftliche Ordnung der Diogenesbriefe,"
an excursus to his "Seneca-Studien." *Jahrbücher für
classische Philologie*, Supp. 22 (1896) 85f.

Hahn, C. *De Dionis Chrysostomi orationibus VI, VIII, IX,
X*. Dissertation, Giessen, 1896.

Dyroff, A. "Jahresbericht uber die deutsche Literatur zur
nacharistotelischen Philosophie (1891-1896)." *Archiv
für Philosophie* 13 (1900) 121-41 (esp. 139-41).

Helm, R. *Lucian und Menipp*. Leipzig/Berlin, 1906.

Gerhard, G. A. *Phoinix von Kolophon*. Leipzig/Berlin,
1909. Esp. pp. 67f., 80f., 111, 117, 119f., 127,
143ff., 165f., 171ff.

_____. "Zur Legende vom Kyniker Diogenes." *Archiv für
Religionswissenschaft* 15 (1912) 388-408.

von der Mühll, P. In *Festgabe Hugo Blümner*. Zurich,
1914. Pp. 432f.

Schmid, W. and Stählin, O. *Geschichte der griechischen
Literatur* II.1. 6th edition. Munich, 1920. Pp.
484, 624.

Oltramare, A. *Les origines de la diatribe romaine.*
    Lausanne, 1926. Pp. 21, 40f.

Ueberweg, F. and Praechter, K. *Philosophie des Altertums.*
    Berlin, 1926. Pp. 168-70, 504f., 63f.*, 167*, 183*.

Keyes, C. W. "The Greek Letter of Introduction." *Ameri-*
    can Journal of Philology 56 (1935) 28-44.

Düring, I. *Chion of Heraclea. A Novel in Letters.* Acta
    Universitatis Gotoburgensis. Göteborgs högskolas
    årsskrift 57/5. Göteborg, 1951. Pp. 18f., 23ff.

Tsopanakis, A. "Διορϑώση χωρίου." *Hellenica* 13 (1954)
    174-76.

Caizzi, F. C. *Antisthenis Fragmenta.* Milan, 1966. Pp.
    118, 123, 125.

Radt, S. L. "Zu Plutarchs Vita Alexandri." *Mnemosyne* 20
    (1967) 120-26.

Malherbe, A. J. "'Gentle as a Nurse': The Cynic Back-
    ground to 1 Thess. 2." *Novum Testamentum* 12 (1970)
    212.

4. The Epistles of Heraclitus

There are nine letters ascribed to Heraclitus of
Ephesus (sixth-fifth centuries B.C.), all of them generally regarded to be spurious. Strictly speaking, only
seven of the letters purport to have been written by
Heraclitus, *Epp.* 1 and 3 pretending to have come from the
pen of Darius the Persian king, a contemporary of Heraclitus.

Jacob Bernays first drew attention to the letters,
and maintained that they were not all written by the same
person.[1] Differences were observed within the first three
letters which describe Heraclitus's and Hermodorus's relationship to the Persian Empire as a rhetorical theme.
Epp. 1 and 3 differ sharply in tone. Since *Epp.* 1 and 2
are incorporated by Diogenes Laertius (9.13f.), they must
have existed comparatively early, probably in the first
century A.D. To these two letters an unskilled rhetorician is thought to have added *Ep.* 3. Bernays noted similarities between *Epp.* 4, 7 and 9, especially their criticism of immorality and traditional cult. These features
led him to advance the theory, seldom accepted by serious
scholars of the letters,[2] that in their present form they
are Jewish in authorship. *Ep.* 4, according to Bernays, is
an interpolated version of an originally pagan letter. In
its present form it dates from the first century A.D.
Epp. 4 and 7 are then ascribed to one author and *Ep.* 9 to
another. Despite the similarities between *Epp.* 9 and 8,
he attributes the latter to an untalented rhetorician
writing in the first century A.D. It is obvious from
their content that *Epp.* 5 and 6 belong together, and it is
not impossible that the author of the original version of
Ep. 4 may have been responsible for them. Thus all the
letters, with the possible exception of *Ep.* 3, come from
the first century. All scholars since Bernays have in
general accepted his dating of the letters, and, with some
modifications, his view of their multiple authorship.

Heinemann admits that *Epp*. 1-3 are different from the
others, and that they may come from one or two authors.[3]
Epp. 5 and 6 belong together, as do *Epp*. 4 and 7. But
Epp. 4, 5 and 6 belong together, and *Ep*. 9 could have come
from the same hand. *Ep*. 8 is somewhat different, but it
could have come from the same circle. Our collection,
according to Heinemann, therefore comes from at least two,
and probably more than two authors.

Kirk also identifies *Epp*. 1-3 as a separate group,
and regards *Ep*. 3 as a possible imitation of the first
two.[4] The rest he takes to show individual characteristics, but he is more impressed by their similarities than
by the differences between them. They were probably all
produced by the same rhetorical school.

Taran, too, agrees that *Epp*. 1 and 2 came from the
same author, and is uncertain whether *Ep*. 3 does.[5] All
three, however, are regarded as coming from the same
school, which shows a biographical interest in Heraclitus,
specifically in his relationship to Darius. *Epp*. 4-6 and
Epp. 7-9 form distinct groups. The former is concerned
with Euthycles' accusation against Heraclitus while the
latter refers to the activity of Hermodorus as a legislator. Both groups, however, can be differentiated from
Epp. 1-3 by their style, yet while it is thus not impossible that the same author wrote all six letters, it is
more probable that they come from different authors of the
same school.

In the most recent extensive treatment of the letters,
Attridge also separates *Epp*. 1 and 2 from the rest.[6] He
groups *Epp*. 3, 4, 7 and 8, which deal with the exile of
Hermodorus, with *Ep*. 9, which describes the circumstances
of that exile, and is therefore regarded as an appropriate
opening for the collection. He points out that in the
manuscripts that contain it, *Ep*. 9 always appears first.
Epp. 5 and 6 have different addresses, and deal with Heraclitus's attitude toward medicine. However, they do cor-
respond in some particulars, for example in piety and the

reference to the setting up of altars, to epistles in the
group dealing with Hermodorus's exile, and this suggests
that *Epp.* 5 and 6 were either composed as part of that
group or were written to harmonize with it.

Attridge's main interest is in the philosophical and
religious affiliations of the letters, especially *Epp.* 4
and 7. He goes to great pains to show that these letters
are Cynic-Stoic in thought and not Jewish, as Bernays has
maintained. That matter must certainly be regarded as
having been laid to rest. A major contribution of Attridge's work lies in the text-critical part of his study.
In establishing a new critical text, he considers the
newly discovered PGen 271 of great significance. This
papyrus, dated by its editors on palaeographic grounds to
the second century A.D. or earlier,[7] contains a longer
version of *Ep.* 7. Attridge regards this form of the letter to have been the original, a judgment not shared by
Taran, who has also published a new critical text.[8] The
papyrus does, however, provide further evidence that this
letter is to be assigned to the same period as the majority of the others, namely the first century and a half of
the Empire.

Notes

[1]J. Bernays, *Die heraklitischen Briefe* (Berlin, 1869).

[2]For the history of the discussion (and the misuse of
the letters), see Harold W. Attridge, *First Century Cynicism in the Epistles of Heraclitus* (Harvard Theological
Studies 29; Missoula, Montana, 1976).

[3]I. Heinemann, "Herakleitos, Briefe des," *Pauly-
Wissowa Realencyklopädie*, Supp. 5 (1931) 228-32.

[4]G. S. Kirk, *Heraclitus: The Cosmic Fragments* (Cambridge, 1954) 29f.

[5]R. Mondolfo and L. Taran, *Eraclito, Testimonianze e
Imitazione* (Biblioteca di studi superiori 54; Florence,
1972) 300-302.

[6]Attridge, *First Century Cynicism*, 11f.

[7]V. Martin, "Un recueil de diatribes cyniques: Pap.
Gen. 271," *Museum Helveticum* 16 (1959) 77-117; P. Pho-
tiades, "Les diatribes cyniques du papyrus Genève 271,"
Museum Helveticum 16 (1959) 118-40; J. T. Kakridis, "Zum
Kynikerpapyrus (Pap. Genev. inv. 271)," *Museum Helveticum*
17 (1960) 34-36; idem, "Weiteres zum Kynikerpapyrus (Pap.
Genev. inv. 271)," *La Parola del Passato* 16 (1961) 383-86.

[8]Attridge, *First Century Cynicism*, 298.

Bibliography

The bibliography of E. Roussos, *Heraklit-
Bibliographie* (Darmstadt, 1971) 88f. is
superseded by the extensive, annotated one of
Attridge. Only items omitted by Attridge are
listed under *Studies*.

Text and Translation

Mondolfo, R. and Taran, L. *Eraclito, Testimonianze e Imi-
    tazioni*. Biblioteca di studi superiori 54. Florence,
    1972. The section dealing with the letters is by
    Taran. Introduction, critical text, Italian transla-
    tion, and excellent commentary, especially on philo-
    sophical matters; text used by permission of La Nuova
    Italia Editrice. For a critical review, especially of
    the text, see M. Marcovich in *Gnomon* 47 (1975) 531-34.

Attridge, Harold W. *First Century Cynicism in the Epistles
    of Heraclitus*. Harvard Theological Studies 29.
    Missoula, Montana, 1976. Introduction, critical text,
    English translation, and bibliography; to be consulted
    for information on earlier editions and translations
    (Latin and German), to which should be added the fol-
    lowing edition, utilized by neither Attridge or Taran.

Boissonade, I. F. *Eunapii Sardiani vitas sophistarum et
    fragmenta historiarum*. Amsterdam, 1822. Pp. 424-30.

Studies

Gerhard, G. A. *Phoinix von Kolophon*. Leipzig/Berlin,
    1909. Pp. 35, 67, 173f., 165, and passim.

Weinreich, O. "De H. quae fertur epistula IV et de ara H.
    dedicata." *Archiv für Religionswissenschaft* 18
    (1915) 18-21.

Ueberweg, F. and Praechter, K. *Philosophie des Altertums*.
    Berlin, 1926. Pp. 54, 505, 43*, 167*, 183*.

Kirk, G. S. *Heraclitus: The Cosmic Fragments*. Cambridge,
    1954. Pp. 29f.

Zoubos, A. N. *Bemerkungen über die pseudoheraklitischen Briefe*. Munich, 1954.

Marcovich, M. "Herakleitos." *Pauly-Wissowa Realencyklopädie*, Supp. 10 (1965) 317.

Dörrie, H. "Herakleitos." *Der kleine Pauly* II (1967) 1048.

5. The Epistles of Socrates and the Socratics

The thirty-five letters contained in this collection
are preserved in one manuscript, Codex Vaticanus graecus
64 (1969-70), on which all the other manuscripts of the
letters are dependent.[1] The order of the letters in this
manuscript is not that of the author or editor, a situation further complicated by Leon Allazzis, the editor of
the first printed edition.[2] He placed *Epp.* 21-23, which
stand at the head of the collection in the manuscript, in
their present position, and removed *Epp.* 33 and 34 from
elsewhere to their present position before *Ep.* 35, because
he could not translate these three letters or make sense
out of them.[3] Orelli[4] and Hercher[5] in turn inserted two
letters ascribed to Plato, which have nothing to do with
the collection, after *Ep.* 24. Köhler, whose text is
printed and whose numbering is followed in this volume,
retained this order, but excluded the Platonic letters.[6]

All the letters were not written by the same person.
Ep. 28, a letter of Speusippus to Philip, may very well be
genuine.[7] *Ep.* 35, dealing with the necessity of keeping
the doctrine of the school secret, really belongs with the
Pythagorean literature. The remaining letters, acknowledged since Bentley to be spurious,[8] fall into two groups,
those attributed to Socrates (*Epp.* 1-7), and those to his
disciples (*Epp.* 8-27, 29-34). On the basis of their content, language, and style, the two groups can be assigned
to different authors.[9]

Common to *Epp.* 1-7 are the extensive use of Xenophon
(of Plato's writings only the *Apology* can be shown to have
been used), the strong didactic tendency which makes
philosophical discourses out of two of the letters (*Epp.*
1 and 6), the predilection for Cynic thought and concepts,
and the lack of interest in unnecessary historical details. The author is an accomplished writer in the Attic
style. A reference to the letters of Socrates in a papyrus from the third century A.D. establishes the *terminus
ante quem* for this group,[10] but it is likely that they come
from the first century or even earlier.[11]

The letters attributed to Socrates' disciples have
different characteristics from the first group. They are
less didactic, and show greater interest in historical
detail. The author wants to write a novel in letters,[12]
accordingly individuals appear and act in them in keeping
with what is known about them from the biographical tradition. Thus, for example, Aristippus is made to write in
Doric in *Epp.* 9, 11, 13, 16, but since it is known that he
also wrote in Attic (Diogenes Laertius 2.83), he is presented as writing in Attic in *Ep.* 27. The author tries to
harmonize or hide the differences among or the contrasts
between members of the Socratic circle, but he could not
do away with the opposition between Aristippus and Antisthenes. He shows a latent aversion to Cynicism of the
rigorous type, and is sympathetic to Aristippus. The historical, geographical, and prosopographic details which he
parades, are taken especially from the Platonic letters,
and from Xenophon and a handbook on Greek philosophy which
is similar to that of Diogenes Laertius but more extensive
in content. His language is Atticistic with an admixture
of Platonic turns of phrase and technical terminology.
That he had thoroughly studied rhetorical letter theory is
evident from the fact that he had worked into *Ep.* 33:1 a
rule that we know from Cicero, *Ad fam.* 2.4, 1.[13]

The *terminus a quo* for the Socratic letters is established by the fact that *Epp.* 22 and 23 seem to use Plu-
tarch's *Quomodo adulator ab amico internoscatur* (67CE),
and *Epp.* 11 and 27 his *De tranquillitate animi* (470F, 469C).
They would thus appear to have been written after the early
part of the second century A.D. Furthermore, the author
may have used Diogenes, *Epp.* 29 and 32 in *Epp.* 8 and 12,
and Crates, *Epp.* 7 and 32 in *Ep.* 21, which cannot, however,
be dated with any certainty. The *terminus ante quem* is
established by Stobaeus (fifth century A.D.), who cites a
line from *Ep.* 12 (3.17, 10 Vol. 3.492, 1-4 W.-H.). Since
the latest author Stobaeus excerpts is Themistius (fourth
century A.D.), one is justified in dating the letters

earlier, around 200 A.D. or a little later. It is possible, but uncertain, that the author of this group had
the letters of Socrates before him.[14] His knowledge of
Plato and his esteem for him makes it probable that he had
some contact with the Platonic school.

The purposes of the two groups appear to have been
different. The interest of *Epp*. 1-7 is not in Socrates as
a person but as an ethical paradigm. The didactic, or
rather, paraenetic tendency, is especially clear in *Epp*.
1 and 6, where the letter form is simply a cover for a
well developed diatribe. The author of the Socratic letters, on the other hand, has a striking conciliatory tendency.[15] While his work does appear as a kind of epistolary novel, the immediate purpose of the letters is difficult to determine. Their value, however, does not lie
only in their literary qualities. The conciliatory efforts of the author do not obscure the differences between
the various types of Cynicism represented by the Socratics
in the correspondence. The letters thus provide valuable
evidence for an attempt to bring rigoristic and hedonistic
Cynicism into harmony, and are thus a major source for the
history of Cynicism.[16]

Notes

[1] See J. Sykutris, "Die handschriftliche Ueberlieferung
der Sokratikerbriefe," *Philologische Wochenschrift* 48
(1928) 1284-95. Sykutris has done the most thorough work
on the letters. His various publications referred to in
this volume were prolegomena to a critical edition of the
letters which in turn was planned as a part of a new,
critical edition of *Epistolographi Graeci*. Neither work
was completed before his death. This introduction to the
letters is heavily indebted to his article, "Sokratiker-
briefe," *Pauly-Wissowa Realencyklopädie*, Supp. 5 (1931)
981-87, where he modifies his earlier opinion that Codex
Helmstadiensis 806 was not dependent on Cod. Vat. gr. 64.

[2] Leon Allazzis, *Socratis, Antisthenis et aliorum
Socraticorum epistolae* (Paris, 1637).

[3]The unintelligibility of the three letters also
forced Orelli, Hercher, and Köhler to forego attempts at
translation. J. Sykutris, *Die Briefe des Sokrates und die
Sokratiker* (Studien zur Geschichte und Kultur des Altertums 18; Paderborn, 1933) 101f., provides a new text and
paraphrase of *Ep.* 35, which are followed in this volume.
His comments on *Epp.* 33 and 34 (ibid., 92-101) similarly
form the basis for the hesitant attempt at translation of
those letters offered here.

[4]Johann Conrad Orelli, *Socratis et Socraticorum,
Pythagorae et Pythagoreorum, quae feruntur epistulae*
(Leipzig, 1815).

[5]R. Hercher, *Epistolographi Graeci* (Paris, 1871).

[6]L. Köhler, "Die Briefe des Sokrates und die Sokratiker," *Philologus*, Supp. 20/2 (Leipzig, 1928). For critical reviews, especially of her text, see W. Nestle in
Philologische Wochenschrift 48 (1928) 1577f.; L. Castig-
lioni in *Gnomon* 6 (1930) 217-19; A. E. Taylor in *Classical
Review* 43 (1929) 22f.

[7]Argued extensively by E. Bickermann and J. Sykutris,
"Speusipps Brief an König Philipp," *Berichte über die
Verhandlungen der Sächsischen Akademie der Wissenschaften*,
Phil.-hist. Kl. 80/3 (Leipzig, 1928) 1-86. For an earlier
German translation and long discussion, see K. G. Boeh-
necke, *Demosthenes, Lykurgos, Hypereides und ihr Zeit-
alter* (Berlin, 1864) 442-81.

[8]R. Bentley, *A Dissertation Upon the Epistles of
Phalaris, Themistocles, Socrates, Euripides* (1699; edited,
with introduction and notes, by Wilhelm Wagner; Berlin,
1874).

[9]See Sykutris, *Briefe des Sokrates*, 106-21. On the
language and style, see W. Obens, *Qua aetate Socratis et
Socraticorum epistulae quae dicuntur scriptae sint* (Dissertation, Münster, 1912).

[10]L. Mitteis and U. Wilcken, *Grundzüge und Chrestomathie der Papyruskunde* I.2 (Leipzig/Berlin, 1912) 182ff.

[11]Sykutris, *Briefe des Sokrates*, 111f.; H. Dörrie,
"Sokratiker-Briefe," *Der kleine Pauly* V (1975) 257f.,
dates all the letters perhaps as early as the first century B.C. Obens, *Qua aetate Socratis*, thinks that they
were all produced by an Atticistic school in the second
century A.D.

[12]See also K. von Fritz, "Quellenuntersuchungen zu
Leben und Philosophie des Diogenes von Sinope," *Philologus*,
Supp. 18 (1926) 67.

[13]On the author's awareness of epistolary theory, see
Sykutris, *Briefe des Sokrates*, 118f.; Köhler, "Briefe des
Sokrates," 128. Different epistolary types can be identified within the corpus, for example, *Ep.* 21 is a letter
of consolation, and *Ep.* 18 (cf. *Ep.* 19) is an invitation
(the form is not exactly that of the papyrus letters
studied by Chan-Hie Kim, "The Papyrus Invitation," *Journal
of Biblical Literature* 94 [1975] 391-402). Among the letters of Socrates, *Ep.* 2 (cf. *Ep.* 6) is a letter of recom-
mendation (cf. Chan-Hie Kim, *The Familiar Letter of Recom-
mendation* [SBLDS 4; Missoula, Montana, 1972]).

[14]See Sykutris, *Briefe des Sokrates*, 112f.

[15]Ibid., 107f., 113f.

[16]See Ronald F. Hock, "Simon the Shoemaker as an
Ideal Cynic," *Greek, Roman, and Byzantine Studies* 17 (1976)
41-53. On rigorism and hedonism in Cynicism, see G. A.
Gerhard, *Phoinix von Kolophon* (Leipzig/Berlin, 1909);
idem, "Zur Legende vom Kyniker Diogenes," *Archiv für
Religionswissenschaft* 15 (1912) 388-408.

Bibliography

Text and Translation

Allazzis, Leon. *Socratis, Antisthenis et aliorum Socrati-
     corum epistolae.* Paris, 1637. Text, Latin transla-
     tion (except for *Epp.* 33-35), and commentary.

Savage, John. *A Select Collection of Letters of the
     Antients.* London, 1703. Pp. 268-72. English para-
     phrases of parts of *Epp.* 5, 8 and 9.

Orelli, Johann Conrad. *Socratis et Socraticorum, Pytha-
     gorae et Pythagoreorum, quae feruntur epistulae.*
     Leipzig, 1815. Text, Latin translation (except for
     Epp. 33-35), and commentary. He also includes (pp.
     327-428) *dissertationes* on the letters by Allazzis,
     John Pearson, Gottfried Olearius, Richard Bentley,
     and Christopher Meiners.

Roberts, William. *History of Letter-Writing from the
     Earliest Period to the Fifth Century.* London, 1843.
     Pp. 86f. English translation of *Ep.* 21.

Boehnecke, K. G. *Demosthenes, Lykurgos, Hypereides und
     ihr Zeitalter.* Berlin, 1864. Pp. 442-81. German
     translation of and extensive commentary on *Ep.* 28.

Hercher, R. *Epistolographi Graeci.* Paris, 1871. Greek
     text with Latin translation (except for *Epp.* 33-35).

Mullach, F. W. A. *Fragmenta philosophorum graecorum* III.
    Paris, 1881. Pp. 82-90. Prints *Epp*. 18-30 as Frag-
    ments 82-90, with Latin translation and commentary.

Jacoby, F. *Fragmenta der Griechischen Historiker*. Berlin,
    1926. IIA/69, pp. 35-37; C, pp. 21f. Sections of
    Ep. 28.

Bickermann, E. and Sykutris, J. "Speusipps Brief an König
    Philipp." *Berichte über die Verhandlungen der Säch-
    sischen Akademie der Wissenschaften*. Phil.-hist. Kl.
    80/3 (Leipzig, 1928) 1-86. Introduction, text,
    German translation, and extensive commentary on *Ep*.
    28.

Köhler, L. "Die Briefe des Sokrates und die Sokratiker,"
    Philologus, Supp. 20/2 (Leipzig, 1928). Text, German
    translation (except for *Epp*. 33-35), commentary, and
    short index of Greek words; text printed in this
    volume is used by permission of Akademie Verlag.

Sykutris, J. "Die handschriftliche Ueberlieferung der
    Sokratikerbriefe." *Philologische Wochenschrift* 48
    (1928) 1284-95. Basic; describes the manuscripts
    and editions of the text, and provides a stemma of
    the tradition; a preparation for his edition of the
    letters, which apparently never appeared before his
    death.

_____. *Die Briefe des Sokrates und die Sokratiker*.
    Geschichte und Kultur des Altertums 18. Paderborn,
    1933. Introduction, commentary on all the letters.
    Greek text of *Ep*. 35, and numerous emendations sug-
    gested of the text of the other letters; modification
    of some positions taken in "Die handschriftliche
    Ueberlieferung" (pp. 7f.). For a critical review,
    see W. Crönert in *Gnomon* 12 (1936) 146-52.

Keyes, Clinton W. "The Greek Letter of Introduction."
    American Journal of Philology 56 (1935) 37f. English
    translations of *Epp*. 2, 3, 25 (Hercher), and 28 (be-
    ginning).

Studies

Bentley, Richard. *A Dissertation Upon the Epistles of
    Phalaris, Themistocles, Socrates, Euripides and Upon
    the Fables of Aesop*. London, 1699. Edited, with
    introduction and notes, by Wilhelm Wagner (Berlin,
    1874).

Orelli, Johann Conrad. *Memnonis historiarum Heracleae
    Ponti excerpta servata a Photio graece cum versione
    Laur. Rhodomanni* (Leipzig, 1816) 325-36. Prints an
    Epistola Critica, with critical exegetical comments
    on the Socratic epistles, by Johannes Caspar Orelli.

Boissonade, M. "Notice des lettres de Crates le Cynique
    contenus dans le manuscrit 483 du Vatican." *Notices
    et Extraits des Manuscrits de la Bibliothèque du Roi*
    XI/2 (1827) 47ff.

Hercher, R. "Zu den griechischen Epistolographen."
    Hermes 4 (1870) 427f.

_____. "Zu griechischen Prosaikern." *Hermes* 6 (1872)
    55f.

von Wilamowitz-Moellendorff, U. "Phaidon von Elis."
    Hermes 14 (1879) 187-93.

Bernays, J. *Phokion und seine neueren Beurteiler.*
    Berlin, 1881. Pp. 116ff.

Dümmler, F. *Akademika.* Giessen, 1889. Pp. 3ff.

Susemihl, F. *Geschichte der griechischen Litteratur in
    der Alexandrinerzeit* II. Leipzig, 1892. Pp. 586ff.

Capelle, W. *De cynicorum epistulis.* Dissertation, Göt-
    tingen, 1896. Pp. 9f.

Crönert, W. *Kolotes und Menedemus.* Leipzig, 1906. Pp.
    86, 426.

Gerhard, G. A. *Phoinix von Kolophon.* Leipzig/Berlin,
    1909. Pp. 89, 111, 127, 174, and passim.

Ritter, C. *Neue Untersuchungen über Platon.* Munich,
    1910. Pp. 379-97.

Dittmar, H. *Aischines von Sphettos.* Philologische Unter-
    suchungen 21. Berlin, 1912. Pp. 196ff.

Gerhard, G. A. "Zur Legende vom Kyniker Diogenes."
    Archiv für Religionswissenschaft 15 (1912) 388-408.

Mitteis, L. and Wilcken, U. *Grundzüge und Chrestomathie
    der Papyruskunde* I.2. Leipzig/Berlin, 1912. Pp.
    182ff.

Obens, W. *Qua aetate Socratis et Socraticorum epistulae
    quae dicuntur scriptae sint.* Dissertation, Münster,
    1912.

Schering, O. *Symbola ad Socratis et Socraticorum epistu-
    las explicandas.* Dissertation, Greifswald, 1917.

Klek, J. *Symbuleutici qui dicitur sermonis historia crit-
    ica.* Rhetorische Studien 9. Paderborn, 1919. Pp.
    102-106.

Pavlu, J. In Χάρισμα. *Festgabe des Vereins klassischer Philologen in Wien* (1924) 33-42.

von Fritz, K. "Quellenuntersuchungen zu Leben und Philosophie des Diogenes von Sinope." *Philologus*, Supp. 18 (1926) 67.

Sykutris, J. "Epistolographie." *Pauly-Wissowa Realencyklopädie*, Supp. 5 (1931) 185-220.

von Fritz, K. "Phaidon von Elis und der 12. und 13. Sokratikerbrief." *Philologus* 90 (1935) 240-44.

Mannebach, E. (ed.). *Aristippi et Cyrenaicorum Fragmenta*. Leiden, 1961. Passim.

Caizzi, F. C. *Antisthenis Fragmenta*. Milan, 1966. Pp. 119, 124f.

Hock, Ronald F. *The Working Apostle: An Examination of Paul's Means of Livelihood*. Yale Ph.D. dissertation, New Haven, 1974.

Dörrie, H. "Sokratiker-Briefe." *Der kleine Pauly* V (1975) 257f.

Hock, Ronald F. "Simon the Shoemaker as an Ideal Cynic." *Greek, Roman, and Byzantine Studies* 17 (1976) 41-53.

THE EPISTLES OF ANACHARSIS

Translated by

Anne M. McGuire

1. Ἀνάχαρσις Ἀθηναίοις

Γελᾶτε ἐμὴν φωνήν, διότι οὐ τρανῶς Ἑλληνικὰ
γράμματα λέγει. Ἀνάχαρσις παρ' Ἀθηναίοις σολοικίζει,
Ἀθηναῖοι δὲ παρὰ Σκύθαις. οὐ φωναῖς διήνεγκαν ἄν-
5 θρωποι ἀνθρώπων εἰς τὸ εἶναι ἀξιόλογοι, ἀλλὰ γνώμαις,
αἷσπερ καὶ Ἕλληνες Ἑλλήνων. Σπαρτιᾶται οὐ τρανοὶ
ἀττικίζειν, ἀλλ' ἔργοις λαμπροὶ καὶ εὐδόκιμοι. οὐ
ψέγουσι Σκύθαι λόγον, ὃς ἂν ἐμφανίζῃ τὰ δέοντα, οὐδ'
ἐπαινοῦσιν, ὅταν μὴ ἐφικνῆται τοῦ δέοντος. πολλὰ καὶ
10 ὑμεῖς οἰκονομεῖτε οὐ προσέχοντες φωνῇ ἄρθρα οὐκ
ἐχούσῃ. εἰσάγεσθε ἰατροὺς Αἰγυπτίους, κυβερνήταις
χρῆσθε Φοίνιξιν, ὠνεῖσθε ἐν ἀγορᾷ οὐ διδόντες πλεῖον
τῆς ἀξίας τοῖς ἑλληνιστὶ λαλοῦσιν. οὐδὲ ὀκνηρῶς
λαμβάνετε παρὰ βαρβάρων, ἐὰν πρὸς τρόπου πωλῶσι.
15 βασιλεῖς Περσῶν κἀκείνων φίλοι μέγα φρονοῦντες, ὅταν
βούλωνται πρὸς Ἑλλήνων πρεσβευτὰς Ἑλληνικῇ φωνῇ
φθέγγεσθαι, ἀναγκάζονται σολοικίζειν, ὧν ὑμεῖς οὔτε
βουλὰς οὔτε ἔργα καταμέμφεσθε. λόγος δὲ κακὸς οὐ
γίνεται, ὅταν βουλαὶ ἀγαθαὶ ὦσι καὶ ἔργα καλὰ λόγοις
20 παρακολουθῇ. Σκύθαι δὲ κρίνουσι λόγον φαῦλον, ὅταν
διαλογισμοὶ φαῦλοι γίνωνται. πολλῶν καθυστερήσετε,
ἂν δυσχεραίνητε φωναῖς βαρβάροις καὶ μετὰ τοῦτο μὴ
ἀποδεχόμενοι τὰ λεγόμενα. πολλοὺς γὰρ ποιήσετε
ὀκνηροὺς εἰσηγεῖσθαι ὑμῖν τὰ συμφέροντα. διὰ τί βαρ-
25 βαρικὰ τιμᾶτε ὑφάσματα, φωνὴν δὲ βάρβαρον οὐ δοκιμά-
ζετε; αὐλούντων καὶ ᾀδόντων φωνὰς ζητεῖτε ἐμμελεῖς,
καὶ ποιητῶν ἔμμετρα ποιούντων ἐπιλαμβάνεσθε, εἰ μὴ
ἀναπληροῦσι γράμμασιν Ἑλληνικοῖς τὰ μέτρα. λεγόντων
δὲ θεωρεῖτε αὐτὰ τὰ λεγόμενα.

1. Anacharsis to the Athenians

You laugh at my speech, because I do not pronounce the Greek sounds clearly. In the opinion of the Athenians, Anacharsis speaks incorrectly, but in the opinion of the Scythians, the Athenians do. It is not in their speech that men differ among themselves in their importance, but rather in their judgments, in which, indeed, even Greeks differ from Greeks. In speaking Attic, the Spartans are not clear, but in their actions they are illustrious and honored. The Scythians do not censure a speech which may clarify needful things, nor do they commend one when it does not aim at what is needful. You also do many things without paying attention to whether someone's speech is inarticulate. You bring in Egyptian doctors, you make use of Phoenician skippers, you shop in the marketplace without giving more to the Greek speakers than their goods are worth. You buy without any hesitation from non-Greeks, if they sell for a suitable price. Whenever the princes of Persia and their friends high-mindedly wish to speak to the Greek ambassadors in Greek, they are compelled to speak incorrectly, and yet you find fault with neither their intentions nor with their actions. A speech is not poor if good intentions stand behind it and good actions follow upon the words. But the Scythians judge a speech poor only when its arguments are poor. You will lag behind in many things if you detest foreign speech and, in consequence, do not understand what is being said. For you will be inordinately reluctant to introduce things that are useful to you. Why do you value foreign woven fabrics, yet disapprove of foreign speech? You demand that the sounds of the flute players and of the singers be harmonious, and you attack poets who compose meters if they do not fill the verses with Greek sounds. Look, rather, when people speak, at the things that are actually said.

τὸ γὰρ τέλος τούτων εἰς ὄνησιν. καὶ βαρβάροις
πειθόμενοι οὐκ ἐπιτρέψετε γυναιξὶ καὶ τέκνοις μὴ
προσέχουσιν ὑμῖν, ἐὰν σολοικίζητε. κρεῖσσον γὰρ
σολοικίζουσι πειθαρχοῦντας σῴζεσθαι ἢ τρανῶς ἀττικί-
5 ζουσιν ἐπακολουθοῦντας μέγα βλάπτεσθαι. ἀπαιδεύτων
ταῦτά ἐστι καὶ ἀπειροκάλων, ἄνδρες Ἀθηναῖοι.
σώφρων γὰρ οὐδεὶς ἂν διανοηθείη ταῦτα.

2. Ἀνάχαρσις Σόλωνι

       Ἕλληνες σοφοὶ ἄνδρες, οὐδέν γε σοφώτεροι βαρ-
10 βάρων. τὸ γὰρ ἐπίστασθαι καλὸν εἰδέναι οὐκ ἀφείλοντο
θεοὶ βαρβάρων. πεῖραν δ' ἔξεστι λαμβάνειν ἐξετάζοντας
λόγοις, εἰ καλὰ φρονοῦμεν, καὶ βασανίζειν εἰ συμφω-
νοῦμεν λόγοις πρὸς ἔργα, εἰ ὅμοιοί ἐσμεν τοῖς ἀγαθῶς
ζῶσι. στῆλαι δὲ καὶ κόσμος σώματος μὴ γινέσθωσαν
15 ἐμπόδια ὀρθῆς κρίσεως. ἄλλοι γὰρ ἄλλως κατὰ νόμους
πατέρων κεκοσμήκασι τὰ σώματα. σημεῖα δὲ ἀσυνεσίας
τὰ αὐτὰ βαρβάροις καὶ Ἕλλησιν, ὁμοίως δὲ καὶ συνέ-
σεως. σὺ δέ, διότι Ἀνάχαρσις ἐλθὼν ἐπὶ σὰς θύρας
ἠβούλετό σοι ξένος γενέσθαι, ἀπηξίωσας καὶ ἀπεκρίνω
20 ἐν οἰκείᾳ χώρᾳ με δεῖν ξενίαν συνάπτειν. εἰ δέ τίς
σοι κύνα Σπαρτιάτην ἐδωρεῖτο, οὐκ ἂν προσέτασσες
ἐκείνῳ ἀνδρὶ κύνα τοῦτον εἰς Σπάρτην ἀγαγόντα δοῦναι
σοι. πότε δὲ καὶ ἐσόμεθα ἑτέροις ξένοι, ἐπειδὰν
ἕκαστος τοῦτον τὸν λόγον λέγῃ; ἐμοὶ μὲν οὐ καλῶς
25 ἔχειν ταῦτα δοκεῖ, Σόλων, Ἀθηναῖε σοφέ. καί με
κελεύει θυμὸς πορεύεσθαι πάλιν ἐπὶ σὰς θύρας οὐκ
ἀξιώσοντα ἃ καὶ πρότερον, ἀλλὰ πευσόμενον πῶς ἔχει,
ἅπερ ἀπεφήνω ὑπὲρ ξενίας.

For the performance of these things is to your advantage.
If you listen to foreigners, you will not allow your wives
and children to disregard you if you speak incorrectly.
For it is better to be saved by obeying people who speak
incorrectly than to suffer great harm by following people
who speak Attic precisely. Men of Athens, these are the
concerns of the uneducated and of people who are ignorant
of what is good. For no one of sound mind would think
such things.

2. Anacharsis to Solon

The Greeks are wise men, yet in no way are they wiser
than non-Greeks. For the gods did not withhold from non-
Greeks the ability to know the good. It is possible,
through reasoned examination, to test whether we think
good thoughts, and to investigate whether our words cor-
respond to our actions, and whether we are like those who
live morally. But columns and adornment of the body
should not become impediments to correct judgment, for
others have adorned their bodies, each in a different way,
according to the customs of their fathers. The signs of
stupidity are the same for non-Greeks as for Greeks, as
are the signs of understanding. But as for you, because
it was Anacharsis who came knocking on your doors with the
desire to become your houseguest, you refused and replied
that I should seek hospitality in my own land. But if
anyone offered you a Spartan dog, you certainly would not
ask that man to bring the dog to Sparta in order to give
it to you! When will we ever be guests to others, if each
one makes the same argument? To me, Solon, you wise Athenian, this does not appear to be right. And my spirit bids
me to come again to your doors, not to ask what I did earlier, but to learn what the case is with respect to what
you declared about hospitality.

3. Ἀνάρχασις Ἱππάρχῳ τυράννῳ

Οἶνος πολὺς ἄκρατος ἀλλότριον τοῦ καλῶς τίθεσθαι
τὰ καθήκοντα. συγχεῖ γὰρ φρένας, ἐν αἷς ἵδρυται
ἀνθρώποις τὸ λογίζεσθαι. τὸν δὲ ὀρεγόμενον μεγάλων
5   οὐκ εὐχερὲς καλῶς πρᾶξαι, ἃ ἐπιβάλλεται, ἐὰν μὴ
νήφοντα βίον καὶ μεριμνητικὸν ἐνστήσηται. ἀφεὶς
οὖν κύβους καὶ μέθην τρέπου πρὸς τὰ δι' ὧν ἄρξεις,
κατὰ τρόπον εὐεργεσίας πατρὸς ἑαυτοῦ φίλους καὶ
προσαίτας εὖ ποιῶν. εἰ δὲ μή, πρὸς τῷ αἰσχρὸς εἶναι
10 κινδυνεύσεις ἰδίῳ σώματι. τότε μνησθήσονταί σου
φίλοι ἀνδρὸς Σκύθου Ἀναχάρσιδος.

4. Ἀνάχαρσις Μηδόκῳ

Φθόνος καὶ πτόησις μεγάλα τεκμήρια φαύλης ψυχῆς.
φθόνῳ μὲν γὰρ ἕπεται λύπη εὐπραγίας φίλων καὶ πολιτῶν,
15 πτοήσει δὲ ἐλπίδες κενῶν λόγων. Σκύθαι οὐκ ἀποδέχον-
ται τούτους ἄνδρας, ἀλλὰ χαίρουσί τε τοῖς εὖ πράττουσι καὶ ζητοῦσιν, ὧν εὔλογον αὐτοῖς τυχεῖν. μῖσος δὲ
καὶ φθόνον καὶ πᾶν δύσκολον πάθος ὡς πολέμια ψυχῆς
ἀποδιοπομποῦντες παντὶ σθένει διατελοῦσιν.

3. Anacharsis to the Tyrant Hipparchus

Much undiluted wine is an enemy of properly perform-
ing one's duties. For it confounds one's mind, in which
men's ability to reason is situated. It is not easy for
the person who strives for great things to accomplish what
he attempts unless he enters upon a sober and careful life.
So, renounce dice games and drunkenness, and turn to the
things through which you will rule, doing good, as you
follow the custom of your father's beneficence, to your
friends as well as beggars. But if you do not, you will
be close to being base and will be in bodily danger. Then
your friends will remember Anacharsis the Scythian.

4. Anacharsis to Medocus

Envy and passion are clear signs of an inferior soul.
For, on the one hand, grief at the success of friends and
fellow citizens follows upon envy, and, on the other,
hopes based on empty words follow upon passion. The
Scythians do not approve of these men, but they delight in
those who do well and they seek only after those things
which they can reasonably expect to acquire. They reso-
lutely reject hate and envy and every troublesome passion
because they are hostile to one's entire moral drive.

5. Ἀνάχαρσις Ἅννωνι

Ἐμοὶ μὲν περίβλημα χλαῖνα Σκυθική, ὑπόδημα
δέρμα ποδῶν, κοίτη δὲ πᾶσα γῆ, δεῖπνον ἄριστον·
γάλα, τυρός, κρέας, πᾶν ὄψον πεῖνα. ὡς οὖν ἄγοντός
5   μου σχολήν, ὧν οἱ πλεῖστοι ἕνεκεν ἀσχολοῦνται, παραγενοῦ πρός με, εἴ τινά μου χρείαν ἔχεις. δῶρα δ᾽
οἷς ἐντρυφᾶτε ἀντιδωροῦμαί σοι. σὺ δὲ δὸς Καρχηδο-
νίοις ἢ χάριν σὴν ἀνάθες θεοῖς.

6. Ἀνάχαρσις υἱῷ βασιλέως

10   Σοὶ μὲν αὐλοὶ καὶ βαλλάντιον, ἐμοὶ δὲ βέλη καὶ
τόξα. διὸ εἰκότως σὺ μὲν δοῦλος, ἐγὼ δὲ ἐλεύθερος.
καὶ σοὶ μὲν πολλοὶ πολέμιοι, ἐμοὶ δὲ οὐδείς. εἰ
δ᾽ ἐθέλεις ῥίψας τὸ ἀργύριον φέρειν τόξα καὶ φαρέτραν
καὶ πολιτεύεσθαι μετὰ Σκυθῶν, ὑπάρξει καὶ σοὶ τὰ
15   αὐτά.

5. Anacharsis to Hanno

For me, a Scythian cloak serves as my garment, the
skin of my feet as my shoes, the whole earth as my resting
place, milk, cheese and meat as my favorite meal, hunger
as my main course. Therefore, since I am free from those
things for which most people sacrifice their leisure, come
to me, if you need anything of mine. For the gifts in
which you delight, I will give you others in return. But
you, give them to the Carthaginians or dedicate your
thankfulness to the gods.

6. Anacharsis to the Son of the King

You have flutes and a purse, but I have arrows and
bows. Therefore, with good reason you are a slave, but I
am free. And you have many enemies, but I have none. But
should you be willing to throw away your money, to carry
bows and a quiver, and to live as a free citizen with the
Scythians, then these same conditions will obtain for you,
too.

7. Ἀνάχαρσις Τηρεῖ Θρακὶ χαλεπῷ δεσπότῃ

Οὐδεὶς ἄρχων ἀγαθὸς ἀπολλύει ἀρχομένους, οὐδὲ
ποιμὴν ἀγαθὸς πρόβατα λυμαίνεται. σοὶ δὲ πᾶσα μὲν
χώρα ἔρημος ἀρχομένων καὶ κακῶς προστατευθεῖσα ὑπ'
5   ἀρχόντων. πᾶς δὲ οἶκος ἰδιώτης εἰς ταπεινὸν συνέσ-
ταλται, ὥστε μὴ δύνασθαι σοῖς πράγμασι χρήσιμος
εἶναι. φείδεσθαι δὲ ἄμεινόν σε, ὧν ἂν ᾖς κύριος.
εἰ μὴ γὰρ ἴδια κτήματα ἐπαύξεται σῇ βασιλείᾳ, καὶ
διαμενεῖ. νῦν δὲ σπανίζῃ μὲν ἀνδρῶν εἰς πόλεμον,
10 ἁρπάζεις δὲ χρημάτων, οἷς διοικεῖς σου στρατιώτας
καὶ δικαίως θεωροῦντας ἓν σῶμα. ἐὰν μὴ καταλίπῃς
τροφὴν ἀρκοῦσαν, ἔπτηξαν. καὶ ἐνδύντες δενδρήεσιν
ὄρεσιν ἐν ἐρήμοις πεφυκόσιν, ἐν τούτοις οἰκήσουσι
καὶ ἐργάσονται τὰ τῶν μελισσῶν.

15   8. Ἀνάχαρσις Θρασυλόχῳ

Κύων ψυχῇ καλὸν ζῷον, μνημονεύων εὐεργεσιῶν.
φυλάσσει εὐεργετῶν οἰκίαν διατηρῶν εὐνομίαν ἕως
θανάτου. σὺ δ' ὑπολείπῃ κυνὸς εὐεργεσιῶν δυναμένου
συλλογισμῷ ἐξισοῦσθαι ἀνθρώποις. ζητεῖ οὖν λόγος
20 ἐμός, τίνος ἂν γένοιο θυμῷ δίκαιος, ὅταν πρὸς τοὺς
εὐεργέτας λέοντος ψυχὴν φορῇς. πειρῶ οὖν συνήθειαν
ἐμὴν ἣν εἴχομεν πρός σε σῴζειν. καὶ γὰρ ἐλπίδες
καλαὶ ἐν ἀνδρὶ τοιούτῳ.

7. Anacharsis to Tereus, the Cruel Despot of Thrace

No good ruler ruins his subjects, nor does a good
shepherd harm his sheep. But your whole land is empty of
subjects and poorly managed by your officials. Every private estate is reduced to such a low state that it can be
of no service to your affairs. It would be better for you
to be sparing of the people over whom you would have authority. For even if your private possessions do not
increase as a result of the misuse of your sovereignty,
they will at least last. But as it is now, you need men
to carry on a war, yet you plunder the funds with which
you support your soldiers and those people who dutifully
look to one person alone. If you do not leave them sufficient food, they become alarmed, and they flee, going into
deserted places in wooded mountains. There they dwell and
perform the tasks of bees.

8. Anacharsis to Thrasylochus

The dog is a good animal at heart, in that he remembers kindnesses. He guards the house of his benefactors,
maintaining its order until he dies. But you fall short
of the kindnesses of a dog, who can, in his reasoning,
equal men. Therefore, I ask myself with whom you might be
just in your anger, when you possess the heart of a lion
in your relationship with benefactors. Endeavor therefore
to preserve the close association we had with you. For
good hopes arise in a man who does so.

9. Ἀνάχαρσις Κροίσῳ

Οἱ ἐν Ἕλλησι ποιηταὶ λόγῳ κόσμον διανέμοντες
Κρόνου παισὶν ἀδελφοῖς λῆξιν τῷ μὲν οὐρανοῦ, τῷ δὲ
θαλάττης, τρίτῳ δὲ ζόφου προσέθεσαν. τοῦτο μὲν
5   ἰδιοπραγίας Ἑλληνικῆς. κοινωνίαν γὰρ οὐδεμίαν
χρήματος ἐπιστάμενοι τὸ ἑαυτῶν κακὸν θεοῖς προσέ-
νειμαν. γῆν δὲ ὅμως ἐξαίρετον καὶ οὗτοι κοινὴν
ἅπασιν ὑπελείποντο.
Φέρε τοῦτο πῇ ποτε φέρει τὸ νόημα φροντίσωμεν.
10 πάντας ἐβούλοντο θεοὺς τιμὰς πρὸς ἀνθρώπων ἔχειν
καὶ πάντας ἀγαθῶν δοτῆρας καὶ κακῶν ἀποτρόπους
ὑπάρχειν. κοινὸν δὲ θεῶν κτῆμα γῆ, κοινὸν καὶ
ἀνθρώπων τὸ πάλαι ἦν. χρόνῳ δὲ παρηνόμησαν, ἴδια
ἐπονομάζοντες τεμένη θεοῖς τὰ πάντων κοινά. θεοὶ δὲ
15 ἀντὶ τούτων δῶρα πρέποντα ἀντεδωρήσαντο ἔριν καὶ
ἡδονὴν καὶ μικροψυχίαν ἀνθρώποις· ἀπὸ τούτων μιγνυ-
μένων τε καὶ διακρινομένων τὰ πάντα ἔφυ κακὰ τοῖς
πᾶσι θνητοῖς· ἄροτοι, σπόροι, μεταλλεῖαι, πόλεμοι.
καρπούς τε γὰρ ἐπεισενεγκόντες πολλαπλασίους ἀποφέ-
20 ρονται μικρά, τέχναις τε ποικίλλοντες ὀλιγόβιον
εὕρηνται τρυφήν. γῆς τε χρώματα διαφόρως μαστεύοντες
θαῦμα πεποίηνται. τόν τε πρῶτον εὑρόντα τὸ ὀλίγον
τοῦτο μακαριστότατον ἄγουσι. καὶ οὐκ ἴσασι παίδων
τρόπον ἑαυτοὺς ἐξαπατῶντες. πόνῳ γὰρ τὸ μηδὲν ἐκτι-
25 μήσαντες, ἔπειτα τὸν πόνον αὐτὸν θαυμάζουσι.
Τοῦτό σοι πλείστων ἀνθρώπων ἤκουσα ῥυῆναι τὸ
κακόν. ἀπὸ τοῦδε τἆλλα. οὐ γὰρ ὁ μέγας πλοῦτος
οὐδὲ οἱ ἀγροὶ τὴν σοφίαν ἐπρίαντο. τὸ σῶμα γὰρ οἷς
ἂν πλείστων ἀλλοτρίων ὑποπλησθῇ, καὶ νοσημάτων
30 ὑποπίμπλασθαί φασι. καὶ τὴν ταχίστην ἀποχέτευσιν

9. Anacharsis to Croesus

The Greek poets in their poetry distributed the universe among the sons of Chronos, and assigned to one the
sphere of heaven, to the second that of the sea, and to
the third that of the nether darkness. This distribution
arose from the Greeks' pursuit of their own interests.
For as they know nothing of mutual participation in anything, they ascribe their own evil to the gods. The earth,
however, even they excepted and left it the common possession of all.

Come, let us consider the consequences of this
thought. They wished all the gods to be honored by men,
and all of them to be dispensers of good and averters of
evil. The earth was long ago the common possession of the
gods and of men. In time, however, men transgressed by
dedicating to the gods as their private precincts what was
the common possession of all. In return for these, the
gods bestowed upon men fitting gifts: strife, desire for
pleasure, and meanness of spirit. From a mixture and a
separation of these grew all the evils which afflict all
mortals: tilling the soil, sowing, metals, and wars. For
although they sowed very liberally, they harvested but
little, and although they worked at various crafts, they
found only a short-lived luxuriousness. They sought the
treasures of the earth in various ways, and deemed their
search a wonderful thing! They regard as most blessed the
first man who devised this silly little undertaking. They
do not know that like children they deceive themselves.
For first they prized nothing that comes by toil, and then
they admire toil itself.

I have heard that this evil which befalls most men
has befallen you, too. From this evil, others follow.
For neither great wealth nor possession of fields has ever
bought wisdom. For, it is said, those persons whose
bodies are filled with many foreign things will also be
filled with diseases. And they urge those who desire to

ποιεῖσθαι κελεύουσιν, οἷς ὑγιαίνειν ἔρως ἐστίν.
ἀλλὰ σωμάτων μὲν δι᾽ ἡδονὰς ἀμέτρους ἰατροὺς ἔχετε,
ψυχῆς δὲ οὐκ ἔχετε. σοφὸν δὲ ἡδονήν σε ἐκβαλεῖν.
ὅτε σοι τὸ πολὺ χρυσίον ἐρρύη, τότε συνερρύηκεν ἅμα
5   τῷ χρυσίῳ καὶ ἡ δόξα τοῦ χρυσίου καὶ ὁ φθόνος καὶ ἡ
τῶν βουλομένων ἀπενέγκασθαι παρὰ σοῦ τὸ χρυσίον
ἐπιθυμία. εἰ μὲν οὖν ἀπεκάθαρας σαυτὸν τοῦ νοσήμα-
τος, ὑγιὴς ἂν ἦσθα, ἐλευθέρως λέγων καὶ ἄρχων.
τοῦτο γαρ ἐστι τὸ ὑγιαίνειν βασιλέως, ὃ κεκτημένος
10   ἔνδον οὐ θαυμαστὸν εἰ καὶ τὰ καλὰ ἐκτήσω. ἀκρατῆ
δέ σε λαβοῦσα ἐπήμηνε δοῦλον ἀντ᾽ ἐλευθέρου ποιήσασα
ἡ νόσος. ἀλλὰ θυμὸν ἀγαθὸν ἔχε, πυρὸς ἐν ὕλῃ
γενομένου λαβὼν εἰκόνα, ὃ σποδιὰν τίθησι τὰ κεκαυμένα,
νέμεται δὲ τῆς ἀκαύστου. καὶ τὰ σὰ πάλαι κακὰ εἰς
15   τοὺς σὲ καὶ τὰ σὰ ἔχοντας μετῴκισται. ἐκείνοις
προσδόκα τὰς ἀνίας δευτέροις ἥξειν. ἄκουσον δὲ
ἐμῆς ὄψεως ἱστορίαν.

Μέγα ῥεῦμα διεξέρχεται τὴν Σκυθῶν χῶραν, τοῦτο
ὃ δὴ Ἴστρον ὀνομάζουσιν. ἐν τούτῳ φορτηγοὶ ναῦν
20   ἔρματι περιβαλόντες ἐπειδὴ οὐδὲν προσαρκέσειν
ἐδύναντο, ἀπῇεσαν ὀλοφυρόμενοι. λῃσταὶ οὖν τὸ
ἐκείνων κακὸν οὐ κατανοήσαντες κενῇ προσπλέοντες
νηί, κᾆτ᾽ ἀφειδῶς ἐνετίθεντο τῶν φορτίων, ἅμα καὶ
τὰ φορτία τῆς νεὼς μετέφερον καὶ τὸ πάθος ἔλαθον
25   μετενεγκόντες. ἡ μὲν γὰρ ἅτε κενωθεῖσα ἀνεκουφίσθη
καὶ πλόιμος ἦν. ἡ δὲ τὸν ἐκείνης φόρτον ὑποδῦσα
ταχέως εἰς βυθὸν ᾔει χρημάτων ἀλλοτρίων ἁρπαγῇ.

Τοῦτο δύναται εἰσρεῖν τὸν ἔχοντα αἰεί. Σκύθαι
δὲ πάντων ἐκτὸς ἔστησαν τούτων. γῆν ἔχομεν πᾶσαν
30   πάντες. ὅσα δίδωσιν ἐκοῦσα, λαμβάνομεν, ὅσα κρύπ-
τει, χαίρειν ἐῶμεν. βοσκήματα ἀπὸ θηρίων σῴζοντες,

be healthy to escape as quickly as possible. Because of
your immoderate enjoyment of pleasure you have physicians
for your bodies, but not for your souls. It would be wise
for you to renounce pleasure. When much gold flows toward
you, the fame that attaches to gold and the envy and desire of those who wish to rob you of your gold have flowed
toward you, too, together with the gold. If, therefore,
you had purified yourself of the disease, you would have
become healthy, speaking and ruling freely. For this is
what it means for a king to be healthy. If you had this
inward possession, it would be no wonder if you also acquired the virtues. But the disease, laying hold of you
in your incontinence, plunged you into ruin, and made you
a slave instead of a free man. But be of good courage and
consider the image of a fire which originates in a forest
and turns what catches on fire to ashes, but which is fed
by what is unburnt. So the evils which were yours long
ago have passed over to those who have a hold on you and
your possessions. Expect that the sorrows will come to
those after you, and hear a story which I myself witnessed.

Through the land of the Scythians there flows a great
river, which is called the Danube. On this river, some
merchants ran their ship aground on a reef. Since they
could not budge it in any way, they went away lamenting.
So, when robbers, without understanding the problem of
these men, sailed up with an empty ship, they freely load-
ed cargo, and at once transferred the cargo from the
strange ship, unaware of the calamity as they made the
transfer. For as the one ship was emptied, it started to
float and became seaworthy. But the ship taking on the
other's cargo quickly sank to the bottom because of the
robbery of foreign goods.

This can always happen to the person who has possessions. But the Scythians have stood apart from all of
these things. All of us possess the whole earth. What it
freely gives, we accept. What it hides, we dismiss from
our minds. We protect our cattle against wild beasts, and

γάλα καὶ τυρὸν ἀντιλαμβάνομεν. ὅπλα ἔχομεν οὐκ ἐπ'
ἄλλους, ἀλλ' ὑπὲρ ἑαυτῶν ἐὰν δέῃ. ἐδέησε δὲ οὐδέπω.
οἱ αὐτοὶ γὰρ ἀγωνισταὶ καὶ ἆθλα τοῖς ἐπελευσομένοις
προκείμεθα. τοῦτο δὲ οὐδὲ πολλοὶ τὸ ἆθλον ἀσπάζον-
5   ται. τὰ αὐτὰ καὶ Σόλων, ἀνὴρ Ἀθηναῖος, συνεβού-
λευσέ σοι, σκοπεῖν κελεύων τὴν τελευτήν, οὐ τὸ νῦν
ἀποβὰν λέγων, ἀλλ' ἐξ οὗ καλῶς τελευτήσεις, τοῦτο
προτιμᾶν ἔλεγεν. ἔλεγε δὲ οὐ τὴν ἀντικρυς. οὐ γὰρ
ἦν Σκύθης. σὺ δ', εἴ σοι φίλον, τὴν ἐμὴν συμβουλὴν
10   καὶ παρὰ Κῦρον φέρε καὶ παρὰ πάντας τυράννους.
μᾶλλον γὰρ ἀκμάσει τοῖς ἐν ἀρχῇ τῶν ἀπολωλότων.

10. Ἀνάχαρσις Κροίσῳ

Ἐγώ, βασιλεῦ Λυδῶν, ἀφῖγμαι εἰς τὴν τῶν
Ἑλλήνων διδαχθησόμενος ἤθη τὰ τούτων καὶ ἐπιτηδεύ-
15   ματα. χρυσοῦ δ' οὐδὲν δέομαι, ἀλλ' ἀπόχρη με
ἐπανήκειν ἐς Σκύθας ἄνδρα ἀμείνονα. ἥκω γοῦν ἐς
Σάρδεις πρὸ μεγάλου ποιούμενος ἐν γνώμῃ τοι γενέσθαι.

in return receive milk and cheese. We have weapons, not
to attack other people, but to defend ourselves, if it
should be necessary. And it has not as yet been necessary.
For we are set before those who would attack us as combat-
ants and as prizes of combat at the same time. For not
many men welcome this prize of combat kindly. These same
things Solon, the Athenian, also advised you, urging you
to consider the end. He was not speaking of what trans-
pires in the present, but he was saying that you should
prefer that by means of which you will finish your life
well. He did not say this openly, for he was not a Scythian. But as for you, if it pleases you, take my advice to
Cyrus and to all tyrants. For it will flourish better
among those in power than among those who are ruined.

10. Anacharsis to Croesus

I, King of the Lydians, have come to the land of the
Greeks to be taught their customs and way of life. I have
no need of gold, but am content to return to the Scythians
a better man. Therefore, I have come to Sardis, considering it an honor to make your acquaintance.

THE EPISTLES OF CRATES

Translated by

Ronald F. Hock

1. ῾Ιππαρχίᾳ

᾽Επάνηκε ταχέως. ἔτι δύνασαι Διογένην καταλαβεῖν ζῶντα (ἐγγὺς γὰρ ἤδη ἐστὶ τῆς τοῦ βίου τελευτῆς,
χθές γέ τοι παρὰ τοσοῦτον ἐξέπνευσεν), ἵνα καὶ
5 ἀσπάσῃ αὐτὸν τὸ ἔσχατον ἄσπασμα καὶ γνῷς ὅσον
δύναται καὶ ἐν τοῖς φοβερωτάτοις φιλοσοφία.

2. Τοῖς ἑταίροις

Μὴ πάντας αἰτεῖτε τὰ ἀναγκαῖα, μηδὲ παρὰ πάντων
τὰ διδόμενα δέχεσθε (οὐ γὰρ θεμιτὸν ἀρετὴν ὑπὸ κακίας
10 τρέφεσθαι), μόνους δὲ καὶ παρὰ μόνων τῶν μεμυημένων
φιλοσοφίαν, καὶ ὑμῖν ἐξέσται ἀπαιτεῖν τὰ ἴδια καὶ μὴ
δοκεῖν αἰτεῖν τὰ ἀλλότρια.

3. Τοῖς αὐτοῖς

Μελέτω ὑμῖν τῆς ψυχῆς, τοῦ δὲ σώματος ὅσον
15 ἀνάγκη, τῶν δ᾽ ἔξωθεν μηδ᾽ ὅσον· εὐδαιμονία γὰρ οὐχ
ἡδονή, δι᾽ ἣν τῶν ἐκτὸς χρεία, ἀρετὴ δὲ μετ᾽ οὐδενὸς
τῶν ἐκτὸς τελεία.

1. To Hipparchia

Return quickly. You can still find Diogenes alive (for he is already near the end of life; yesterday, at any rate, he all but expired) in order to greet him for the last time and to learn how much philosophy can do even in the most terrifying circumstances.

2. To His Students

Do not beg the necessities of life from everyone, nor accept from everyone what is given to you (for it is not right for virtue to be supported by vice). Rather, beg only from those men and accept gifts only from those who have been initiated into philosophy. Then it will be possible for you to demand back what belongs to you and not to appear to be begging what belongs to others.

3. To the Same

Take care of your soul, but take care of the body only to the degree that necessity requires, and of externals not even that much. For happiness is not pleasure, on account of which we need externals, while virtue is complete without any externals.

4. Ἑρμαΐσκῳ

Εἴθ' αἱρετὸν πόνος, εἴτε φευκτόν, πόνει, ἵνα
μὴ πονῇς· διὰ γὰρ τοῦ μὴ πονεῖν οὐ φεύγεται πόνος,
τῷ δὲ ἐναντίῳ καὶ διώκεται.

5. Τοῖς ἑταίροις

Καλὸν νόμος, ἀλλ' οὐ κρείττων φιλοσοφίας· ὃ
μὲν γὰρ βιάζεται μὴ ἀδικεῖν, ἡ δὲ διδάσκει. ὅσῳ
δὲ χεῖρόν ἐστιν ἀνάγκη τι ποιεῖν τοῦ ἑκουσίως,
τοσούτῳ καὶ νόμος φιλοσοφίας, ὥστε διὰ ταῦτα
φιλοσοφεῖτε καὶ μὴ πολιτεύεσθε. κρεῖττον γὰρ δι'
οὗ διδάσκονται ἄνθρωποι δικαιοπραγεῖν ἐπίστασθαι
ἢ δι' οὗ ἀναγκάζονται μὴ ἀδικεῖν.

6. Τοῖς αὐτοῖς

Φιλοσοφεῖτε πολλάκις ἢ ἀναπνεῖτε (αἱρετώτερον
γὰρ τὸ εὖ ζῆν, ὃ ποιεῖ φιλοσοφία, τοῦ ζῆν, ὃ ποιεῖ
ἀναπνοή), καὶ μὴ ὡς οἱ ἄλλοι, ἀλλ' ὡς ἤρξατο μὲν
Ἀντισθένης, ἐτελείωσε δὲ Διογένης. εἰ δὲ δύσκολον
τὸ ὧδε φιλοσοφεῖν, ἀλλὰ συντομώτερον. πρὸς δὲ
εὐδαιμονίαν, ὡς ἔλεγε Διογένης, κἂν διὰ πυρὸς
βαδιστέον.

4. To Hermaiscus

Whether toil is something to be chosen or to be avoided, continue to toil away, in order that you might not toil. For by not toiling toil is not avoided; on the contrary, it is even pursued.

5. To His Students

Law is a good thing, but it is not superior to philosophy. For the former compels a man not to do wrong, but the latter teaches him not to do wrong. To the degree that doing something under compulsion is worse than doing it willingly, to that degree law is worse than philosophy. For this reason do philosophy and do not take part in government. For it is better to know the means by which men are taught to do right than to know the means by which they are compelled not to do wrong.

6. To the Same

Do philosophy more frequently than you breathe (for living well, which philosophy accomplishes, is preferable to simply living, which breathing accomplishes), and not as the others do philosophy, but as Antisthenes began to do philosophy and as Diogenes perfected it. But if doing philosophy in this way is unpleasant, at least it is shorter. As Diogenes used to say, one must proceed toward happiness, even if it is through fire.

7. Τοῖς πλουσίοις

Ἀπάγξασθε, ὅτι θέρμους καὶ ἰσχάδας καὶ ὕδωρ
ἔχοντες καὶ ἐξωμίδας Μεγαρικὰς πλεῖτε καὶ πολλὰ
γεωργεῖτε καὶ προδίδοτε καὶ τυραννεῖτε καὶ φονεύετε
5   καὶ ὅσα ἄλλα τοιαῦτά ἐστι ποιεῖτε, δέον ἠρεμεῖν.
ἡμεῖς δὲ εἰρήνην ἄγομεν τὴν πᾶσαν, παντὸς κακοῦ
ἐλεύθεροι γενόμενοι ὑπὸ τοῦ Σινωπέως Διογένους,
καὶ ἔχοντες μηδὲν πάντ' ἔχομεν, ὑμεῖς δὲ πάντ'
ἔχοντες οὐδὲν ἔχετε διὰ φιλονεικίαν καὶ φθόνον καὶ
10   φόβον καὶ κενοδοξίαν.

8. Διογένει

Ἀπὸ μὲν δὴ τοῦ πλούτου ἤδη ἐλευθεριάζομεν, ἡ
δὲ δόξα ἡμᾶς οὐδέπω ἔτι καὶ νῦν μεθίεται τῆς δου-
λείας, καίτοι νὴ τὸν Ἡρακλέα ἡμῶν πάντα ποιούντων
15   εἰς τὸ ἀφεθῆναι παρ' αὑτῆς. ἄλλως δὲ καὶ τῆσδε
ἐμαυτὸν τῆς δεσποίνης λυτρώσομαι καὶ πλεύσομαι
Ἀθήναζε φέρων σοι δωρεὰν ἀντὶ τῆς ἐλευθερίας, εἰς
ἣν ἐξείλετο ἡμᾶς ὁ παρὰ σοῦ λόγος, ἐμαυτὸν κρείττονα
τῶν πάντων κτημάτων.

7. To the Wealthy

Go hang yourselves, for although you have lupines, dried figs, water, and Megarian tunics, you engage in trade and cultivate much land, you are guilty of treachery, you exercise tyranny and commit murder, and you perpetrate whatever other such things there are--despite the fact that one should live quietly. But as for us, we observe complete peace since we have been freed from every evil by Diogenes of Sinope, and although we possess nothing, we have everything, but you, though you have everything, really have nothing because of your rivalry, jealousy, fear, and conceit.

8. To Diogenes

We are indeed already free from wealth, but fame has up to this point not yet released us from bondage to her, although, by Heracles, we have done everything to be set free from her. Anyway, I shall redeem myself also from this mistress and shall sail to Athens to offer myself to you as a gift which is superior to all possessions in return for the freedom for which your word has set us free.

9. Μνασοῖ

Μὴ ἀπέχου τοῦ καλλίστου κόσμου, ἀλλὰ κόσμει
σαυτὴν ἑκάστης ἡμέρας, ἵνα διαφέρουσα ᾖς. κάλλιστος
δὲ κόσμος ἐστὶν ὁ κάλλιστα κοσμῶν, κάλλιστα δὲ κοσμεῖ
5 ὁ κοσμιωτάτην ποιῶν, κοσμιωτάτην δὲ ποιεῖ κοσμιότης,
ᾗ μοι δοκοῦσι καὶ ἡ Πηνελόπη καὶ Ἄλκηστις κεκοσ-
μῆσθαι καὶ ἔτι καὶ νῦν ἐπ᾿ ἀρετῇ ὑμνεῖσθαι καὶ
τιμᾶσθαι. ἵν᾿ οὖν καὶ σὺ ταύταις ἐνάμιλλος γένῃ,
πειρῶ τούτων ἀντέχεσθαι τῶν παραινουμένων.

10   10. Λύσιδι

Ἀκήκοά σε, ὦ Λῦσι, ἀπὸ τοῦ ἀγῶνος τοῦ ἐν
Ἐρετρίᾳ συνεχῶς μεθύσκεσθαι. εἰ δὲ ταῦτά ἐστιν
ἀληθῆ, πάρεστί γέ σοι μὴ καταφρονῆσαι ὧν Ὅμηρος ὁ
σοφὸς λέγει. φησὶ γάρ
15   οἶνος καὶ κένταυρον ἀγακλυτὸν Εὐρυτίωνα ἄασε
καὶ Κύκλωπα ὑπὲρ ἄνθρωπον καὶ τὸ μέγεθος καὶ τὴν
ἰσχὺν φοροῦντα. εἰ οὖν καὶ τοὺς ἰσχυροτέρους καὶ
μείζους ἡμῶν κακῶς διατίθησι, πῶς οἴει ἡμᾶς αὐτὸν
διαθήσειν; οἶμαι μὲν γὰρ ἀθλίως. ὅπως οὖν μὴ γένη-
20 ται μηδὲν δυσχερὲς ἀπ᾿ αὐτοῦ, παραινῶ σοι μαθόντα
εὐχρήστως αὐτῷ χρῆσθαι. (2) ὡς ἄτοπόν ἐστι, τῷ μὲν
πλήκτρῳ μὴ εἴκειν οἴεσθαι δεῖν, ὃ τοὺς χρωμένους
αὐτῷ καλῶς οὐκ ἐξίστησι τῶν φρενῶν οὐδ᾿ εἰς μανίαν
ἐμβάλλει, τῷ δὲ οἴνῳ οἴεσθαι εἴκειν δεῖν καὶ χρῆσθαι
25 αὐτῷ. (ἢ τῷ πλήκτρῳ ἀποβαίνει τοσοῦτον μεῖζον; καὶ
τὴν μελέτην αὐτοῦ ποιητέον.) πειρῶ δὴ τοῖς ἐγκρατέσι
τῶν ἀνδρῶν ὁμιλῶν ἐγκρατῶς χρῆσθαι μανθάνειν, ὅπως

9. To Mnasos

Do not abstain from the most beautiful ornament, but adorn yourself every day so that you may stand out. The most beautiful ornament is the one that decorates you most beautifully, but the one that decorates you most nobly is the one that makes you decorous, and it is decorum that makes you most decorous. Both Penelope and Alcestis, I think, adorned themselves with it and even now they are praised and honored for their virtue. In order, then, that you, too, might become like them, try to hold fast to this advice.

10. To Lysis

I have heard, Lysis, that you have constantly been drunk ever since the contest in Eretria. If this is true, it behooves you not to despise what the wise Homer says. For he says,

Wine destroyed even a centaur, the renowned
Eurytion (*Od*. xxi.295),

and also Cyclops, even though he possessed superhuman size and strength. Therefore, if wine adversely affects those who are stronger and greater than we are, how do you think it will affect us? Wretchedly, I think. In order, then, that nothing unpleasant happen because of it, I advise you to learn to put it to good use. (2) So, it is absurd to think that one should not succumb to the plectrum, which does not drive those who use it well out of their minds nor throw them into madness, but to think that one should succumb to wine and use it. (Or does something so much worse result from the plectrum? Also be careful in using it.) Now, try to learn to use it temperately, and in the company of temperate men, so that the gift of God might

ἂν τό γε δῶρον τοῦ θεοῦ μὴ ἀτιμάζοντι εἰς κεφαλήν σοι
γένηται, ἀλλὰ τιμῶντι ἡδοναὶ ἀμεταμέλητοι καὶ ὠφέλειαί
σοι ἀπ' αὐτοῦ ὦσιν, ὅταν ἄλλως πᾶς μετ' ἐγκρατείας
περαινομένας εὐσχημόνως σε καὶ δικαίως ποιῇ βιοτεύειν,
5   μηδὲν ἄσχημον μηδὲ φαῦλον ἐν τῷ βίῳ διαπραττόμενον,
ἀλλὰ πάντα τὰ δίκαια λέγοντα καὶ πράττοντα. (3) ὧν
παρουσίᾳ ἄνθρωποι λέγονται τρισευδαίμονες γίνεσθαι,
τρισσῶν αὐτοῖς ἀγαθῶν πληθυνόντων ἐν τῷ βίῳ· οἷς γὰρ
τά τε περὶ ψυχὴν ἐγκρατῶς διάκειται, τά τε περὶ τὸ
10   σῶμα ὑγιεινῶς, τά τε περὶ κτῆσιν αὐτάρκως, πῶς ἂν οὐ
τρισευδαίμονες εἶεν; ὅπως οὖν τούτων τῶν ἀγαθῶν
ἀπολαύῃς, παραινῶ σοι μὴ ὀλιγωρεῖν τῶν ἐπεσταλμένων.

11. Τοῖς ἑταίροις

Ἀσκεῖτε ὀλίγων δεηθῆναι (τοῦτο γὰρ ἐγγυτάτω
15   θεοῦ, τὸ δ' ἐναντίον μακροτάτω), καὶ ὑμῖν ἐξέσται
μέσοις γενομένοις θεῶν καὶ ἀλόγων ζῴων τῷ κρείττονι
γένει καὶ μὴ τῷ χείρονι ὁμοίους γενέσθαι.

12. Ὠρίωνι

Οὐ ποιεῖ ἀγρὸς σπουδαίους, οὐδὲ ἄστυ φαύλους,
20   ἀλλ' αἱ σὺν τοῖς ἀγαθοῖς καὶ κακοῖς διατριβαί. ὥστ'
εἰ βούλει ἀγαθοὺς καὶ μὴ κακοὺς γενέσθαι σοι τοὺς
παῖδας, πέμπε μὴ εἰς ἀγρόν, ἀλλ' εἰς φιλοσόφου, ἵνα
καὶ αὐτοὶ βαδίζοντες τὰ καλὰ ἐμάθομεν. ἀσκητὸν γὰρ
ἀρετὴ καὶ οὐκ αὐτόματος ἐμβαίνει τῇ ψυχῇ ὥσπερ κακία.

not come down on your head because you dishonor it, but so
that, because you do honor it, the pleasures that come
from it might be enjoyed without regret and might be beneficial to you, especially when everyone causes you to live
decently and justly, with temperance in the pleasures that
are being limited, as you do nothing indecent or bad in
your life, but say and do everything that is just. (3) By
their presence men are said to become thrice-blessed as
three benefits accrue to them in life. For how would
those men not be blessed who have temperate souls, healthy
bodies, and sufficient possessions? In order, therefore,
that you may enjoy these benefits, I exhort you not to
slight these precepts.

11. To His Students

Practice being in need of only a few things (for this
is the closest thing to God, while the opposite is the
farthest), and it will be possible for you, because you
are midway between gods and irrational beasts, to become
like the superior race and not like the inferior.

12. To Orion

It is not the country that makes good men, nor the
city bad ones, but rather the time spent with good men and
bad. Consequently, if you want your sons to become good
men and not bad, send them, not to the country, but to a
philosopher's school, where we, too, went and learned the
fine things of life. For virtue is something acquired by
practice and does not spontaneously enter the soul as evil
does.

13. Εὐμόλπῳ

Ἄδοξος στολὴ Διογένειος, ἀλλ᾽ ἀσφαλής, καὶ
πιστότερος ὁ χρώμενος αὐτῇ τῶν τὰ Καρχηδονίων
φορούντων· καὶ λιτὸς ὁ βίος, ἀλλ᾽ ὑγιεινότερος τοῦ
5   Περσικοῦ· καὶ ἐπίπονος ἡ διαγωγή, ἀλλ᾽ ἐλευθεριω-
τέρα τῆς Σαρδαναπάλλου. ὥστε εἰ κρεῖττον τὸ ἀσφαλὲς
τῆς Καρχηδονίας στολῆς καὶ ὑγίεια τοῦ λαμπροῦ βίου
καὶ ἐλευθερία τῆς ἐπονειδίστου διαγωγῆς, καὶ ἡ ταῦτα
φιλοσοφία ποιοῦσα τῶν πάντων ἐστὶ κρείττων, καὶ εἰ μὴ
10   ἡ κατ᾽ ἄλλους, ἀλλ᾽ ἡ κατὰ Διογένην τὸν εὑρόμενον τὴν
σύντομον ὁδὸν ἐπ᾽ εὐδαιμονίαν.

14. Τοῖς νέοις

Ἐθίζεσθε ἐσθίειν μᾶζαν καὶ πίνειν ὕδωρ, ἰχθύος
δὲ καὶ οἴνου μὴ γεύεσθε· ταῦτα γὰρ τοὺς μὲν γέροντας
15   ἀποθηριοῖ ὥσπερ τὰ παρὰ τῆς Κίρκης φάρμακα, τοὺς δὲ
νέους ἀποθηλύνει.

15. Τοῖς ἑταίροις

Φεύγετε μὴ μόνον τὰ τέλη τῶν κακῶν, ἀδικίαν καὶ
ἀκρασίαν, ἀλλὰ καὶ τὰ τούτων ποιητικά, τὰς ἡδονάς·
20   μόναις γὰρ ταύταις καὶ παρούσαις καὶ ἐλπιζομέναις
ἐνατενιεῖτε, ἄλλῳ δὲ οὐδενί. καὶ διώκετε μὴ μόνον τὰ
τέλη τῶν ἀγαθῶν, ἐγκράτειαν καὶ καρτερίαν, ἀλλὰ καὶ
τὰ τούτων ποιητικά, τοὺς πόνους, καὶ μὴ διὰ τὸ τραχὺ
αὐτῶν φεύγετε· <οὐ γὰρ μεγάλῳ τινὶ ἀντικαταλλάξετε
25   χείρω; ἀλλ᾽ ὅσον χρύσεα χαλκείων, πόνων ἀρετήν.>

─────────────────────────
24   <οὐ γὰρ...ἀρετήν> Capelle

13. To Eumolpus

The cloak of Diogenes is disgraceful but secure, and
the one who uses it is more trustworthy than those who
wear the robes of the Carthaginians. And his life is
simple but healthier than that of the Persian. And his way
of life is toilsome but freer than that of Sardanapalus.
Consequently, if security is better than the Carthaginian
robe, health than the magnificent life, and freedom than
the disgraceful way of life, the philosophy that brings
about these things is better, too, than all others, and if
it is not the philosophy of others, it is that of Diogenes,
who discovered the short cut to happiness.

14. To the Youths

Accustom yourselves to eat barley cake and to drink
water, and do not taste fish and wine. For the latter,
like the drugs of Circe, make old men bestial and young
men effeminate.

15. To His Students

Shun not only the worst of evils, injustice and self-
indulgence, but also their causes, pleasures. For you
will concentrate on these alone, both present and future,
and on nothing else. And pursue not only the best of
goods, self-control and perseverance, but also their
causes, toils, and do not shun them on account of their
harshness. For would you not exchange inferior things for
something great? As you would receive gold in exchange
for copper, so you would receive virtue in exchange for
toils.

16. Τοῖς ἑταίροις

Ἡ μὲν κυνικὴ φιλοσοφία ἐστὶν ἡ Διογένειος, ὁ δὲ
κύων ὁ κατὰ ταύτην πονῶν, τὸ δὲ κυνίζειν τὸ συντόμως
φιλοσοφεῖν. ὥστε μὴ φοβεῖσθε τὸ ὄνομα, μηδὲ διὰ
5   ταῦτα φεύγετε τὸν τρίβωνα καὶ τὴν πήραν, τὰ θεῶν
ὅπλα· συντόμως γὰρ ἐκφέρεται τοῖς διὰ τὸ ἦθος τιμίοις.
ὥσπερ οὖν, εἰ ἀγαθοί, οὐκ ἄν κακοὶ λεγόμενοι ἠσχάλλετε,
οὕτως μηδὲ νυνί, ὅτε καὶ τὸ φιλοσοφεῖν συντόμως
κυνίζειν λέγεται καὶ ὁ ὧδε φιλοσοφῶν κύων καὶ ἡ
10   φιλοσοφία κυνική. δόξα γὰρ τὸ ὅλον τοῦτο. δόξῃ δὲ
καὶ ἀδοξίᾳ δουλεύειν, καὶ τοῦτ᾽ ἐν σκιαῖς, ὥς φασι,
τοῖς ὀνόμασι, πάντων χαλεπώτατον. πειρᾶσθε οὖν καὶ
τούτων καὶ τῶν ὁμοίων καταφρονεῖν.

17. Τοῖς αὐτοῖς

15   Οἱ μὲν ἰατροὶ μίαν ἔγραψαν κοιλιακὴν διάθεσιν,
ἥν ἔλεγον ποιεῖν ἀπεψίαν, Διογένης δὲ ἑτέραν, ἥν
ἔλεγε ποιεῖν λιμόν. ἀλλ᾽ ἐπὶ τῇ προτέρᾳ φάρμακον
αἰτεῖν παρὰ τῶν ἰατρῶν οὐκ ἄδοξον, ἀλλὰ τῇ ἑτέρᾳ.
ὥστε διὰ τοῦτο καταφρονεῖτε τῶν τοιαῦτα αἰσχρὰ
20   λεγόντων καὶ ἄδοξα, καὶ αἰτεῖτε κατ᾽ ἴσον τὴν μᾶζαν
τοῖς καταποτίοις· οὐ γὰρ αἰσχρὸν τὸ αἰτεῖν, ἀλλὰ τὸ
μὴ παρέχειν ἑαυτὸν ἄξιον τοῦ διδομένου. ἔστι δὲ τὸ
δι᾽ ἀπεψίαν ἢ λιμὸν ἐπὶ ῥᾴστων· ἡ μὲν γὰρ γίνεται
διὰ γαστριμαργίαν παρὰ κακίας, ἡ δὲ δι᾽ ἔνδειαν παρ᾽
25   ἀπορίας.

16. To His Students

Cynic philosophy is Diogenean, the Cynic is one who toils according to this philosophy, and to be a Cynic is to take a short cut in doing philosophy. Consequently, do not fear the name, nor for this reason shun the cloak and wallet, which are the weapons of the gods. For they are quickly displayed by those who are honored for their character. Therefore, just as you, if you were good, would not be distressed at being called bad, so do not be distressed even now when taking the short cut to philosophy is called "living like a dog" and such a philosopher is called a "dog," and such a philosophy "doggish." For all this is merely opinion, and to be enslaved to opinion and disgrace, and that to names, "mere shadows," as they say, is most irksome of all. Try, therefore, to despise both these and similar things.

17. To the Same

Doctors have written about one condition of the bowels which, they say, causes indigestion, while Diogenes has written about another which, he says, causes hunger. For the former condition it is not disgraceful to ask doctors for medicine, yet it is for the latter condition. So for this reason despise those who say such base and disreputable things, and beg bread as well as pills. For it is not begging that is base, but not showing oneself as worthy of what is given. It is characteristic of unscrupulous men to beg on account of indigestion rather than hunger, for the former is caused by gluttony that results from wickedness, but the latter by need that results from poverty.

18. Τοῖς νεανίσκοις

Ἐθίζεσθε ψυχρῷ λούεσθαι καὶ πίνειν ὕδωρ καὶ
ἐσθίειν μὴ ἀνιδρωτὶ καὶ ἀμπέχεσθαι τρίβωνα καὶ κατα-
τρίβεσθαι ἐπὶ γῆς, καὶ οὐδέποτε ὑμῖν κλεισθήσεται τὰ
5   βαλανεῖα, αἱ δ' ἄμπελοι καὶ τὰ πρόβατα ἀφορήσει καὶ
τὰ ὀψοπώλια καὶ κλινοπώλια πενητεύσει ὥσπερ τοῖς
μεμαθηκόσι θερμῷ μὲν λούεσθαι, πίνειν δ' οἶνον καὶ
ἐσθίειν μὴ πονήσαντας καὶ ἀμπέχεσθαι ἀλουργῆ καὶ
ἀναπαύεσθαι ἐπὶ κλίνης.

10   19. Πατροκλεῖ

Μὴ λέγε τὸν Ὀδυσσέα πατέρα τῆς κυνικῆς τὸν
πάντων μαλακώτατον ἑταίρων καὶ τὴν ἡδονὴν ὑπὲρ πάντα
πρεσβεύοντα, ὅτι ποτὲ τὰ τοῦ κυνὸς ἐνεδύσατο· οὐ γὰρ
ἡ στολὴ ποιεῖ κύνα, ἀλλ' ὁ κύων στολήν, ὅπερ οὐκ ἦν
15   Ὀδυσσεύς, ἡττώμενος μὲν ἀεὶ ὕπνου, ἡττώμενος δὲ
ἐδωδῆς, ἐπαινῶν δὲ τὸν ἡδὺν βίον, πράττων δὲ οὐδὲν
οὐδέποτε ἄνευ θεοῦ καὶ τύχης, αἰτῶν δὲ πάντας καὶ
τοὺς ταπεινούς, λαμβάνων δ' ὁπόσ' ἂν τις χαρίσαιτο.
λέγε δὲ Διογένη τὸν μὴ ἅπαξ κυνικὴν στολὴν ἐνδυσά-
20   μενον, ἀλλὰ τὸν ὅλον βίον, κρείττω καὶ πόνου καὶ
ἡδονῆς, τὸν ἀπαιτοῦντα καὶ οὐκ ἐκ τοῦ ταπεινοῦ, τὸν
τἀναγκαῖα πάντα προϊέμενον, τὸν ἐφ' ἑαυτῷ θαρροῦντα,
τὸν μηδέποτε εὐχόμενον ἐλεεινὸν ἐς τιμὰς ἐλθεῖν,
ἀλλὰ σεμνὸν καὶ τῷ λόγῳ πιστεύοντα καὶ οὐ δόλῳ οὐδὲ
25   τόξῳ, τὸν οὐκ ἐπὶ τῷ ἀποθανεῖν καρτερικόν, ἀλλ' ἐπὶ
τῷ τὴν ἀρετὴν ἀσκῆσαι ἀνδρεῖον· καὶ ἐξέσται σοι μὴ
τὸν Ὀδυσσέα ζηλοῦν, ἀλλὰ τὸν Διογένη, τὸν πολλοὺς
καὶ ὅτε ἔζη ἐξελόμενον ἐκ κακίας εἰς ἀρετὴν καὶ ὅτε
τέθνηκε δι' ὧν κατέλιπεν ἡμῖν λόγων.

18. To the Youths

Accustom yourselves to wash with cold water, to drink only water, to eat nothing that has not been earned by toil, to wear a cloak, and to make it a habit to sleep on the ground. Then the baths will never be closed to you, the vineyards and flocks fail, the fish shops and couch shops go broke, as they will to those who have learned how to wash with hot water, to drink wine, to eat without having toiled, to wear purple clothing, and to rest on a couch.

19. To Patrocles

Do not call Odysseus, who was the most effiminate of all his companions and who put pleasure above all else, the father of Cynicism because once he put on the garb of the Cynic. For the cloak does not make a Cynic, but the Cynic the cloak. Such was not the case with Odysseus, since he always succumbed to sleep, succumbed to food, praised the sweet life, never did anything without God and fortune, begged from everyone--even from the humble, and accepted whatever anyone gave. Rather, call Diogenes the father of Cynicism. He put on the cloak not just once but throughout his life, he was superior to both toil and pleasure, he demanded his support but not from the humble, he abandoned all necessities, he had confidence in himself, he prayed that he might never attain to honors out of pity but as a revered man, he trusted in reason and not in guile or bow, he was brave not only at the point of death but was also courageous in his practice of virtue. And it will be proper for you to emulate, not Odysseus, but Diogenes who delivered many from evil to virtue, both when he was alive and after he died through the teachings he left behind for us.

20. Μητροκλεῖ

Χωρισθέντος σοῦ παρ' ἡμῶν ἐπ' οἴκου κατέβην εἰς
τὴν τῶν νέων παλαίστραν καὶ ἀλειψάμενος ἔτρεχον. καί
με οἱ νέοι κατιδόντες ἐγέλων, ἐγὼ δὲ ἵνα μὴ θᾶττον
5   καταπαύσωμαι τῶν γυμνασίων, ἐπεκελευόμην ἐμαυτῷ
λέγων "Κράτης, πονεῖς ὑπὲρ ὀφθαλμῶν, ὑπὲρ κεφαλῆς,
ὑπὲρ ὤτων, ὑπὲρ ποδῶν." οἱ δέ μου ταῦτα ἐπήκουσαν,
καὶ οὐκέτι ἐπεγέλων, ἀλλ' ἐγχειρήσαντες καὶ αὐτοὶ
τρέχειν ἤρξαντο, καὶ ἐξ ἐκείνου οὐκέτι μόνον ἠλεί-
10 φοντο ἀλλὰ καὶ ἐγυμνάζοντο, καὶ διὰ ταῦτα οὐκ ἐπιν-
νόσως διῆγον, ὥσπερ πάλαι, ἐμοί τε χάριν ἐγίνωσκον
ὡς αἰτίῳ τῆς ὑγιείας, καὶ οὐκ ἀπελείποντο, ἀλλ'
εἵποντο ὅπου ἂν βαδίζοιμι, ἐπακροώμενοι καὶ μιμούμενοι ἃ λέγοιμι καὶ πράττοιμι.
15   Ταῦτα ἐπέσταλκά σοι, ἵνα καὶ σὺ μὴ καθ' ἑαυτὸν
τρέχῃς, κεῖθι δὲ ἔνθα οἱ νέοι διατρίβουσιν, ὧν ἐχρῆν
τι ἡμᾶς προμηθεῖσθαι, ἐπεὶ διδάσκει καρτερίαν τάχιον
τὸ ἔργον τοῦ λόγου, ὅπερ ἐν μόνῃ τῇ Διογένους ἐστὶ
φιλοσοφίᾳ.

20   ## 21. Μητροκλεῖ τῷ κυνί

Ἕως ἂν φοβῇ τὸν κύνα, τοῦτο προσαγορεύω· φαίνει
δὲ φοβούμενος ἕως τούτου. καὶ αὐτὸς δ' ἐπιστέλλων
ἡμῖν κύνα ἐπέγραψας. καὶ τἆλλα δὲ ὧδε ποιεῖν μαθήσῃ,
μὴ φοβεῖσθαι ἐθιζόμενος, μὴ μόνον λογικεύεσθαι· μακρὰ
25 γὰρ ἡ διὰ τῶν λόγων ὁδὸς ἐπ' εὐδαιμονίαν, ἡ δὲ διὰ
τῶν καθ' ἡμέραν ἔργων μελέτη σύντομος. ἀλλ' οἱ
πολλοὶ ἐπὶ τὸ αὐτὸ τοῖς κυσὶν ἱέμενοι ἐπειδὰν ἐπι-
βλέψωσι τὸ χαλεπὸν αὐτῆς, φεύγουσι τοὺς ἐπιφωνοῦντας.
ἀλλὰ διὰ μὲν ταύτην τὴν ὁδὸν τὸν κύνα οὐ γενέσθαι
30 δεῖ, ἀλλὰ γεννηθῆναι· φύσει γὰρ ἡ μελέτη μᾶλλον
ἀνυσιμωτέρα ἢ ἡ ὁδὸς αὕτη.

20. To Metrocles

After you left us for home, I went down to the palaestra of the young men and, after anointing myself with oil,
went running. When the young men caught sight of me, they
broke up laughing, but I, lest I cease too quickly from exercising, exhorted myself, saying: "Crates, you are toiling
for the eyes, for the head, for the ears, for the feet."
They heard me saying this and laughed no more; rather,
they, too, made a start and began to run, and from that
time on they no longer merely anointed themselves with oil,
but also kept exercising. For that reason they are not
always sick, as formerly. They thanked me for being the
cause of their health and did not leave me but continued
to follow me wherever I went, listening to me and imitating what I said and did.

I am writing this to you so that you, too, might run,
not by yourself, but where the young men spend their time.
We must provide for them, since action teaches endurance
more quickly than words, a tenet found only in the philosophy of Diogenes.

21. To Metrocles the Cynic

So long as you fear the name "Cynic," I am going to
call you by this name, and you are still plainly afraid of
it. You yourself, when writing, have addressed us as "Cynics." And you will learn how to do the other things in
this manner if you make it a habit not to be afraid of words
nor merely to use them. For the way that leads to happiness
through words is long, but that which leads through daily
deeds is a shortened regimen. But the masses, although they
desire the same end as the Cynics, flee those who preach the
regimen, when they see how difficult it is. One must not
become a Cynic because of this way, but must be born one. For
the regimen is naturally more effective than the way itself.

22. Μετροκλεῖ

Μὴ πάντας αἴτει, ἀλλὰ τοὺς ἀξίους, μηδὲ παρὰ
πάντων τὸ ἴσον λάμβανε, ἀλλὰ τριώβολον μὲν παρὰ τῶν
σωφρόνων, μνᾶν δὲ παρὰ τῶν ἀσώτων· οὐ γὰρ παρ' αὐτῶν
ἔστι πάλιν λαβεῖν, ὡς παρὰ τῶν σωφρόνων, ὧδε δαπανών-
5   των.

23. Γανυμήδει

Ἕως ἂν φοβῇ τὸν τρίβωνα καὶ τὴν πήραν καὶ τὴν
βακτηρίαν καὶ τὴν κόμην, φιλῇς δὲ τὰ ἀλουργῆ καὶ τὴν
τρυφήν, οὐ παύσει τοὺς ἐραστὰς ἐπισυρόμενος, ὥσπερ ἡ
10   Πηνελόπη τοὺς μνηστῆρας. ὥστ' εἰ μή σοι ὄχλος οἱ
τοιοῦτοι τῶν ἀνθρώπων, χρῶ ᾧ προῄρησαι βίῳ· εἰ δ'
ἔστιν, ὡς πείθομαι, καὶ οὐ μικρός, τοὺς μὲν ἄλλους
βοηθοὺς χαίρειν ἔα δι' ὧν πολλάκις ἐπειράθης αὐτοὺς
ἀπελάσαι σαυτοῦ καὶ οὐκ ἴσχυσας, ἔνδυσαι δὲ τὰ
15   Διογένεια ὅπλα, οἷς κἀκεῖνος ἀπήλασε τοὺς ἐπιβου-
λεύοντας, καὶ πείθου μηδένα ἔτι πελάσειν σοι τῶν
ἐραστῶν· δεινὰ γὰρ ταῦτα καταγωνίσασθαι τοὺς τοιούτους ἐχθροὺς καὶ ἀποκρύψαι τὸν μὴ ἐθέλοντα τούτοις
ἐκ τοῦ ἐμφανοῦς μάχεσθαι, ὥσπερ ἄιδος κυνῆ τὸν
20   περικείμενον αὐτήν.

22. To Metrocles

Do not beg from everyone but only from the worthy, and do not take the same amount from everyone, but accept a triobol from the prudent and a mina from spendthrifts. For one cannot again receive anything from them, as one can from the prudent, since they squander their money so recklessly.

23. To Ganymedes

So long as you fear the cloak and wallet and staff and long hair, and as long as you love purple robes and luxury, you will not cease leading on lovers, as Penelope did her suitors. And so, if such men are not troublesome to you, enjoy the life you have chosen. But if, as I am persuaded, they are not a little troublesome to you, dismiss the other aides through whom you frequently, but without success, tried to drive them away from yourself, and put on the weapons of Diogenes, with which he did drive away those who had designs on him. Rest assured that none of the lovers will ever approach you again. For these weapons are terribly effective at overcoming such foes and at concealing the one who does not wish to fight openly with them, just as the helmet of Hades conceals the one who wears it.

24. Θεσσαλοῖς

Οὐ γεγόνασιν οἱ ἄνθρωποι τῶν ἵππων χάριν, ἀλλ'
οἱ ἵπποι τῶν ἀνθρώπων, ὥστε πειρᾶσθε ὑμῶν ἢ τῶν
ἵππων ἐπιμελεῖσθαι. ἐπεὶ εὖ ἴστε ὅτι ἕξετε ἵππους
5   πολλοῦ ἀξίους, αὐτοὶ ὀλίγου ἄξιοι ὄντες.

25. Ἀθηναίοις

Πυνθάνομαι ὑμᾶς ἀπορεῖν χρημάτων. τοὺς ἵππους
οὖν ἀπόδοσθε καὶ εὐπορήσετε. ὅταν δὲ χρεία ᾖ ἵππων,
τοὺς ὄνους χειροτονήσατε ἵππους εἶναι· τοῦτο γὰρ
10   συνηθὲς ὑμῖν ἐν παντί, μὴ τοὺς ἐπιτηδείους πρὸς τὰς
χρείας ἀλλὰ τοὺς κεχειροτονημένους ποιεῖσθαι. ἀλλ'
εἰ μὲν ἐν τοῖς μείζοσι τὸ μὴ ὄν, ὅμως τὴν χρείαν οὐ
διαφθείρει, μηδ' ἐν τοῖς ἐλάττοσι προσδοκᾶτε. ὥστε
διὰ τοῦτο πείσθητέ μοι, καὶ τοὺς ἵππους, ἐπειδὰν
15   ἀργυρίων δέησθε καὶ πόρος ἄλλοθεν μὴ ᾖ, ἀπόδοσθε,
τοὺς δὲ ὄνους, ὅταν χρεία ᾖ, χειροτονήσατε ἵππους
εἶναι.

24. To the Thessalians

Men were not created for the sake of horses, but
horses for the sake of men. So, try to take care of
yourselves rather than the horses. Otherwise, know for
certain that you will have horses worth very much, whereas
you yourselves will be worth very little.

25. To the Athenians

I hear that you are in need of money. Therefore,
sell your horses and you will have money. Then, whenever
there is a need for horses, vote that your asses are
horses. For this has become your custom in every matter:
not to do what is proper for your needs but to do what has
been voted upon. But if there is a lack of realism in
important matters, it nevertheless does not do away with
the need, even in minor matters. So for this reason obey
me and sell your horses whenever you are in need of money
and have no other resources, and when there is a need vote
that your asses are horses.

26. Τοῖς αὐτοῖς

Μὴ θαυμάζετε, εἰ Διογένης, πάντα τοῦ σπουδαίου
εἶναι λέγων, προσιὼν οὐκ ᾔτει ὑμᾶς, ἀλλ' ἀπῄτει.
οὐ γὰρ ὅτι πάντα τοῦ θεοῦ ἐστὶ θαυμάζετε, ἀλλ'
5   ὁμολογεῖτε, κἄν τις ὑμᾶς κατ' ὄναρ ἐμπελάσας θῦσαι
προστάττῃ, αὐτῷ θύετε, καὶ οὐ λέγετε μεταιτεῖν τὸν
Ἥλιον ὑμᾶς, ἀλλὰ τὰ αὐτοῦ ἀπαιτεῖν. ἔπειτα τοῦ
θεοῦ λέγοντες πάντα οὐκ ἀσχάλλετε, ὅταν τι ἀπαιτῆσθε
ὑπ' αὐτοῦ. τὸ αὐτό ἐστι καὶ ἐπὶ τοῦ σπουδαίου.
10 πάντα λέγετε τοῦ θεοῦ καὶ κοινὰ τὰ τῶν φίλων καὶ
φίλον τῷ θεῷ μόνον τὸν σπουδαῖον, ἀλλ' ὅταν ἀπαιτήσῃ
παρά τινος ὑμῶν τὸν ὀβολόν, ὡς τὰ αὐτῶν μεθιέμενοι
συμφοράζετε.

27. Τοῖς αὐτοῖς

15 Διογένης ὁ κύων ἔλεγε πάντα τοῦ θεοῦ καὶ κοινὰ
τὰ τῶν φίλων, ὥστε πάντα εἶναι τοῦ σπουδαίου, καὶ
τὸν τούτων τι τῶν λημμάτων ἐκ τοῦ λόγου ἀθετοῦντα
ὅρκια συγχεῖν οὐ τὰ Ἀχαιῶν καὶ Τρώων, ἀλλὰ τὰ τοῦ
βίου, ὥστε πειθόμενοι τῷ λόγῳ μὴ χαλεπαίνετε, ὅταν
20 αἰτῆσθε παρὰ τῶν σπουδαίων τὸ τριώβολον· οὐ γὰρ τὰ
αὐτῶν, ἀλλὰ τὰ ἐκείνων ἀποδίδοτε.

26. To the Same

Do not be amazed if Diogenes, saying that all things
belong to the wise man, approached you and did not ask you
for something but demanded back what was due him. For you
are not amazed that all things belong to God. On the contrary, you admit that even if someone appears to you in a
dream and orders you to sacrifice, you would sacrifice to
him. Moreover, you do not say that Helios begs from you
but rather that he demands back what belongs to him. Then,
having said that all things belong to God, you are not
vexed whenever he demands something of you. The same
thing is true also in the case of the wise man. You say
that all things belong to God, that friends have things in
common, and that only the wise man is a friend of God, yet
whenever the wise man demands an obol from any of you, how
you wail at having to let go of it, as though it were yours!

27. To the Same

Diogenes the Cynic used to say that all things belong
to God and that friends have things in common, so that all
things belong to the wise man. He also used to say that
the one who rejects any of the assumptions of this argument violates not the treaty of Achaea and Troy but that
of life itself. Therefore, heed the argument and do not
be angry whenever you are asked for a triobol by wise men.
For you are giving back not what is yours but what is
theirs.

28. Ἱππαρχία

Αἱ γυναῖκες ἀνδρῶν οὐκ ἔφυσαν χείρους. Ἀμαζό-
νες γοῦν αἱ τοσαῦτα ἔργα ἀσκήσασαι ἐν οὐδενὶ ἀνδρῶν
ἐμειονέκτησαν. ὥστε εἰ μέμνησαι τούτων, μὴ ἀπολιποῦ
5   τούτων· οὐ γὰρ ἂν πείσειας ἡμᾶς, ὡς παρ' ἑαυτῇ
θρύπτει. αἰσχρὸν δὲ ὡς ἐπὶ τούτῳ συγκυνίζειν καὶ
ἐν πύλαις εὐδοκιμήσασαν τῷ γαμέτῃ καὶ τῷ πλούτῳ νῦν
μετανοεῖν καὶ ἐκ μέσης τῆς ὁδοῦ ἀναστρέφειν.

29. Τῇ αὐτῇ

10   Οὐκ ἀπὸ τοῦ ἀδιαφορεῖν περὶ πάντα κυνικὴν τὴν
φιλοσοφίαν ἡμῶν ἐκάλεσαν ἀλλ' ἀπὸ τοῦ σφοδρῶς ὑπο-
μένειν τὰ ἄλλοις διὰ μαλακίαν ἢ δόξαν ἀνυπομόνητα,
ὥστε διὰ τοῦτο καὶ οὐ διὰ τὰ πρῶτα κεκλήκασι κύνας
ἡμᾶς. μένε οὖν καὶ συγκύνιζε (οὐ γὰρ ἔφυς χείρων
15   ἡμῶν· οὐδὲ γὰρ αἱ κύνες τῶν κυνῶν), ἵνα σοι γένηται
καὶ ἀπὸ τῆς φύσεως ἐλευθερωθῆναι, ὥστε ἀπὸ τοῦ
νόμου ἢ διὰ κακίαν πάντες δουλεύουσιν.

28. To Hipparchia

Women are not by nature worse than men. The Amazons, at any rate, who have accomplished such great feats, have not fallen short of men in anything. So, if you remember these deeds, do not leave them undone. For you would not convince us that you are enfeebled at home! Furthermore, it would be shameful, since you have taken up the Cynic life with your husband, both in the portals and with respect to your wealth, to change your mind now and to turn back half way down the road.

29. To the Same

It is not because we are indifferent to everything that others have called our philosophy Cynic, but because we robustly endure those things which are unbearable to them because they are effeminate or subject to false opinion. It is for this latter reason and not for the former that they have called us Cynics. Stand fast, therefore, and live the Cynic life with us (for you are not by nature inferior to us, for female dogs are not by nature inferior to male dogs), in order that you might be freed even from nature, since all are slaves either by law or through wickedness.

30. Τῇ αὐτῇ

῎Επεμψα σοι τὴν ἐξωμίδα, ἣν ὑφηναμένη μοι
ἔπεμψας, ὅτι ἀπαγορεύεται τοῖς καρτερίᾳ χρωμένοις
τοιαῦτα ἀμπέχεσθαι, καὶ ἵνα σε τούτου τοῦ ἔργου
5   ἀποπαύσαιμι, εἰς ὃ πολλῇ σπουδῇ ἐξῆλθες, ἵνα τις
δόξῃς φίλανδρος τοῖς πολλοῖς εἶναι. ἐγὼ δὲ εἰ μὲν
διὰ ταῦτά σε ἡγόμην, εὖ γε ποιεῖς καὶ αὐτὴ διὰ
τούτων ἐπιδεικνυμένη μοι· εἰ δὲ διὰ φιλοσοφίαν,
ἧς καὶ αὐτὴ ὠρέχθης, τὰ τοιαῦτα σπουδάσματα ἔα
10 χαίρειν, πειρῶ δὲ εἰς τὰ κρείττω τῶν ἀνθρώπων τὸν
βίον ὠφελεῖν. ταῦτα γὰρ ἔμαθες καὶ παρ᾽ ἐμοὶ καὶ
παρὰ Διογένει.

31. Τῇ αὐτῇ

Λόγος ψυχῆς ἡγεμὼν καλὸν ἔργον καὶ μέγιστον
15 ἀγαθὸν ἀνθρώποις. ζήτει οὖν, ὅτῳ τρόπῳ κτήσῃ
τοῦτον· ἀνθέξῃ γὰρ εὐδαίμονος βίου καὶ κτήματος.
ζήτει δὲ ἄνδρας σοφούς, κἂν δέῃ ἐπ᾽ ἔσχατα γῆς
ἀφικνεῖσθαι.

30. To the Same

I am returning the tunic that you wove and sent to
me because those of us who live a life of perseverance
are forbidden to wear such things, and I do so in order
that I may cause you to desist from this task which you
have undertaken with much zeal so that you might appear
to the masses to be someone who loves her husband. Now
if I had married you for this reason, you would certainly
be acting properly and your zeal would be very apparent
to me in this. But since I married you for the sake of
philosophy, for which you yourself have yearned, renounce
such pursuits and try to be of greater benefit to human
life. For this you learned both from me and from Diogenes.

31. To the Same

Reason is a guide of the soul, a beautiful work, and
the greatest good to men. Therefore, seek how to acquire
this for yourself. For then you will hold fast to a happy
life along with this possession. And seek wise men, even
if you have to go to the ends of the earth.

32. Τῇ αὐτῇ

῏Ηκόν τινες παρὰ σοῦ κομίζοντες ἐξωμίδα καινήν,
ἣν ἔφασκον ποιῆσαί σε, ἵνα ἔχοιμι ἐς τὰ χειμάδια.
ἐγὼ δὲ ὅτι μέν σοι μέλω, ἀπεδεξάμην σε, ὅτι δὲ ἔτι
5   ἰδιωτεύεις καὶ οὐ φιλοσοφεῖς, εἰς ὃ σε προυτρεψάμην,
μέμφομαι. ἔτι οὖν καὶ νῦν ἐπάνηκε, εἴ σοι ὄντως
μέλει καὶ οὐ καλλωπίζῃ ἐπὶ τούτῳ, καὶ σπούδαζε δι᾽
ἃ ἐπεθύμησας ἡμῖν συνελθεῖν πρὸς γάμον ταῦτα πράττειν, ταλασίας δὲ τὰς μικρὰς ὠφελείας ἔα ποιεῖν
10   ταῖς ἄλλαις γυναιξίν, αἳ μηδενὸς τῶν αὐτῶν σοι
ὠρέχθησαν.

33. Τῇ αὐτῇ

᾿Επυθόμην σε ἀποτεκεῖν καὶ εὐμαρῶς· σὺ μὲν γὰρ
οὐδὲν ἡμῖν ἐδήλωσας. χάρις δὲ θεῷ καὶ σοί. πέπει-
15   σαι ἄρα ὅτι τὸ πονεῖν αἴτιόν ἐστι τοῦ μὴ πονεῖν·
οὐδὲ γὰρ ἂν ὧδέ γ᾽ εὐμαρῶς ἀπέτεκες, εἰ μὴ κύουσα
ἐπόνεις ὥσπερ οἱ ἀγωνισταί. ἀλλ᾽ αἱ πολλαὶ γυναῖκες,
ἐπειδὰν κύωσι, θρύπτονται· ἐπειδὰν δὲ ἀποτέκωσιν,
αἷς δ᾽ ἂν συμβῇ περισωθῆναι, νοσερὰ τὰ βρέφη γεννῶν-
20   ται. ἀλλ᾽ ἐπιδείξασα, εἰ ὅπερ ἐχρῆν ἥκειν ἀφῖκται,
μελέτω σοι τούτου τοῦ σκυλακίου ἡμῶν· μελήσει δέ,
ἐὰν ἀσφαλῶς σαυτῇ παραπλησίως ἐπεισέλθῃς. (2) ἔστω
οὖν λουτρὸν μὲν ψυχρόν, σπάργανα δὲ τρίβων, τροφὴ
δὲ γάλακτος ὅσον γε μὴ ἐς κόρον, βαυκαλήσεις δὲ ἐν
25   ὀστρακίῳ χελώνης· τοῦτο γάρ φασι καὶ πρὸς νοσήματα
παιδικὰ διαφέρειν. ἐπειδὰν δὲ ἐς τὸ λαλεῖν ἢ περι-
πατεῖν ἔλθῃ, κοσμήσασα αὐτὸ μὴ ξίφει, ὥσπερ ἡ Αἴθρα
τὸν Θησέα, ἀλλὰ βακτηρίᾳ καὶ τρίβωνι καὶ πήρᾳ, τοῖς
μᾶλλον δυναμένοις φυλάττειν ἀνθρώπους ξιφῶν, πέμπε
30   ᾿Αθήναζε. τὰ δ᾽ ἄλλα ἡμῖν μελήσει πελαργὸν ἐς τὸ
γῆρας ἑαυτῶν ἀντὶ κυνὸς θρέψαι.

32. To the Same

Some have come from you bringing a new tunic, which,
they say, you made so that I might have it for the winter.
Because you care for me, I approved of you, but because
you are still uneducated and not practicing the philosophy
for which I have tutored you, I censure you. Therefore,
give up doing this right now, if you really care, and do
not pride yourself in this kind of activity, but endeavor
to do those things for which you wanted to marry me.
And leave the wool-spinning, which is of little benefit,
to the other women, who have aspired to none of the
things you do.

33. To the Same

I hear that you have given birth--and that quite
easily, for you have said nothing to me. Thanks be to
God and to you. You believe, it seems, that toiling is
the cause of your not having to toil. For you would not
have given birth so easily unless, while pregnant, you had
continued to toil as the athletes do. Most women, however,
whenever they are pregnant, are enfeebled; and when they
give birth, those who happen to survive bring forth sickly
babies. Having shown that what had to come has arrived,
take care of this little puppy of ours. And you will take
care of him, if you enter into child rearing with your
usual concern. (2) Therefore, let his bath water be cold,
his clothes be a cloak, his food be milk, yet not to excess. Rock him in a cradle made from a tortoise shell,
for this, they say, protects against childhood diseases.
When he is able to speak and walk, dress him, not with a
sword, as Aethra did with Theseus, but with a staff and
cloak and wallet, which can guard men better than swords,
and send him to Athens. As for the rest, I shall take
care to rear a stork for our old age instead of a dog.

34. Μητροκλεῖ

Ἴσθι με συμφορᾷ κεχρῆσθαι πυθόμενον Διογένη ἐς
ληστρικὰ ἁλῶναι, καὶ εἰ μή τις τῶν αἰχμαλώτων
λυτρωθεὶς ἦλθεν Ἀθήναζε, ἔτι ἂν ἦν καὶ νῦν ἐν τοῖς
5   ὁμοίοις. νῦν δ᾽ ἀφικόμενος οὗτος ἰάσατό με, διηγη-
σάμενος ὡς "ἤνεγκε τὴν συμφορὰν πρᾴως, ὥστε ποτὲ καὶ
εἶπε τοῖς λησταῖς ὀλιγωροῦσιν ἡμῶν, 'ὦ οὗτοι, τί
δήποτε; εἰ μὲν σῦς ἤγετε εἰς ἐμπορίαν, ἐπεμελεῖσθε
ἂν αὐτῶν, ἵνα ὑμῖν πλεῖον ἀργύριον πωλούμενοι
10   ἐνέγκωσιν· ἡμῶν δέ, οὓς καὶ αὐτοὺς μέλλετε ὥσπερ σῦς
πιπράσκειν, καταμελεῖτε. (2) ἢ οὐ δοκεῖτε καὶ ἡμᾶς
πλεῖον εὑρίσκειν, ἐὰν παχεῖς ὁρώμεθα, ἔλαττον δὲ ἐὰν
λεπτοί; ἐπεὶ ἄνθρωποι οὐκ ἐσθίονται, οὐκ οἴεσθε
δεῖν καὶ ἀνθρώπων ἐπιμελεῖσθαι ὧδε; ἀλλ᾽ ἴστε γε
15   ὡς πάντες οἱ ἀγοράζοντες τὰ ἀνδράποδα εἰς ἓν τοῦτο
βλέπουσιν, εἰ παχὺ τὸ σῶμα καὶ μέγα. ἐρῶ δὲ ὑμῖν
καὶ αἰτίαν, ὅτι καὶ ἄνθρωπον διὰ τὴν τοῦ σώματος
χρείαν ἀγοράζουσι καὶ οὐ τῆς ψυχῆς.' ἐξ ἐκείνου οἱ
λησταὶ οὐκέτι ἠμέλουν ἡμῶν, ἐπὶ τούτῳ δὲ καὶ ἡμεῖς
20   αὐτῷ χάριν ἐγινώσκομεν.
(3) "Ὡς δὲ ἥκομεν ἐς τινα πόλιν, ἵνα ἠδυνάμεθα
κέρμα γενέσθαι αὐτοῖς, προήγαγον ἡμᾶς ἐς ἀγοράν,
εἶτα ἡμεῖς μὲν ἐστῶτες ἐδακρύομεν, ὃ δὲ ἄρτου ἐπι-
λαβόμενος ἤσθιε καὶ ἡμῖν προσώρεγεν. ἀπονευόντων
25   δὲ ἡμῶν προσδέξασθαι ἔφη

καὶ γάρ τ᾽ ἠύκομος Νιόβη ἐμνήσατο σίτου

καὶ τοῦτο μετὰ παιδιᾶς καὶ γέλωτος εἰπὼν 'οὐ
παύσεσθε' ἔφη 'εἰρωνευόμενοι καὶ κλαίοντες ἐπὶ τῷ
μέλλειν δουλεύειν, ὥσπερ πρὶν ἁλῶναι εἰς τοὺς
30   ληστὰς ἐλεύθεροι ὄντες καὶ οὐ δοῦλοι καὶ τῶν γε
φαύλων δεσποτῶν; νυνὶ μὲν γὰρ κληρώσεσθε ἴσως
δεσπότας μετρίους, οἳ ἐκκόψουσιν ὑμῶν τὴν τρυφήν,
ὑφ᾽ ἧς διεφθάρητε, ἐμποιήσουσι δὲ καρτερίαν καὶ

34. To Metrocles

You should know that I was quite upset when I heard
that Diogenes had fallen into the hands of pirates, and
unless one of the captives had been set free and come to
Athens, I would even now be in the same condition. But as
it is, this man has reached Athens and relieved me by nar-
rating how "Diogenes bore the misfortune easily, so that
once he even said to the pirates when they were neglecting
us, 'Hey, you guys, what do you think you're doing? If
you were driving hogs to market, you would take care of
them so that they might bring you a better price when
sold. But us, whom you are also going to sell like hogs,
you neglect. (2) Don't you think that we, too, will fetch
more if we look stout, less if skinny? Is it because men
are not eaten that you think it unnecessary to take care
of them, too, in this way? On the contrary, you surely
know that all who buy slaves look for this one thing,
whether the body is big and strong. And I will even tell
you the reason, namely, that they buy a man, too, because
they need his body and not his soul.' From that time on
the pirates no longer neglected us, and for this we have
him to thank.

(3) "When we came to a certain city where we could
fetch a profit for them, they led us to the market place.
Then we stood still and cried, but he grabbed some bread,
ate it, and offered us some. But when we declined to
accept it, he said,

'Even fair-haired Niobe remembered food'
(Hom., *Il*. xxiv.602)

and then he said this in sport and ridicule: 'Won't you
stop feigning ignorance and crying over your imminent
slavery, as if you were really free before you fell into
the hands of pirates and were not slaves even to worse
masters? For now perhaps you will be allotted moderate
masters who will cut out of you the luxury by which you
were ruined, and who will instill in you perseverance and

ἐγκράτειαν, τὰ τιμιώτατα ἀγαθά.' (4) ταῦτα οὖν
διεξιόντος οἱ ὠνηταὶ ἐστῶτες τῶν λόγων ἠκροῶντο
καὶ αὐτὸν ἐθαύμαζον τῆς ἀπαθείας, τινὲς δὲ καὶ
ἠρώτων εἴ τι ἐπίσταται. ὃ δὲ ἔλεγεν ἐπίστασθαι
5   ἀνθρώπων ἄρχειν, 'ὥστε εἴ τις ὑμῶν κυρίου δεῖται,
συμφωνείτω προσιὼν τοῖς πωληταῖς.' κἀκεῖνοι ἀναγε-
λάσαντες ἐπὶ τουτῳ 'καὶ τίς' ἔφασαν 'ἐστίν, ὃς ἂν
ἐλεύθερος κυρίου δεῖται;' 'πάντες' εἶπεν 'οἱ φαῦλοι
καὶ τιμῶντες μὲν ἡδονήν, ἀτιμάζοντες δὲ πόνον, τὰ
10 μέγιστα τῶν κακῶν δελέατα.'

(5) "Διὰ ταῦτα περιμάχητος ἐγένετο ὁ Διογένης
καὶ οὐκέτι ἐπράθη, ἀλλ' οἱ λῃσταὶ καθελόντες αὐτὸν
ἀπὸ τοῦ λίθου ἦγον οἴκαδε παρ' αὐτούς, ὑπισχνούμενοι,
εἰ ἐπιδείξαι τι αὐτοῖς ὧν πωλούμενος ἔλεγεν εἰδέναι,
15 ἀφήσειν."

Διὰ ταῦτα οὔτε αὐτὸς ἐπανελθὼν οἴκαδε τὸ λύτρον
ἐπόρισα, οὔτε σοι ἐπέστειλα πορίζειν. ἀλλὰ χαῖρε
καὶ σύ, ὅτι ζῇ ἁλοὺς εἰς τὰ λῃστρικὰ καὶ ὅτι ἃ μὴ
ὑπὸ πολλῶν ἐπιστεύετο εἶναι ἐφάνη.

self-control, the most honored of goods.' (4) Then, as
he went through these things in detail, the buyers stood
and listened to his words and were amazed at his freedom
from emotion, though some also asked him whether he was
skilled at anything. And he said that he was skilled at
ruling men. 'So, if any of you needs a master, let him
come forward and strike a bargain with the sellers.' But
they laughed at him and said, 'And who is there who, since
he is free, needs a master?' 'All,' he said, 'who are
base and who honor pleasure and despise toil, the greatest
incitements to evils.'

(5) "For this reason Diogenes became highly prized
and was no longer up for sale. Instead, the pirates took
him down from the platform and led him to their house,
promising to release him if he would share with them some
of the things he said he knew when he was being sold."

For this reason I myself did not return home and
furnish the ransom, nor am I writing you to furnish it.
Rather, you, too, must rejoice, because he lives in spite
of having fallen into the hands of pirates, and because
what was not believed by the masses appeared to be so.

35. Ἀπέρει εὖ πράττειν

Τὸ μὲν σύντομον καὶ ἁρμοστὸν πρὸς πᾶσαν περί-
στασιν, ὦ τιμιώτατε ἄνερ, ὁ τῶν ἀρχαίων χρησμὸς
ἔφησε τὰ ἀναγκαῖα μὴ φεύγειν· τὸν γὰρ φεύγοντα τὰ
5   ἄφυκτα ἀνάγκη δυστυχεῖν, καὶ τὸν ὀρεγόμενον τῶν
ἀδυνάτων ἀνάγκη αὐτῶν ἀτυχεῖν. ἴσως μὲν οὖν δόξω
σοι ἀκαιρότερος εἶναι καὶ σχολαστικώτερος. καὶ
τοῦτο μὲν οὐκ ἀπολογοῦμαι· ὅμως δέ, εἰ δοκεῖ, ἐμοῦ
μὲν καταγίνωσκε, πρόσεχε δὲ τοῖς ἀρχαίοις. ἐγὼ γὰρ
10 ἀπ' ἐμαυτοῦ τεκμαίρομαι, ὅτι τότε θλιβόμεθα ἄνθρωποι,
ὅταν ἀπερίστατον βίον ζῆν ἐθέλωμεν. (2) τοῦτο δέ
ἐστι τῶν ἀμηχάνων· ἀνάγκη μὲν γὰρ ζῆν μετὰ σώματος,
ἀνάγκη δὲ καὶ μετ' ἀνθρώπων, αἱ δὲ πλεῖται περιστά-
σεις γίνονται ἔκ τε τῆς ἀνοίας τῶν συμβιούντων καὶ
15 πάλιν ἐκ τοῦ σώματος. ἐὰν μὲν οὖν ἐπιστήμων τις ἐν
τούτοις ἀναστρέφηται, οὗτός ἐστιν ἄλυπος καὶ ἀτάρα-
χος, ὁ μακάριος ἀνήρ· ἐὰν δὲ καὶ ταῦτα ἀγνοῇ, οὐ
μήποτε παύσηται αἰωρούμενος κεναῖς ἐλπίσι καὶ ἐπιθυ-
μίαις συνεχόμενος. σὺ οὖν, εἰ μὲν ἀρέσκη τῷ τῶν
20 πολλῶν βίῳ, ἐκείνοις συμβούλοις χρῶ, καὶ γὰρ εἰσι
τετριμμένοι μᾶλλον ἐν τούτοις· εἰ δέ σε ὁ Σωκράτους
καὶ Διογένους ἀρέσκει βίος, τὰ τῶν τραγῳδῶν ἄλλοις
παρεὶς σαυτὸν ἐπάνηκε ἐπὶ τὸν ἐκείνων ζῆλον.

36. Δεινομάχῳ

25 Οὐ μόνον τῶν αἰτούντων Διογένης ἀπεφήνατο
ἀργυρικὸν τὸ πτωχικὸν τὸ κυνικόν, ἀλλὰ καὶ τῶν
διδόντων τὸ ἐλεητικὸν τὸ σπουδαῖον. ὥστε τοῦτο
εἰδὼς μὴ πάντας προσιὼν αἴτει, οὐ γὰρ λήψῃ, μόνον
δὲ τὸν σπουδαῖον. τοῦτον γὰρ καὶ λέγομεν εὐδαίμονα
30 ἀκούειν, τῶν δ' ἄλλων οὐδένα.

35. To Aper, do well

The oracle of the ancients, honored Sir, has given advice that is concise and fitting in regard to every circumstance: Do not flee from what is necessary. For the one who flees from what is inevitable must be unhappy, and the one who desires what is impossible must fail to obtain it. Perhaps, then, I shall seem to you to be rather importunate and pedantic, and I do not defend myself against this charge. And yet, if it does seem so to you, condemn me, but pay attention to the ancients. For I have concluded from my own case that we men are distressed precisely when we wish to live a life without hardship. (2) But this wish is impossible. For we must live with the body, and we must live with men as well, and most hardships issue from the folly of those who live in society and, in turn, from the body. If, therefore, a wise man lives by these principles, he is free from pain and confusion, a happy man. But if he is ignorant of these principles, he will never cease from being dependent on vain hopes and from being constrained by desires. As for you, then, if you are satisfied with the life of the masses, make use of those advisors, for in fact they are more expert in these matters. But if the life of Socrates and Diogenes pleases you, leave the writings of the tragic poets to others and devote yourself to emulating those men.

36. To Dinomachus

Diogenes declared that not only should those who beg for silver have the Cynic fitness to be a beggar but those, too, who give should have the compassion of the wise man. So, since you know this, do not approach and beg from everyone, for you will not receive anything from them, but beg only from the wise man. For we can say that this man and none of the others is called happy.

THE EPISTLES OF DIOGENES

Translated by

Benjamin Fiore, S.J.

1. Σινωπεῦσιν

Ὑμεῖς μὲν ἐμοῦ φυγὴν κατεψηφίσασθε, ἐγὼ δὲ
ὑμῶν μονήν. οἰκήσετε οὖν διὰ τοῦτο ὑμεῖς μὲν
Σινώπην, ἐγὼ δὲ Ἀθήνας, τοῦτ' ἔστιν ὑμεῖς μὲν μετὰ
5 τῶν ἐμπόρων, ἐγὼ δὲ μετὰ Σόλωνος καὶ τῶν τὴν Ἑλλάδα
ἠλευθερωκότων ἀπὸ τῶν Μηδικῶν, καὶ ὑμεῖς μὲν
Ἡνιόχοις καὶ Ἀχαιοῖς χρώμενοι, ἀνθρώποις ἐκ τοῦ
ἐχθροῦ γένους Πανέλλησιν, ἐγὼ δὲ Δελφοῖς καὶ
Ἠλείοις, μεθ' ὧν καὶ θεοὶ πολιτεύονται. (2) ἀλλ'
10 ὤφελε τοῦτο μὴ νῦν ὑμῖν δόξαι, ἀλλ' ἔτι πάλαι καὶ
ἐπὶ τοῦ πατρὸς Ἱκέτου. νυνὶ δὲ ἓν τοῦτο δέδοικα,
μὴ διὰ τὴν πατρίδα ἀπιστηθῶ μέτριος εἶναι. τὸ μὲν
οὖν πρὸς ὑμῶν με φυγαδευθῆναι συνηγορεῖ, καὶ πιστεύω
αὐτῷ μᾶλλον τοῦ ἑτέρου· κρεῖττον γὰρ παρὰ πολὺ δια-
15 βάλλεσθει πρὸς ὑμῶν ἢ ἐπαινεῖσθαι. ὅμως μέντοι
δέδοικα τοῦτο, μή με ὁ κοινὸς περὶ τῆς πατρίδος
λόγος βλάψῃ. ἄλλου δέ τινος οὐδεὶς λόγος· κρεῖττον
γὰρ ὁπουδήποτε οἰκεῖν ἢ σὺν ὑμῖν οὕτως ἡμῖν προσε-
νεχθεῖσιν.

20 ## 2. Ἀντισθένει

Ἀνέβαινον εἰς ἄστυ ἐκ Πειραιῶς, καὶ περιτυγχά-
νει μοι μειράκια ἄττα θρυπτόμενα <κακ' ὁμαδοῦντ'> ἀπὸ
συμποσίου τινὸς ἐγηγερμένα, καὶ ἐν σφίσιν αὐτοῖς,
ἐπεὶ ἀγχοῦ ἐγενόμην, "ἀνάγωμεν" ἔλεγον "ἀπὸ τοῦ κυνός."
25 κἀγὼ ἐπεὶ τοῦτο ἤκουσα "θαρρεῖτε" ἔφην, "οὗτος ὁ κύων
τεῦτλα οὐ δάκνει." οἳ δ', ὡς τοῦτο ἔλεξα, ἐπαύοντο
ἀλύοντες καὶ τοὺς στεφάνους οὓς εἶχον περὶ τῇ κεφαλῇ
καὶ τῷ τραχήλῳ διαρρήξαντες ἐξέβαλον καὶ τὰς χλανίδας
εὐκόσμως περιεβάλοντο καὶ ἥσυχοι εὖ μάλα ἕως εἰς ἄστυ
30 ἠκολούθουν, ἐπακροώμενοι τῶν λόγων οὓς πρὸς ἐμαυτὸν
διεξῄειν.

---

22 <κακ' ὁμαδοῦντ'> Emeljanow

1. To the Sinopians

You condemned me to exile but I sentence you to remain at home. Thus, you will live in Sinope and I in Athens; that is, you in the company of merchants, I with Solon and those who have liberated Greece from the Persians. Moreover, you deal with the Heniochians and Achaeans, a stock of people which is at enmity with all the Greeks; but I with the Delphians and Eleans, with whom even the gods associate. (2) Would that you had thought it best to pass this judgment not just now but long ago, even in the days of my father Hicetas! But this one thing I now fear, that because of my native land it might not be believed that I am a moderate man. That you banished me, then, does argue in my defense and I place more faith in it than in the other alternative, for it is far better to be slandered by you than to be praised by you. Nonetheless I still fear that what is commonly said about my native land might harm me. But I take no account of anyone else, for it is better to dwell anywhere else than with you, since you treated me as you did.

2. To Antisthenes

I was going up to the city from Piraeus when some young men crossed my path. Coming from some party or other, they were making a spectacle of themselves and raising hell. As I drew near they said to each other, "Let's move away from the dog." But when I heard this I said, "Don't be afraid, this dog doesn't bite beets." At this remark of mine their excitement dissolved and, tearing up the wreaths that they had on their heads and around their necks, they threw them away. Then they drew their capes around themselves decently and accompanied me up to the city, keeping very quiet and listening to my words as I thought aloud.

3. Ἱππαρχίᾳ

Ἄγαμαί σε τῆς ἐπιθυμίας, ὅτι τε φιλοσοφίας
ὠρέχθης γυνὴ οὖσα, καὶ ὅτι τῆς ἡμετέρας αἱρέσεως
ἐγενήθης, ἣν διὰ τὸ αὐστηρὸν καὶ οἱ ἄνδρες κατεπλάγη-
5   σαν. ἀλλ' ὅπως καὶ τέλος ἐπιθῇς τῇ ἀρχῇ σπούδασον.
ἐπιθήσεις δὲ εὖ οἶδα, εἰ Κράτητός τε τοῦ συνευνέτου
μὴ ἀπολείποιο, ἡμῖν τε τοῖς εὐεργέταις τῆς φιλοσοφίας θαμινῶς ἐπιστέλλοις· δύνανται γὰρ αἱ ἐπιστολαὶ
πολλὰ καὶ οὐχ ἥττονα τῆς πρὸς παρόντας διαλέξεως.

10   4. Ἀντιπάτρῳ

Μὴ μέμφου με, ὅτι σοι μεταπεμπομένῳ ἡμᾶς ἐπὶ
Μακεδονίαν οὐκ ἐπείσθημεν, μηδ' ὅτι τοὺς Ἀθήνησιν
ἅλας προυκρίναμεν τῆς παρὰ σοῦ τραπέζης· οὐ γὰρ δι'
ὑπεροψίαν τοῦτ' ἐπράξαμεν, ἀλλ' οὐδὲ διὰ φιλοδοξίαν,
15   δι' ἣν τάχ' ἴσως ἕτεροι ἂν ἐποίησαν, ἵνα τινὲς τοῖς
πολλοῖς μεγάλοι δόξωσι, βασιλεῦσι δυνάμενοι ἀντιλέ-
γειν, ἀλλ' ὅτι ἡμῖν παρὰ τὰς ἐν Μακεδονίᾳ τραπέζας
οἱ Ἀθήνησιν ἅλες εἰσὶ σύμφυλοι. φυλακῇ οὖν τῆς
οὐσίας μᾶλλον ἀντείπομεν <σοι> καὶ οὐχ ὑπεροψίᾳ.
20   συγγίγνωσκε οὖν· καὶ γὰρ εἰ πρόβατα ἦμεν, συνέγνως
ἂν μὴ πεισθεῖσιν, ὅτι οὐκ ἔστι προβάτου τε τροφὴ καὶ
βασιλέως ἡ αὐτή. ἔα οὖν ἕκαστον ὅπου ἂν δύνηται ζῆν,
ὦ μακάριε· βασιλικὸν γὰρ τοῦτο καὶ οὐ τὸ ἕτερον.

---

19   <σοι> Emeljanow

3. To Hipparchia

I admire you for your eagerness in that, although you
are a woman, you yearned for philosophy and have become
one of our school, which has struck even men with awe for
its austerity. But be earnest to bring to a finish what
you have begun. And you will cap it off, I am sure, if
you should not be outstripped by Crates, your husband,
and if you frequently write to me, your benefactor in
philosophy. For letters are worth a great deal and are
not inferior to conversation with people actually present.

4. To Antipater

Do not find fault with me for not heeding you when
you summoned me to Macedonia, or for judging the men of
Athens a salt preferable to your table. For I did not do
this out of arrogance or love of glory. Perhaps others
would act from this motive, in order that they might appear extraordinary in the eyes of the masses for their
ability to speak out against kings. But for me, compared
with the tables of Macedon, the men of Athens are the more
naturally suitable salt. Thus I spoke out against you rather in defense of true nature than in arrogance. Pardon
me, therefore. For truly if we were sheep you would pardon
us if we did not obey, since the food for a flock is not
the same as that for a king. So permit each one to live
wherever he can, my dear sir, for this, and not the other,
is the royal attitude.

5. Περδίκᾳ

Εἰ μὲν ταῖς δόξαις ἤδη πολεμεῖς, λέγω δὲ τοῖς
ἰσχυροτέροις ἐχθροῖς καὶ πλείονα καταβλάπτουσί σε
Θρᾳκῶν τε καὶ Παιόνων, <καταστρεφόμενος> τὰ τῶν
5   ἀνθρώπων πάθη μεταπέμπου με· δύναμαι γὰρ εἰς τὸν πρὸς
ταῦτα πόλεμον καὶ στρατηγεῖν. εἰ δ' ἔτι σοι τὰ πρὸς
ἀνθρώπους ἔργα λείπεται καὶ τούτου τοῦ πολέμου σχεδὸν
<οὐκ> αἰσθάνῃ, ἔα μὲν ἡμᾶς Ἀθήνησι καθέζεσθαι, μετα-
πέμπου δὲ τοὺς Ἀλεξάνδρου στρατιώτας, οἷς κἀκεῖνος
10 ἐπικούροις χρώμενος Ἰλλυριοὺς καὶ Σκύθας ὑπέταξεν.

—— 4   <καταστρεφόμενος> Emeljanow   8   <οὐκ> Emeljanow

6. Κράτητι

Χωρισθέντος σου εἰς Θήβας ἀνέβαινον ἐκ Πειραιῶς
ὑπὸ μέσην ἡμέραν, καὶ διὰ τοῦτο λαμβάνει με δίψος
15 καρτερόν. ὥρμησα οὖν ἐπὶ τὴν Πάνοπος κρήνην. καὶ
ἕως ἐγὼ τὸ ποτήριον ἐκ τῆς πήρας ἐξῆρουν, ἧκέ τις
θέων θεράπων τῶν τὴν χώραν ἐργαζομένων καὶ συνάψας
κοίλας τὰς χεῖρας ἤρύετο ἀπὸ τῆς κρήνης καὶ οὕτως
ἔπινε, καὶ ἐγώ, δόξαν μοι ποτηρίου σοφώτερον εἶναι,
20 οὐκ ἠδέσθην διδασκάλῳ αὐτῷ τῶν καλῶν χρήσασθαι. (2)
ἀπορρίψας οὖν τὸ ποτήριον ὃ εἶχον, καὶ σοὶ εὑρών
τινας ἐπὶ Θηβῶν ἀνερχομένους τὸ σοφὸν τοῦτο ἐπέσταλκα,
οὐδὲν βουλόμενος τῶν καλῶν δίχα σοῦ ἐπίστασθαι.
ἀλλὰ καὶ σὺ διὰ τοῦτο πειρῶ εἰς τὴν ἀγορὰν ἐμβάλ-
25 λειν, ἵνα πολλοὶ διατρίβουσιν ἄνθρωποι. ἔσται γὰρ
ἡμῖν οὕτω καὶ ἄλλα σοφὰ παρὰ τῶν κατὰ μέρος εὑρεῖν·
πολλὴ γὰρ ἡ φύσις, ἣν ἐκβαλλομένην ὑπὸ τῆς δόξης ἐκ
τοῦ βίου ἐπὶ σωτηρίᾳ ἀνθρώπων κατάγομεν ἡμεῖς.

5. To Perdiccas

If you are now battling appearances, enemies which,
in my view, are more formidable and inflict more damage
on you than the Thracians and Paeonians, and if you are
trying to subdue the human passions, summon me, for I can
wage war against these just like a general. But if there
still remains business with other men for you to attend to,
and if you do not sense this battle close at hand, permit
me to stay in Athens and summon Alexander's soldiers, the
ones he used as auxiliaries to subdue the Illyrians and
Scythians.

6. To Crates

After you left for Thebes, I was making my way up from
Piraeus at midday. Because of the hour a powerful thirst
seized me, so I hurried to the well of Panops. While I
was taking my cup out of my wallet, a servant of some field
workers came running up and, cupping his hands, dipped water for himself from the well and drank in that manner.
Now since this seemed wiser to me than using a cup, I was
not ashamed to use him as a teacher of good practices.
(2) So I threw away the cup which I had, and having found
some people on their way up to you at Thebes, I am sending
this bit of wisdom along, since I do not wish to know anything good without your knowing it too.
Therefore, you too must try to venture forth into
the market place where many people pass their time. For
we will have occasion in this way to discover yet other
wise things from them, one after another. Nature is
mighty and, since it has been banished from life by appearance, it is what we restore for the salvation of mankind.

7. Ἱκέτῃ

Μὴ ἀνιῶ, ὦ πάτερ, ὅτι κύων λέγομαι καὶ ἀμπέχομαι
τρίβωνα διπλοῦν καὶ πήραν φέρω κατ' ὤμων καὶ ῥάβδον
ἔχω διὰ χειρός· οὐ γὰρ ἄξιον ἐπὶ τοῖς τοιούτοις
5   ἀνιᾶσθαι, μᾶλλον δὲ ἥδεσθαι, ὅτι ὀλίγοις ἀρκεῖται ὁ
παῖς σου, ἐλεύθερος δέ ἐστι δόξης, ᾗ πάντες δουλεύουσιν Ἕλληνές τε καὶ βάρβαροι· τὸ γὰρ ὄνομα πρὸς τῷ
μὴ συμπεφυκέναι τοῖς πράγμασι, σύμβολον δ' εἶναι ἔν-
δοξόν πώς ἐστι. καλοῦμαι γὰρ κύων ὁ οὐρανοῦ, οὐχ ὁ
10 γῆς, ὅτι ἐκείνῳ εἰκάζω ἐμαυτόν, ζῶν οὐ κατὰ δόξαν,
ἀλλὰ κατὰ φύσιν ἐλεύθερος ὑπὸ τὸν Δία, εἰς αὐτὸν ἀνα-
τεθεικὼς τἀγαθὸν καὶ οὐκ εἰς τὸν πλησίον· (2) τὴν δὲ
στολὴν καὶ Ὅμηρος γράφει Ὀδυσσέα τὸν τῶν Ἑλλήνων
σοφώτατον φορῆσαι, ἡνίκα οἴκαδε ἐπανῄει ἐξ Ἰλίου
15 Ἀθηνᾶς ὑποθημοσύνῃσιν, καὶ οὕτω καλή ἐστιν, ὡς μὴ
ἀνθρώπων εὕρημα εἶναι ὁμολογεῖσθαι, ἀλλὰ θεῶν.

φᾶρος μέν οἱ πρῶτα χιτῶνά τε εἵματ' ἔδωκε
λευγαλέα, ῥυπόωντα, κακῷ μεμορυγμένα καπνῷ·
ἀμφὶ δέ μιν μέγα δέρμα ταχείης ἔσσ' ἐλάφοιο
20   ψιλόν, δῶκε δέ οἱ σκῆπτρον καὶ ἀεικέα πήρην,
πυκνὰ ῥωγαλέην, ἐν δὲ στρόφος ἦεν ἀορτήρ.

θάρρει οὖν, ὦ πάτερ, ἐπὶ τῷ ὀνόματι, ὃ καλοῦσιν ἡμᾶς,
καὶ ἐπὶ τῇ στολῇ, ἐπεὶ ὁ μὲν κύων ἐστὶ πρὸς θεῶν, ἡ
δὲ εὕρημα τοῦ θεοῦ.

7. To Hicetas

Do not be upset, Father, that I am called a dog and
put on a double, coarse cloak, carry a wallet over my
shoulders, and have a staff in my hand. It is not worth
while getting distressed over such matters, but you should
rather be glad that your son is satisfied with little,
while being free from popular opinion, to which all,
Greeks and barbarians alike, are subservient. Now the
name, besides not being in accord with my deeds, is a sign
that is notable as it is. For I am called heaven's dog,
not earth's, since I liken myself to it, living as I do,
not in conformity with popular opinion but according to
nature, free under Zeus, and crediting the good to him and
not to my neighbor. (2) As for my clothing, even Homer
writes that Odysseus, the wisest of the Greeks, so dressed
while he was returning home from Ilium under Athena's
direction. And the vesture is so fine that it is commonly
acknowledged to be a discovery not of men but of the gods.

> First she gave him a cloak, tunic and mantle,
> seedy, dirty, stained by filthy smoke. She put
> around him a large, hairless hide of swift deer
> and gave him a staff and a poor leather pouch,
> riddled with holes, with a knapsack strap on
> it. (Hom. *Od.* xiii.434-38)

Take heart, Father, at the name which they call me, and at
my clothing, since the dog is under the protection of the
gods and his clothing is god's invention.

8. Εὐγνησίῳ

ʽΗκον εἰς Κόρινθον ἐκ Μεγάρων καὶ διαπορευόμενος
τὴν ἀγορὰν παρίσταμαι διδασκαλείῳ τινὶ παίδων, καί
μοι ἐπεὶ οὐκ εὖ ἐρραψῴδουν, ἔδοξε πυθέσθαι τίς ἦν ὁ
5   διδάσκων αὐτούς. καὶ ἀπεκρίναντο "Διονύσιος ὁ τῆς
Σικελίας τύραννος." κἀγὼ δόξας αὐτοὺς ἐρεσχελεῖν
πρός με καὶ τοῦτο οὐχ ἁπλῶς ἀποκεκρίσθαι, παρελθὼν
ἐπί τι βάθρον ἐκάθισα, εὐκόσμως ἀναμένων αὐτόν·
ἐλέγετο γὰρ πρὸς ἀγορὰν ὡρμηκέναι. καὶ δὴ οὐ διαγί-
10   νεται πολὺς χρόνος, καὶ ἐπιστρέφεται ὁ Διονύσιος,
κἀγὼ ἐξαναστὰς προσαγορεύω τε αὐτὸν καὶ ἐπιλέγω "ὡς
οὐκ εὖ, Διονύσιε, διδάσκεις." (2) ὁ δέ με δόξας
συνάχθεσθαι αὐτῷ ἐπὶ τῇ πτώσει τῆς τυραννίδος καὶ τῷ
παρόντι σχήματι τοῦ βίου, τοιαῦτα εἶπεν· "ὦ Διόγενες,
15   εὖ ποιεῖς συναλγῶν ἡμῖν." κἀγὼ "προσέθηκα <τὸ 'οὐκ
εὖ' τὸ ἀληθές.> ἀλλ' ἐγὼ μὲν οὐχ ὅτι τῆς τυραννίδος
ἀφῄρησαι ἄχθομαι, ὦ Διονύσιε, ἀλλ' ὅτι ἐλευθεριάζεις
ἐν τῇ ʽΕλλάδι τὰ νῦν, καὶ περισέσωσαι ἀπὸ τῶν ἐν
Σικελίᾳ κακῶν, οἷς ἔδει σε ἐναποθανεῖν τοσαῦτα ἐργα-
20   σάμενον φαῦλα γῆν καὶ θάλατταν."

_____
15   <τὸ 'οὐκ εὖ' τὸ ἀληθές> Emeljanow

8. To Eugnesius

I arrived in Corinth from Megara and, while going
through the market place, I came to a certain school for
children. Since, in my opinion, they were not reciting
well, I thought it best to ask who it was that was teaching them. They answered, "Dionysius, the tyrant of Sicily."
Now I thought they were joking with me and had not replied
candidly. So I went and sat down on a bench, respectfully
waiting for him, for he was said to be hurrying toward the
market place. To be sure, it was not long before Dionysius returned. I stood up and addressed him, calling him
by name. "Dionysius, how awful that you are teaching!"
(2) But he thought I was commiserating with him in his
fall from power and the present condition of his life. He
said, "O Diogenes, you do well to share in my suffering."
But I answered, "I applied the word 'awful' and meant it.
But I am not upset because you have been deprived of abso-
lute power, Dionysius, but because you now live as a free
man in Greece and have escaped with your life from the
troubles in Sicily. You should have died in them after
having worked so much ill on land and sea."

9. Κράτητι

ʽΕπυθόμην σε τὴν οὐσίαν ἄπασαν κατενεγκεῖν εἰς
τὴν ἐκκλησίαν καὶ παραχωρῆσαι τῇ κατρίδι καὶ στάντα
ἐν μέσῳ κηρῦξαι "Κράτης Κράτητος Κράτητα ἀφίησιν
5   ἐλεύθερον." ἡσθῆναι οὖν ἐπὶ τῇ δωρεᾷ τοὺς πάντας
ἀστοὺς καὶ ἀγασθῆναι ἡμᾶς τοὺς τῶν τοιούτων ἀνθρώπων
ποιητάς, ἐθελῆσαι δὲ διὰ τοῦτο μεταπέμψασθαι ἡμᾶς
ʼΑθήνηθεν, σὲ δὲ ἐπιστάμενον τὴν ἡμετέραν κρίσιν
κωλῦσαι. ἐνταῦθα μὲν οὖν ἐπαινῶ σε τοῦ νοῦ, ἐπὶ δὲ
10   τῇ παραδόσει τῆς οὐσίας καὶ ἄγαμαι, ἐπεὶ θᾶττον ἢ
προσεδόκησα κρείττων ἐγένου τῶν δοξῶν. ἀλλὰ διὰ
ταχέων ἐπάνηκε· ἔτι γάρ σοι δεῖ πρὸς τἆλλα συνασκή-
σεως, καὶ χρονίζειν ἔνθα μὴ εἰσὶν ὅμοιοι οὐκ ἀσφαλές.

10. Μητροκλεῖ, <εὖ πράττειν>

15   Μὴ μόνον ἐπὶ τῇ στολῇ καὶ τῷ ὀνόματι καὶ τῇ
διαίτῃ θάρρει, Μητρόκλεις, ἀλλὰ καὶ ἐπὶ τῷ αἰτεῖν
ἀνθρώπους τὰ σωτήρια· οὐ γὰρ αἰσχρόν. βασιλεῖς γέ τοι
καὶ δυνάσται παρὰ τῶν ὑποτεταγμένων αἰτοῦσι χρήματα,
στρατιώτας, ναῦς, σῖτον, καὶ οἱ κάμνοντες παρὰ τῶν
20   ἰατρῶν φάρμακα καὶ οὐ μόνον πυρετοῦ, ἀλλὰ καὶ φρίκης
καὶ λοιμοῦ, καὶ οἱ ἐρασταὶ παρὰ τῶν παιδικῶν φιλήματα
καὶ ἐπαφήματα, τὸν δὲ ʽΗρακλέα παρὰ τῶν ἀναισθήτων
φασὶ καὶ ἰσχὺν λαμβάνειν. οὐ γὰρ προῖκα οὐδ᾽ ἐπὶ
χείρονι ἀνταλλαγῇ, ἀλλ᾽ ἐπὶ τῇ σωτηρίᾳ πάντων ἔστιν
25   αἰτεῖν, ἀνθρώπους τὰ πρὸς τὴν φύσιν, καὶ ἐπὶ τῷ ταὐτὰ
ποιεῖν ʽΗρακλεῖ τῷ Διὸς καὶ ἔχειν ἀμείβεσθαι πολὺ
κρείττονα ὧν λαμβάνεις αὐτός. (2) τίνα ταῦτα; μὴ
πρὸς τὴν ἀλήθειαν εἶναί σοι τὴν μάχην τοῦτο πράσσον-
τι, ἀλλὰ πρὸς τὴν δόξαν.

---

14 <εὖ πράττειν> Hercher

9. To Crates

I heard that you brought all your property to the
assembly, delivered it over to your fatherland, and,
standing in the midst of the people, cried out, "Crates,
son of Crates, sets Crates free." Thus the whole citizen-
ry were pleased at the gift and wondered about me, the
person who creates men of this sort. They, therefore,
wished to send for me from Athens; but you, aware of my
mind on the matter, prevented them. So I commend you for
your good sense in this, and am delighted with your sur-
render of your property, since you became superior to
popular opinion faster than I expected. But do return
quickly, for you still need training in other matters, and
it is not safe to linger where there is no one like you.

10. To Metrocles, do well

Be bold, not only with regard to your dress, name,
and way of life, Metrocles, but also in begging people for
sustenance, for it is not at all disgraceful. To be sure,
kings and lords ask for money, soldiers, ships, and food
from their subjects. And those who are sick ask remedies
of their doctors, not only for intermittent fever but also
for chills and the plague. Those fond of boys request
kisses and caresses from them, and they say that Heracles
even received strength from people without common sense.
It is all right to beg, if it is not for a free gift or
for something worse in exchange, but for the salvation of
everyone; that is, to ask people for things that accord
with nature, and to ask with a view to doing the same
things as Heracles, the son of Zeus, and to be able to
give back something much better than what you receive
yourself. (2) What would this be? That in doing this you
are not battling against truth but against popular opinion.

ἢ πάντη μάχου, κἂν μηδέν σε ἐπείγῃ· καλὸν γάρ τι ἔθος
καὶ ὁ πρὸς τὰ τοιαῦτα πόλεμος. Σωκράτης δὲ ἔλεγε
μὴ αἰτεῖν τοὺς σπουδαίους, ἀλλὰ ἀπαιτεῖν· εἶναι γὰρ
αὐτῶν τὰ πάντα ὡς καὶ τῶν θεῶν. καὶ τοῦτ' ἐπειρᾶτο
5 συνάγειν ἐκ τοῦ κυρίους μὲν ὑπάρχειν τῶν πάντων τοὺς
θεούς, κοινὰ δ' εἶναι τὰ τῶν φίλων, φίλον δ' εἶναι
τῷ θεῷ τὸν σπουδαῖον. αἰτήσεις τοίνυν τὰ ἴδια.

11. Κράτητι, <εὖ πράττειν>

Καὶ τοὺς ἀνδριάντας τοὺς ἐν ἀγορᾷ προσιὼν αἴτει
10 τὰ ἄλφιτα. καλὴ γάρ που καὶ ἡ τοιαύτη μελέτη·
ἐντεύξῃ γὰρ ἀνθρώποις ἀπαθεστέροις ἀνδριάντων. καὶ
ὅταν σου μᾶλλον γάλλοις καὶ κιναιδολόγοις μεταδιδῶσι,
μὴ θαύμαζε· τιμᾷ γὰρ ἔκαστος τὸν πλησίον ἑαυτοῦ καὶ
οὐ τὸν πόρρω· εἰσὶ δὲ οἱ τοῖς πολλοῖς ἀρέσκοντες
15 γάλλοι μᾶλλον ἢ φιλόσοφοι.

8   <εὖ πράττειν> Hercher

Fight against this everywhere, even if nothing is pressing upon you, for the battle against things like this, too, is a good habit. Socrates used to say that sages do not beg but demand back, for everything belongs to them, just as it does to the gods. And this he tried to infer from the premises that the gods are masters of all, that the property of friends is held in common, and that the sage is a friend of god. Therefore, you will be begging for what is your own.

11. To Crates, do well

Ask for bread even from the statues in the market place as you enter it. In a way, such a practice is good, for you will meet men more unfeeling than statues. And whenever they give something to eunuchs and to the authors of obscenity rather than to you, do not be surprised. For each person pays honor to the one who is close to him and not someone far off. And it is eunuchs rather than the philosophers who pander to the masses.

12. Τῷ αὐτῷ, <εὖ πράττειν>

Οἱ πολλοὶ ἐπὶ τὸν εὐδαιμονισμόν, ὅταν μὲν σύντομον ὁδὸν ἐπ' εὐδαιμονίαν φέρουσαν ἀκούσωσιν, ἵενται
καθάπερ ἡμεῖς ἐπὶ φιλοσοφίαν· ὅταν δ' ἐπὶ τὴν ὁδὸν
5   ἀφίκωνται καὶ αὐτῆς τὴν χαλεπότητα θεάσωνται, ὡς
ἀσθενοῦντες ὀπίσω ἀναχωροῦσιν, εἶτα μέμφονταί που
οὐχ αὐτῶν τὴν μαλακίαν, ἀλλὰ τὴν ἡμῶν ἀπάθειαν. ἔα
οὖν τούτους μὲν ὅπως ἐσπούδασαν ταῖς ἡδοναῖς συγκαθεύ-
δειν· καταλήψεται γὰρ <οὕτως> ζῶντας οὐκ εἰς ὃν ἡμᾶς
10 διαβάλλουσι πόνος, ἀλλ' οἱ μείζονες, δι' οὓς πάσῃ
περιστάσει δουλεύουσιν αἰσχρῶς. σὺ δὲ ἐπίμενε ἐν τῇ
ἀσκήσει ὥσπερ ἦρξω, καὶ σπούδαζε κατ' ἴσον ἡδονῇ
ἀντιτάττεσθαι καὶ πόνῳ, ἐπεὶ καὶ κατ' ἴσον ἀμφότερα
πολεμεῖν ἡμῖν πέφυκε καὶ εἰς τὰ πρῶτα ἐμποδίζειν, ἣ
15 μὲν διὰ τὸ ἐπὶ τὰ αἰσχρὰ ἄγειν, ὃ δὲ διὰ τὸ ἀπὸ τῶν
καλῶν ἀπάγειν τῷ φόβῳ.

---

1   <εὖ πράττειν> Hercher
9   <οὕτως> Emeljanow

13. Ἀπολήξιδι, <χαίρειν>

Ἀπεθέμην τὰ πολλὰ τῶν τὴν πήραν βαρυνόντων,
πίνακα μὲν διδαχθεὶς ἐν ἄρτῳ τὸ κοῖλον εἶναι, ποτή-
20 ριον δὲ τὰς χεῖρας. καὶ οὐκ ἔστιν αἰσχύνη τὸν ἐπισ-
τάτην εἰπεῖν ὅτι "παῖς ἦν ἔτι," οὐκ ἔδει δὲ τὴν
εὕρεσιν εὔχρηστον οὖσαν διὰ τὴν ἡλικίαν παρελθεῖν,
ἀλλὰ προσδέξασθαι.

---

17 <χαίρειν> Hercher

12. To the same, do well

Just as we do toward philosophy, the masses hasten
eagerly toward what they think is happiness, whenever
they hear of a short cut leading to it. But when they
come up to the road and survey its ruggedness, they draw
back as though they were sick, and then somehow voice a
complaint not about their own weakness, but about our indifference to hardship. So let them sleep with their
pleasures as they were eager to do. For if they lead
[such] lives, greater hardships will overtake them than
those of which they accuse us. By reason of these they
become base slaves to every circumstance. But as for you,
continue in your training, just as you began, and earnest-
ly pursue a balanced resistance to both pleasure and hardship. For it is natural for us to war equally against
both and, first and foremost, to shackle them, the one
because it leads to shameful deeds, the other because it
leads away from noble acts through fear.

13. To Apolexis, greetings

I have laid aside most of the things that weigh down
my wallet, since I learned that for a plate a hollowed out
loaf of bread suffices, as the hands do for a cup. And
there is no shame in the master's saying, "I was still a
child." Nor ought we to slight, because of its age, a
discovery which is still very serviceable, but ought
rather to welcome it.

14. 'Αντιπάτρῳ, <χαίρειν>

Μέμφῃ μου τὸν βίον ὡς ἐπίπονον καὶ διὰ χαλεπότητα ὑπ' οὐδενὸς ἐπιτηδευθησόμενον· ἐγὼ δὲ ἑκὼν αὐτὸν
ἐπέτεινα, ἵνα γνῶσιν οἱ μιμούμενοί με μὴ τέλεον
5   ἡδυπαθεῖς εἶναι.

1 <χαίρειν> Hercher

15. 'Αντιπάτρῳ, <χαίρειν>

'Ακούων λέγειν σε μηδέν με ποιεῖν παράδοξον
διπλοῦν τρίβωνα φοροῦντα καὶ πήραν ἐξημμένον, ἐγὼ δὲ
θαυμαστὸν μὲν οὐδὲν εἶναί φημι τούτων, καλὸν δ'
10   ἑκάτερον αὐτῶν ἀπὸ διαθέσεως ἐπιτηδευόμενον· οὐ γὰρ
μόνον τὸ σῶμα ταύτῃ δεῖ κεχρῆσθαι τῇ λιτότητι, ἀλλὰ
καὶ τὴν ψυχὴν σὺν αὐτῷ, οὐδ' ἐπαγγέλλεσθαι μὲν πολλά,
πράττειν δὲ τὰ μηδὲν ἀρκοῦντα, ἀλλὰ τῷ βίῳ τὸν λόγον
ἀκόλουθον ἐπιδείκνυσθαι. ἃ δὴ πειρῶμαι ποιεῖν καὶ
15   μαρτυρεῖν μοι--ἴσως ὑπολήψῃ με λέγειν τὸν 'Αθηναίων
δῆμον ἢ τὸν Κορινθίων, ἀδίκους μάρτυρας; τὴν ἐμαυτοῦ
ψυχήν φημι, ἣν οὐκ ἔστι λαθεῖν ἁμαρτάνοντα.

6 <χαίρειν> Hercher

16. 'Απολήξιδι, <χαίρειν>

'Ενέτυχόν σοι περὶ οἰκήσεως, καὶ χάρις ὑποσχο-
20   μένῳ, κοχλίαν δὲ θεασάμενος ηὗρον οἴκησιν ἀλεξάνεμον
τὸν ἐν τῷ Μητρῴῳ πίθον. ἀπολέλυσο οὖν τῆς ὑπηρεσίας
ταύτης καὶ σύγχαιρε ἡμῖν τὴν φύσιν ἀνευρίσκουσιν.

18 <χαίρειν> Hercher

14. To Antipater, greetings

You find fault with my way of life on the grounds
that it is toilsome and will be cultivated by no one because of its austerity. But I purposely increased its
intensity, so that whoever imitates me might know not to
enjoy any luxury at all.

15. To Antipater, greetings

I hear that you say I am doing nothing unusual in
wearing a double, ragged cloak and carrying a wallet. Now
I admit that none of these is extraordinary, but each of
them is good when undertaken out of conscious determination. For not only is it necessary that the body exercise
this simplicity, but the spirit should too, along with it.
That is to say, it should not promise much and then do
what is not sufficient, but should demonstrate that the
spoken claims conform to the way of life. In fact, it is
this that I try to do and witness in my case. Will you
perhaps take me to be speaking of the people of Athens or
Corinth as unjust witnesses? I am speaking of my own
spirit, whose notice I cannot escape when I do wrong.

16. To Apolexis, greetings

I asked you about a dwelling. Thank you for undertaking to arrange one. But when I saw a snail, I found a
house to keep off the wind. I mean the earthenware jug in
the Metroon. So consider yourself discharged from this
service and rejoice with me over my discovery of nature.

17. 'Ανταλκίδη, <χαίρειν>

'Ακούω σε γράφειν περὶ ἀρετῆς πρὸς ἡμᾶς καὶ
τοῖς γνωρίμοις ἐπαγγέλλεσθαι ὅτι διὰ τῆς γραφῆς
πείσεις ἡμᾶς φρονεῖν περὶ σοῦ τι. ἐγὼ δὲ οὐδὲ τὴν
5   τοῦ Τυνδάρεω θυγατέρα ἐπαινῶ τὴν εἰς τὸν οἶνον τὸ
νηπενθὲς βαλοῦσαν φάρμακον (ἔδει γὰρ αὐτὸ προσενέγ-
κασθαι χωρὶς οἴνου), οὐδὲ σέ, ὃς παρόντων μὲν ἡμῶν
οὐδὲν ἐπεδείξω σπουδῆς ἄξιον, διὰ γραμμάτων δὲ ὑπολαμβάνεις ἡμᾶς πείσειν, ἃ μνήμας μὲν ἂν σώζοι τῶν
10   οὐκ ὄντων, ἀρετῆς δὲ ζώντων καὶ οὐ παρόντων οὐκ ἂν
εἴη δηλωτικά. ταῦτά σοι γράφειν ἔσχον, ἵνα μὴ διὰ
τῶν ἀψύχων ἡμῖν προσφωνῇς, ἀλλὰ παρὼν αὐτός.

––––––––––
1 <χαίρειν> Hercher

18. 'Απολήξιδι, <χαίρειν>

Μηνόδωρον φιλόσοφον παρεκάλεσάν με συστῆσαί σοι
15   Μεγαρικοὶ νεανίσκοι, γελοιοτάτην σύστασιν· ὅτι μὲν
γὰρ ἄνθρωπός ἐστιν, ἐκ τῶν εἰκόνων εἴσῃ, εἰ δὲ καὶ
φιλόσοφος, διὰ βίου καὶ λόγου. ὁ γὰρ καθ' ἡμᾶς
σπουδαῖος δι' ἑαυτοῦ συνίσταται.

––––––––––
13 <χαίρειν> Hercher

17. To Antalcides, greetings

I hear that you are writing to me about virtue and are announcing to your friends that by means of your letter you will persuade me to have some regard for you. But I do not praise the daughter of Tyndareus who put the sorrow-quelling drug into wine (for it should have been brought separate from the wine). Nor do I praise you. For while I was present you exhibited nothing worthy of esteem, but now you suppose that you will convince me through letters. Letters might preserve the memory of those who are no longer alive, but would not reveal the virtue of those alive but not present. I am obliged to write this to you, so that you will not address me through inanimate means, but will be present in person.

18. To Apolexis, greetings

The Megarian youths appealed to me to introduce Menodorus the philosopher to you, a very ridiculous introduction, for you will know that he is a man from his portraits, and from his life and words whether he is also a philosopher. For, in my opinion, the sage provides his own introduction.

19. Ἀναξιλάῳ <τῷ σοφῷ, χαίρειν>

Πυθαγόρας ἑαυτὸν ἔλεγεν Εὔφορβον γεγενῆσθαι τὸν
Πάνθου, ἐγὼ δὲ νέον ἐμαυτὸν ἐπέγνων Ἀγαμέμνονα·
σκῆπτρόν τε γάρ ἐστί μου τὸ βάκτρον καὶ χλαμὺς ὁ
5   διπλοῦς τρίβων, ἡ δὲ πήρα παρὰ δέρματος ἀλλαγὴν
ἀσπίς. εἰ δὲ μὴ καρηκομόω, νέος ἦν ὁ Ἀγαμέμνων,
γέρων δ᾽ ἂν γενόμενος ἐψιλοκόρρησε. τοιαῦτα γὰρ
ἄξιον καὶ φρονεῖν καὶ λέγειν πρὸς τὸν "αὐτὸς ἔφα"
λέγοντα.

‾‾‾‾‾‾‾‾
1   <τῷ σοφῷ, χαίρειν> Hercher

10   20. Μελησίππῳ, <χαίρειν>

Ἤκουόν σε λελυπῆσθαι ὅτι τὰ Ἀθηναίων τέκνα
πληγὰς ἡμῖν ἐνέτεινε μεθύοντα, καὶ δεινὰ πάσχειν,
εἰ σοφία πεπαρῴνηται. εὖ δ᾽ ἴσθι ὅτι τὸ Διογένους
μὲν ἐπλήγη σῶμα ὑπὸ τῶν μεθυόντων, ἀρετὴ δὲ οὐκ
15   ᾐσχύνθη, ἐπεὶ μήτε κοσμεῖσθαι πέφυκεν ὑπὸ φαύλων
μήτε αἰσχύνεσθαι. Διογένης μὲν δὴ οὐχ ὑβρίσθη, κακῶς
δ᾽ ἔπαθεν ὁ Ἀθηναίων δῆμος, ἐν ᾧ τινες ἔδοξαν
ἀρετῆς ὑπεριδεῖν. διὰ γοῦν τὴν ἑνὸς ἀφροσύνην κατὰ
δήμους ἀφραίνοντες ἀπόλλυνται, βουλευόμενοι τὰ μὴ
20   προσήκοντα καὶ στρατευόμενοι δέον ἡρεμεῖν. εἰ δὲ
τὴν ἀρχὴν τὴν ἀπόνοιαν ἔστησαν, οὐκ ἂν ἐπὶ ταῦτα
ἐχώρουν.

‾‾‾‾‾‾‾‾
10   <χαίρειν> Hercher

19. To Anaxilaus the wise, greetings

Pythagoras used to say that he had once been Euphor-
bus, the son of Panthus; but I have recently come to
recognize myself to be Agamemnon, since for a scepter I
have my staff and for a mantle the double, ragged cloak,
and by way of exchange, my leather wallet is a shield. As
to the fact that I do not have a full head of hair, Agamemnon was young but had he grown old he would have been
bald headed. So it is fitting both to think and say such
things in reply to one who declares, "He himself said."

20. To Melesippus, greetings

I heard that you are grieved that the Athenian
youths, drunk with wine, laid blows on me, and that you
suffer great distress that wisdom should be treated with
drunken violence. But be well aware that although
Diogenes' body was beaten by the drunkards, his virtue was
not dishonored, since it is in its nature not to be
adorned or shamed by evil men. Diogenes certainly was not
insulted, but the Athenian public, some of whom resolved
to show contempt for virtue, suffered terribly. Really,
through the foolishness of one person foolish men throughout the populace come to ruin, since they plan improper
actions and wage war when they should be at peace. But
had they checked their madness from the start, they would
not have come to this.

21. Ἀμυνάνδρῳ, <χαίρειν>

Γονεῦσι χάριτας οὐχ ἑκτέον οὔτε τοῦ γενέσθαι,
ἐπεὶ φύσει γέγονε τὰ ὄντα, οὔτε τῆς ποιότητος· ἡ γὰρ
τῶν στοιχείων σύγκρασις αἰτία ταύτης. καὶ μὴν καὶ
5   τῶν κατὰ προαίρεσιν ἢ βούλησιν οὐδεμία χάρις· ἡ γὰρ
γένεσις ἀφροδισίων ἐστὶ παρακολούθημα, ἅπερ ἡδονῆς
ἕνεκεν, οὐ γενέσεως ἐπιτηδεύεται. ταύτας τὰς φωνὰς
ὁ τῆς ἀπαθείας προφήτης ἐγὼ ἀποφθέγγομαι ἐναντίας τῷ
τετυφωμένῳ βίῳ. εἰ δέ τισιν εἶναι φαίνονται σκληρό-
10 τεραι, φύσις αὐτὰς σὺν ἀληθείᾳ βεβαιοῖ καὶ ὁ βίος ὁ
τῶν μὴ κατὰ τῦφον, ἀλλὰ κατ᾽ ἀρετὴν βιούντων.

_____
1   <χαίρειν> Hercher

22. Ἀγησιλάῳ, <χαίρειν>

Ἐμοὶ τὸ μὲν ζῆν οὕτως ἐστὶν ἀβέβαιον, ὡς μὴ
πιστεύεσθαι παραμενεῖν ἕως τὴν ἐπιστολήν σοι γράψω·
15 πήρα δὲ ἱκανὸν αὐτοῦ ταμιεῖον, τὰ δὲ τῶν νομιζομένων
θεῶν μείζονα ἢ κατ᾽ ἀνθρώπους. ἓν δὲ μόνον ἐμαυτῷ
βέβαιον σύνοιδα, τὴν μετὰ τὴν γένεσιν φθοράν. Ταῦτ᾽
ἐπιστάμενος αὐτός τε τὰς κενὰς ἐλπίδας ἱπταμένας
περὶ τὸ σωμάτιον ἀποφυσῶ, καὶ σοὶ παραγγέλλω μὴ πλέον
20 ἀνθρώπου φρονεῖν.

_____
12 <χαίρειν> Hercher

21. To Amynander, greetings

One need not thank one's parents, either for the fact of being born, since it is by nature that what exists came into being; or for the quality of one's character, for it is the blending of the elements that is its cause. Furthermore, no thanks is required even for the things done by deliberate choice or willed purpose. For birth is a consequence of sexual activity, which is engaged in for the sake of pleasure, not procreation. As the prophet of indifference I speak these words plainly, which are opposed to the deluded life. But if they seem to be rather hard to some, nature yet confirms them with truth, as does the life of those who live, not under delusion, but in accord with virtue.

22. To Agesilaus, greetings

To me life is so uncertain that I am not sure of lasting till I finish writing you this letter. But life has a sufficient store in a wallet. The equipment provided by those esteemed gods is greater than people think. For myself, I am conscious of but one thing certain, that death follows birth. Aware of this, I myself blow away the empty hopes that fly around my poor body and I enjoin you not to be overwise for a man.

23. Λακύδα, <χαίρειν>

Εὐαγγελίζῃ μοι βασιλέα Μακεδόνων σπουδάζειν περὶ
τὴν θέαν ἡμῶν, εὖ δὲ ἐποίησας προσθεὶς τῷ βασιλεῖ
τοὺς Μακεδόνας· τὰ γὰρ ἡμέτερα ᾔδεις ἀβασίλευτα.
5   ἰδεῖν δὲ τὸν ἐμὸν τύπον μηδεὶς ὡς ξένον βουλέσθω· εἰ
δὲ μεταλαβεῖν Ἀλέξανδρος βίου καὶ λόγων βούλεται,
λέγε αὐτῷ, ὅτι ὅσον ἐξ Ἀθηνῶν εἰς Μακεδονίαν, τοσοῦτον καὶ ἐκ Μακεδονίας εἰς Ἀθήνας.

1   <χαίρειν> Hercher

24. Ἀλεξάνδρῳ, <χαίρειν>

10   Εἰ θέλεις καλὸς κἀγαθὸς γενέσθαι, ἀπορρίψας ὃ
ἔχεις ἐπὶ τῆς κεφαλῆς ῥάκος παραγενοῦ πρὸς ἡμᾶς. ἀλλ'
οὐ μὴ δυνηθῇς κρατῇ γὰρ ὑπὸ τῶν Ἡφαιστίωνος μηρῶν.

9   <χαίρειν> Hercher

25. Ἵππωνι

Παρεκάλεις με ἐπιστεῖλαί σοι, ὅ τι ποτὲ ἔγνωκα
15   περὶ θανάτου καὶ ταφῆς, ὡς οὐκ ἂν τέλειος φιλόσοφος
γενόμενος, εἰ μὴ καὶ τὰ μετὰ τὸ ζῆν παρ' ἡμῶν μάθοις.
ἐγὼ δ' ἱκανὸν ἡγοῦμαι τὸ κατ' ἀρετὴν καὶ φύσιν ζῆσαι
καὶ τοῦτ' ἐφ' ἡμῖν εἶναι. ὥσπερ δὲ τὰ πρὸ τῆς γενέσεως παρακεχώρηται τῇ φύσει, οὕτω καὶ τὰ μετὰ τὸ ζῆν
20   ἐπιτρεπτέα ταύτῃ· αὕτη γὰρ ὡς ἐγέννησε, καὶ διαλύσει.
μηδὲν δὲ εὐλαβηθῇς ὅπως ποτὲ ἀναίσθητος ὦ. ἐγὼ γοῦν
ἔγνωκα ἀποπνεύσαντί μοι παρατεθῆναι τὸ βάκτρον, ἵνα
τὰ δοκοῦντά με λυμαίνεσθαι ζῷα ἀπελαύνοιμι.

23. To Lacydes, greetings

You bring me the good news that the king of the
Macedonians is eager to see me, but you did well to add
"the Macedonians" to "the king," for you know that my
affairs are free of royal domination. But let no one be
inclined to consider my example as strange. If one is
inclined to share Alexander's life and discourse, tell him
that it is as far from Athens to Macedonia as it is from
Macedonia to Athens.

24. To Alexander, greetings

If you wish to become good and upright, throw aside
the rag you have on your head and come to me. But you
certainly cannot, for you are held fast by the thighs of
Hephaestion.

25. To Hippon

You have urged me to write you what I have come to
know at one time or another about death and burial, as if
you would not become an accomplished philosopher unless you
learned from me even about the things that will take place
after life. But I deem it enough to live according to virtue and nature, and that this is in our power. As conditions before birth submit to nature, so even must those
after life be consigned to it. For as nature begets, it
also destroys. But have no worry about my being at any
time unconscious of feeling. I know for a fact that I
shall be furnished with a staff after breathing my last,
that I might drive away the animals that would defile me.

26. <Κράτητι>

Μέμνησο ὅτι τῆς πενίας τὴν ἀρχὴν ἔδωκά σοι διὰ
βίου, καὶ πειρῶ μήτε αὐτὸς ταύτην ἀποθέσθαι μήτε ὑπ'
ἄλλου ἀφαιρεθῆναι αὐτήν· εἰκὸς γὰρ τοὺς ἐν Θήβαις
5   ἐκπεριελθεῖν σε πάλιν κακοδαιμονίζοντας. σὺ δὲ τὸν
τρίβωνα λεοντῆν νόει, τὸ δὲ βάκτρον ῥόπαλον, τὴν δὲ
πήραν γῆν καὶ θάλατταν, ἀφ' ἧς τρέφῃ· οὕτω γὰρ ἂν
Ἡράκλειον διανασταίη σοι φρόνημα καὶ πάσης τύχης
κρεῖττον. ἢν δέ σοι τῶν θέρμων ἢ καὶ τῶν ἰσχάδων
10   περιῇ, καὶ ἡμῖν πέμπε.

1   <Κράτητι> Emeljanow

27. Ἀννικέριδι, <χαίρειν>

Λακεδαιμόνιοι καθ' ἡμῶν ἐψηφίσαντο ὡς μὴ τῆς
Σπάρτης ἐπιβαίνοιμεν. ἀλλὰ σύ γε μηδὲν εὐλαβηθῇς·
ὀνόματι γὰρ ἀποκέχρησαι κυνισμοῦ. ἀξιελέητοί γε μὴν
15   οἱ μὴ νοοῦντες, ἃ δοκοῦσιν ἀσκεῖν, ὑπ' ἐμοῦ μόνου
κατορθοῦσθαι. βίου τε γὰρ λιτότητα οὐκ οἶδ' εἴ τις
ἐμοῦ μᾶλλον ἤσκησεν· ὑπομονήν τε τῶν δεινῶν τίς ἂν
καυχήσαιτο Διογένους παρόντος; ἀκόλουθα γοῦν καὶ
ταῦτα τούτοις· ἀτείχιστον δοκοῦντες δι' ἀνδρείαν
20   οἰκεῖν τὴν Σπάρτην ἀφύλακτον τὴν ψυχὴν τοῖς πάθεσιν
ἐκδεδώκασι, μηδένα κατ' αὐτῶν βοηθὸν ἐπιστήσαντες.
φοβεροὶ οὖν τοῖς ὁμόροις φανέντες ὑπὸ τῶν ἐν αὐτοῖς
νοσημάτων πολεμοῦνται. ἐξελαυνέτωσαν οὖν ἀρετήν,
ὑφ' ἧς <μόνη δύναιτ' ἂν ἐρρῶσθαι ἡ ψυχὴ> καὶ τῶν
25   νοσημάτων ἀπηλλάχθαι.

11   <χαίρειν> Hercher
24   <μόνη...ψυχή> Emeljanow

26. To Crates

Remember that I started you on your life-long poverty.
Try neither to lay it aside yourself nor to let it be taken
away by someone else. For it is likely that the Thebans
will again surround you, deeming you unhappy. But as for
you, consider the ragged cloak to be a lion's skin, the
staff a club, and the wallet land and sea, from which you
are fed. For thus would the spirit of Heracles, mightier
than every turn of fortune, stir in you. Now if you have
any lupines or dried figs left, send them to me.

27. To Anniceris, greetings

The Spartans voted against me, resolving that I
should not set foot in Sparta. But you, at any rate,
should have no worry, for you have made full use of the
name of Cynicism. Pitiable indeed are those people who do
not understand that the things they seem to be practicing
are in fact brought to perfection by me alone. For I do
not know whether anyone has practiced simplicity of life
more than I. Who would boast of patience under frightful
circumstances with Diogenes present? It follows that, although they seem to live in unwalled Sparta by relying on
their manly strength for their defense, they have actually
surrendered their unprotected spirits to the passions,
setting up no auxiliary force against them. While they
appear fearful to their neighbors, they suffer attack from
diseases within themselves. So, let them drive away virtue, by which alone the spirit could be strengthened and
set free from its diseases.

28.

Διογένης ὁ κύων τοῖς καλουμένοις Ἕλλησιν
οἰμῴζειν. Ὑπάρχει δὲ τοῦθ᾽ ὑμῖν, κἂν ἐγὼ μὴ λέγω·
ὄντες γὰρ ταῖς μὲν ὄψεσιν ἄνθρωποι, ταῖς δὲ ψυχαῖς
5   πίθηκοι, προσποιεῖσθε μὲν πάντα, γινώσκετε δὲ οὐδέν·
τοιγάρτοι τιμωρεῖται ὑμᾶς ἡ φύσις· νόμους γὰρ ὑμῖν
αὐτοῖς μηχανησάμενοι μέγιστον καὶ πλεῖστον τῦφον ἐξ
αὐτῶν διεκληρώσασθε, μάρτυρας τῆς ἐμπεφυσιωμένης
κακίας λαβόντες. καὶ οὐδέποτε ἐν εἰρήνῃ, ἀλλ᾽ ἐν
10   πολέμῳ τὸν ὅλον βίον καταγηρᾶτε, κακοὶ κακῶν ἐπιτήδειοι ὄντες, καὶ ἀλλήλοις φθονοῦντες, ἐὰν μικρῷ
μαλακώτερον ἱμάτιον ἄλλον ἴδητε ἔχοντα ἢ κερμάτιον
μικρῷ πλέον ἢ ἐν λόγῳ δριμύτερον ἢ μᾶλλον πεπαιδευμέ-
νον. (2) οὐδὲν γὰρ διακρίνετε ὑγιεῖ λόγῳ, ἀλλ᾽ εἰς
15   εἰκότα καὶ πιθανὰ καὶ ἔνδοξα κατολισθάνοντες πάντα
μὲν αἰτιᾶσθε, οὐδὲν δὲ οἴδατε, οὔθ᾽ οἱ πρόγονοι ὑμῶν
οὔθ᾽ ὑμεῖς, ἀλλὰ ὑπὸ ἀγνοίας καὶ ἀφροσύνης καταμωκώ-
μενοι στρεβλοῦσθε, καλῶς ποιοῦντες. μισεῖ δ᾽ ὑμᾶς οὐ
μόνον ὁ κύων, ἀλλὰ καὶ ἡ φύσις αὐτή· μικρὰ μὲν γὰρ
20   εὐφραίνεσθε, πολλὰ δὲ λυπεῖσθε καὶ πρὸ τοῦ γῆμαι καὶ
γήμαντες, ὅτι γε ἐγήματε ὄντες ἐξώλεις καὶ δυσάρεστοι.
ὅσους δὲ καὶ οἵους ἄνδρας ἀπεκτείνατε, τοὺς μὲν ἐν
πολέμῳ πλεονέκται ὄντες, τοὺς δὲ ἐν τῇ καλουμένῃ
εἰρήνῃ αἰτίαν ἐπενεγκόντες. (3) οὔκουν πολλοὶ μὲν
25   ἐπὶ τῶν σταυρῶν κρέμανται, πολλοὶ δὲ ὑπὸ τοῦ δημίου
ἀπεσφαγμένοι, ἕτεροι δὲ φάρμακον πιόντες δημοσίᾳ, οἳ
δ᾽ ἐπὶ τοῦ τροχοῦ, δηλονότι ἄδικοι δόξαντες εἶναι;
πότερον οὖν ἐπιχειρητέον, ὦ κακαὶ κεφαλαί, παιδεῦσαι
τούτους ἢ ἀποκτεῖναι; νεκρῶν μὲν γὰρ ἡμῖν οὐδεμία
30   δήπου χρεία, εἰ μὴ ὥσπερ ἱερείων σάρκας ἐσθίειν
μέλλομεν, ἀνδρῶν δὲ ἀγαθῶν πάντως ἐστὶ χρεία, ὦ κακαὶ
κεφαλαί. ἀγραμμάτους μὲν καὶ ἀμούσους παιδεύετε

28.

Diogenes the Dog to the so-called Greeks, a plague on
you! And this is already beginning to infect you, even if
I should say nothing more. For although to all appearances
you are men, you are apes at heart. You pretend to everything, but know nothing. Therefore, nature takes vengeance
on you, for in contriving laws for yourselves you have allotted to yourselves the greatest and most pervasive delusion that issues from them, and you admit them as witnesses
to your ingrained evil. Nor are you ever at peace, but
you grow old in war your whole life long, evil persons fit
for evil. You envy each other, when you see someone else
who has a slightly finer mantle or a little more small
change, or who has a more striking turn of phrase, or who
had a better education. (2) You decide nothing by sound
reason, but you censure everything as you sink to what is
likely and plausible and generally approved. You know
nothing--as your ancestors did not, neither do you--but,
being made a mockery of by your ignorance and senselessness, you become perverted, a fine way of acting! It is
not only the Dog that hates you; nature itself does too.
For little do you enjoy, but you are much distressed both
before and after the wedding day, since indeed you were
already spoiled and hard to please before you married.
Look at the number and the quality of the men you killed!
Some you killed in your greed during war, others in so-
called peacetime, after hurling charges at them. (3) Were
not many hung on crosses, and did not many have their
throats cut by the public executioner, while others drank
a drug administered by the executioner, and some died on
the rack? Of course, they seemed to be guilty! But, you
blockheads, should one not attempt to educate such people
rather than kill them? For without doubt we have no need
of corpses, unless we intend to eat them as the flesh of
sacrificial victims. But there is most certainly a need
for good men, you blockheads. You educate the unlettered

γράμματα τὰ καλούμενα μουσικά, ἵνα ὑπάρχωσιν ὑμῖν,
ὅταν ποτὲ χρεία ᾖ τούτων, ἄνδρας δὲ ἀδίκους διὰ τί
οὐ παιδεύσαντες χρῆσθε τούτοις, ὁπόταν ᾖ χρεία
δικαίων; ἐπεὶ καὶ ἀδίκων χρείαν ἔχετε, ὅταν βούλησθε
5 ὑφελέσθαι πόλιν ἢ στρατόπεδον;

(4) καὶ οὔπω μέγα τοῦτο ὅταν μετὰ βίας πράττητε
τὰ καλά, καὶ τὰ κρείσσονα λεηλατούμενα πάρεστιν ὁρᾶν,
καὶ οἷς μὲν ἄν, ὦ κακαὶ κεφαλαί, ἐπιχειρήσητε, τούτους ἀδικεῖτε <καὶ κολάζετε>. καίτοι αὐτοὶ μείζονος
10 τιμωρίας ἄξιοι ὄντες. ἔν τε τοῖς γυμνασίοις, ὅταν
ᾖ τὰ καλούμενα Ἕρμαια ἢ Παναθήναια, καὶ ἐν μέσῃ τῇ
ἀγορᾷ ἐσθίετε καὶ πίνετε, μεθύετε, περαίνετε, γυναι-
κοπαθεῖτε. εἶτ' ἐνασεβεῖτε ὑμεῖς ἔτι καὶ κρύφα καὶ
φανερῶς ποιεῖτε ταῦτα. οὐδὲν μὲν μέλει τῷ κυνί, ὑμῖν
15 δὲ πάντα ταῦτα ἐπιμελῆ ἐστιν.

(5) καὶ ὅπου κύνας εἴργετε βίου φυσικοῦ καὶ
ἀληθοῦς, πῶς εἰς αὐτοὺς οὐκ ἂν πλημμελήσαιτε; κἀγὼ
μὲν ὁ κύων τῷ λόγῳ, ἡ δὲ φύσις τῷ ἔργῳ ὁμοίως πάντας
ὑμᾶς τιμωρεῖται· ὁμοίως γὰρ πᾶσιν ὑμῖν θάνατος ἐπι-
20 κρέμαται, ὃν ὑμεῖς φοβεῖσθε. καὶ πολλάκις εἶδον
πτωχοὺς ὑγιαίνοντας δι' ἔνδειαν, πλουσίους δὲ νοσοῦν-
τας δι' ἀκρασίαν τῆς δυστυχοῦς γαστρὸς καὶ πόσθης·
χαρισάμενοι γὰρ τούτοις ὀλίγον ἐγαργαλίσθητε χρόνον
ὑφ' ἡδονῆς μεγάλας καὶ ἰσχυρὰς ἐναποδεικνυμένης
25 ἀλγηδόνας. (6) καὶ οὐδὲν ὠφελήσει ὑμᾶς οὔτε οἰκία
οὔτε τὰ ἐν αὐτῇ κιονόκρανα, ἀλλ' ἐν ταῖς χρυσαῖς καὶ
ἀργυραῖς κλίναις κατακείμενοι στρεβλοῦσθε καλῶς
ποιοῦντες, οὐδ' ἰσχυροποιεῖσθαι δύνασθε, ἵνα τὰ τῶν
ἀγαθῶν λείψανα μετὰ τῶν λαχάνων καταφάγητε κακοὶ
30 κακῶν ἐπιτήδειοι ὄντες. ἀλλ' εἰ νοῦν ἔχετε, ὥσπερ
οὐκ ἔχετε, ἐὰν μεθύητε, Σωκράτει τε τῷ σοφῷ πεισθέντες κἀμοὶ κοινῇ βουλῇ συνελθόντες ἡβηδὸν σύμπαντες
ἢ σωφρονεῖν μάθετε ἢ ἀπάγξασθε· οὐ γὰρ δυνατὸν εἶναι
ἄλλως ἐν τῷ ζῆν, εἰ μὴ θέλετε ὥσπερ ἐν συμποσίῳ,

---

9 <καὶ κολάζετε> Emeljanow

and unrefined in the so-called liberal arts, that they
might be available to you whenever you need them. But why
do you not educate unjust men and use them whenever you
need just men? As when you need unjust men, whenever you
wish to suborn a city or encampment?

(4) But this is not at all a matter of great consequence. Whenever you enact good things by force, one can
see even superior things despoiled. And, you blockheads,
whomever you lay your hands on, you wrong and chastise.
And yet you yourselves deserve greater punishment. Whenever the so-called festival of Hermes or the Panathenaean
games are held, both in the gymnasia and right in the
market place, you eat and drink, get drunk, have intercourse, and act effeminately. Then you act profanely and,
furthermore, do these things both in secret and in the
open. The Dog cares nothing for these things, but you are
anxious for them all.

(5) And where you bar Cynics from a natural and true
way of life, how would you not offend them? I, the Cynic,
for my part punish you in word, but nature likewise punishes all of you in deed, for death, which you fear,
dangles over you equally. Now I have often seen beggars
enjoying health because of want, and rich people ailing
from the intemperance of their unfortunate stomach and
penis. For while you gratified these you were titillated
for a short time by pleasure, which then displays great
and grievous pains. (6) And neither a house nor the capi-
tals on its columns will benefit you at all, but stretched
out on gold and silver couches you are being pulled out of
joint, and rightly so. Nor can you be strengthened, so as
to eat up the remnants of the good along with the greens,
you who are evil and deserve evil. If you have any sense,
as you do not when you are drunk, obey Socrates the wise
and me, and come together in common council, all of you
from the youth upward, and either learn self-control or
hang yourselves. It is impossible to live in any other
way, unless you want to live as in a drinking party until,

ἕως ἂν ὑπερπιόντες καὶ ὑπερμεθυσθέντες ὑπὸ ἱλίγγων
καὶ στρόφων συνεχόμενοι ὑφ' ἑτέρων ἄγησθε καὶ μὴ
αὐτοὶ δύνησθε σωθῆναι.

  (7) σπαταλῶσι δ' ὑμῖν καὶ ἐνθυμουμένοις, ὅσα γε
5 τὰ ἀγαθὰ ὧν δεσπόται λέγεσθε εἶναι, ἔρχονται οἱ
κοινοὶ δήμιοι, οὓς ὑμεῖς καλεῖτε ἰατρούς, οἷς ἃ ἂν
ἐπὶ τὴν γαστέρα ἐπέλθῃ, ταῦτα λέγουσι καὶ πράττουσιν.
οὗτοι δὲ καλῶς ποιοῦντες τέμνουσι καὶ κάουσι καὶ
δεσμεύουσι φάρμακά τε διδόασι καὶ ἔσω καὶ ἔξω τοῦ
10 σώματος. κἂν ὑγιασθῆτε, οὐδὲ τοῖς καλουμένοις
ἰατροῖς χάριν ἔχετε, ἀλλὰ τοῖς θεοῖς φατὲ δεῖν ἔχειν
χάριν· ἐὰν δὲ μή, τοῖς ἰατροῖς ἐγκαλεῖτε. πλεῖον δ'
ἔμοιγε πάρεστι τὸ εὐφραίνεσθαι τοῦ λυπεῖσθαι καὶ τὸ
εἰδέναι τοῦ ἀγνοεῖν· (8) διετέλεσα γὰρ ἐντυγχάνων
15 Ἀντισθένει τῷ σοφῷ, ὃς μόνοις τοῖς εἰδόσιν αὐτὸν
διεῖλε καὶ τοῖς ἀλλοτρίοις τοῖς οὐκ εἰδόσι φύσιν,
λόγον, ἀλήθειαν παρεξέβη, οὐδὲν φροντίσας κνωδάλων
νηπίων μὴ ἐπισταμένων, ὡς εἴρηται ἐν ἐπιστολῇ,
λόγους κυνός. βαρβάροις δὲ οὖσιν οἰμώζειν λέγω, ἕως
20 ἂν ἑλληνιστὶ μαθόντες Ἕλληνες ἀληθινοὶ γένησθε· νῦν
μὲν γὰρ πολὺ χαριέστεροί εἰσιν οἱ καλούμενοι βάρβαροι
καὶ τόπῳ ἐν ᾧ εἰσὶ καὶ τρόπῳ, καὶ οἱ μὲν καλούμενοι
Ἕλληνες στρατεύουσιν ἐπὶ τοὺς βαρβάρους, οἱ δὲ
βάρβαροι διαφυλάττειν οἴονται δεῖν τὴν ἑαυτῶν, πάντες
25 ὄντες αὐτάρκεις. ὑμῖν δὲ ἱκανὸν οὐδέν· καὶ γὰρ
φιλόδοξοι καὶ ἄλογοι καὶ ἀχρήστως τρεφόμενοί ἐστε.

after drinking too much and getting roaring drunk, you feel gripped by whirling and rolling, and are led away by others, and are unable to be saved yourselves.

(7) If you indulge yourselves, and think about how many good things there are of which you are said to be the masters, the public executioners, whom you call doctors, will come to you. They call by name whatever enters into the stomach and set to work. Working appropriately, they cut, cauterize, bind up, and apply medication both inside and outside the body. And should you regain your health, you have no thanks for the so-called doctors, but say that one must thank the gods. But if you do not, you blame the doctors. But I, at any rate, am more capable of gladness than sadness, and knowledge than ignorance. (8) For I continued to talk with the wise Antisthenes, who carried on philosophical discourse only with those who knew him. He avoided the others who did not know nature, reason, and truth, and paid no attention to the childish beasts who do not understand the words of a Cynic, as is said in the letter. I call a plague on you real barbarians, until you learn in the Greek way and become true Greeks. For now those who are called barbarians are much more refined both in the place where they live and in their way of life. Those who are called Greeks war against the barbarians, while the barbarians think it necessary only to protect their own land, since they are content with what they have. But nothing is enough for you, for you are lovers of glory, irrational, and ineptly brought up.

29. Διονυσίῳ

Ἐπειδὴ δέδοκταί σοι ἐπιμέλειάν ποιήσασθαι
σεαυτοῦ, πέμψω σοι ἄνθρωπον οὐδὲν μὰ Δία Ἀριστίππῳ
καὶ Πλάτωνι ὅμοιον, ἀλλ' ἕνα τῶν Ἀθήνησι παιδαγωγῶν
5   ἐξ ὧν ἔχω, δριμύτατα μὲν βλέποντα, ὀξύτατα δὲ
βαδίζοντα, σκῦτος δὲ ἀλγεινότατον φέροντα, ὅς σε μὰ
Δία ἐπιτρέψει τὸ μὴ καθ' ὥραν ἀναπαύεσθαι καὶ πρωὶ
ἐγείρεσθαι, παύσας φόβων καὶ δειμάτων, ἐν οἷς ὢν
οἴει τι μᾶλλον διὰ δορυφόρους ἢ τῆς ἀκροπόλεως τὴν
10   εὐερκίαν ἀποστήσεσθαι αὐτῶν, δι' ὧν μόνων ἀεὶ πάρεστι
καὶ σοὶ δὲ ὅσῳ μᾶλλον καὶ πλείω καὶ μείζω τοιαῦτα
κατασκευάζῃ, πλείους καὶ μείζους ἀπορίαι καὶ δείματα
τῆς ψυχῆς ἀποβαίνουσι.

(2) πάντα οὖν ταῦτα περιαιρήσεται καὶ θάρσος
15   ἐμποιήσας ἀποστήσει τῆς μαλακίας· τί γὰρ ὄφελος
ἀνδρὸς μὴ ἐλευθέρου; ἔστι δέ τοι αὐτὸ τοῦτο ἡ δουλεία, οἷς μετὰ δέους ὁ βίος παρεσκεύασται. ἕως μὲν
οὖν ταύτας σὺ τὰς συνουσίας ἔχῃς, οὐκ ἀνήσει σε
τούτων τι τῶν κακῶν· ἐὰν δὲ τὸν ἐξωμέα λάβῃς, ὅς σου
20   τὰς πλευρὰς ἀποκαθαρεῖ καὶ παύσει δείπνων μαγειρικῶν,
ἐν ὁποίοις δὲ καὶ αὐτὸς διαιτᾶται τρόποις καταστήσει
σε, σωθήσῃ, ὦ δείλαιε.

(3) νυνὶ δὲ τοιούτους ηὕρηκας ἀνθρώπους, οἳ ἂν
μάλιστά σε διαλυμαίνοιντο καὶ διαφθείρειεν· οὐ γὰρ
25   ὅπως ἀγαθόν τι παρασκευάσωσί σοι, ἀλλ' ὅπως δειπνή-
σωσί τι σκοποῦσι καὶ ὅ τι κερδανοῦσι ζητοῦσιν, οὐδὲν
ἀφαιρούμενοί σου τῶν ὑπαρχόντων κακῶν, ἀλλὰ τῶν ὄντων
ἀφαιρούμενοι καὶ προσκαταλύοντες τῶν οἰκείων ἐθῶν.
καὶ οὕτως ἀναίσθητος εἶ, ὃς οὐδὲ ἐκεῖνο ἀκούεις οὕτως
30   ἐν μέσῳ καὶ πανταχοῦ τῆς Ἑλλάδος λεγόμενον,

29. To Dionysius

Since you have resolved to take care of yourself, I will send a man to you who is not, by Zeus, like Aristippus and Plato, but is one of the paedagogues of Athens that I engage. He has very keen powers of vision, moves very swiftly, and carries a very painful whip. He will direct you, by Zeus, not to take your rest early, but to rise early, and will give you rest from your fears and terrors. When you are surrounded by them, you think that somehow you will rather elude them with the aid of bodyguards or the security of a citadel. But it is through these alone that the fears are always present. And the more you furnish more numerous and stronger defenses of this sort for yourself, the more numerous and stronger are the perplexities and terrors of the soul that result.

(2) Therefore, he will take away all these fears and, instilling courage, will turn you from softness. For what good is a man who is not free? Without a doubt, this very condition is slavery, when people make provision for their life in the grips of fear. Until, then, you have habitual associations like this, none of these evils will let you loose. But if you receive the man clad in a sleeveless vest, who will purge your sides and keep you away from gourmet dinners, and will instead establish you in the way of life that he himself pursues, then you will be saved, you poor soul.

(3) As it is, you have found the kind of people who would certainly corrupt and destroy you. For they are not looking out for any good they might do you, but rather how they might get a meal, and they are searching for whatever personal gain they might make. They remove none of your present troubles but make off with some of your possessions and, in addition, corrupt the standards of your household. Now you are so senseless that you do not hear what is said in the very center of Greece as well as everywhere in it:

ἐσθλῶν μὲν γὰρ ἄπ' ἐσθλὰ μαθήσεαι, ἢν δὲ
κακοῖσι συμμίσγῃς, ἀπολεῖς καὶ τὸν ἐόντα
νόον.

(4) ὧν σοι οὐδὲν βαρύτερόν ἐστιν, ὦ δείλαιε, τῶν
5   πατρῴων καὶ τυραννικῶν τρόπων, οὐδέ ἐστιν ὅ τι σε
ἀεὶ ἄλλο μᾶλλον ἀπόλλυσιν. ἀλλ' οὐδὲ ἄνθρωπον δύνῃ
ἐξευρεῖν ἐπὶ τοῦτο, ὅστις σε ἀποστήσει ὥσπερ τῆς
ἱερᾶς νόσου καλουμένης τῆς τυραννίδος· ἅπαντα γὰρ
ποιεῖς, ὅσα ἄνθρωπος μαινόμενος ποιεῖ, μόνου δὲ
10   ἀποστὰς τούτου σωθείης ἄν. ἀλλ' οὔτε οἱ συνόντες
ὁρῶσιν ὅσον τὸ κακὸν ἔχεις, οὔτε αὐτὸς αἰσθάνῃ,
οὕτως ἐκ πολλοῦ τέ σου καὶ σφόδρα ἧπται ἡ νόσος.
σκύτους οὖν δεῖ σοι καὶ σεσπότου, οὐχ ὅς σε θαυμάσει
καὶ κολακεύσει· ὡς ὑπό γε τοιούτου ἀνθρώπου πῶς ἄν
15   τίς ποτε ὠφεληθείη, ἢ πῶς ὁ τοιοῦτος ὠφελήσειέ τινα;
εἰ μὴ ὥσπερ ἵππον ἢ βοῦν κολάζοι τε ἅμα καὶ σωφρονί-
ζοι, φροντίζοι τε τῶν δεόντων.

(5) ἀλλὰ σύ γε πόρρω ἥκεις διαφθορᾶς. οὐκοῦν
ἀναγκαῖον τομάς τε καὶ καύσεις καὶ φαρμακείας
20   ποιεῖσθαι. σὺ δὲ ὥσπερ τὰ παιδία πάππους τινὰς καὶ
τίτθας εἰσηγάγου, καὶ σοί φασι "δέξαι, τέκνον,
ἔγχεαι, εἴ τί με φιλεῖς, μικρὸν ἔτι μόνον τουτὶ
πρόσφαγε." εἰ οὖν σοι ἅπαντες καὶ πᾶσαι συνελθόντες
κατηρῶντο, οὐκ ἂν συμφορώτερα τῇ νόσῳ ἐποίεις. ἀλλὰ
25   τί; οὐ γὰρ μήποτε σὺ ἐθελήσεις τὰ θρῖα τῶν σύκων
ἐπιτρώγειν, ἀλλ' ὥσπερ πρόβατον οὐκ ἂν ἀποσταίης τῶν
ὡρίμων. οὐκ ἔστιν οὖν σοι οὔτε χαίρειν οὔτε
ἐρρῶσθαι, ὦ φίλτατε.

> For you will learn good things from good men, but
> if you mix with the bad, you will destroy even
> the good sense that you have. (Theognis, *El*. 1.
> 35-36)

(4) Poor soul, there is no harsher burden for you than the ways of your forefathers and of the tyrants. There is nothing else which more consistently destroys you. Yet you cannot find a man with this purpose, that he preserve you from the sacred sickness which is also called tyranny. For you do everything that a madman does, although you would be saved if you held back from this alone. However, your companions do not see the extent of your evil, nor do you yourself perceive it, for so long and so thoroughly has the sickness gripped you. Consequently you need a whip and an overlord and not someone who will admire and flatter you. Indeed, how would anyone ever be benefited by this sort of person, and how would such a person benefit anyone? Only if he chastise him like a horse or an ox and at the same time recall him to his senses and pay heed to what is lacking.

(5) But you are in an advanced state of corruption. Therefore, cutting, cautery and medication must be employed. But you, like little children, have brought in for yourself a number of grandparents and wetnurses who say to you, "Here, my child, fill your cup if you love me. Eat just this little bit more." And so, if all men and women assembled and called down curses on you, you couldn't do more to further the disease alone. But what then? You will surely never want to eat the fig leaves, but like a sheep you would not turn from the ripe fruit. So, my dearest friend, you can neither enjoy yourself nor become strong.

30. 'Ικέτη, <εὖ πράττειν>

Ἧκον, ὦ πάτερ, 'Αθήναζε, καὶ πυθόμενος τὸν
Σωκράτους ἑταῖρον εὐδαιμονίαν διδάσκειν, εἰσῆλθον
παρ' αὐτόν. ὃ δὲ ἐτύγχανε τότε σχολάζων περὶ ταῖν
5   ὁδοῖν ταῖν φερούσαιν, ἔλεγε δὲ αὐτὰς εἶναι δύο καὶ
οὐ πολλάς, καὶ τὴν μὲν σύντομον, τὴν δὲ πολλήν·
ἐξεῖναι οὖν ἑκάστῳ ὁποτέραν βούλοιτο βαδίζειν. κἀγὼ
ταῦτα ἀκούσας τότε μὲν κατεσίγησα, τῇ δὲ ἐξῆς,
ἐπειδὴ πάλιν εἰσιόντων ἡμῶν παρ' αὐτὸν περὶ ταῖν
10 ὁδοῖν παρεκάλεσα αὐτὸν ἐπιδεῖξαι ἡμῖν, καὶ ὃς μάλ'
ἑτοίμως ἀπαναστὰς τῶν θάκων ἧγεν ἡμᾶς εἰς ἄστυ καὶ
δι' αὐτοῦ εὐθὺς εἰς τὴν ἀκρόπολιν. (2) καὶ ἐπεὶ
ἀγχοῦ ἐγενόμεθα, ἐπιδείκνυσιν ἡμῖν δύο τινὲ ὁδὼ
ἀναφερούσα, τὴν μὲν ὀλίγην προσάντη τε καὶ δύσκολον,
15 τὴν δὲ πολλὴν λείαν τε καὶ ῥαδίαν. καθιστὰς ἅμα γὰρ
"αἱ μὲν εἰς τὴν ἀκρόπολιν" εἶπε "φέρουσαι ὁδοί εἰσιν
αὗται, αἱ δὲ ἐπὶ τὴν εὐδαιμονίαν τοιαῦται· αἱρεῖσθε
δὲ ἕκαστος ἣν ἐθέλετε, ξεναγήσω δ' ἐγώ." τότε οἱ μὲν
ἄλλοι τῆς ὁδοῦ τὸ δύσκολον καὶ πρόσαντες καταπλαγέν-
20 τες ὑποκατεκλίνησαν καὶ τὴν μακρὰν καὶ λείαν παρεκάλουν αὐτὸν διάγειν, ἐγὼ δὲ κρείττων γενόμενος τῶν
χαλεπῶν τὴν προσάντη καὶ δύσκολον· ἐπὶ γὰρ εὐδαιμονίαν ἐπειγομένῳ κἂν διὰ πυρὸς ἢ ξιφῶν βαδιστέον
εἶναι.
25   (3) ἐπεὶ δὲ ταύτην εἱλόμην τὴν ὁδόν, ἀφαιρεῖταί
μου τὸ ἱμάτιον καὶ τὸν χιτῶνα καὶ περιβάλλει μοι
τρίβωνα διπλοῦν καὶ ἀποκρήμνησί μου τοῦ ὤμου πήραν,
ἐμβαλὼν εἰς αὐτὴν ἄρτον καὶ τρίμμα καὶ ποτήριον καὶ
τρυβλίον, ἔξωθεν δὲ αὐτῇ παρήρτησε λήκυθον καὶ
30 στλεγγίδα, δίδωσι δέ μοι καὶ βακτηρίαν. καὶ ἐγὼ
τούτοις ἐκοσμήθην, ἠρόμην δὲ αὐτόν, διὰ τί με τρίβωνα
περιέβαλε διπλοῦν. ὃ δὲ ἔφη "ἵνα σε πρὸς ἄμφω
συνασκήσω, καὶ καῦμα τὸ ἀπὸ θερείας καὶ ψῦχος τὸ ἀπὸ
χειμῶνος."
35   "τί γὰρ" ἔφην, "ὃ ἁπλοῦς τοῦτο οὐκ ἐποίει;"

-----

1 <εὖ πράττειν> Hercher

30. To Hicetas, do well

I came to Athens, Father, and, when I heard that the
companion of Socrates was teaching about happiness, I went
to listen to him. Now he happened to be lecturing at the
time about the two roads that lead to it. He said that
they are two and not many: the one a short cut, and the
other the long way. Consequently each person can proceed
along whichever of the two he wishes. I remained silent
at the time that I heard this, but when we returned to him
on the next day, I urged him to speak to us about the two
roads. He quite readily rose from his seat and led us to
town and straight through it to the acropolis. (2) And
when we were near, he pointed out to us a certain pair of
roads leading upward: the one short, rising up against the
hill and difficult; the other long, smooth and easy. And
as soon as he had brought us down, he said, "Such are the
roads leading to the acropolis, and the ones to happiness
are like them. Each of you, choose the one you want and
I will guide you." Then the others, fearstruck at the
difficulty and steepness of the road, backed down and
urged him to lead them along the long and smooth one. But
since I was superior to the hardships, I chose the steep
and rough road, for the person hurrying on toward happiness must proceed even if it be through fire and sword.

(3) And after I chose this road, he took off my
mantle and tunic, put a double, coarse cloak around me,
and hung a wallet from my shoulder, putting bread, drink,
a cup, and a bowl into it. He attached an oil flask and a
scraper on the outside of it, and gave me a staff too.
Furnished with this equipment, I asked him why he put a
double, coarse cloak on me. He explained, "So that I might
assist you in your training for both eventualities: the
burning heat of summer and the cold of winter."

"What?," I said. "Did not the single one do this?"

(4) "οὐ μὲν οὖν" εἶπεν, "ἀλλὰ θέρους μὲν
ῥᾳστώνην, χειμῶνος δὲ πλείονα ἢ κατ᾽ ἄνθρωπον
ταλαιπωρίαν."

"τὴν δὲ πήραν διὰ τί μοι περιτέθεικας;"

5   "ἵνα πάντη τὴν οἰκίαν" εἶπε "περιφέρης."

"τὸ δὲ ποτήριον καὶ τὸ τρυβλίον διὰ τί ἐνέβαλες;"

"ὅτι δεῖ σε" εἶπε "καὶ πίνειν καὶ ὄψῳ χρῆσθαι,
ὄψῳ ἑτέρῳ" ἔφη, "κάρδαμον μὴ ἔχοντα."

"τὴν δὲ λήκυθον καὶ τὴν στλεγγίδα πρὸς τί

10   ἀπήρτησας;"

"τὴν μὲν ἀρωγόν" ἔφη "πόνων, τὴν δὲ γλοίου."

"ἡ δὲ βακτηρία πρὸς τί;" ἔφην.

"πρὸς τὴν ἀσφάλειαν" εἶπε.

"ποίαν τήνδε;"

15   "πρὸς ἣν οἱ θεοὶ αὐτῇ ἐχρήσαντο, πρὸς τοὺς
ποιητάς."

31. Φαινύλῳ, <εὖ πράττειν>

Ἀνέβαινον Ὀλυμπίαζε μετὰ τὸν ἀγῶνα, τῇ δ᾽
ὑστεραίᾳ κατὰ τὴν ὁδὸν ὑπήντησέ μοι Κίκερμος ὁ παγ-

20   κρατιαστής, κατεστεμμένος τῷ Ὀλυμπιακῷ στεφάνῳ, καὶ
σὺν αὐτῷ τῶν οἰκείων πολὺς ὅμιλος πορευόμενος οἴκαδε.
κἀγὼ, ὡς πλησίον ἐγένετό μου, λαβόμενος αὐτὸν τῆς
χειρός "ἔκστηθι" εἶπον, "ὦ ἄθλιε, τῆς ταλαιπωρίας καὶ
λῆξον τοῦ τύφου, ὅς σε Ὀλυμπίαζε ἀναβάντα ἀνεπίγνωσ-

25   τον τοῖς γονεῦσιν ἀπάγει. καὶ φράσον ἐπὶ τίνι δὴ
μέγα φρονῶν κατέστεψαι μέν" ἔφην "τῷδε τῷ στεφάνῳ τὴν
κεφαλήν, φοίνικα δὲ διὰ τῶν χειρῶν φέρεις, ὄχλον δὲ
τοσοῦτον ἐπισύρῃ."

(2) καὶ ὃς ἀπεκρίνατο "ἐπὶ τῷ νενικηκέναι παγ-

30   κράτιον τοὺς ἐν Ὀλυμπίᾳ πάντας."

"ὦ τοῦ θαύματος" ἔφην, "καὶ τὸν Δία καὶ τὸν
ἀδελφόν;"

―――――――――――――――――――――
17 <εὖ πράττειν> Hercher

(4) "Not at all," he replied.   "It does bring relief during the summer, but in the winter it causes more bodily hardship than a person can put up with."

"But why did you put the wallet around me?"

"So that you might carry your house with you everywhere," he explained.

"And the cup and bowl, why did you throw them in?"

"Since you have to drink and use an appetizer," he said, "some other appetizer if you don't have mustard."

"The oil flask and scraper, why did you hang them alongside?"

"The one is useful for hard work," he said, "the other for oil and dirt."

"The staff, what is that for?" I asked.

"For security," he answered.

"How's that?"

"For what the gods use it, against the poets."

31. To Phaenylus, do well

I was going up to Olympia after the games, and on the day following it Cicermus, the pancratiast, met me along the road. He was crowned with the Olympic wreath and with him was a sizeable crowd of friends on their way home. Now when he came near me I took him by the hand and said, "Hey sport, retire from this wretched exercise and put an end to the delusion which brings you home from your trip to Olympia a stranger to your own parents. And tell me, on what do you pride yourself," I went on, "that you crown your head with this wreath, bear the palm in your hands, and drag this crowd along after you?"

(2) He answered, "For having beaten everyone in the pancratium in Olympia."

"Oh what a wonder!" I exclaimed.   "Zeus too and his brother?"

"οὐ μὲν οὖν" ἔφη.

"ἀλλὰ τοὺς καθ᾽ ἕνα προκαλούμενος;"

"οὐ γάρ" εἶπεν.

"ἄλλους ἄρα δήπουθεν καὶ ἄλλους κληρωσάμενος
5 ἐπαγκρατίασας;"

"πάνυ γε."

"εἶτα πῶς τοὺς ὑπ᾽ ἄλλων ἐκβληθέντας ἐτόλμησας
λέγειν αὐτὸς νενικηκέναι; τί δαί; ἄνδρες ἦσαν μόνον
οἱ παγκρατιάζοντες Ὀλυμπίασι;"
10 "καὶ παῖδες" εἶπεν.

"καὶ τούτους ἐνίκησας ἀνδρισάμενος;"

οὐκ ἔφη· "οὐ γὰρ ἦσαν ἐκ τοῦ ἐμοῦ κλήρου."

"τί γάρ, σὺ τοὺς ἐκ τοῦ ἰδίου κλήρου πάντας
ἐνίκησας;"
15 "πάνυ γε."

"λέγε μοι" ἔφην, "οὐχ ὁ σὸς κλῆρος ὁ τῶν
τελείων ἦν;"

"τῶν τελείων" εἶπεν.

"Κίκερμος δὲ ποῖον κλῆρον ἠγωνίζετο;"
20 "ἐμὲ λέγεις; τῶν τελείων" εἶπεν.

"ἆρ᾽ οὖν Κίκερμον ἐνίκησας;"

"οὐ μὲν οὖν" εἶπεν.

(3) "εἶτα σὺ μήτε τοὺς παῖδας νενικηκὼς μήτε
τοὺς τελείους πάντας τολμᾷς λέγειν νενικηκέναι;
25 τίνας δ᾽ εἶχες" ἔφην "τοὺς ἀντιπάλους;"

"ἄνδρας" εἶπεν "ἐπιφανεῖς τῶν ἐκ τῆς Ἑλλάδος
καὶ Ἀσίας."

"ἆρα κρείττονας σαυτοῦ ἢ ἴσους ἢ χείρονας;"

"κρείττονας."
30 "κρείττονας λέγεις τοὺς ἡττηθέντας ὑπὸ σοῦ;"

"ἴσους" εἶπε.

"καὶ πῶς τοὺς ἴσους ἠδυνήθης ἡττῆσαι σεαυτοῦ
μὴ χείρονας γενομένους;"

"ἥττους" εἶπεν.

"Not at all," he said.

"But those you did beat, was it by challenging them one by one?"

"Not exactly," he answered.

"Well, then, you won the pancratium beating some, I presume, and having the others allotted to you. Right?"

"Yes."

"Then how dare you say that you yourself have beaten those eliminated by others? What then? Did only men participate in the pancratium at Olympia?"

"Boys too," he added.

"And you fought and won over these although you have already grown to manhood?"

"No," he said, "for they were not in my allotted group."

"What then? Did you beat everyone in your own group?"

"Certainly."

"Tell me," I said, "wasn't your group that of the adults?"

"It was," he answered.

"Now take Cicermus, what kind of group did he vie with?"

"Do you mean me? A group of adults," he explained.

"So you beat Cicermus?"

"Not at all," he insisted.

(3) "And you, who have beaten neither the boys nor all the adults, dare to say that you are the victor? Whom did you have as adversaries?" I asked.

"Men," he answered, "renowned in Greece and Asia."

"Were they superior to you, equal, or weaker?"

"Superior."

"You say that those worsted by you were superior?"

"Equal," he said.

"And how were you able to beat your equals without their being weaker than you?"

"Inferior," he said.

"εἶτα οὐ παύσῃ ἐπὶ τῷ τοὺς ἥττονας κατηγωνίσθαι
μέγα φρονῶν; ἢ σὺ μὲν τοῦτο δύνασαι μόνος ποιῆσαι,
ὁ τυχὼν δ᾽ οὐκ ἂν δύναιτο; τί δ᾽; οὐκ ἔστιν ὅστις
οὐ τοὺς χείρονας ἑαυτοῦ δυνάμει ἐπικρατεῖ. (4) ἔα
5   γοῦν ταῦτα, ὦ Κίκερμε, τὰ πολλὰ χαίρειν καὶ ἀγωνίζου
μὴ παγκράτιον, μηδὲ πρὸς ἀνθρώπους, ὧν χείρων ἔσῃ
μετ᾽ οὐ πολὺ εἰς γῆρας ἀφικόμενος, ἧκε δὲ ἐπὶ τὰ
ὄντως καλὰ καὶ μάθε μὴ ὑπὸ ἀνθρωπίων τυπτόμενος
καρτερεῖν, ἀλλ᾽ ὑπὸ τῆς ψυχῆς, μηδ᾽ ἱμᾶσι μηδὲ
10   πυγμαῖς, ἀλλὰ πενίᾳ, ἀλλ᾽ ἀδοξίᾳ, ἀλλὰ δυσγενείᾳ,
ἀλλὰ φυγαδείᾳ. τούτων γὰρ ἀσκήσας καταφρονεῖν μακα-
ρίως μὲν ζήσεις, ἀνεκτῶς δὲ ἀποθανῇ· ἐκεῖνα δὲ ζηλῶν
ζήσεις ταλαιπώρως."
    ταῦτά μου διεξιόντος αὐτῷ τόν τε φοίνικα εἰς τὴν
15   γῆν κατέβαλε καὶ τὸν στέφανον τῆς κεφαλῆς ἀφείλετο
καὶ οἷός τε ἦν τὴν ὁδὸν ἀναλύειν.

32. Ἀριστίππῳ, <χαίρειν>

    Ἐπυθόμην σε σχολάσαι <βασκαίνειν> καθ᾽ ἡμῶν καὶ
παρὰ τῷ τυράννῳ ὀνειδίζειν ἑκάστοτε τὴν ἐμὴν πενίαν,
20   ὅτι ἡμᾶς ποτὲ κατέλαβες ἐπὶ τῆς κρήνης σέρεις ἀπο-
κλύζοντας ὄψον τῷ ἄρτῳ. ἐγὼ δὲ ἄγαμαι, πῶς, ὦ μακά-
ριε, τοῖς τὰ ἄξια ἐπαινοῦσι πενίαν κακίζεις, καὶ
ταῦτα Σωκράτους κατακηκοώς, τοῦ τὸν αὐτὸν μὲν τρίβωνα
χειμῶνος καὶ θέρους καὶ ἄλλοτε ἀμπεχομένου, τὸν αὐτὸν
25   δὲ πρὸς τὰς γυναῖκας κοινὸν ἔχοντος, ὄψον δὲ οὐκ ἐκ
τῶν κήπων φέροντος οὐδ᾽ ἐκ τῶν μαγειρείων, ἀλλ᾽ ἀπὸ
τῶν γυμνασίων. ἀλλ᾽ ἔοικας ταῦτα ἐπιλελησμένῳ διὰ
τὰς Σικελικὰς τραπέζας.

17   <χαίρειν> Hercher
18   <βασκαίνειν> Emeljanow

"Then won't you stop bragging about beating those weaker than you? Or are you the only man who can do this, whereas the average person would not be able to? There is no one who doesn't prevail over those weaker than himself in strength. (4) In any case, Cicermus, say goodby to most of this and don't compete in the pancratium, nor against men to whom you will be inferior before long, when you reach old age. But come to what is really honorable and learn to be steadfast under blows, not of puny men, but of the spirit, not through leather straps or fists, but through poverty, disrepute, lowly birth, and exile. For when you have trained to despise these things, you will live happily and will die in a tolerable way. But if you strive after those things, you will live in endless suffering."

While I was expounding these things to him, he dropped the palm to the ground, took the wreath off his head, and was able to go off on his way.

32. To Aristippus, greetings

I learned that you have devoted yourself to slandering me and to reproaching my poverty at every opportunity you have before the tyrant, saying that you once caught me at the well washing off chicory as an appetizer for my bread. But I am amazed, my fine friend, at how you abuse the poverty of those who commend worthy practices, especially since you have heard and followed the same recommendations from Socrates, who wore the same coarse cloak winter, summer and at all other times. He held the same common rights to be applicable to his wives and did not get his appetizers from the gardens or kitchens, but from the gymnasia. But you seem to have forgotten these facts because of the Sicilian banquets.

(2) κἀγὼ οὐχ ὑπομνήσω σε πόσου ἄξιόν ἐστι πενία
μάλιστα ᾿Αθήνησιν, οὐδὲ ἀπολογήσομαι περὶ αὐτῆς (οὐ
γὰρ εἰς σὲ κἀγὼ ἀνατίθεμαι τὸ ἐμαυτοῦ ἀγαθόν, ὥσπερ
καὶ σὺ εἰς ἑτέρους· ἀπόχρη οὖν μοι μόνῳ ἐπίστασθαι
5 ὑπὲρ αὐτοῦ), ὑπομνήσω δέ σέ ποτε περὶ Διονυσίου καὶ
τῶν μακαρίων αὐτοῦ συνουσιῶν, αἵ σε εὐφραίνουσιν,
ὁπότε ἐσθίων καὶ πίνων τὰ πολυτελῆ δεῖπνα καὶ ἃ
μήποτε ἡμῖν παρείη ἀνθρώπους ἑκάστοτε τοὺς μὲν μαστι-
γουμένους, τοὺς δὲ ἀνασκολοπιζομένους, τοὺς δὲ εἰς
10 τὰς λατομίας ἀπαγομένους βλέπεις, καὶ τῶν μὲν γυναῖκας ἀφαιρουμένας εἰς ὕβριν τῶν δὲ παῖδας, καὶ πλέονας
τῶν δούλων, οὐχ ἑνὸς μόνον οὐδ᾿ αὐτοῦ τοῦ τυράννου,
ἀλλὰ πολλῶν καὶ ἀνοσίων, καὶ πίνοντα πρὸς ἀνάγκην καὶ
μένοντα καὶ πορευόμενον καὶ ἀποδρᾶναι μὴ δυνάμενον
15 διὰ τὰς χρυσᾶς πέδας.
     (3) ταῦτ᾿ ἔγωγε ἀντ᾿ ἐκείνων τῶν ὀνειδῶν ὑπομι-
μνήσκω. ὁπόσῳ ζῶμεν σέρεις πλύνειν ἐπιστάμενοι, τὰς
δὲ Διονυσίου θύρας θεραπεύειν ἀγνοοῦντες ὑμῶν, φημί,
κρεῖττον τῶν Διονυσίῳ συμβουλευόντων καὶ ἐπιτασσόντων
20 Σικελίᾳ πάσῃ. ἀλλ᾿ εἴη σοι, κἂν ὁπόσα γε λέγῃς πρὸς
ἡμᾶς ἀποθαρρυνόμενος, καὶ νοεῖν καὶ μὴ στασιάζεσθαι
πρὸς τὰ πάθη τὸν λόγον· καλὰ γὰρ τὰ παρὰ Διονυσίῳ
μέχρι λόγου, ἐλευθερία δὲ ἡ ἐπὶ Κρόνου καὶ ἡ φιλητιος
μαζαβλωρος...

(2) But I will not remind you how much poverty is
valued, especially at Athens, nor shall I defend myself
for it (for in my case I do not impart my own good to you,
as you give your goods to others. So it is enough for me
alone to know for certain about it). But I shall remind
you a bit about Dionysius and his blessed company, which
delights you. I mean the occasions when you are eating
and drinking at extravagant dinners, the likes of which
would never be held in my presence, when you see some men
being whipped, others fixed to a stake, others driven to
the stone quarries, and the wives of some taken away for
wanton purposes, as are the children of others, and many
of the slaves, not just of one man or of the ruler himself,
but of many unholy men. And when you see someone forced
to drink, lingering, then going his way, but unable to
flee because of his golden shackles.

(3) I, for one, remind you of these things in return
for those reproaches. How much better do we live, who
know how to wash chicory but do not know how to dance at-
tendance at the doors of Dionysius! I declare, we live
better than you who advise Dionysius and give orders to
all of Sicily. But however much you rail against us in
your extreme boldness, you should have sense, nor should
reason rise up against the passions. For the things in
Dionysius' court are fine according to all reports, but
the freedom in the time of Chronos...

33. Φανομάχῳ, <εὖ πράττειν>

Ἐκαθήμην ἐν τῷ θεάτρῳ βιβλίδια κολλῶν, ἀφικόμενος δὲ Ἀλέξανδρος ὁ Φιλίππου στὰς ἐν τῷ καταντικρὺ
πλησίον ἐμοῦ τὸν ἥλιον ἀφείλετό μου, κἀγὼ διὰ τὸ
5   μηκέτι πως ὁρᾶν τὰ διασπάσματα τῶν βιβλιδίων ἀνέβλεψα
καὶ τότε ἔγνων αὐτὸν παρόντα. ὡς δέ με καὶ αὐτός,
ἐπεὶ ἀνέβλεψα, προσηγόρευσε καὶ τὴν δεξιὰν ὤρεξεν, ὡς
δὲ καὶ αὐτὸν ἐγὼ διὰ τοῦτο ἀντιπροσηγόρευσα καὶ εἶπον
τοιοῦτον. "ἀληθῶς ἀνίκητος εἶ, μειράκιον, ὅτε καὶ
10   θεοῖς τὰ ἴσα δύνασαι· ἰδοὺ γάρ, ὃ φασι τὴν σελήνην
τὸν ἥλιον διατιθέναι ἐν τῷ γενέσθαι αὐτῷ καταντικρύ,
καὶ σὺ ταὐτὸ τοῦτο εἴργασαι, ἐπεὶ δεῦρο εἰσελθὼν ἐμοὶ
παρέστης."
    (2) καὶ ὁ Ἀλέξανδρος "σκώπτεις" εἶπεν, "ὦ
15   Διόγενες."
    "τί τοῦτ᾽" ἔφην "λέγεις; οὐ γάρ ἐστιν ὁρᾶν σοι
ὅτι τοῦ ἔργου μὲν ἀπολείπομαι διὰ τὸ μὴ βλέπειν ὥσπερ
ἐν νυκτί; διαφέρον δ᾽ οὐδέν μοι τὰ νῦν σοι προσδια-
λέγεσθαι, διαλέγομαι."
20   "οὐδέν" εἶπε "σοι διαφέρει Ἀλέξανδρος ὁ βασιλεύς;"
    "οὐδ᾽ ὅσον" ἔφην· "πολεμεῖται γὰρ τῶν ἐμῶν οὐδέν,
οὐδὲ καθαρπάζεται, καθάπερ τὰ Μακεδόνων καὶ τὰ Λακεδαιμονίων ἢ τινων ἄλλων, ἐν οἷς ἑκάστῳ χρεία βασιλέως."
    "διὰ μέντοι πενίαν" ἔφη "διαφέρω <σοι>."
25   "ποίαν" ἔφην "πενίαν;"
    "τὴν σὴν πενίαν" εἶπε, "δι᾽ ἥνπερ οὕτως εἶ
μεταίτης ἐνδεῶν πάντων."
    (3) "οὗτοι" ἔφην "τοῦτ᾽ ἐστὶ πενία τὸ μὴ ἔχειν
χρήματα, οὐδὲ κακὸν τὸ μεταιτεῖν, ἀλλὰ τὸ ἐπιθυμεῖν
30   πάντων, ὅπερ ἐστὶν ἐν ὑμῖν, καὶ τὸ βίᾳ. διὰ τοῦτο
τῇ μὲν ἐμῇ πενίᾳ κρῆναί τε καὶ γῆ εἰσιν ἐπίκουροι,
ναὶ μὴν καὶ τὰ σπήλαια καὶ τὰ νάκη,

─────────
1   <εὖ πράττειν> Hercher
24 <σοι> Schafstaedt & Emeljanow

33. To Phanomachus, do well

I was seated in the theater gluing together pages of
a book, when Alexander, the son of Philip, came up and
stood right opposite near me, and blocked my sunlight. I
looked up, because I could no longer see the joins of the
pages at all, and recognized him at my side. When he also
recognized me as I looked up, he greeted me and offered me
his right hand. And so I greeted him in return and spoke
to this effect. "You are truly invincible, my boy, since
you are capable of the same things as the gods. For look,
they say of the moon, that it disposes of the sun by getting in its way, and you have done the same thing by coming here and standing near me."

(2) Then Alexander said, "Diogenes, you are joking."

"What do you mean?" I retorted. "First of all, can't
you see that I am kept from my work because I can't see,
as though it were night. And secondly, although it means
nothing to me to be discussing these things with you now,
I am in fact doing so."

"Nothing?" he said. "Is that what Alexander the king
matters to you?"

"Not even a little," I said. "For he does not war
against anything that belongs to me, nor does he carry it
off, as he does the possessions of the Macedonians, the
Lacedaemonians, or any others, each of whom needs a king
in these matters."

"But I do matter to you by reason of poverty," he
countered.

"What sort of poverty?" I asked.

"Your poverty," he explained, "because of which you
are thus a beggar for all your needs."

(3) "Poverty," I replied, "does not consist in not
having money, nor is begging a bad thing, but poverty con-
sists in desiring everything, and that is in your power to
do, and to do so with vigor. Therefore, springs and earth
are allies to my poverty, yes even caves and goat skins are.

καὶ πολεμεῖται μὲν διὰ ταύτην οὐδὲ εἷς οὔτε ἐν γῆ
οὔτε ἐν θαλάσσῃ, ἀλλ' ὡς ἐγεννήθημεν, ἴσθι, καὶ
ζῶμεν· τῇ δὲ ὑμετέρᾳ τάξει οὔτε γῆ εὑρίσκεται ἐπί-
κουρος οὔτε θάλαττα, (4) ἀλλὰ δὴ ταῦτα μὲν ὡς ὄντα
5 <παραλείπετε>, ἀναβαίνετε δὲ ἐπὶ τὸν οὐρανὸν καὶ
οὐδὲ Ὁμήρῳ πείθεσθε τούτων μὴ ἐπιθυμεῖν τῷ εἰς
σωφροσύνην τὰ τῶν Ἀλωειδῶν πάθη ἀναγράψαντι."
     ταῦτ' ἐμοῦ πολλῷ παραστήματι διεξερχομένου
πολλή τις αἰδὼς τὸν Ἀλέξανδρον εἰσῆλθε, καὶ ἀποκλί-
10 νας πρὸς ἕνα τῶν ἑταίρων εἶπεν "ἀλλ' εἰ μὴ ἔφθην
Ἀλέξανδρος γενέσθαι, Διογένης ἂν ἐγενόμην." καὶ
ἐξαναστήσας με ἀπῆγεν σὺν ἑαυτῷ, παρακαλῶν συστρα-
τεύεσθαι, καὶ μόλις ἀφῆκεν.

_____
5 <παραλείπετε> Emeljanow

34. Ὀλυμπιάδι, <εὖ πράττειν>

15   Μὴ ἀνιῶ πρὸς τοὺς συνήθεις, Ὀλυμπιάς, ὑπὲρ
ἐμοῦ, ὅτι τρίβωνα ἀμπέχομαι καὶ ἄλφιτα ἐπιπωλούμενος
ἀνθρώπους μεταιτῶ· οὐ γάρ ἐστι ταῦτα αἰσχρὰ οὐδ'
ἐλευθέροις, ὡς φῆς, ὕποπτα, καλὰ δὲ καὶ οἷα ὅπλα
εἶναι κατὰ δοξῶν τῶν πολεμουσῶν τῷ βίῳ. κἀγὼ ταῦτα
20 ἔμαθον οὐ παρὰ Ἀντισθένους πρώτου τὰ μαθήματα, ἀλλὰ
θεῶν καὶ ἡρώων καὶ τῶν τὴν Ἑλλάδα ἐπεστροφότων ἐπὶ
σοφίαν, Ὁμήρου καὶ τῶν τραγῳδοποιῶν, (2) οἵτινες
Ἥραν τε τὴν Διὸς παράκοιτιν ἔφασαν εἰς ἱέρειαν μετα-
μορφωθεῖσαν τοιοῦτον βίου σχῆμα ἀναλαβεῖν "νύμφαις
25 κρηνιάσιν, κυδραῖς θεαῖς, ἀγείρουσαν Ἰνάχου
Ἀργείου ποταμοῦ παισὶν βιοδώροις," Τήλεφόν τε τὸν
Ἡρακλέους, ἡνίκα εἰς Ἄργος παρεγένετο, πολὺ χείρονι
σχήματι τοῦ ἡμετέρου ἐμφανισθῆναι "πτώχ' ἀμφίβληστρα
σώματος λαβόντα ῥάκη ἀλιτήρια ψύχους," Ὀδυσσέα τε
30 τὸν Λαέρτου ἐξ Ἰλίου οἴκαδε ὑποστρέψαντα φάρει ῥωγαλέῳ,

_____
14 <εὖ πράττειν> Hercher

And no one fights me because of it, neither on land nor
sea. But as I was born, mark well, so also do I live.
To your position, however, the earth is found to be no
ally, nor is the sea. (4) But you leave these aside as
mundane and make for heaven. And you do not even heed
Homer, who warns us not to desire all this, when he describes the sufferings of the Aloadaeans in order to pro-
mote self-control."

While I was expounding on all these points with great
inspiration, a great sense of awe came over Alexander and,
leaning toward one of his companions, he said, "Had I not
been born Alexander first, I would have been Diogenes."
And making me rise, he tried to lead me away with him,
urging me to campaign with him. But reluctantly he let
me go.

34. To Olympias, do well

Do not complain to my associates, Olympias, that I
wear a worn-out cloak and make the rounds of people begging for barley meal. For this is not disgraceful nor, as
you claim, suspect behavior for free men. Rather, it is
noble and can be armament against the appearances which
war against life. Now I did not learn these lessons from
Antisthenes first, but from the gods and heroes and those
who converted Greece to wisdom, like Homer and the tragic
poets. (2) For they said that Hera, the wife of Zeus,
after being transformed into a priestess, took up a way of
life of this sort, collecting alms for the "nymphs of the
spring, noble goddesses, life-giving offspring of Inachus,
the Argive river." And that Telephus, the son of Heracles,
when he came to Argos, appeared in a condition much worse
than ours, with beggarly rags thrown around his body as a
help against the cold. And that Odysseus, son of Laertes,
returned home from Ilium in a torn cloak, caked with

ἱπνοῦ καὶ καπνοῦ ἀναμέστῳ. ἆρά σοι ἔτι δοκεῖ ἡ ἐμὴ
στολὴ καὶ τὸ μεταιτεῖν αἰσχρὰ εἶναι ἢ καλὰ καὶ ἀγαστὰ
βασιλεῦσιν καὶ παντὶ νοῦν ἔχοντι αἱρετὰ εἰς εὐτέλειαν;
       (3) καὶ Τήλεφος μέν, ἵνα ὑγιείας τύχῃ, τούτῳ τῷ
5   σχήματι τοῦ βίου ἐναπεκρύψατο, Ὀδυσσεὺς δ᾽, ἵνα τοὺς
μνηστῆρας ἐκ πολλοῦ ἀδικοῦντας ἀποκτείνῃ· ἐγὼ δὲ ἵνα
τύχω μὲν εὐδαιμονίας ἧς μικρὰ μοῖρά ἐστι τὸ Τηλέφειον
ἀγαθόν, ἕλω δὲ τὰς ψευδεῖς δόξας δι᾽ ἃς οὐχ ἕνα δεσ-
πότην ᾑρήμεθα, διαφύγω δὲ νόσους καὶ τοὺς ἐπ᾽ ἀγορᾶς
10 συκοφάντας, περιέλθω δὲ ἐλεύθερος ὑπὸ τὸν Δία πατέρα
ἐπὶ ὅλης γῆς, μηδένα φοβούμενος τῶν μεγάλων δεσποτῶν.
       εἰ μὲν οὖν <ἐξίαμαι> σε, μῆτερ, ἐπιδείξας τοὺς
κρείττονας ἐμοῦ τρίβωνας ἀμπεχομένους καὶ πήραν
φοροῦντας καὶ παρὰ τῶν χειρόνων ἄλφιτα μεταιτοῦντας,
15 θεοῖς χάρις· εἰ δὲ μή, μάτην ἀνιάσῃ.

----

12 <ἐξίαμαι> Emeljanow

35. Σωπόλιδι, <εὖ πράττειν>

       Ἧκον εἰς Μίλητον τῆς Ἰωνίας, διαπορευόμενος δὲ
τὴν ἀγορὰν <προσήκουσα> παίδων μὴ εὖ ῥαψῳδούντων.
προσελθὼν οὖν τῷ διδασκάλῳ ἠρόμην αὐτόν "διὰ τί
20 κιθαρίζειν οὐ διδάσκεις;"
       ὃ δὲ ἀπεκρίνατο "ὅτι οὐκ ἔμαθον."
       "εἶτα" ἔφην "πῶς τοῦτο μέν, ὅτι οὐκ ἔμαθες, οὐ
διδάσκεις, γράμματα δέ, ἃ μὴ ἔμαθες, σὺ διδάσκεις;"
       πάλιν δὲ προελθὼν μικρὸν εἴσειμι εἰς τὸ τῶν νέων
25 γυμνάσιον, θεασάμενος δὲ ἐν τῷ αἰθρίῳ κακῶς σφαιρί-
ζοντά τινα, προσελθὼν τῷ παλαιστροφύλακι "πόσον"
εἶπον "ἀποτεταγμένον ἐστὶν ἐπιτίμιον κατὰ τοῦ
ἀλειψαμένου καὶ μὴ σφαιρίσαντος;"

----

16 <εὖ πράττειν> Hercher
18 <προσήκουσα> Emeljanow

kitchen dirt and smoke. Now do my clothing and begging
still seem disgraceful to you or are they noble and admirable to kings and to be taken up by every sensible
person for frugality's sake?

(3) Telephus concealed himself in this way of life to
find health, and Odysseus did so to kill the suitors for
their wrongdoings over a long period of time. But I do
this to find happiness, of which the good sought by Telephus is only a small part; to do away with false opinions,
because of which we have taken more than one despot for
ourselves; to escape diseases and slanderers in the market
place; and to go about the whole earth a man free under
father Zeus, afraid of none of the great lords.

So, mother, if I have cured you of your pain by
pointing out those who wear cloaks more ragged than mine,
carry a wallet and beg for barley meal from their infer-
iors, thanks be to god. But if not, you shall be upset
to no purpose.

35. To Sopolis, do well

I came to Miletus from Ionia and, as I was going
through the market place, among other things I heard children reciting incorrectly. So I went up to the teacher
and asked him, "Why don't you teach cithara playing?"

He answered, "Because I never learned how to play
myself."

"Then how is this?" I asked. "Since you didn't learn,
you don't teach; but you do teach letters, which you never
learned yourself?"

Continuing on a bit, I came to the young men's gymnasium, and, upon seeing someone in the open court playing
ball poorly, I went up to the custodian of the palaestra
and asked, "How much is the penalty fixed against someone
oiled for sport but not playing ball?"

ὃ δέ "ὀβολός" ἔφη.

"ἐκεῖνος ὁ νεανίας" ἔφην δείξας τὸν ἄνθρωπον
"μηδενὸς ὄντος ἐπιτιμίου αὐτῷ ὑπ᾽ ἀνάγκης ἐμπαίζει."

(2) ἀποθέμενος οὖν καὶ αὐτὸς τὸν τρίβωνα καὶ τὴν
5   στλεγγίδα ἐκλύσας παρελθὼν ἠλειψάμην, καὶ οὐ διαγίγ-
νεται χρόνος συχνὸς καὶ κατὰ τὸ ἐπιχώριον εὐθέως
παρελθών τις εἷς τῶν νέων, σφόδρα ἀστεῖος τὴν ὄψιν,
ἀγένειος, προσαναδίδωσί μοι τὴν χεῖρα, διαπειρώμενος
εἰ ἐπίσταμαι τὰ παλαιστρικά. κἀγὼ ἕως μέν τινος
10   προσεποιούμην ὑπὸ αἰδοῦς μὴ εἰδέναι· ὡς δὲ ἐπηπείλησε
καταναλίσκειν με, ἠρξάμην συνανατρίβεσθαι αὐτῷ
νομίμως. εἶτα ὁ γνώμων μοί πως ἀνίσταται (τὸ γὰρ
ἕτερον ὄνομα δέδια διὰ τοὺς πολλοὺς εἰπεῖν), καὶ ὧδε
μὲν τὸ μειράκιον ὑπ᾽ αἰδοῦς καταλιπόν με ἄπεισιν, ἐγὼ
15   δὲ ἑστὼς ἐτριβόμην πρὸς ἐμαυτόν.

(3) ἐπεὶ δὲ προσεῖδέ με ὁ παλαιστροφύλαξ, προσελθὼν ἐπέπληττεν, κἀγὼ πρὸς αὐτόν "εἶτα σὺ παρεὶς τῷ
νόμῳ μάχεσθαι νῦν ἐμοὶ διαφέρῃ; εἰ μὲν ἔθος ἦν τὸ
καταλειφομένους πταρμικὸν ὀσφραίνεσθαι, οὐκ ἂν
20   ἠσχάλλες, εἴ τις τῶν ἀλειφομένων ἐν τῷ γυμνασίῳ
ἐπτάρνυτο· νυνὶ δὲ ἄχθῃ, εἴ τις καλοῦ συνανακυλιομέ-
νου αὐτόματος ἐστύθη; ἢ δοκεῖς τὰς μὲν ῥῖνας ὅλως
ἐπὶ τῇ φύσει εἶναι, ταυτὶ δ᾽ ἡμῶν ἐπὶ τῇ προαιρέσει;
οὐ παύσῃ" ἔφην "τοιαῦτα σφαδάζων πρὸς τοὺς εἰσιόντας;
25   εἰ δέ σοί τίς ἐστι λόγος ἵνα μὴ γίγνοιτο τοῦτ᾽ ἐν τῷ
γυμνασίῳ, μεταιρεῖς ἐκ τοῦ μέσου τοὺς νέους. ἀλλ᾽
οἴει, ὅτι δυνήσεταί σοι ὁ νόμος, ἐὰν συνανακυλίηται
τοῖς ἀνδράσι τὰ μειράκια, δεσμοὺς καὶ κύφωνας τῇ
στυτικῇ φύσει περιβαλεῖν;"
30   ταῦτ᾽ ἐμοῦ λέξαντος καὶ ὁ παλαιστροφύλαξ ᾤχετ᾽
ἀπιών, κἀγὼ ἀναλαβὼν τὸν τρίβωνα καὶ τὴν πήραν
ἐξῆλθον ἐπὶ θάλασσαν.

"An obol," he answered.

"That young man," I said, pointing the individual out, "is fooling around, with no penalty enforced against him."

(2) Then I too removed my ragged cloak, untied the scraper, and went up and oiled myself. Much time did not pass before one of the young men, following the local custom, came right up to me, very handsome in appearance, beardless, and he thrust his hand toward me, trying to see if I was acquainted with wrestling. And for a time I pretended out of modesty not to know anything. But when he threatened to finish me off, I began to move into various holds with him, following the normal procedure. Then my pointer somehow became erect (I'm afraid to mention the other name on account of the general public), and with this the lad left me and went away in embarrassment. But I stood there and rubbed myself.

(3) Now when the custodian of the palaestra caught sight of me, he came up and upbraided me. But I said to him, "So, then, after allowing the match to go on in the normal way, will you now take issue with me? If it were usual for those oiling themselves to smell something that induces sneezing, you would not be annoyed if one of those smeared with oil sneezed in the gymnasium. But are you now upset that someone quite spontaneously experiences an erection while rolling around with a handsome lad? Or do you suppose that, while the nostrils are completely responsive to nature, this other part of us is in the power of our deliberate choice? Won't you stop," I added, "struggling so convulsively against those who come in here? And if you have some reason for this not to occur in the gymnasium, then remove the young men from your midst. But do you think that your regulation will be able to place bonds and restraints upon excitable nature when boys happen to roll around with adults?"

After I said this, the custodian of the palaestra went his way and I took up my poor cloak and wallet and went off to the sea.

36. Τιμομάχῳ, <εὖ πράττειν>

Ἧκον εἰς Κύζικον καὶ διαπορευόμενος τὴν ὁδὸν
ἐθεασάμην ἐπί τινος θύρας ἐπιγεγραμμένον "ὁ τοῦ Διὸς
παῖς καλλίνικος Ἡρακλῆς ἐνθάδε κατοικεῖ, μηδὲν
5   εἰσίτω κακόν." ἐπιστὰς οὖν ἀνεγίγνωσκον καὶ παρε-
ρχόμενόν τινα ἠρόμην "τίς ἢ πόθεν ὁ ταύτην τὴν οἰκίαν
οἰκῶν;"

ὃ δέ με δόξας πυνθάνεσθαι διὰ τὰ ἄλφιτα ἀπεκρίνατο "φαῦλος ἄνθρωπος, ὦ Διόγενες· ἀλλ᾽ ἀπάναγε
10 ἐνθένδε."

κἀγὼ πρὸς ἐμαυτὸν "ἀλλ᾽ ἔοικεν" ἔφην "οὗτος,
ὅστις ποτ᾽ ἔστιν, ἐξ ὧν λέγει ἑαυτῷ τὴν θύραν ἀποκ-
λεῖσαι." καὶ μικρὸν προελθὼν ἑτέραν θύραν θεωρῶ
τὸ αὐτὸ ἰαμβεῖον ἔχουσαν ἐπιγεγραμμένον. (2) "ἐν
15 ταύτῃ" ἔφην "τίς ἐστιν ὁ κατοικῶν;"

"τελώνης" εἶπεν, "ἄνθρωπος ἀγοραῖος ὤν."

"ταύτην οὖν αἱ τῶν πονηρῶν" ἔφην "θύραι μόνον
ἔχουσι τὴν ἐπιγραφὴν ἢ καὶ αἱ τῶν σπουδαίων;"

"πάντων" εἶπεν.

20 "εἶτα διὰ τί" ἔφην, "εἰ ὑμᾶς ὠφελεῖ τοῦτο, οὐχὶ
ταῖς πύλαις ἐπεγράψατε αὐτὸ ταῖς τῆς πόλεως, ἀλλὰ
ταῖς οἰκίαις, εἰς ἃς μηδὲ χωρῆσαι δύναται ὁ Ἡρακλῆς;
ἢ τὴν μὲν πόλιν βούλεσθε ἔχειν κακῶς, τὰς δὲ οἰκίας
οὔ; ἢ τὰ μὲν κοινὰ ὑμᾶς κακὰ οὐ δύναται καταβλάπ-
25 τειν, τὰ δ᾽ ἴδια;"

"οὐκ ἔχω" εἶπε, "Διόγενες, περὶ τούτων ἀποκρίνασθαί σοι."

"τί δέ" ἔφην "οἴεσθε ὑμεῖς οἱ Κυζικηνοὶ κακὸν
εἶναι;"

30 "νόσον, πενίαν, θάνατον, τὰ τοιαῦτα" ἔφησεν.

(3) "εἶτ᾽ οἴεσθε ταῦτα, εἰ μὲν εἰς τὴν οἰκίαν
εἰσέλθοι, καταβλάψειν ὑμᾶς, εἰ δὲ μὴ εἰσέλθοι, μὴ
καταβλάψειν;"

"πάνυ γε" ἔφη.

35 "εἶεν" ἔφην, "ταῦτα δ᾽ οὐχ ἁπτόμενα βλάψειν
ἀνθρώπους;"

---

1 <εὖ πράττειν> Hercher

36. To Timomachus, do well

I came to Cyzicus and, while making my way along the
road, I saw this written on a doorway: "The son of Zeus,
the gloriously triumphant Heracles, lives here. Let no
evil enter." So, stopping, I read this out and asked a
passerby, "Who lives in this house, and where is he from?"

But, thinking that I was asking with an eye toward a
handout of bread, he answered, "A worthless man, Diogenes.
Go on away from here."

Then I said to him, "But this man, whoever he is,
seems, from what he says, to have barred the door to himself." Then after going on a bit, I saw another door with
the same iambic verse written on it. (2) I asked, "Who
lives in this house?"

"A tax collector," he said, "a vulgar individual."

I said, "So, do only the doors of the good for noth-
ings have this inscription, or do the doors of people of
character also have it?"

"They all do," he answered.

"Then why," I asked, "if this benefits you, did you
not write it on the gates of the city, instead of only on
the houses, into which not even Heracles can enter? Or do
you want the city to be in a sorry state but not the
houses? Or are the public evils unable to harm you, but
only the private ones?"

"Diogenes," he answered, "I have no reply for you on
these matters."

"But what," I continued, "do you citizens of Cyzicus
consider to be evil?"

"Sickness, poverty, death, things of that sort," he
said.

(3) "Then you believe that if these should enter your
house they will harm you; but if not, they will do you no
injury?"

"Certainly," he answered.

"So be it," I went on. "But these evils, don't they
take hold in order to injure people?"

"ἁπτόμενα γάρ" εἶπεν.

"ἆρ᾽ οὖν" ἔφην "εἰς μὲν τὰς οἰκίας ἐπειδὰν
εἰσέλθῃ, ἅπτεται ὑμῶν, εἰς δὲ τὴν ἀγορὰν ἐπειδὰν εἰσ-
βάλῃ, τότε οὐχ ἅπτεται; ἢ ἔστιν ὅστις ἀπολέγει αὐ-
5   τοῖς ἐπὶ μὲν τῇ ἀγορᾷ μὴ ἅπτεσθαι ὑμῶν, ἐν δὲ ταῖς
οἰκίαις;"

"οὐκ ἔχω" εἶπεν "οὐδὲ ἐνθάδε ἀποκρίνασθαί σοι."

"τί δέ" ἔφην, "ταῦτα ἐπειδὰν εἰς τὰς οἰκίας ὑμῶν
εἰσέλθῃ, καταβλάπτει ὑμᾶς ἢ ἐπειδὰν εἰς ὑμᾶς αὐτούς;"
10   "εἰς ἡμᾶς" εἶπεν.

(4) "εἶτ᾽" ἔφην "παρὸν ὑμῖν αὐτοῖς ἐπιγράφειν τὸ
ἰαμβεῖον ταῖς θύραις ἐπιγράφετε; πῶς δέ" ἔφην "ὁ
Ἡρακλῆς εἷς ὢν ἐν τοσαύταις δύναται παροικεῖν οἰκίαις; κινδυνεύει γὰρ καὶ τοῦτο τὴν μωρίαν τῆς πόλεως
15   ἐνδείκνυσθαι."

"τίνα οὖν τις" εἶπεν, "ὦ Διόγενες, ἑτέραν ταύτης
εὐφημοτέραν ποιήσαιτ᾽ ἂν ἐπιγραφήν;"

"χρὴ γὰρ" ἔφην "πάντως ἐπιγεγράφθαι τῇ θύρᾳ;"

"πάνυ γε" εἶπεν.

20   "μάθε" ἔφην, "Πενία ἐνθάδε κατοικεῖ, μηδὲν
εἰσίτω κακόν."

"εὐφήμει" εἶπεν, "ἄνθρωπε, ἀλλ᾽ αὐτὸ τοῦτο
κακόν ἐστι."

"κακόν" ἔφην "καθ᾽ ὑμᾶς, καὶ μὴ παρ᾽ ἐμοῦ
25   μανθάνειν."

"'ἀλλὰ Λινδίων τοὺς βόας κατέφαγε.' πενία
δὲ πρὸς θεῶν κακὸν οὐκ ἔστιν;" εἶπε.

"τί ποιοῦσαν αὐτήν" ἔφην "κακὸν λέγεις;"

"λιμόν" εἶπε, "ψῦχος, καταφρόνησιν."

30   (5) "ἀλλ᾽ οὐδέν γε τούτων ὧν φῂς πενία ἄρα οὔτε
λιμός· πολλὰ γὰρ ἐν τῇ γῇ φύεται, δι᾽ ὧν ὅ τε λιμὸς
θεραπεύεται τό τε ψῦχος, ἐπεὶ οὐδὲ τὰ ἄλογα γυμνὰ
ὄντα αἰσθάνεται ψύχους."

"ἀλλὰ τὰ μὲν ἄλογα οὕτως ἡ φύσις" εἶπεν "ἐποίησεν."

35   "ἀνθρώπους δὲ ὁ λόγος οὕτως ποιεῖ" ἔφην.

"ἀλλ᾽ οὐ προσποιοῦνται πολλοὶ συνιέναι διὰ μαλακίαν.

"They do indeed," he replied.

"Thus," I said, "when they enter the homes, they seize you; but when they invade the market, then they do not take hold? Or is there someone who forbids them to touch you both in the market place and in the homes?"

"I don't have any answer for you on this point," he admitted.

"What then?" I asked. "Do these ills harm you when they enter your houses, or when they enter into yourselves?"

"Into us," he answered.

(4) "So," I said, "although it is possible to inscribe the iambic verse in your very selves, you write it on the doors? But," I went on, "how is Heracles, although he is one man, able to sojourn in so many houses? For this may very likely give proof of the city's folly."

He retorted, "Diogenes, then what other, more auspicious inscription than this could anyone compose?"

"Is it altogether necessary," I asked, "that there be something written on the door?"

"Certainly," he replied.

"Listen to this one," I offered. "Poverty lives here, let no evil enter."

"Don't say that," he cautioned. "That itself is evil."

"Evil in your view," I corrected, "but you don't learn that from me!"

"'But he devoured the oxen of the Lindians.' Now isn't poverty an evil to the gods?" he asked.

"What does it do that you call it an evil?"

"It causes hunger, cold, contempt."

(5) "But none of these things which you mention is tied to poverty. Now hunger isn't, for many things spring up in the earth through which hunger is provided for; and cold too, since the animals, though they are naked, do not feel the cold."

"But nature made the animals like this," he countered.

"And reason makes people thus," I said, "but many because of their moral weakness pretend not to understand.

ἀλλ' εἰσὶ καὶ ἐνθάδε ἐπίκουροι αἵ τε δοραὶ τῶν ζῴων
καὶ τὰ νάκη τῶν προβάτων καὶ οἱ τοῖχοι τῶν σπηλαίων
καὶ τῶν οἴκων. οὐ μὴν οὐδὲ καταφρόνησιν ἐργάζεται
πενία. Ἀριστείδου γέ τοι τοῦ τοὺς φόρους τάξαντος
5   οὐδεὶς κατεφρόνει πένητος ὄντος, οὔτε Σωκράτους τοῦ
Σωφρονίσκου· οὐ γὰρ αὐτὰ ἦσαν βλάβαι, ἀλλὰ μοχθηρία.
(6) τί δέ" ἔφην, "<ἀλλ' ἢ> ταῦτα ἔδρα ἡ πενία παρ'
ὑμῖν <οἰκοῦσα>; οὐκ ἦν <αἰρετή, ἄλλα> σφοδρότερα
κακὰ ἀπελαύνουσα ὑμῶν;"
10   "ποῖα ἄττα;" εἶπεν.

"φθόνους, μίση, συκοφαντίας, τοιχωρυχίας, ἀπε-
ψίας, στρόφους, ἄλλα χαλεπὰ νοσήματα, πενίαν ἄρα ἐπιγράφετε οἰκεῖν παρ' ὑμῖν, καὶ οὐ τὸν Ἡρακλέα. καὶ
γὰρ ἃ μὲν δύναται ὁ Ἡρακλῆς ἀναιρεῖν οὐ φοβεῖσθε,
15   ὕδρας, ταύρους, λέοντας, κερβέρους, ἔνια δὲ καὶ αὐτοὶ
θηρᾶσθε· ἃ δὲ πενία ἀπελαύνει, ταῦτα δεινά· πενίαν
μὲν ὀλίγα δαπανῶντες θρέψετε φύλακα αὐτῶν, τὸν δὲ
Ἡρακλέα πολλά."

"ἀλλὰ δύσφημόν ἐστι πενία" εἶπεν, "ὁ δὲ Ἡρακλῆς
20   εὔφημον."

"σοί" ἔφην "εἰ πενία ἐστὶ δύσφημον, Αὐγείᾳ δὲ
καὶ Διομήδει τῷ Θρᾳκὶ καὶ ἄλλοις ὁ Ἡρακλῆς."

"οὐ πείθεις με" εἶπεν, "ὦ Διόγενες, 'πενίαν'
ἐπιγράψαι, ὥσθ' ἕτερόν τι σκέπτου, ἵνα σοι πεισθῶ
25   τὸν ''Ἡρακλέα' ἐξαλεῖψαι."

"ἔσκεμμαι" ἔφην. "ἄκουε λόγον" εἶπον, "'Δικαιοσύνη ἐνθάδε κατοικεῖ, μηδὲν εἰσίτω κακόν.'"

"ἐνταῦθα μὲν" ἔφη "πείθομαί σοι, καὶ τὸν ''Ἡρακλέα' οὐκ ἐξαλείψω, συνεπιγράψω δὲ τὴν 'δικαιοσύνην.'"
30   "ὀρθῶς" ἔφην, "τοῦτο ποίει καὶ ἐπιγράψας κάθευδε
ἀναπεσὼν ὥσπερ Ὀδυσσεὺς μηκέτι μηδὲν φοβούμενος."

"ποιήσω" εἶπε, "σοὶ δὲ χάριν τούτου γνώσομαι νῦν
τε καὶ εἰσαεί, Διόγενες, ἀσφαλισαμένῳ ἀπὸ τῶν φαύλων
ἡμᾶς."
35   ταῦτ' ἐν Κυζίκῳ, φίλε Τιμόμαχε, ἠὐθύνθη ἡμῖν.

_____
7   <ἀλλ' ἢ> Westermann & Emeljanow
8   <οἰκοῦσα> Schafstaedt & Emeljanow
8   <αἰρετή, ἄλλα> Westermann & Emeljanow

But even here there are allies: animal hides, woolly sheep-
skins, and the walls of caves and houses. Nor indeed does
poverty produce contempt. Surely no one despises Aris-
tides, who fixed the scale of taxes although he was a poor
man. Nor Socrates, son of Sophroniscus. Poor circumstances are not a source of damages, but depravity is.
(6) What things other than these," I asked, "would poverty
be doing if it dwelt with you? Would it not be desirable
if it were to drive away other more violent evils from you?"

"What sort of evils?" he asked.

"Jealousies, hatreds, calumnies, burglaries, indigestion, colic, other troublesome afflictions. So write that
Poverty lives among you, and not Heracles. For you are
not even afraid of the things that Heracles can slay:
water serpents, bulls, lions, cerberuses. You even hunt
some of these yourselves. But what poverty keeps away,
these things are fearful. With little expense you will
make poverty grow as a guardian for yourselves, but Heracles at great cost."

"But poverty has a bad reputation," he complained,
"and Heracles a good one."

I rejoined, "If poverty has a bad reputation with you,
so does Heracles with Augeas, Diomedes the Thracian, and
others."

"Diogenes," he said, "you haven't convinced me to inscribe 'Poverty'. Look then for something else so that I
might obey you and erase 'Heracles'."

"I have looked," I answered. "Listen to this saying:
'Justice lives here, let no evil enter'."

He said, "Here I'm won over by you. But I won't
erase 'Heracles'. I'll write 'Justice' along with him."

"Do this right," I cautioned. "And after inscribing
it lie down and sleep, like Odysseus, no longer afraid of
anything."

"I'll do it," he said, "and will acknowledge my thanks
to you for this now and always, Diogenes. For you made me
safe from evils."

This, dear Timomachus, was the guidance I gave at Cyzicus.

37. Μονίμῳ, <εὖ πράττειν>

Ἀπαναστάντος τῆς Ἐφέσου ἔπλευσα καὶ αὐτὸς εἰς
Ῥόδον, σπουδάζων τὸν τῶν Ἁλίων ἀγῶνα θεάσασθαι.
ἀποβὰς δὲ τῆς νεὼς ἀνέβαινον εἰς ἄστυ καὶ παρὰ
5   Λακύδην τὸν ξένον· ὁ δὲ τυχὸν ἴσως, ἐπεὶ ἔγνω με
καταπλεύσαντα, τὴν ἀγορὰν ἐξέκλινεν, ἐγὼ δὲ ἐπεὶ
περιελθὼν τὴν πόλιν οὐδαμῇ αὐτῷ ἐνέτυχον, ἔγνων δὲ
πυθόμενος ὡς εἴη κατὰ ἄστυ, ἐπὶ τὴν τῶν θεῶν ξενίαν
ἅσμενος ἱκόμην καὶ παρὰ τούτοις ἐσκήνωσα. ἡμέρᾳ δὲ
10   τρίτῃ σχεδὸν ἢ τετάρτῃ ἐντυχών μοι κατὰ τὴν ὁδὸν τὴν
ὡς ἐπὶ τὸ στρατόπεδον φέρουσαν προσηγόρευσε καὶ ἐπὶ
τὴν ξενίαν παρεκάλει ἔρχεσθαι.

(2) κἀγὼ οὐδέν τι μηνίσας αὐτῷ διὰ τοσούτου μοι
ἐντυχόντι "αἰσχρὸν μέν" ἔφην "τοὺς θεοὺς καταλιπεῖν,
15   οἵ με, ἐπεὶ ἡ σὴ ξενία καταπλεύσαντι ἐκλείσθη, ἐδέ-
ξαντο· ἀλλ' ἐπεὶ δύνανται οὗτοι ἐπὶ μηδενὶ τῶν τοιούτων ἀσχάλλειν, ἡμεῖς δὲ διὰ τὸ ἀσθενές, βαδίζωμεν.
πρότερον δέ, εἴ σοι δοκεῖ, ἀναβάντες γυμνασώμεθα· οὐ
γὰρ χρῆν οἶμαι, εἰ παρὰ σὲ τήμερον μέλλω κατάγεσθαι
20   καταλιπὼν τοὺς κρείττονας ξένους, τοῦ σώματος ἀμελεῖν."

"ἀλλὰ καλῶς" ἔφη, "Διόγενες, λέγεις, καὶ οὐ βιά-
ζομαί σε τοὺς θεοὺς <ἐξελᾶν>."

(3) ἐγὼ δὲ ἀναβὰς εἰς τὸ στρατόπεδον περιεπάτησα,
καὶ τότε κατέβην εἰς τὴν οἰκίαν τοῦ Λακύδου. τῷ δὲ
25   ἄρα ἦν παρασκευὴ οὐχ ὅση πρὸς τὴν φύσιν ἀποχρῆναι ἧς
ἡμεῖς ἐδεόμεθα, ἀλλ' ὁπόση πρὸς τὴν δόξαν ἧς οἱ ἄλλοι
ἡττῶνται· κλῖναι γὰρ ἐξέστρωτο σφόδρα πολυτελεῖς καὶ
τράπεζαί τινες ἐν τῷ καταντικρὺ ἔκειντο, αἱ μὲν ἐκ
βαριασνοου, αἱ δὲ ἐκ σφενδαμνίνων ξύλων, ἀργυρωμάτων
30   ἀνάπλεῳ, ἐπὶ δὲ τούτοις θεράποντες εἰστήκεσαν οἱ μὲν
χέρνιβας ἔχοντες, οἱ δὲ ἄλλα διακονήματα. εἰς ταῦτα
ἀπιδὼν "ἀλλὰ ἐγὼ μέν" ἔφην "ἧκον εἰς τὴν ξενίαν τὴν
σήν, Λακύδη, ὠφεληθησόμενος, σὺ δὲ ἐπ' ἐμὲ ὅσα οἱ
ἐχθροὶ παρεσκεύασαι.

---
1   <εὖ πράττειν> Hercher
22   <ἐξελᾶν> Emeljanow

37. To Monimus, do well

After you packed up and left Ephesus, I myself sailed
to Rhodes, eager to witness the contest at the festival of
the sun. Disembarking, I went up to town to the house of
Lacydes my host. When he learned that I had put into port,
perhaps by chance he avoided the market place. Now, when
I did not meet him anywhere, although I made the rounds of
the city, but knew from inquiry that he was in town, I
came up and asked for the hospitality of the gods. So I
lodged with them. Then, on about the third or fourth day,
when he happened to meet me on the road which leads up to
the military camp, he greeted me and urged me to come and
share his hospitality.

(2) Now since I felt no anger toward him for meeting
me after so long, I said, "It's disrespectful to leave the
gods, who received me after your hospitality was barred to
me when I came ashore. But since they cannot take offense
at anything of this sort, though we do because of our weakness, let's go. But first, if you think it's a good idea,
let's go and exercise. For if I'm going to come and lodge
at your house today, leaving superior hosts, I don't think
I should neglect my body."

"Well put, Diogenes," he said, "but I am not forcing
you to slight the gods."

(3) So I went up to the military camp, walked about,
and then went down to Lacydes' house. His furniture was
not the kind that sufficed for our natural needs, but was
all that appearance required, to which others are slaves.
For the couches were expensively covered and a number of
tables lay facing them, some made of (*bariasnous*), others
of maple wood, laden with silver plate. And in addition
to these, servants stood by, some holding finger bowls,
others utensils of various kinds. Looking at these things
I said, "But I have come to share your hospitality, Lacydes,
in order to derive some benefit from it. However, you have
made the kind of preparations against me that enemies do.

(4) ταῦτα μὲν οὖν κέλευε ἄλλῃ μεταίρεσθαι, ἡμᾶς δὲ
κατάκλιναι, ὡς Ὅμηρος τοὺς ἥρωας ἐν Ἰλιάδι κατέκλι-
νεν, ἐπὶ ῥινοῦ βοὸς ἀγραύλοιο, ἢ ὡς Λακεδαιμόνιοι ἐπὶ
στιβάδος, καὶ ἔα τὸ σῶμα ἐφ᾽ ὧν ἔμαθε κατακλίνεσθαι.
5   θέραψ δ᾽ οὐδὲ εἷς ἔστω ἐνταῦθα διακονούμενος· ἀποχρή-
σουσι γὰρ αἱ χεῖρες ἐς τοῦτο, καὶ γὰρ τούτου ἕνεκα
ἡμῖν προσετέθησαν ὑπὸ τῆς φύσεως. ποτήρια δ᾽ ἔστω,
οἷς πιόμεθα, τὰ ἐκ πηλοῦ λεπτὰ καὶ εὔωνα, πόμα δὲ
ὕδωρ ναματιαῖον, τροφαὶ δὲ ἄρτος καὶ ὄψον ἅλες ἢ
10 κάρδαμον.

       "τοιαῦτα ἐγὼ παρὰ Ἀντισθένει παιδευόμενος ἔμαθον
ἐσθίειν καὶ πίνειν, οὐχ ὡς φαῦλα ἀλλ᾽ ὡς κρείττονα τῶν
ἑτέρων καὶ μᾶλλον δυνάμενα ἐν τῇ ὁδῷ εὑρίσκεσθαι τῇ
φερούσῃ ἐπ᾽ εὐδαιμονίαν, ἣν δὴ πάντων τιμιωτάτην χρημά-
15 των θετέον. [ἐν τόπῳ ὀχυρωτάτῳ καὶ ἀποκρημνοτάτῳ μίαν
ὁδὸν προσάντη καὶ τραχεῖαν ἱδρύσασθαι.] (5) ταύτην
οὖν τὴν ὁδὸν διὰ τὸ δύσκολον μόλις ἂν δύνασθαι γυμνὸν
ἕκαστον ἀναβῆναι, καὶ οὐχ ὅτι φέροντά τι σὺν ἑαυτῷ
καὶ βαρούμενον μόγῳ καὶ δεσμοῖς περισωθῆναι, ἀλλ᾽ οὐδὲ
20 'τῶν ἀναγκαίων' τι μετιόντα, ποιῆσαι δ᾽ ἐν τῇ ὁδῷ τροφὴν
μὲν πόαν ἢ κάρδαμα, πόμα δὲ εὐπαλὲς ὕδωρ, <καὶ ταῦτα>
μάλιστα δ᾽ ὅπῃ δέοι τοῦ ῥᾷστα βαδίσαι. [γυμναστέον
ἐσθίειν μὲν κάρδαμον, πίνειν δὲ ὕδωρ, ἀμπέχεσθαι δὲ
τρίβωνα κοῦφον.]

25   "<ἀποδειξάμενος δὲ τὸ ἀποδύεσθαι πρὸς τὴν ἄθλησιν>,
[ἑστῶτα δὲ ἐπὶ ἄκρον τὸν Ἑρμῆν ἐκτινάσσειν τοὺς βαδί-
ζοντας, μή τι ἔχοντες ἐφόδιον βέβηλον οἴκοθεν βαδί-
ζωσιν.] (6) ἐγώ τοι παρὰ Ἀντισθένει πρῶτον ἀσκήσας
ἐσθίειν τε καὶ πίνειν ἧκον τὴν ἐπ᾽ εὐδαιμονίαν ὁδὸν
30 σπεύδων ἀπνευστί, παρελθὼν δὲ ἵνα ὑπῆρχεν ἡ εὐδαιμονία
ἔφην 'ὑπέμεινα, εὐδαιμονία, διὰ σὲ καὶ μέγα <ἀγαθὸν>
κακὸν ὕδωρ πίνειν καὶ κάρδαμον ἐσθίειν καὶ ἐπὶ γῆς
κοιμᾶσθαι.'

15 [ἐν...ἱδρύσασθαι] gloss, Nihard & Emeljanow
21 <καὶ ταῦτα> Emeljanow
22 [γυμναστέον...κοῦφον] gloss, Nihard & Emeljanow
25 <ἀποδειξάμενος...ἄθλησιν> Emeljanow
26 [ἑστῶτα...βαδίζωσιν] gloss, Nihard & Emeljanow
31 <ἀγαθόν> Emeljanow

(4) So, order that these be removed somewhere else, and
have us recline, as Homer made his heroes in the *Iliad* recline, on the hide of oxen from the fields, or as the
Spartans do, on a bed of straw. So let the body recline
on what it has grown accustomed to. And don't let even a
single waiter stand here in service. For our hands will
be adequate for this, and indeed they were given to us by
nature for this purpose. Let the cups we drink from be
the clay kind, meager and cheap; and our drink be spring
water and the food bread, and the appetizer salt or water-
cress.

"These things I learned to eat and drink, while being
taught at the feet of Antisthenes, not as though they were
poor fare but that they were superior to the rest and more
likely to be found on the road leading to happiness, which
should be regarded as the most esteemed of all possessions.
In a very secure and precipitous place, one road, steep and
rugged, is laid out. (5) And so, because of its ruggedness, an individual, stripped for action, would barely be
able to ascend this road. And if a person were carrying
something with him and were weighed down with trouble and
obligations, he would not be saved, nor would the person
pursuing something 'necessary.' Then, too, a person would
have to make the grass or cresses along the road his food
and common water his drink, and these especially where it
would be necessary to proceed most expeditiously. One must
train oneself to eat cresses and drink water, and to wear
a light, ragged cloak.

"Demonstrating how to strip for the contest, while
Hermes stood at the summit and made a thorough search of
those advancing, lest they proceed from home with improper
supplies for the journey, (6) I, after first practicing how
to eat and drink in the company of Antisthenes, reached the
road to happiness in breathless haste. And arriving at
where happiness really was, I said, 'For your sake, Happiness, and for the sake of the greater good, I persisted in
drinking water, eating cresses, and lying on the ground.'

"ἢ δὲ ἠμείψατό με 'ἀλλ' ἐγώ τοι' ἔφη 'σοι ταῦτα
ποιήσω δίχα ταλαιπωρίας ἡδύτερα τῶν τοῦ πλούτου
ἀγαθῶν, ὃν μᾶλλον οἱ ἄνθρωποι ἐμοῦ πρεσβεύουσι, καὶ
οὐκ αἰσθάνονται τύραννον ἑαυτοῖς ἐπιτρέφοντες.'

5   "ἐξ ἐκείνου ἐγώ, ἐπεὶ ταῦτα τῆς εὐδαιμονίας
διαλεγομένης ἤκουσα, οὐκέτι ταῦτα ὡς ἀσκήματα ἤσθιον
καὶ ἔπινον, ἀλλ' ὡς ἡδονάς, κρατεῖ δέ με πρὸς ταύτην
τὴν δίαιταν καὶ τὸ ἔθος, οὗ πᾶς ἀπολειπόμενος βλάπτε-
ται. (7) παρατίθει οὖν ἡμῖν καὶ σὺ τοιαῦτα δεῖπνα,
10   μιμούμενος τὸ κάλλιστον τῶν ἐν τῷ βίῳ, εὐδαιμονίαν,
τὰ δὲ πλούτου ἵει εἰς τοὺς ἁμαρτάνοντας αὐτῆς τῆς
ὁδοῦ. ἀλλ' εἰ τοῦτό σοι" ἔφην "δοκοίη, ἴσθι καὶ
τοῦτ'" εἶπον. "ἀεὶ τοιούτοις με δείπνοις θοίνα, τοῦ
τε λοιποῦ τοιαῦτα παρέχου τοῖς ξένοις. καὶ οὐδέποτε
15   παρόντας μὲν αὐτοὺς ἐκκλινεῖς, ὑστερίζοντας δέ τινας
αὐτῶν ζητήσεις, <ἐλέγχους> γὰρ εἰς βελτίων."

ταῦτά μοι, ἐν Ῥόδῳ ἐπεὶ ἐγενόμην, πρὸς Λακύδην
τὸν ξένον ὡμιλήθη.

―――――
16   <ἐλέγχους> Emeljanow

"She answered me and said, 'I will make these things, far from a hardship, more pleasant to you than the goods of wealth, which people rank first, ahead of me. But they are not aware that they are nurturing a tyrant for themselves.'

"And from the time when I heard Happiness discussing this, I no longer ate and drank these things as an exercise but as a pleasure. Now the force of habit also held me to this diet, and anyone lacking this is handicapped. (7) Therefore, you too, set dinners like this before me, imitating the fairest thing in life, Happiness. As for the objects of wealth, send them to those who miss the road to happiness. But if this should seem right to you," I continued, "note the following as well. Always entertain me with such banquets and, from now on, offer meals like this to your guests. Never avoid those who are present, and make inquiries after those who are late in coming. In this way you are above reproach."

This is what I said to Lacydes, my guest-friend, while I was on Rhodes.

38.

Σὺ μέν, ἐπεὶ οἱ ἀγῶνες ἀνεβλήθησαν, καταλιπὼν
ᾤχου τὴν 'Ολυμπίαν, ἐγὼ δὲ διὰ τὸ ἐκτόπως εἶναι
φιλοθεάμων κατέμεινα τὴν ἄλλην θεώμενος πανήγυριν.
5   διέτριβον δὲ ἐν τῇ ἀγορᾷ, ἵνα ὁ ἄλλος ὅμιλος, καὶ
περιιὼν ἄνω κάτω προσέσχον ὁτὲ μὲν τοῖς πωλοῦσιν, ὁτὲ
δὲ τοῖς ῥαψῳδοῦσιν ἢ φιλοσοφοῦσιν ἢ μαντευομένοις.
καὶ ποτε διεξιόντος τινὸς περὶ ἡλίου φύσεως καὶ δυνά-
μεως καὶ πάντας ἀναπείθοντος παρελθὼν εἰς τὸ μέσον
10 "ποσταῖος," ἔφην "φιλόσοφε, ἀπὸ τοὐρανοῦ καταβέβηκας;"
ὁ δέ μοι οὐκ εἶχεν ἀποκρίνασθαι. οἳ δὲ καταλιπόντες
αὐτὸν οἱ περιεστῶτες ᾤχοντο ἀπιόντες, ὁ δέ γε κατα-
λειφθεὶς μόνος τὰς εἰκόνας τοῦ οὐρανοῦ συνετίθει εἰς
τὸ κιβώτιον.
15   (2) ἀπ' ἐκείνου προσίσταμαι μάντει, ὁ δὲ ἐκάθητο
ἐν τῷ μέσῳ κατεστεμμένος μείζονα τοῦ εὑραμένου τὴν
μαντείαν 'Απόλλωνος. ἠρόμην οὖν καὶ τοῦτον παρελθὼν
"πότερον ἄριστος εἶ μάντις ἢ φαῦλος;" τοῦ δὲ εἰπόντος ὅτι ἄριστος, ἅμα ἐκτείνας τὴν βακτηρίαν "τί μέλλω
20 δῆτε ποιεῖν; ἀπόκριναι, πότερον τύπτειν σε ἢ οὔ;"
μικρὸν πρὸς αὐτῷ γενόμενος "οὔ" φησί, τύπτω τ'
ἐγὼ γελάσας αὐτὸν καὶ οἱ περιεστῶτες ἀνέκραγον.
"τί" ἔφην "ἐβοήσατε; ἐπεὶ κακὸς μάντις ἐφάνη,
καὶ ἐπλήχθη."
25   (3) ὡς δὲ καὶ τοῦτον καταλιπόντες οἱ περιεστῶτες
ἀπηλλάγησαν, ἄνθρωποι καὶ ἄλλοι οἱ ἐν τῇ ἀγορᾷ, ἐπεὶ
ταῦτα ἤκουσαν, διέλυσαν τοὺς κύκλους καὶ εἵποντο ἐξ
ἐκείνου, καὶ πολλάκις μὲν διαλεγομένου μου περὶ καρτερίας ἐπακολουθοῦντες ἐπηκρῶντο, πολλάκις δὲ καρτε-
30 ροῦντος ἢ διαιτωμένου παρετύγχανον. ἐκόμιζον δέ μοι
διὰ ταῦτα οἳ μὲν ἀργύρια, οἳ δὲ ἄξια ἀργυρίου, πολλοὶ
δὲ καὶ ἐπὶ δεῖπνον ἐκάλουν, ἐγὼ δὲ παρὰ μὲν τῶν

38.

After the games were adjourned, you left and went to
Olympia. But since I am unusually fond of spectacles, I
stayed behind to witness the rest of the festal assembly.
I was passing time in the market place, where the rest of
the crowd was, and, while I was strolling back and forth,
I turned for a time toward those selling things, and then
to those reciting, or philosophizing, or prophesying. And
at one point, while someone was going on in detail about
the nature and power of the sun, and was convincing everyone, I came up into their midst and said, "How many days
has it been, philosopher, since you've come down from
heaven?" But he had no answer for me. Now those standing
around him abandoned him and went on their way. But he,
left alone, started gathering the models of heaven into
his little wooden chest.

(2) After that I stood near a diviner. He was seated
in the middle of a crowd, wearing a wreath larger than
Apollo's, who discovered the art of divination. So draw-
ing near I questioned this man too. "Are you a very good
diviner or a poor one?" At his answer that he was very
good I brandished my staff. "What, then, am I going to
do? Answer. Will I strike you or not?"

He reflected to himself for a moment and said, "You
won't." But strike him I did, with a laugh, while those
standing around roared.

I said, "Why did you cry out? Since he was obviously
an inept diviner, he was beaten."

(3) As the bystanders left this man as well and went
away, other people too in the market place broke up the
circles they were in, when they heard about these inci-
dents, and followed me from then on. And those following
me often listened to me discussing patient endurance, and
they often happened to be present as I actually exercised
patient endurance or pursued that pattern of life. Because
of this some gave me money, others things worth money, and
many invited me to dinner. But I took from moderate people

μετρίων ἐλάμβανον τὰ πρὸς τὴν φύσιν ἀποχρῶντα, παρὰ
δὲ τῶν φαύλων οὐδὲν προσιέμην, καὶ παρὰ μὲν τῶν ἐπισταμένων μοι χάριν ἐπὶ τῷ καὶ τὸ πρῶτον λαβεῖν καὶ
πάλιν ἐλάμβανον, παρὰ δὲ τῶν μὴ ἐπισταμένων οὐκέτι.
5   (4) ἐξήταζον δὲ καὶ τὰς δωρεὰς τῶν δωρεῖσθαί μοι
ἐθελόντων τὰ ἄλφιτα, καὶ παρὰ μὲν τῶν ὠφελουμένων
ἐλάμβανον, τῶν ἄλλων δὲ οὐδὲν προσιέμην, οὐκ οἰόμενος
καλὸν εἶναι λαμβάνειν παρὰ τοῦ μηδὲν παρειληφότος.
ἐδείπνουν δὲ οὐ παρὰ πᾶσι, παρὰ μόνοις δὲ τοῖς θερα-
10 πείας δεομένοις.   ἦσαν δ᾽ οὗτοι οἱ τοὺς Περσῶν βασιλεῖς μιμούμενοι.

κai δή ποτε εἰσελθὼν πρὸς μειράκιον τῶν σφόδρα
εὐπόρων κατακλίνομαι ἔν τινι ἀνδρῶνι πάντη κεκαλλωπισ-
μένῳ γραφαῖς τε καὶ χρυσῷ, ὡς μηδὲ ὅπου πτύσῃ τις
15 τόπον εἶναι.   (5) ἐπιστὰν οὖν μοι ἐπὶ τὴν φάρυγγα,
ἐχρεμψάμην, περιελάσας δὲ τὰ ὄμματα εἰς τὰ κύκλῳ,
ἐπεὶ ὅπου πτύσαιμι τόπον οὐκ εἶχον, εἰς αὐτὸν ἔπτυσα
τὸν νεανίσκον.   τοῦ δὲ μεμψαμένου ἐπὶ τούτῳ "εἶτα"
ἔφην "οὗτος," εἰπὼν αὐτὸν ἐξ ὀνόματος, "ἐμὲ μέμφῃ
20 τοῦ γενομένου καὶ οὐ σεαυτὸν τοὺς μὲν τοίχους καὶ τὰ
ἐδάφη κοσμήσαντα τοῦ ἀνδρῶνος, σαυτὸν δὲ μόνον ἀπο-
λιπόντα ἀκόσμητον εἰς τὸ ἐμπτύεσθαι χωρίον ἐπιτήδειον;"

"ταῦτ᾽" ἔφη "πρὸς τὴν ἀπαιδευσίαν φαίνῃ λέγων
25 ἡμῶν, ἀλλ᾽ οὐκ ἐξέσται σοι τοῦτο πάλιν εἰπεῖν· οὐ γὰρ
μὴ ἀπολειφθῶ σου ἕνα πόδα."

ἀπὸ τῆς αὔριον δὴ ἐξ ἐκείνου διανείμας τὴν
οὐσίαν τοῖς αὐτοῦ ἐμοὶ ἀναλαβὼν τὴν πήραν καὶ διπλώ-
σας τὸν τρίβωνα εἵπετο.   ταῦτα μετὰ τό σε ἀπαλλαγῆναι
30 ἐπράχθη ἡμῖν ἐν Ὀλυμπίᾳ.

what was suitable to nature, but from the worthless I accepted nothing. And from those who felt gratitude toward
me for accepting the first time, I accepted again as well;
but never again from those who did not feel thankful. (4)
I scrutinized even the gifts of those who wished to present me barley meal, and accepted it from those who were
being benefited. But from the others I took nothing,
since I thought it improper to take something from a person who had himself not received anything. I did not dine
with everyone, but only with those in need of therapy.
These are the ones who imitate the kings of the Persians.

And indeed, once when I went to the house of a lad,
the son of extremely prosperous parents, I reclined in a
banquet hall adorned all about with inscriptions and gold,
so that there was no place where you could spit. (5)
Therefore, when something lodged in my throat, I coughed
and glanced around me. Since I had no place to spit, I
spit at the lad himself. When he rebuked me for this, I
retorted, "Well then, So-and-So (speaking to him by name),
do you blame me for what happened and not yourself? It
was you who decorated the walls and pavement of the banquet hall, leaving only yourself unadorned, as a place fit
to spit onto!"

He answered, "You appear to be criticizing my lack of
education, but you won't be able to say this anymore. I
don't intend to fall one step behind you."

From the next day, after he distributed his property
to his relatives, he took up the wallet, doubled his coarse
cloak, and followed me. These things happened to me in
Olympia after you departed.

39. Μονίμῳ, <εὖ πράττειν>

Μελέτω σοι καὶ τῆς μετοικίας τῆς ἐντεῦθεν,
μελήσει δέ, εἰ μελετήσειας ἀποθνήσκειν, τοῦτ' ἔστι
χωρίζειν τὴν ψυχὴν ἔτι ζῶν ἀπὸ τοῦ σώματος. τοῦτο
γὰρ δοκῶ μοι καὶ οἱ περὶ Σωκράτη θάνατον ἐκάλουν, καὶ
5   γάρ ἐστιν ἡ μελέτη ἐν τῷ ῥάστῳ. φιλοσόφει δὲ καὶ
διασκέπτου, τί πρὸς σὲ (οὐχ οὕτως καὶ τί κατὰ φύσιν
καὶ τί κατὰ νόμον;) ἐν τούτῳ γὰρ μόνῳ χωρίζεται ψυχὴ
ἀπὸ σώματος, ἐν δὲ τοῖς ἄλλοις οὐδαμῶς, ἀλλὰ καὶ ὅταν
βλέπῃ καὶ ὅταν ἀκούῃ καὶ ὅταν ὀσφραίνηται καὶ ὅταν
10 γεύηται, σύνεστιν ὥσπερ μιᾶς αὐτῷ κορυφῆς ἐξημμένη.
γίγνεται γοῦν, ὅταν μὴ μελετήσωμεν ἀποθνήσκειν,
χαλεπὴν τελευτὴν ἀναμένειν· ἡ γὰρ ψυχὴ ὥς τινων
παιδικῶν ἀπολειπομένη συμφοράζει καὶ μετὰ ἀχθηδόνος
15 πολλῆς ἀπολύεται.
τότε καὶ ἐν τῇ ὁδῷ πολλὰ κάμνει. (2) ἀφίεται
γὰρ ἀξενάγητος ὅποι ποτὲ φέρεσθαι εἰς κρημνοὺς ἢ
χάσματα ἢ ποταμούς, ἕως ἐπὶ τὸ ἔσχατον ἐνεχθῇ. <ὅταν
δὲ καὶ φιλοσόφων ψυχαῖς ἐντύχῃ>, φεύγουσι γὰρ αὐτήν,
20 ὅτι οἴονται πολλὰ ἐξημαρτηκέναι ἐν τῷ ζῆν παραχωρή-
σασαν τῷ χείρονι τὴν τοῦ ὅλου ἀρχήν, δι' ἣν πολλὰ
ἠναγκάσθη ὡς ἐν πονηροκρατίᾳ ἄδικα πρᾶξαι. ὅταν δὲ
μελετήσωμεν τὴν καλὴν μελέτην, γίγνεται καὶ ὁ βίος
ἡδὺς καὶ ἡ τελευτὴ οὐκ ἀηδὴς καὶ ἡ ὁδὸς ῥάστη·
25 ξεναγεῖ γὰρ πᾶσα ἡ ἐντυχοῦσα τὴν τοιαύτην ψυχὴν ἐπὶ
τὰ εὔπορα καὶ ὥσπερ καλὴν ἄγραν ἐπιφανῶς ἄγει λαβο-
μένη παρὰ τοὺς κάτω τῶν καλῶν δικαστάς, αὐτή τε ὡς
ἂν μεμελετηκυῖα καὶ μόνη ζῆν οὐκ ἀηδίζεται καταλι-
ποῦσα τὸ σῶμα.

---

1 <εὖ πράττειν> Hercher
18 <ὅταν...ἐντύχῃ> transposed by Nihard & Emeljanow

39. To Monimus, do well

Take care, also, for your migration from here. And
you will take such care, if you practice how to die, that
is, how to separate the soul from the body, while you are
still alive. For this, I think, is what the associates of
Socrates, too, call death. And really, the practice is
very easy. Examine methodically and consider well what
death means to you. (Don't we do the same when we ask
what is according to nature and what according to conven-
tion?) For in death alone is the soul separated from the
body, while in other experiences it is not at all. When a
person sees, hears, smells, or tastes, the soul is joined
to him as if dependent from a single apex. And so it happens that when we do not practice for death a difficult
end awaits us. For the soul bemoans its ill fortune, as
if it were leaving behind some darling boys, and it is
released with much pain.

And then it labors a great deal along the way. (2)
For it is sent off without a guide to wherever it is carried, to crags, or chasms, or rivers, until it is brought
to its final destination. But whenever it meets the souls
of philosophers, they flee from it, since they know that
it has erred greatly in life by conceding the direction of
the whole self to the worst part of its nature. And because of this regime, it was forced to do numerous wrongs,
as though under a corrupt government. But whenever we
exercise the proper care, life also becomes sweet, the end
is not unpleasant, and the road is very easy. For every
practice that encounters such a soul guides it onto easily
traveled routes and conducts it ceremoniously, like a
prize catch, leading it to the judges of good deeds below.
And as if the soul were practiced at living all alone, it
does not loathe leaving its body behind.

(3) ἔστι δὲ καὶ διὰ τοῦτο καὶ πολλή τις ταῖς
τοιαύταις ψυχαῖς ἐν ᾅδου τιμή ὅτι ἄρα οὐκ ἦσαν
φιλοσώματοι.   δόξα γάρ ἐστι τὰς φιλοσωμάτους ψυχὰς
φαύλας τε εἶναι καὶ ἐνελευθέρους, τὰς δὲ μὴ τοιαύτας
ἀγαθάς τε καὶ ὑψαύχενας (ζῶσι γὰρ ἡγούμεναι πάντων
καὶ ἐπιτάττουσι ἀρχικῶς), διά τε ταῦτα ἀναιρεῖσθαι
μόνα τὰ δίκαια καὶ ῥᾷστα, τῶν δὲ ἐναντίων μηδὲ ἕν,
ἐφ' ἃ τὸ σῶμα ἀναγκάζει τὴν ψυχὴν ἥδεσθαι διὰ τὴν
περιπεπλασμένην αὐτοῖς ἡδονὴν ἰχθύος τρόπον ἢ ἄλλου
τινὸς ἀλόγου πρὸς τὴν τοῦ χείρονος ἀρχὴν γεγενημένου.

(4) ταῦτά σοι ἕψεται μελετήσαντι ἀποθνήσκειν,
ὅταν δέῃ μετοικεῖν ἐνθένδε.   καὶ τὸ πρῶτον ἡδὺς ὁ
βίος· ζήσῃ γὰρ ἐλεύθερος, ἄρχων καὶ οὐκ ἀρχόμενος,
βραχὺ μὲν καὶ ὅσον τῷ σώματι περισπώμενος, καὶ τοῦτ'
εἰς τὴν τοῦ ὅλου ἁρμονίαν, σιωπῶν δὲ βασιλεύων καὶ
θεωρῶν, ἃ θεοὶ ἀνθρώποις τοῖς μετρίοις κατεσκεύασαντο
ἀπεχομένοις τοῦ ἀγρίου βίου, ἐν ᾧ ἁρπαγαὶ καὶ ἀλληλοκ-
τονίαι οὐ περὶ μεγάλων οὐδὲ θείων, περὶ μικρῶν δὲ καὶ
κοινῶν, οὐ πρὸς ἀνθρώπους μόνον, ἀλλὰ καὶ τὰ ἄλογα.
περὶ γὰρ τοῦ πλείονα ἔχειν καὶ ἐσθίειν καὶ πίνειν καὶ
ἀφροδισιάζειν οἱ πάντες φαῦλοί εἰσι καὶ τοῖς ἀλόγοις
σύμφοροι.

(3) Therefore there is even a certain high honor paid such souls in Hades, since they were not at all indulgent of their bodies. For opinion has it that the souls that indulge the body are worthless and servile, while the souls that are not like these are good and carry their heads high (for they live as leaders of all, giving commands with sovereign authority), undertaking as a consequence of this only what is just and very easy to accomplish. But they don't take up even one of the opposite sort of things, those in which the body compels the soul to take delight on account of the pleasure that clings to them, like a fish or any other animal destined to live under the domination of its worst elements.

(4) If you have practiced how to die, this exercise will accompany you whenever you have to migrate from here. First, life will be sweet, for you shall live free, a master and not someone in subjection, and in a short time you will strip away all that relates to the body. Now this leads to the harmony of the whole, when one keeps silent, exercises dominion, and considers what the gods have provided for men who are moderate and restrain themselves from the wild life. In the latter, robberies and mutual slaughter are committed, not for great and godly reasons, but for trifling and common ones, and not against men only but against animals as well. For when it is a question of possessing more, eating, drinking, and indulging in one's lusts, they are all worthless and no different from animals.

40. Διογένης ὁ κύων Ἀλεξάνδρῳ

Ἐμεμψάμην καὶ Διονυσίῳ καὶ Περδίκκᾳ, λέγω δὲ
καὶ σοὶ ὅτι δοκεῖτε τὸ ἄρχειν εἶναι μάχεσθαι τοῖς
ἀνθρώποις. τὸ δὲ πλεῖστον διαφέρει· τὸ μὲν γὰρ ἀφρο-
5   σύνη ἐστί, τὸ δ᾽ ἐπίστασθαι τοῖς ἀνθρώποις χρῆσθαι
καὶ ἕνεκά τι τοῦ βελτίστου πράττειν. σκόπει οὖν ἀνθ᾽
ὧν νῦν ἐγχειρεῖς οὐδὲν εἰδὼς ποιεῖν ἐπιτρέψαι τινὶ
σαυτὸν ἀνθρώπῳ, ὅστις σε ὥσπερ ἰατρὸς νοσοῦντα ἐκθε-
ραπεύσας ἀπαλλάξει τῆς νῦν πολλῆς καὶ κακῆς δόξης.
10   σὺ γὰρ ὅπως μέν τινα κακὸν ἀπεργάσῃ ζητεῖς, εὖ δ᾽ ἂν
οὐδὲ βουλόμενος ἔχοις οὐδένα ποιῆσαι. (2) ἔτι δὲ τὸ
κρατεῖν καὶ τὸ ὑφ᾽ ἑαυτῷ ἔχειν τινὰς οὐ τοιοῦτόν
ἐστιν, οἷον μετὰ τῶν κακίστων ἀνθρώπων ἄγειν καὶ
φέρειν ἀεὶ τοὺς παρατυγχάνοντας. τοῦτο γὰρ οὐδὲ τῶν
15   θηρίων τὰ βέλτιστα ποιεῖ, ἀλλ᾽ οὐδὲ οἱ λύκοι, ὧν ζῷον
οὐδέν ἐστιν πονηρότερον οὐδὲ κακουργότερον, οὓς σύ
μοι δοκεῖς ὑπερβεβλῆσθαι ἀμαθίᾳ. τοῖς μὲν γὰρ ἐξαρ-
κεῖ μόνοις πονηροῖς εἶναι, σὺ δὲ καὶ πρὸς μισθὸν
διδοὺς ἀνθρώποις τοῖς πονηροτάτοις τούτοις τε παρέ-
20   χεις ἐξουσίαν μηδὲν ὑγιὲς πράττειν καὶ αὐτὸς ὅμοια
τούτοις ἐγχειρεῖς ποιεῖν καὶ μείζω.

(3) κατάγνωθι οὖν, ὦ ᾽γαθέ, καὶ ἐν σαυτῷ γενοῦ
ἔτι μᾶλλον. ποῦ γῆς εἶ ἄρα; καὶ τί σοι δύναται τὰ
κατασκευάσματα ταῦτα καὶ ἡ σπουδὴ ἡ ἐπὶ τούτοις; οὐ
25   γὰρ οἴει δήπου βελτίων τινὸς εἶναι ἀνθρώπου τοιαῦτα
ποιῶν. εἰ δὲ μηδενὸς εἶ βελτίων, <μὴ> τούτοις
<ἐκπόνει>. τί οἴει σοι τὰ γινόμενα εἶναι ἀλλ᾽ ἢ
συμφορὰν καὶ φόβους καὶ κινδύνους μεγάλους; καίτοι
οὐκ οἶδα ἐγὼ ὅπως ἂν ἔτι μείζω ἀτυχήματα ἀτυχήσαις
30   τῶν νῦν. τίς γὰρ ἄνθρωπος μὴ δίκαιος οὐκ ἂν ἀτυχοῖ;
τίς κακὸς καὶ βίαιος οὐκ ἂν κακὸν πράττοι καὶ μηδὲν
ἀγαθὸν ἔχοι; καὶ τοῦτο τὸ ζῆν δοκεῖ τί σοι εἶναι καὶ

─────────
26   <μὴ> Emeljanow
27   <ἐκπόνει> Emeljanow

40. Diogenes the Cynic to Alexander

I blamed both Dionysius and Perdiccas, and I say the same to you, that you think that to rule means to make war on people. But they are entirely different. For the one is senselessness, while the other is to know how to deal with men and to do something for the most noble reason. Therefore, instead of those things which you in your ignorance are presently trying to do, look to entrust yourself to some person who, like a doctor, curing an ill person, will free you from the currently prevalent but harmful opinion. For you are on the lookout for a way to harm someone, but, even if you wanted to, you would not be able to do anybody any good. (2) And yet to rule and to have subjects under oneself is not the same as associating with the worst men and always waylaying those who happen by. Not only do the most noble of the animals not do this, but not even wolves do, and no animal is more wicked and harmful than they. But you seem to have outdone them in stupidity. For it is quite enough for them to be wicked by themselves; but, by giving a salary besides to very wicked men, you present them with the opportunity of doing no good. And you yourself have a hand at doing things like this and worse.

(3) So be your own accuser, my good man, and be still more introspective. Where on earth are you? And what can these provisions and your exertion over them do for you? For you don't think that in doing these things you are in any way better than any other person. But if you are better than no one, do not work hard at these things. Why do you think that what happens to you will be anything other than misfortune, fears, and great dangers? Really, I don't know how there would be still greater misfortunes than those you now experience. For what unjust person would not be unfortunate? What evil and violent individual would not do evil and admit of nothing good? What do you

περὶ τοῦδε κίνδυνός σοι εἶναι μάλιστα παθεῖν τι
τοιαυτὶ ποιοῦντι;

    (4) καὶ <ὡς> οὐκ οἴει σοι <τούτους> ἐπιβουλεῦσαι
μάλιστα, εἴπερ τῶν πολλῶν ἐστιν ἐξαμαρτάνειν; οὐ
5   τοίνυν ἔχοις ἂν ἐπιδεῖξαι ὅπως τοιοῦτος ὢν ἐπικέχρη-
σαι ἀνθρώπῳ χρηστῷ, τοιούτοις δὲ ἐπιχρώμενος οἷος
πρῶτός γ' ἂν αὐτὸς καὶ μέγιστα κακὰ παθεῖν καὶ νῦν
μηδὲν ἀγαθὸν πάσχειν, μηδέ σοι ἀρκέσειν τὰ τείχη·
ῥᾳδίως τὰ κακὰ ὑπεράλλεται καὶ παραδύεται. σκόπει
10   δ' οἷον καὶ αἱ νόσοι ποιοῦσιν· οὐδένα γὰρ πυρετὸν
οὐδὲ τεῖχος εἴργει, οὐδὲ ξενικὸν τὸν κατάρρουν, ὥστε
μὴ οὐχ οὕτω διατεθῆναι τῶν τυράννων ὅντινα βούλει,
ὥσπερ ἂν τὸν ἀποροῦντα δοκοῦντα ἄνθρωπον. τίνος οὖν
σοι καὶ ὑγιειναὶ φυλακαὶ παρεσκευασμέναι ἕνεκεν ἀλλ'
15   ἢ ἀμαθίας, ὅπως ὡς μάλιστα ταύτην διαφυλάττωσι, καὶ
πλείστοις ᾖς ἐν κακοῖς καὶ ἐν φόβοις; (5) ἢ γὰρ οἴει
ἄλλοθέν ποθεν τοῖς ἀνθρώποις εἶναι τὰ κακὰ ἢ ἐξ ὧν
ἂν μὴ εἰδῶσιν ὅ τι ἂν αὐτοῖς ᾖ πρακτέον; πάνυ οὖν
μοι δοκεῖς καὶ σὺ τῶν τυράννων εἶναι· οὗτοι γὰρ οὐδὲ
20   τῶν παίδων πλείω νοῦν ἔχουσι. παῦσαι, οὖν, ὦ 'γαθέ,
καὶ εἴ τί σοι βούλει ἀγαθὸν εἶναι, σκόπει πόθεν τι
πράξεις τῶν δεόντων· τοῦτο δὲ οὐδέποτε ἂν δυνηθείης
μὴ διδαχθείς.

    ἆρα οὖν εἴ τινά σοι τῶν Ἀθήνησι δικαστῶν πέμ-
25   ψαιμι; οἳ γὰρ ὁσημέραι τοῦτο πράττουσι περὶ τῶν
ἀδίκων, οἴονται καὶ αὐτοὶ μέγιστοι εἶναι καὶ τοὺς
ἄλλους παρέχεσθαι μηδὲν κακὸν μήτε ἔχοντας μήτε
πράττοντας. ἐρρῶσθαι δὲ ἢ χαίρειν οὐ θέμις μοι
γράφειν, ἕως ἂν ᾖς τοιοῦτος καὶ μετὰ τοιουτοτρόπων
30   βιοῖς.

_____
3 <ὡς> Emeljanow
3 <τούτους> Boissonade & Emeljanow

think this life is? Do you not risk suffering for it by
being engaged in activities like these?

(4) Nonetheless you think that these men are especially capable of plotting against you, don't you, if indeed it is possible for so many to miss their aim? You
would therefore be unable to show how a man like you has
had dealings with an honest person. But, dealing with
such people as you do, you would be able to show how you
first have suffered the greatest evils yourself, how you
experience nothing good, and how walls will not be sufficient protection for you. For evils easily leap over them
or crawl in underneath. Consider the evil that diseases
work. For a wall shuts out no fever at all, nor does a
mercenary force the catarrh, so they do not hinder any
tyrant whatsoever from being so handled by the diseases,
just as they do not with the man who seems to be without
any resources. What other motive is there for which you
are furnished guardians for your health than ignorance,
that they may guard it as closely as possible, and you may
still be encumbered by countless evils and fears? (5) Or
do you think that people's evils originate from any other
source than from their not knowing what they have to do?
Therefore, you, too, certainly seem like one of the tyrants
to me. For they have no more sense than children. So
stop, my good man, and even if what you wish for yourself
is good, examine in what way you will obtain what you need.
You will most assuredly never be capable of this without
being taught.

Suppose I send you one or other of the moral judges
at Athens? They do this daily for criminals and believe
that they are very qualified to render others so that they
neither suffer any evil nor perpetrate it. Now it is not
right for me to write salutations and farewell, until you
are a man like this and spend your life with people of
this sort.

41. Μελησίππῳ

Οὐ δοκεῖ μοι πᾶς τὸ καθ' ἡμᾶς ἐν ἀρετῇ δύνασθαι,
ἐπεὶ πολλῶν ἡ πρόθεσις καθαιρετικὴ τῆς ἀξίας γίνεται·
οὐδὲ γὰρ ὁ τοῦ Μέλητος εἰπὼν τὸν Δία πατέρα ἀνδρῶν
5   τε θεῶν τε ἐκύδηνεν ἀλλ' ἐμείωσεν, ἐπεὶ χαλεπόν, εἰ
οὓς οἱ γεννήσαντες διὰ πονηρίαν ἀπολέγονται, Διὸς
εἶναι παῖδας πιστεύομεν. ταῦτα οὖν ὁ κύων μόνα
δυνήσεται, ἃ κατ' ἀρετὴν ἐνεργεῖται.

42. Μελεσίππῃ τῇ σοφῇ, <χαίρειν>

10   ῎Εφθασεν ἡ χείρ μου πρὸ τῆς σῆς ἀφίξεως τὸν
ὑμέναιον ᾆσαι, ἐγίγνωσκε δὲ τὴν ἀφροδισίων ἀποπλήρω-
σιν εὐποριστοτέραν εὑρῆσθαι τῆς κατὰ γαστέρα. ὁ γὰρ
κυνισμός, ὡς οἶσθα, φύσεώς ἐστιν ἀναζήτησις· εἰ δέ
τινες μέμφοιντο τὴν προαίρεσιν ταύτην, ἀξιοπιστότερος
15   ἐπαινῶν ἐγώ.

---

9   <χαίρειν> Hercher

43. Μαρωνίταις, <εὖ πράττειν>

'Ορθῶς ἐποιήσατε τὴν πόλιν μεταχρηματίσαντες καὶ
καλέσαντες ἀντὶ Μαρωνείας ἥτις νῦν καλεῖται 'Ιππαρ-
χίαν, ἐπεὶ κρεῖττον ὑμῖν ἀπὸ 'Ιππαρχίας λέγεσθαι,
20   γυναικὸς μέν, ἀλλὰ φιλοσόφου, ἢ Μάρωνος, ἀνδρὸς
οἰνοπώλου.

---

16   <εὖ πράττειν> Hercher

41. To Melesippus

I do not think that everyone is capable of virtue
as we understand it, for the designs of many people destroy moral values. Now when the son of Meles called Zeus
the father of both men and gods, he did not do him any
honor, but degraded him, since I find it difficult to believe those to be children of Zeus whose own parents re-
pudiate them because of their wickedness. So the Cynic
will be able to do only those things which are executed
according to virtue.

42. To the wise Melesippe, greetings

My hand sounded the wedding hymn first, before your
arrival, and it understood that the satisfaction of sexual
pleasures was found to be more easily procured than that
of the stomach. For Cynicism, as you know, is an investigation of nature. And if some should find fault with this
deliberate choice, yet am I worthy of greater trust in my
praise of it.

43. To the Maroneans, do well

You did well when you changed the name of the city
and, instead of Maroneia, called it Hipparchia, its present name, since it is better for you to be named after
Hipparchia, a woman, it's true, but a philosopher, than
after Maron, a man who sells wine.

44. Μητροκλεῖ, <εὖ πράττειν>

   Οὐ μόνον ἄρτος καὶ ὕδωρ καὶ στιβὰς καὶ τρίβων
σωφροσύνην καὶ καρτερίαν διδάσκουσιν, ἀλλ᾽ εἰ χρὴ
οὕτως φάναι, καὶ ποιμενικὴ χείρ. ὤφελον καὶ τὸν πρὶν
5 ἐκεῖνον βουκόλον ὄντα ἐξεπίστασθαι. ἐπιμέλου οὖν καὶ
ταύτης ἔνθα ἂν ἐπείγῃς· ἔστι γὰρ ἐκ τῆς συντάξεως τοῦ
ἡμετέρου βίου. τὰς δὲ πρὸς τὰς γυναῖκας ἀκρατεῖς
ἐντεύξεις πολλῆς δεομένας σχολῆς ἔα πολλὰ χαίρειν·
οὐ γὰρ σχολή <ἔστιν οὐ μόνον πτωχῷ> αἰτεῖν κατὰ
10 Πλάτωνα, ἀλλὰ τῷ ἐπ᾽ εὐδαιμονίαν σύντομον ἐπειγομένῳ.
ἡ πρὸς γυναῖκας ἔντευξις ὄνησιν φέρει ἀνθρώπων δ᾽
ἰδιωτῶν πολλῶν, οἷς ὁμοίως διὰ ταύτην τὴν πρᾶξιν
ζημία· περιμαθήσεις παρὰ τοῖς μεμαθηκόσιν ἐκ <Πανὸς>
ἐργάσασθαι. σὺ μὴ ἐπιστρέφου, μηδ᾽ εἴ σε διὰ τὸν
15 τοιοῦτον βίον κύνα τινὲς ἢ ἄλλο τι ἀποκαλῶσι χεῖρον.

---

1 <εὖ πράττειν> Hercher
9 <ἔστιν...πτωχῷ> Emeljanow
13 <Πανὸς> Schafstaedt & Emeljanow

45. Περδίκκᾳ, <εὖ πράττειν>

   Αἰσχύνου ἐφ᾽ οἷς γράφων ἀπειλεῖς μοι, ὅτι δῆτά
σοι οὐ πείθομαι χείρων Ἐριφύλης γενέσθαι καὶ χρυσοῦ
ἐμαυτὸν ἀνταλλάξασθαι κακῶς. τοῦτο γὰρ ἀξιοῖς, καὶ
20 λόγοις μὲν ἅπτεσθαί μου οὐκ ἀναβάλλῃ, ἀπειλεῖς δὲ
ἀπειλὴν κανθαρίδος, ἀποκτενεῖν, καὶ οὐκ οἶσθα ὅτι
δράσας τοῦτο ἀντιπείσῃ. ἔστι γάρ τις, ᾧ μέλει περὶ
ἡμῶν, ὃς καὶ τῶν τοιούτων τὴν ἴσην δίκην τοὺς ἄρξαντας
ἀδίκων ἔργων εἰσπράττεται, καὶ ζῶντας μὲν ἁπλοῦν,
25 τελευτήσαντας δὲ δεκαπλάσιον. ταῦτ᾽ ἐγὼ οὐχὶ δεδοι-
κώς σου τὰς ἀπειλὰς ἔγραψα, ἀλλ᾽ οὐ βουλόμενός σε δι᾽
ἐμὲ κακόν τι πρᾶξαι.

---

16 <εὖ πράττειν> Hercher

44. To Metrocles, do well

It is not only bread, water, a bed of straw, and a
coarse cloak that teach moderation and patience, but also,
if one may speak in this way, the hand of the shepherd.
Would that I knew that famous fellow in the past who was
a cattle-herd. So attend to this, wherever you are rush-
ing to, for it has to do with putting our life in order.
As for intemperate intercourse with women, which demands
a lot of spare time, bid it farewell. For there is no
spare time, either for a poor man to beg, as Plato says,
nor for the person hastening on the short cut to happiness.
Intercourse with women provides enjoyment to the general,
uninformed public. But they, in like manner, are damaged
because of this practice; but you will learn in the company of those who have learned from Pan to do the trick
with their hands. As for you, then, do not turn back even
if they call you a dog or some other worse name because of
this sort of life.

45. To Perdiccas, do well

Be ashamed at the threats you wrote me, since you
haven't convinced me at all that I am worse than Eriphyle
and that I have bartered myself venally for gold. You
think this fit, and you probably won't put off assaulting
me verbally. You threaten to kill me--the threat of an
insect! Nor are you aware that if you do this you in turn
will suffer. For there is someone who cares about us, and
he exacts equal satisfaction for such deeds from those who
initiate unjust actions. From the living it's a single
penalty, but from the dead ten-fold. I write this not out
of fear of your threats, but wishing that you not do anything wrong on my account.

46. Πλάτωνι τῷ σοφῷ, <χαίρειν>

Διαπτύεις μου τὸν τρίβωνα καὶ τὴν πήραν ὡς ἐμοὶ
μὲν ἐπαχθῆ καὶ χαλεπά, τὸν δὲ βίον οὐδὲν ὠφελοῦντα,
οὐκ εὖ ποιῶν. σοὶ μὲν γὰρ ἐπαχθῆ καὶ χαλεπά, ἔμαθες
5   γὰρ ἀπὸ τυραννικῶν τραπεζῶν ἀμέτρως ἐμφορεῖσθαι καὶ
γαστρὶ προβάτων, ἀλλὰ μὴ ψυχῆς ἀρετῇ, κοσμεῖσθαι· ἐγὼ
δὲ ὡς μετ᾽ ἀρετῆς ταῦτα ἐπιτετήδευκα, τίνα ἂν μείζονα
ἀπόδειξιν ἢ τὸ μὴ μεταβάλλεσθαι πρὸς ἡδυπάθειαν ἐξόν
μοι παρασχοίμην; τόν γε μὴν βίον ἀξιῶ πάντων μᾶλλον
10 ἀνθρώπων ὠφελεῖν οὐ μόνον δι᾽ ὧν ἔχω, ἀλλὰ καὶ δι᾽ ὧν
τοιοῦτος αὐτοῖς φαίνομαι. τίς γὰρ ἂν ἐφ᾽ οὕτως
αὐτάρκη καὶ λιτὸν πολέμιος στρατεύσαιτο; ἐπὶ τίνα δ᾽
ἂν οἱ τοιούτοις ἀρεσκόμενοι βασιλέα ἢ δῆμον πόλεμον
ἐξενέγκαιεν; ἀκόλουθα γοῦν τούτοις, ἐκκεκάθαρται μὲν
15 ἡ ψυχὴ κακῶν, <ἀφέσταται> δὲ κενοδοξίας, ἐπιθυμιῶν
δὲ ἀμετρίαν ἐκβέβληκεν, ἀληθεύειν δὲ δεδίδακται, <καὶ
ἑτέρων> ψευδῶν πάντων ὑπερορᾶν· εἰ δέ σε μὴ πείθει
ταῦτα, ἄσκει φιληδονίαν καὶ κατάπαιζε ἡμῶν ὡς οὐ
μέγα νοησάντων.

---

1   <χαίρειν> Hercher
15 <ἀφέσταται> Emeljanow
16 <καὶ ἑτέρων> Emeljanow

46. To Plato, the Sage, greetings

You scorn my rough cloak and wallet as though they
were burdensome and difficult, and my way of life as of no
benefit, doing no good. Now they are burdensome and difficult to you, for you learned to take your fill without
moderation from the tables of a tyrant, and to adorn yourself with the bellies of sheep, but not with the virtue of
the soul. But as for me, as I practiced these things with
virtue, what greater demonstration could I supply than not
changing toward a life of pleasure, although I could have?
I certainly think that I benefit life more than all other
men, not only through the things I possess, but also
through those things which show them that I am this kind
of man. For what enemy would campaign against a person so
self-sufficient and simple? Against what king or people
would those satisfied with such things begin a war? Con-
sistent with this, my soul has been purified of evils, has
been removed from vainglory, has rejected excess of desires, has been taught to be truthful and to despise all
other falsehood. But if this does not convince you,
practice fondness of pleasure and mock us for not knowing
much.

47. Ζήνωνι, <εὖ πράττειν>

Οὐ γαμητέον οὐδὲ θρεπτέον παῖδας, ἐπεὶ τὸ γένος
ἡμῶν ἀσθενές ἐστιν, ἐπιφορτίζει δὲ γάμος καὶ τέκνα
ἀνίαις τὴν ἀνθρωπίνην ἀσθένειαν. οἱ γοῦν ἐλθόντες
5   ἐπὶ γάμον καὶ τέκνων τροφὴν δι᾽ ἐπικουρίαν, ὕστερον
γνόντες ὡς πλειόνων ὀχληρῶν ἐστὶ ταῦτα, μετανοοῦσιν,
ἐνὸν ἀρχῆθεν πεφευγέναι. ὁ δὲ ἀπαθὴς ἱκανὰ πρὸς
ὑπομονὴν ὑπολαβὼν τὰ οἰκεῖα γάμον καὶ τέκνων ἐκκλίνει
γένεσιν.
10   ἀλλ᾽ ὁ βίος ἔρημος ἀνθρώπων γενήσεται· πόθεν γάρ,
ἐρεῖς, ἡ διαδοχή;
       εἴθε γὰρ ἐπιλείποι βλακεία τὸν βίον, σοφῶν γενο-
μένων πάντων· νῦν δ᾽ ὁ μὲν ἡμῖν πεισθεὶς μόνος ἴσως
ἐπιλείψει, ὁ δὲ σύμπας βίος ἀπειθήσας παιδοποιήσεται.
15   εἰ δὲ καὶ γένος ἀνθρώπων ἐπιλείποι, ἆρα ἄξιον τοσοῦτον ὀλοφύρασθαι, ὅσον καὶ εἰ μυιῶν καὶ σφηκῶν ἐπιλείποι γένεσις; ταῦτα γὰρ τὰ ῥήματα μὴ τεθεαμένων ἐστὶ
τὴν τῶν ὄντων φύσιν.

------

1   <εὖ πράττειν> Hercher

48. ῾Ρήσῳ, <χαίρειν>

20   Φρύνιχος Λαρισαῖος ἀκουστὴς ἡμῶν ποθεῖ τὸ "ἱππό-
βοτον" Ἄργος θεάσασθαι, ὃς ἀπὸ σοῦ δεήσεται φιλόσοφος
ὢν οὐ πολλῶν.

------

19   <χαίρειν> Hercher

47. To Zeno, do well

One should not wed nor raise children, since our race
is weak and marriage and children burden human weakness
with troubles. Therefore, those who move toward wedlock
and the rearing of children on account of the support
these promise, later experience a change of heart when
they come to know that they are characterized by even
greater hardships. But it is possible to escape right
from the start. Now the person insensitive to passion,
who considers his own possessions to be sufficient for
patient endurance, declines to marry and produce children.

But life will become devoid of people. For from
where, you will ask, will the succession of children come?

I only wish that dullness would leave our life, and
that everyone would become wise! For now, perhaps only
the one persuaded by me will go childless, while the
world, unconvinced, will beget children. But even if the
human race should fail, would it not be fitting to lament
this as much as one would if the procreation of flies and
wasps should fail? For this is what people say who have
not observed the true nature of things.

48. To Rhesus, greetings

Phrynichus the Larissaean, a disciple of mine, is
anxious to see Argos, "where horses graze." And he will
not require much from you since he is a philosopher.

49.

Ὁ κύων Ἀρουέκα γνῶναι σαυτόν (οὕτω γὰρ ἂν εὖ
πράττοις), καὶ εἴ τις ἄρα περὶ ψυχῆς νόσος, οἷον
ἀφροσύνη, ταύτης ἰατρὸν λαμβάνειν, τοῖς θεοῖς εὐχό-
5 μενος, ἵνα μὴ δοκοῦντα λαβὼν θάτερον ποιῇς. χρόνιζε
δὲ μὴ οὕτως· οἶνος γάρ σοι θησαυρίζεται, ἀλλὰ μὲν
βλάψεις ὑλήσει. ταῦτα δὲ ποιῶν οὐ μόνον ἐμοὶ φίλος
πολλοῦ ἄξιος, ἀλλὰ καὶ τοῖς ἄλλοις πᾶσι. τὸ δὲ
ἐρρῶσθαί σε καὶ τὸ χαίρειν ἐν τῷ μὴ ἀμελῆσαι τῶν
10 γεγραμμένων ἐπέσταλται.

50. Χαρμίδα, <χαίρειν>

Σοφίσματά μοι καὶ γρίφους ὁ σὸς γνώριμος
Εὐρήμων προύτεινεν ἐξησκημένα ὡς ἔνι μάλιστα. ἐγὼ δὲ
οὐκ ἐπὶ τούτοις ἀξιῶ τὴν ἀρετὴν σεμνύνεσθαι, ἃ ταῖς
15 κεναῖς καὶ δυσανοίκτοις πυξίσιν ἔοικεν, ἀλλ' ἐπὶ τῷ
βίῳ, ὃν γυμνὸν ἐπιδείκνυσθαι πρέπει τοῖς ἐντυγχάνουσι.
μετὰ γοῦν τὰς χαλεπάς τε καὶ κατησκημένας ζητήσεις ὁ
γενναῖος καὶ σοφὸς Εὐρήμων περὶ τῶν μητρῴων πρὸς τὸν
πατέρα μόνον οὐχὶ γυμνὸς ἐπαγκρατίαζε, καὶ τὴν μάχην
20 τοῦ σοφοῦ ἔνιοι τῶν ἐπιτυχόντων φορτικῶν ἀνδρῶν
διέλυον. ἔδει δέ, εἴπερ ἀρετῇ συνετέθραπτο, ἢ τὴν
ἀρχὴν μηδὲ συστῆναι χρημάτων ἐπιθυμίαν περὶ αὑτόν, ἢ
πάσης κακίας ἐστὶν αἰτία, <ἢ διὰ> τῆς σεμνοτάτης
φιλοσοφίας, ἧς ἀφηρῆσθαι τὸ σύμπαν πάθος. οἱ
25 Ἀθηναῖοι δὲ καθ' ὑμᾶς φιλοσοφήσαντες ἐοίκασι τοῖς
ἐπαγγελλομένοις ἄλλους ἰατρεύειν, ἃ μὴ αὐτοὺς ἰᾶσθαι
δεδύνηται.

_____
11 <χαίρειν> Hercher
23 <ἢ διὰ> Marcks & Emeljanow

49.

The Cynic to Aroueca. Know yourself (for thus you
would do well) and, if there is any disease afflicting
your soul, senselessness for example, get a doctor for it.
And pray the gods that you not do more harm than good by
choosing one that only seems to be a good physician. Do
not thus delay, for wine is being stored up for you, but
you will ruin it if you do not filter it. But if you do
this, you will be a valuable friend, not only to me but to
all the others too. My greeting and salutation has been
sent on the condition that you not disregard what is written.

50. To Charmides, greetings

Your pupil Euremus offered me captious arguments and
riddles with as much embellishment as he was capable of.
But I do not think that virtue is dignified by such talk,
which is like decorative boxes that are empty and hard to
open, but rather by a style of life which can properly be
shown naked to those who chance upon it.

Anyway, after those difficult and well exercised inquiries, the noble and wise Euremus fought his father in a
pancratium over his mother's property. But Euremus was not
naked in this contest. Some of the common people who happened to come upon them resolved the wise man's dispute.
But if he was really nurtured on virtue, he should, right
from the start, not have introduced into himself the love
for money, which is the cause of all evil. Or through
philosophy, so highly esteemed, he should have done away
with all his passions. But the Athenians, when they phi-
losophize your way, resemble those who propose to cure
others of what they haven't been able to cure themselves.

51. Ἐπιμενίδῃ, <χαίρειν>

Ἐπιμενίδη σοιασσατοιδιεα δι᾽ ἀρετὴν ἀνατλῆναι
μένοις ἂν οἴκοι τὴν γαστέρα τέρπων καὶ τὸ σωμάτιον
κοσμῶν. ἀκούω γάρ σε ἀρετὴν ἐπαγγέλλεσθαι, καί μοι
5   τὸ πρᾶγμα οὐκ ἐφάνη παράδοξον· εἶναι μὲν γὰρ ἐσθλὸν
κατὰ Σιμωνίδην χαλεπόν, ἐπαγγέλλεσθαι δὲ ῥᾴδιον.

_____
1 <χαίρειν> Hercher

51. To Epimenides, greetings

To Epimenides...(rather than) endure with the help
of virtue, you would remain at home, gratifying your
stomach and adorning your poor body. For I hear that you
are promising virtue; and to me the report did not appear
incredible. For, according to Simonides, it is difficult
to be good, but easy to promise it.

THE EPISTLES OF HERACLITUS

Translated by

David R. Worley

1. Βασιλεὺς Δαρεῖος Ἡράκλειτον Ἐφέσιον
   σοφὸν ἄνδρα προσαγορεύει

Καταβέβλησαι λόγον γραπτὸν περὶ φύσεως δυσνόητόν
τε καὶ δυσεξήγητον. ἔν τισι μὲν οὖν ἑρμηνευόμενος
5 κατὰ λέξιν σὴν δοκεῖ μοι δύναμίν τινα προσφέρεσθαι
θεωρίας κόσμου τοῦ σύμπαντος καὶ τῶν ἀπὸ τούτου συμ-
βαινόντων, ἅπερ ἐστὶν ἐν θειοτάτῃ κείμενα κινήσει,
τῶν δὲ πλείστων ἐποχὴν ἔχειν τὰ πρὸς ζήτησιν καὶ
μάθησιν, ὥστε καὶ τοὺς ἐπὶ πλεῖστον μετεσχηκότας
10 γραμμάτων ἑλληνικῶν καὶ τοὺς ἄλλους τοὺς ἀσχολουμέ-
νους περὶ τὴν τῶν μετεώρων προσοχὴν καὶ φιλομάθειαν
ἀπορεῖσθαι τῆς ἐν ὀρθῇ γνώμῃ παρὰ σοὶ δοκούσης κατα-
γεγράφθαι διηγήσεως. βασιλεὺς οὖν Δαρεῖος Ὑστάσπου
βούλεται σῆς ἀκροάσεως μεταλαβεῖν καὶ παιδείας
15 λογικῆς. ἔρχου δὴ συντόμως πρὸς ἐμὴν ὄψιν καὶ βασί-
λειον οἶκον. Ἕλληνες γὰρ ὡς ἐπὶ τὸ πλεῖστον ἀνε-
πισήμαντοι σοφιζομένοις ἀνδράσιν ὄντες παρορῶσι τὰ
καλῶς ὑπ᾿ αὐτῶν ἐνδεικνύμενα πρὸς καλὴν ἀγωγὴν καὶ
δίαιταν, παρ᾿ ἐμοὶ δὲ ὑπάρξει σοι πᾶσα μὲν προεδρία,
20 καθ᾿ ἡμέραν δὲ καλὴ καὶ σπουδαία προσαγόρευσις καὶ
βίος εὐδόκιμος σαῖς παραινέσεσιν.

186

1. King Darius greets Heraclitus
of Ephesus, a wise man

You have written down a discourse on nature which is difficult to understand and hard to interpret. In certain parts, when interpreted word for word, the discourse does appear to me to exhibit some ability in the philosophical contemplation of the order of the universe and of those things which result from it and are subject to a most divine motion. Most of its parts, however, appear to produce a suspension of judgment in matters that are subject to inquiry and learning. As a result, both those who are very well acquainted with Greek literature as well as others who devote their attention and their love of learning to the observation of celestial phenomena are perplexed over your discourse although it appears to have been written with sound judgment. King Darius, son of Hystaspes, therefore, desires to hear your lectures and oral teaching. So, come quickly to my presence and my palace. For the Greeks usually do not confer distinctions upon scientific men, and they disregard the things that pertain to good conduct and a proper mode of life that such men display. But with me you will have every privilege, a daily greeting that is good and excellent, and a life that befits your precepts.

2. Ἡράκλειτος Δαρείῳ βασιλεῖ πατρὸς
Ὑστάσπεω χαίρειν

Ὁκόσοι τυγχάνουσιν ἐπιχθόνιοι, τῆς μὲν ἀληθείης
καὶ δικαιοπραγίης ἀπέχονται, ἀπληστίῃ δὲ καὶ δοξοκο-
5   πίῃ προσέχουσι κακῆς εἵνεκεν ἀνοίης.   ἐγὼ δὲ ἀμνησ-
τίην ἔχων πάσης πονηρίης καὶ κόρον φεύγων παντὸς
οἰκειεύμενον φθόνον διὰ τὴν ὑπερηφανίην οὐκ ἂν ἀφι-
κοίμην εἰς Περσικὴν χώρην, ὀλίγοις ἀρκεόμενος κατ᾽
ἐμὴν γνώμην.   [ἔρρωσο.]

10   3. Βασιλεὺς Δαρεῖος Ἐφεσίοις

Ἀνὴρ ἀγαθὸς μέγα ἀγαθὸν πόλει· λόγοις καλοῖς
καὶ νόμοις ψυχὰς ἀγαθὰς ποιεῖ καιρίως ἄγων εἰς ἀγαθά.
ὑμεῖς δὲ Ἑρμόδωρον οὐ μόνον αὐτῶν βέλτιστον ἀλλὰ καὶ
Ἰώνων πάντων ἐξεβάλετε ἐκ πατρίδος, αἰσχρὰς αἰτίας
15 ψυχῇ ἀγαθῇ προσάπτοντες.   εἰ μὲν οὖν διεγνώκατε
βασιλεῖ πολεμεῖν δεσπότῃ, ἑτοιμάζεσθε (ἀποστελῶ γὰρ
στρατιάν, ᾗ ὑμεῖς οὐ δυνήσεσθε ἀντιτάσσεσθαι· αἰσχρὸν
γὰρ βασιλεῖ μεγάλῳ μὴ ἀρκέειν φίλοις).   εἰ δὲ μηδὲν
τοιοῦτον ἐγχειρήσετε, κατάξατε Ἑρμόδωρον καὶ ἀπόδοτε
20 αὐτῷ κατρῴαν κτῆσιν, μνημονεύοντες ἃ ὑμᾶς ἐκείνου
εὐνοίᾳ εὐηργέτησα, φόρους ἐλάττους τάξας ὧν ἐφέρετε
καὶ γῆν πολλὴν δοὺς πρὸς ᾗ ἐκέκτησθε.   ὧν οὐκ ἐοίκατε
χάριν ὀφείλειν· οὐ γὰρ ἄν ποτε Ἑρμόδωρον φίλον βασιλέως ἐφυγαδεύσατε.   ἀποστείλατε οὖν ἄνδρας τοὺς
25 ἐροῦντας πρός με τὸ δίκαιον ὑπὲρ ὧν ἐγκαλεῖτε Ἑρμο-
δώρῳ, ἵν᾽ ἐὰν μὲν ἐκεῖνος ἐπιδειχθῇ κακοφρονῶν, ἐπι-
τιμηθῇ, ἐὰν δὲ ὑμεῖς, ἐπὶ νοῦν βέλτιον θῶμαι καὶ εἰς
τὸ λοιπὸν ἁμαρτάνειν κωλύσω εἰς ἀγαθοὺς ἄνδρας· καὶ
γὰρ βασιλεῖ ὑμετέρῳ συμφέρει ταῦτα καὶ ὑμῖν.
30 [ἔρρωσθε.]

2. Heraclitus to King Darius,
Son of father Hystaspes, greetings

All men who dwell on earth keep themselves from
truth and from practicing what is just. Because of their
base folly, they cleave to insatiable desire and vainglory. But as for me, since I have no memory of any
wickedness and in everything flee that satiety which because of arrogance breeds the envy of everyone, I would
not go to the land of Persia, for in accordance with my
judgment, I am satisfied with little. Farewell.

3. King Darius to the Ephesians

A good man is a great credit to a city. With noble
words and laws he makes men good by leading them at the
proper time to the good. Yet you have banished Hermodorus,
the best man, not only among yourselves, but among all the
Ionians, lodging shameful accusations against this noble
man. If, then, you have decided to war against your king
and ruler, be prepared! For I will send an army which you
will not be able to resist. For it is shameful for a great
king not to assist friends. But if you are not undertaking
any such venture, bring Hermodorus back and return his
patrimony to him, remembering what benefits I conferred on
you out of my good will toward him when I levied smaller
taxes than you had paid, and gave you much land in addition to what you already possessed. You do not seem grateful for these benefits; otherwise you would not have banished Hermodorus, who is a friend of the king. Therefore,
send men who will argue the justice of the charge which
you lodged against Hermodorus before me so that, if he is
indeed shown to bear ill will, he might be punished, but
if you are in the wrong, I might improve your judgment and
prevent you from offending good men in the future. For
this is fitting both to your king and to yourselves.

4. Ἡράκλειτος Ἑρμοδώρῳ

Ἤδη μηκέτι τοῖς ἑαυτοῦ χαλέπαινε, Ἑρμόδωρε.
Εὐθυκλῆς ὁ Νικοφῶντος τοῦ συλήσαντος προπέρυσι τὴν
θεὸν ἀσεβείας με γέγραπται, ἄνδρα σοφίᾳ προύχοντα
5   ἀπαιδευσίᾳ νικῶν, ὡς ὅτι ἐπέγραψα τῷ βωμῷ ὃν ἐπέστησα
τὸ ἐμὸν ὄνομα, θεοποιῶν ἄνθρωπον ὄντα ἐμαυτόν. εἶτα
κριθήσομαι ὑπὸ ἀσεβοῦς ἐν ἀσεβέσι. τί οἴει; δόξω
αὐτοῖς εὐσεβὴς εἶναι ἐναντία φρονῶν οἷς αὐτοὶ περὶ
θεῶν νομίζουσιν; εἰ καὶ πεπηρωμένοι ἔκρινον ὄψιν,
10 τυφλότητα ἂν ἔλεγον τὴν ὅρασιν. ἀλλ᾽ ὦ ἀμαθεῖς
ἄνθρωποι, διδάξατε πρῶτον ἡμᾶς τί ἐστιν ὁ θεός, ἵνα
ἀσεβεῖν λέγοντες πιστεύησθε. (2) ποῦ δ᾽ ἐστὶν ὁ
θεός; ἐν τοῖς ναοῖς ἀποκεκλεισμένος; εὐσεβεῖς γε
οἳ ἐν σκότει τὸν θεὸν ἱδρύετε. ἄνθρωπος λοιδορίαν
15 ποιεῖται λίθινος εἰ λέγοιτο, θεὸς δὲ ἀληθεύεται, ὡς
τοῦτο τὸ εὐώνυμον† "ἐκ κρημνῶν γεννᾶται"; ἀπαίδευτοι,
οὐκ ἴστε ὅτι οὐκ ἔστι θεὸς χειρόκμητος, οὐδὲ ἐξ ἀρχῆς
βάσιν ἔχει, οὐδὲ ἔχει ἕνα περίβολον, ἀλλ᾽ ὅλος ὁ
κόσμος αὐτῷ ναός ἐστι ζῴοις καὶ φυτοῖς καὶ ἄστροις
20 πεποικιλμένος; Ἡρακλεῖ ἐπέγραψα τῷ Ἐφεσίῳ τὸν
βωμὸν πολιτογραφῶν ὑμῖν τὸν θεόν, οὐχ Ἡρακλείτῳ.
ἂν δὲ ὑμεῖς ἀξυνετῆτε γράμματα, οὐκ ἐμὴ ἀσέβεια τὸ
ὑμῶν ἀπαίδευτον. μανθάνετε σοφίην καὶ συνίετε. ἀλλ᾽
οὐ θέλετε, οὐδ᾽ ἐγὼ ἀναγκάζω. γηρᾶτε σὺν ἀπαιδευσίᾳ
25 χαίροντες ἰδίοις κακοῖς. (3) Ἡρακλῆς δὲ οὐκ
ἄνθρωπος ἐγεγόνει; ὡς μὲν Ὅμηρος ἐψεύσατο, καὶ
ξενοκτόνος. ἀλλὰ τί αὐτὸν ἐθεοποίησεν; ἡ ἰδία
καλοκαγαθία καὶ ἔργων τὰ γενναιότατα τοσούτους ἐκτε-
λέσαντα ἄθλους. ἐγὼ μὲν οὖν, ὦ ἄνθρωποι, οὐ καὶ
30 αὐτὸς ἀγαθός εἰμι; ἥμαρτον ἐρόμενος ὑμᾶς· καὶ γὰρ
εἰ τὰ ἐναντία ἀποκρίναισθε, ὅμως ἀγαθός εἰμι. καὶ
ἔμοιγε πολλοὶ καὶ

4. Heraclitus to Hermodorus

No longer be angry at your own circumstances, Hermodorus. Euthycles, the son of Nicophon, who only two years ago plundered the goddess, has accused me of impiety. He is prevailing in his ignorance over a man who is pre-eminent in wisdom. He maintains that I wrote my name on an altar that I erected and thus made myself, who am only a man, into a god. I shall, then, be judged by an impious man among impious men. What do you think? Shall I appear to be pious to them while I in fact think the very opposite of what they think about the gods? Indeed, if the blind were to determine what is sight, they would call seeing blindness. O you ignorant men, first teach us who God is so that when you speak of committing impiety you may be trusted. (2) Where is God? Locked up in the temples? Pious, indeed, are you who set up God in darkness! A man feels insulted if he is called a person of stone, but is a god truly spoken of when the honored name, "Out of the cliffs he was born," is applied to him? You ignorant men! Don't you know that God is not made by hands, that he has not from the beginning had a pedestal, and that he does not have a single enclosure but that the whole world, adorned with animals, plants, and stars, is his temple? I inscribed on the altar the words "Heracles the Ephesian," not "Heraclitus," thus making the god your fellow citizen. But if you do not understand your ABC's, the problem is not my impiety but rather your ignorance. Learn wisdom and understand. But you don't want to, and I won't force you. Grow old in your ignorance and delight in your own vices! (3) Was not Heracles born a man? According to Homer's lies he even murdered his guests. What, then, made him a god? His own goodness and the most noble of his works when he had concluded such great labors. Therefore, sirs, am I myself not also good? I made a mistake in even asking you, for even if you answer to the contrary, nevertheless I am good. Indeed, I have perfectly

δυσχερέστατοι ἆθλοι κατώρθωνται. νενίκηκα ἡδονάς,
νενίκηκα χρήματα, νενίκηκα φιλοτιμίαν, κατεπάλαισα
δειλίαν, κατεπάλαισα κολακείαν, οὐκ ἀντιλέγει μοι
φόβος, οὐκ ἀντιλέγει μοι μέθη, φοβεῖταί με λύπη,
5   φοβεῖταί με ὀργή. κατὰ τούτων ἀγών· καὶ αὐτὸς
ἐστεφάνωμαι ἐμαυτῷ ἐπιτάττων, οὐχ ὑπ᾽ Εὐρυσθέως.
(4) οὐ παύσεσθε σοφίαν ὑβρίζοντες καὶ ἴδια ἀμαρτή-
ματα καὶ ἴδια ἐγκλήματα ἡμῖν προστριβόμενοι; εἰ
ἐδύνασθε μετ᾽ ἐνιαυτοὺς ἐκ παλιγγενεσίας πεντακοσίους
10 ἀναβιῶναι, κατελάβετε ἂν Ἡράκλειτον ἔτι ζῶντα, ὑμῶν
δὲ οὐδ᾽ ἴχνος ὀνόματος. ἰσοχρονήσω πόλεσι καὶ χώραις
διὰ παιδείαν οὐδέποτε σιγώμενος. κἂν ἡ Ἐφεσίων
ἀναρπασθῇ πόλις καὶ οἱ βωμοὶ διαλυθῶσι πάντες, αἱ
ἀνθρώπων ψυχαὶ τῆς ἐμῆς ἔσονται χωρία μνήμης. ἄξομαι
15 καὶ αὐτὸς γυναῖκα Ἥβην, οὐ τὴν Ἡρακλέους (ἐκεῖνος
ἀεὶ ἔσται μετὰ τῆς ἑαυτοῦ), ἑτέρα δ᾽ ἡμῖν γενήσεται.
(5) πολλὰς ἀρετὴ γεννᾷ, καὶ Ὁμήρῳ ἔδωκεν ἄλλην καὶ
Ἡσιόδῳ ἄλλην, καὶ ὅσοι <ἂν> ἀγαθοὶ γένωνται, ἑνὶ
ἑκάστῳ συνοικίζει παιδείας κλέος. ἆρ᾽ οὐκ εἰμὶ
20 εὐσεβής, Εὐθύκλεις, ὃς μόνος οἶδα θεόν, σὺ δὲ καὶ
θρασὺς εἶναι οἰόμενος καὶ ἀσεβὴς τὸν μὴ ὄντα δοκῶν;
ἐὰν δὲ μὴ ἱδρυθῇ θεοῦ βωμός, οὐκ ἔστι θεός, ἐὰν δὲ
ἱδρυθῇ μὴ θεοῦ, θεὸς ἔστιν, ὥστε λίθοι θεῶν μάρτυρες;
ἔργα δεῖ μαρτυρεῖν οἷα ἡλίου· νὺξ αὐτῷ καὶ ἡμέρα
25 μαρτυροῦσιν, ὧραι αὐτῷ μάρτυρες, γῆ ὅλη καρποφοροῦσα
μάρτυς, σελήνης ὁ κύκλος, ἐκείνου ἔργον, οὐράνιος
μαρτυρία.

performed many even of the most troublesome labors. I
have overcome pleasures, I have overcome money, I have
overcome ambition, I overthrew cowardice, I overthrew
flattery, fear does not contradict me, drunkenness does
not contradict me, grief fears me, anger fears me. It is
against these that I struggle. And I crowned myself, at
my own behest, and not at that of Eurystheus. (4) Will
you not stop slandering wisdom and attributing your own
mistakes and accusations to us? Were you able to be re-
born and live five hundred years from now you would find
Heraclitus still living but no trace of your name. I
shall live as long as cities and countries, and because of
my education I shall never be silenced. Even if the city
of the Ephesians should be sacked and all its altars torn
down, the souls of men will be a place for my memory. I,
too, shall take Hebe to wife, not the wife of Heracles (he
will always be with his own) but another will be ours.
(5) Virtue begets many daughters. She gave one to Homer,
another to Hesiod, and now gives the renown of education
to every individual who is good. Am I, then, not pious,
Euthycles, I who alone know God, while you are rash and
impious, for while you think that he exists, you suppose
he is what he is not? If an altar of a god is not erected
is there then a god? Are the stones witnesses of the gods?
His works, such as those of the sun, must testify to him.
Night and day testify to him. The seasons are his witnesses. The whole earth is a fruit-bearing witness. The
cycle of the moon, his work, is his heavenly testimony.

5. Ἡράκλειτος Ἀμφιδάμαντι

Νοσοῦμεν, Ἀμφιδάμα, νοῦσον ὕδρωπα, ὥστε ὅσα ἐν
ἡμῖν, ἑκάστου τὸ κράτος νόσημα. ὑπερβολὴ θερμοῦ
πυρετός, ὑπερβολὴ ψυχροῦ παράλυσις, ὑπερβολὴ πνεύμα-
τος πνῖγος, ἡ νῦν ἐμὴ ὑγρὰ νόσος. ἀλλὰ θεῖόν τι
ψυχὴ ἡ ἁρμόζουσα αὐτά. ὑγίεια ἐστὶ τὸ πρῶτον,
ἰατρικώτατον φύσις· οὐ γὰρ εἰκάζει ἡ πρώτη ἀτεχνία
τὸ παρ᾽ αὑτήν, ἀλλὰ ὕστερον ἄλλα μιμούμενοι οἱ ἄνθρωποι ἐπιστήμας καὶ ἀγνοίας ἐκάλεσαν. ἐγὼ εἰ οἶδα κόσμου φύσιν, οἶδα καὶ ἀνθρώπου, οἶδα νόσους, οἶδα
ὑγίειαν. ἰάσομαι ἐμαυτόν, μιμήσομαι θεόν, ὃς κόσμου
ἀμετρίας ἐπανισοῖ ἡλίῳ ἐπιτάττων. (2) οὐχ ἀλώσεται
νόσῳ Ἡράκλειτος, νόσος Ἡρακλείτου ἀλώσεται γνώμῃ.
καὶ ἐν τῷ παντὶ ὑγρὰ αὐαίνεται, θερμὰ ψύχεται. οἶδεν
ἐμὴ σοφίη ὁδοὺς φύσεως, οἶδε καὶ νόσου παῦλαν. ἐὰν
δὲ φθάσαν ὑπέραντλον γένηται τὸ σῶμα, δύσεται εἰς τὸ
εἱμαρμένον. ἀλλὰ οὐ ψυχὴ δύσεται, ἀλλὰ ἀθάνατον οὖσα
χρῆμα εἰς οὐρανὸν ἀναπτήσεται μετάρσιος, δέξονται δε
με αἰθέριοι δόμοι καὶ Ἐφεσίους συκοφαντήσω. πολι-
τεύσομαι οὐκ ἐν ἀνθρώποις, ἀλλ᾽ ἐν θεοῖς, καὶ οὐχ
ἱδρύσω ἄλλων βωμούς, ἀλλ᾽ ἐμοὶ ἄλλοι, οὐδὲ ἀπειλήσει
μοι ἀσέβειαν Εὐθυκλῆς, ἀλλ᾽ ἐγὼ ἐκείνῳ χολήν. (3)
θαυμάζουσι πῶς ἀεὶ σκυθρωπὸς Ἡράκλειτος, οὐ θαυμάζουσι πῶς ἀεὶ πονηροὶ ἄνθρωποι. μικρὰ τῆς κακίας
ὑπανεῖτε, κἀγὼ τάχα μειδιάσω. καίτοι πρᾳότερος ἐν
τῇ νόσῳ νῦν ἐγενόμην, ὅτι οὐκ ἐντυγχάνω ἀνθρώποις,
ἀλλὰ μόνος νοσῶ. τάχα καὶ ψυχὴ μαντεύεται ἀπόλυσιν
ἑαυτῆς ἤδη ποτὲ ἐκ τοῦ δεσμωτηρίου τούτου, καὶ σειο-
μένου τοῦ σώματος ἐκκύπτουσα ἀναμιμνήσκεται τὰ πάτρια
χωρία, ἔνθεν κατελθοῦσα περιεβάλετο

5. Heraclitus to Amphidamas

We are sick with the dropsy, Amphidamas. The over-
powering of any natural condition in us is a disease. An
excess of heat is fever, an excess of cold is paralysis,
an excess of air is suffocation, and my present moistness
is a disease. But that which regulates our conditions,
the soul, is something divine. Health is primary, and
nature has the greatest skill in healing. The original,
unskilled way of healing does not imitate what is contrary
to nature, but later men imitated things of a different
sort, and called their ignorance knowledge. But as for
me, since I understand the nature of the world, I understand
also that of man, I understand diseases, I understand health.
I shall cure myself; I shall imitate God who, by commanding
the sun, brings the excesses of the world into balance.
(2) Heraclitus will not be overcome by disease; disease
will be overcome by the judgment of Heraclitus. Also in
the universe does water dry up and heat become cold. My
wisdom understands the ways of nature, it understands also
how to bring about the end of a disease. But if my body
should become water-logged before I heal it, it will sink
into what is fated for it. Yet my soul will not sink, but,
since it is a thing immortal, it will fly on high into
heaven. The ethereal dwellings will receive me and I
shall prosecute the Ephesians. I shall be a citizen, not
among men, but among the gods. I shall not erect altars
for others, but others will erect them for me. Euthycles
will not threaten me with a charge of impiety, but I shall
threaten him with a charge of anger. (3) They wonder why
Heraclitus is always sullen; they do not wonder why men are
always evil. If you reduced your vice a little, I would
quickly smile. And yet in my disease, I have now become
gentler, because I do not meet men, but am ill all alone.
Perhaps my soul is already prophesying its release from
this prison, and, while the body still moves, peers out
and remembers the homeland from which it had descended and
wrapped around itself a body in a perpetual state of flux

ῥέον σῶμα τεθνειὸς τοῦτο, ὃ δοκεῖ τοῖς ἄλλοις ζῆν ἐν
φλέγμασι καὶ χολῇ καὶ ἰχῶρι καὶ αἵματι, καὶ νεύροις
καὶ ὀστοῖς καὶ σάρκεσι πεπιλημένον. εἰ γὰρ μὴ τὰ
πάθη ἐσοφίζετο τὴν κόλασιν, οὐκ ἂν ἤδη πρόπαλαι κατα-
5 λιπόντες τὸ σῶμα ἐξήλθομεν ἀπ᾽ αὐτοῦ;   [ἔρρωσο.]

6. Τῷ αὐτῷ

Συνῆλθον οἱ ἰατροί, ᾽Αμφιδάμα, καὶ πάνυ προθύμως
γε ἐπὶ τὴν ἐμὴν νοῦσον, οὔτε τέχνην οὔτε φύσιν εἰδό-
τες, ἀλλὰ τὸ μὲν οὐδὲ ἐβούλοντο, τὸ δὲ ἐδόκουν, ἄμφω
10 δὲ ἠγνόουν. οὐδὲν πλέον ἢ κατεμάλαξάν μου τὴν γαστέρα ταῖς ἀφαῖς ὡς ἀσκόν. οἳ δὲ καὶ θεραπεύειν
ἤθελον, ἀλλ᾽ οὐκ ἐπέτρεψα, ἀλλὰ λόγον αὐτοὺς πρότερον
ᾔτουν τῆς νόσου, καὶ οὐκ ἔδοσαν, οὐδὲ περιεγένοντό
μου, ἀλλ᾽ ἐγὼ αὐτῶν. "πῶς ἂν οὖν" ἔφην "δύναισθε
15 αὐληταὶ τεχνῖται εἶναι ὑπὸ μὴ αὐλητοῦ ἡττημένοι;
ἐμαυτὸν ἰάσομαι, ἢ ὑμεῖς, ἐάν με διδάξητε πῶς ἐξ
ἐπομβρίας αὐχμὸν ποιητέον." (2) οἳ δὲ οὐδὲ συνέντες
τὸ ἐρώτημα ἡσύχασαν ἀπορούμενοι ἐπιστήμης ἰδίας.
ἔγνων ὅτι καὶ τοὺς ἄλλους οὐκ αὐτοί, ἀλλὰ τύχη
20 ἰάσαιτο. οὗτοι ἀσεβοῦσιν, ᾽Αμφιδάμα, καταψευδόμενοι
τεχνῶν ἃς οὐκ ἔχουσι, καὶ θεραπεύοντες ἃ μὴ ἴσασι,
καὶ ἀποκτιννύντες ἀνθρώπους, δι᾽ ὀνόματος τέχνης
ἀδικοῦντες καὶ φύσιν καὶ τέχνην. αἰσχρόν ἐστιν
ὁμολογεῖν ἄγνοιαν, αἴσχιον ἐπιστήμην οὐκ ἔχοντα.
25 τί αὐτοῖς ἡδὺ τὸ ψεύδεσθαι ἢ ἵνα δι᾽ ἀπάτης χρηματί-
σωνται; ἀμείνους ἂν ἦσαν μεταιτοῦντες· ἠλεοῦντο γοῦν
ἄν· νῦν δὲ μισοῦνται καὶ βλάπτοντες καὶ ψευδόμενοι.
εὐτελέστεραι αἱ ἄλλαι τέχναι, ταχέως ἐλέγχονται·

and change, a body dead, though appearing to others to be
alive, with phlegms, bile, juices and blood, made solid by
sinews, bones and flesh. For if our emotions had not
cleverly devised punishments would we not long ago have
left the body behind and gone out of it? Farewell.

6. To the Same

The doctors, Amphidamas, have quite eagerly assembled
to diagnose my disease although they understand neither
science nor nature. The one they did not wish to understand, the other they thought they did understand, but
they were ignorant of both. They did nothing more than
soften my belly with their kneading as though it were an
animal hide. Some also wanted to treat me, but I would
not let them, but I first demanded from them an explanation
of my disease which they could not give. They did not
prevail over me, but I prevailed over them. "How," I said,
"could you be skilled flute players if you are bested by a
non flute player? I shall heal myself or you will, if you
teach me how a drought can be made out of a downpour."
(2) Since they did not understand the question they were
silent, at a loss for the proper knowledge. I knew that
it was not they, but chance, which healed the other men.
These men are impious, Amphidamas, because they pretend to
skills they do not have and treat things they do not understand. They murder men, and in the name of science do a
grave injustice to both nature and science. It is a disgrace to admit to ignorance, but it is a greater shame to
claim knowledge when one in fact does not possess it.
What pleasure do they find in lying? Or are they lying in
order to make money through their deceit? They would be
better off begging; at least then they would be pitied.
As it is they are hated for injuring and lying. The other
skills are simpler and are examined quickly; better things

δυσελεγκτότερα τὰ κρείττω.   (3) ἐλελήθεσάν με οἱ
τοιοῦτοι ἐν τῇ πόλει.   οὐδεὶς αὐτῶν ἰατρός, ἀλλὰ
πάντες ἀπατεῶνες καὶ φένακες, σοφίσματα τέχνης
ἀργυρίου πιπράσκοντες.   Ἡρακλεόδωρον ἐμὸν θεῖον
5   οὗτοι ἀπέκτειναν καὶ μισθὸν ἔλαβον, οἳ οὐκ ἐδυνήθησαν
ἐμῆς νόσου λόγον εἰπεῖν, οὐδὲ ἐξ ἐπομβρίας πῶς ἂν
αὐχμὸς γένοιτο.   οὐκ ἴσασιν ὅτι θεὸς ἐν κόσμῳ μεγάλα
σώματα ἰατρεύει.   ἐπανισοῖ αὐτῶν τὸ ἄμετρον, τὰ
θρυπτόμενα ἐνοποιεῖ, τὰ ὀλισθήσαντα ὑποφθὰς πιέζει,
10   συνάγει τὰ σκιδνάμενα, φαιδρύνει τὰ ἀπρεπῆ, κατείργει
τὰ ληφθέντα, διώκει τὰ φεύγοντα, φωτὶ μὲν ἀναλάμπει
τὸ ζοφερόν, περατοῖ δὲ τὸ ἄπειρον, καὶ μορφὴν μὲν
ἐπιβάλλει τοῖς ἀμόρφοις, ὄψεως δὲ ἀναπίμπλησι τὰ
ἀναίσθητα.   (4) διὰ πάσης γὰρ ἔρχεται τῆς οὐσίας
15   πλάττων, ἀρμοζόμενος, διαλύων, πηγνύς, χέων.   τὸ
ξηρὸν εἰς ὑγρὸν τήκει καὶ εἰς λύσιν αὐτὸ καθίστησι,
καὶ λιβάδας μὲν ἐκθυμιᾷ, παχύνει δὲ χαλασθέντα τὸν
ἀέρα, καὶ συνεχῶς τὰ μὲν ἄνωθεν διώκει, τὰ δὲ κάτωθεν
ἱδρύει.   ταῦτα κάμνοντος κόσμου θεραπεία.   τοῦτον ἐγὼ
20   μιμήσομαι ἐν ἐμαυτῷ, τοῖς δ' ἄλλοις χαίρειν λέγω.

are more difficult to examine. (3) Such men have escaped
my notice in the city. None of them is a doctor but all
of them are frauds and quacks who sell the skills of the
profession for money. These men killed my uncle Heracle-
odorus and pocketed a reward; they were unable to explain
my disease or how a drought could come from a downpour.
They do not know that God heals the larger bodies in the
world. He brings their excess into balance, he unifies
things that are shattered, hastens to compress things that
have slipped out of place, he brings together things that
are dispersed, he cleanses things that are unseemly, he
shuts in things that have been carried off, he pursues
things that are fleeing, he illuminates the dark with
light and limits the infinite, he gives form to the form-
less things that lack perception with sight. (4) He per-
vades all existence, moulding, harmonizing, dissolving,
solidifying, liquefying. He melts the dry land into something wet and dissolves it. He turns streams into vapor
and thickens the slackened air. He constantly sets in
motion the things on high, settles those below. These
things are medical treatment for an ill world. I shall
imitate this in myself and say farewell to the others.

7. Ἑρμοδώρῳ

Πυνθάνομαι Ἐφεσίους μέλλειν εἰσηγεῖσθαι νόμον
κατ' ἐμοῦ ἀνομώτατον· οὐδεὶς γὰρ νόμος ἐφ' ἐνός,
ἀλλὰ κρίσις. οὐκ ἴσασιν Ἐφέσιοι ὅτι ἕτερος δικαστὴς
5 νομοθέτου. καὶ τόδε ἄμεινον, ἐπεὶ ἀπαθέστερον πρὸς
ἄδηλον τὸν μέλλοντα πράξειν. ὁ δικάζων δὲ ὁρᾷ τὸν
κρινόμενον, ᾧ συνάπτεται τὸ πάθος. ἴσασί με, Ἑρμόδωρε, συντεχνιτεύσαντά σοι τοὺς νόμους, κἀμὲ ἐλάσαι
βούλονται, ἀλλ' οὐ πρότερόν γε ἢ ἐλέγξαι αὐτούς, ὅτι
10 ἄδικα ἐγνώκασι. τὸν μὴ γελῶντα καὶ πάντα μισανθρω-
ποῦντα πρὸ ἡλίου δύνοντος ἐξιέναι τῆς πόλεως, τοῦτο
νομοθετεῖν βουλεύονται, οὐδεὶς δ' ἐστὶν ὁ μὴ γελῶν,
Ἑρμόδωρε, ἢ Ἡράκλειτος, ὥστε με ἐλαύνουσιν. (2) ὦ
ἄνθρωποι, οὐ θέλετε μαθεῖν, διὰ τί ἀεὶ ἀγελαστῶ; οὐ
15 μισῶν ἀνθρώπους, ἀλλὰ κακίαν αὐτῶν. οὕτω γράψατε τὸν
νόμον, "Εἴ τις μισεῖ κακίαν, ἐξίτω τῆς πόλεως," καὶ
πρῶτος ἔξειμι. φυγαδευθήσομαι οὐ πατρίδος ἀλλὰ
πονηρίας ἄσμενος. μεταγράψατε τὸ διάταγμα, εἰ δὲ
ὁμολογεῖτε Ἐφεσίους κακίαν εἶναι καὶ ὑμᾶς μισῶ.
20 πῶς οὐκ ἂν ἐγὼ δικαιότερον νομοθέτης εἴην τοὺς ποιή-
σαντας Ἡράκλειτον διὰ πονηρίαν ἀγέλαστον ἐξιέναι τοῦ
ζῆν, μᾶλλον δὲ μυρίαις ζημιοῦσθαι, εἰ πλέον ἀνιᾶσθε
ἀργυρίῳ κολαζόμενοι; τοῦτο ὑμῶν ἐστι φυγή, τοῦτο
θάνατος. (3) ἠδικήκατέ με ἀφελόμενοι ὃ θεὸς ἔδωκε
25 καὶ φυγαδεύετέ με ἀδίκως. ἢ τοῦτο ὑμᾶς πρῶτον
ἀγαπήσω, ὅτι μου τὸ ἥμερον ἐξεκόψατε; καὶ οὐ
παύεσθε ἐπαγωνιζόμενοι νόμοις καὶ φυγαδείαις; ἐν
γὰρ τῇ πόλει μένων οὐ πεφυγάδευμαι ἀφ' ὑμῶν; τίνι
συμμοιχεύω, τίνι συμμιαιφονῶ, τίνι συμμεθύω, τίνι
30 συμφθείρομαι; οὐ φθείρω, οὐκ ἀδικῶ οὐδένα τῶν
ἁπάντων, μόνος εἰμὶ ἐν τῇ πόλει. ἐρημίαν αὐτὴν

7. To Hermodorus

I hear that the Ephesians are about to introduce a
most illegal law against me; for no law is directed against
an individual--only a legal judgment is. The Ephesians do
not know that a judge is different from a legislator. And
this is better, since he would be more dispassionate in
dealing with some as yet unknown person who would act in
the future. The judge, however, sees the person who is
being judged, and his feelings are linked up with him.
They know, Hermodorus, that I helped you draft the laws,
and they want to drive me out, but they will not before I
have refuted them for having decreed unjustly that "The
man who does not laugh, and every misanthrope, must leave
the city before sundown." They want to make this a law.
But there is no one who does not laugh, Hermodorus, except
Heraclitus; consequently, they can drive me away. (2) O
you men, don't you want to learn why I never laugh? It is
not because I hate men but because I hate their wickedness.
Write your law in this way: "If anyone hates wickedness,
he must leave the city" and I shall be the first to leave.
I shall gladly be banished, not from my homeland, but from
evil. Correct the edict! But if you admit that Ephesians
are "wickedness," then I do hate you. Would I not more
justly decree: "Those who have made Heraclitus melancholy
by their wickedness must depart this life," or rather
"they are to be fined ten thousand drachmas," since you
suffer more when hit in the purse? This is your exile,
this your death. (3) You have wronged me by depriving me
of what God gave, and you banish me unjustly. Shall I
love you mainly for this, that you have cut out my mild-
ness and that you do not cease attacking me with laws and
banishments? While still in the city have I not been
exiled from you? With whom do I commit adultery? With
whom am I a partner in murder? With whom do I get drunk?
Whose partner in crime am I? I do not corrupt, I do not
wrong anyone at all, I am alone in the city. You have

πεποιήκατε διὰ κακίας. ἡ ἀγορὰ ὑμῶν Ἡράκλειτον
ἀγαθὸν ποιεῖ; οὔκ, ἀλλὰ Ἡράκλειτος ὑμᾶς, πόλιν.
ἀλλ' οὐκ ἐθέλετε. (4) ἐγὼ μὲν βούλομαι καὶ νόμος
εἰμὶ ἄλλων, εἷς <δ'> ὢν οὐκ ἀρκῶ πόλιν κολάζειν.
5   θαυμάζετε εἰ μηδέπω γελῶ, ἐγὼ δὲ τοὺς γελῶντας ὅτι
ἀδικοῦντες χαίρουσι, σκυθρωπάζειν δέον οὐ δικαιοπρα-
γοῦντας. δότε μοι καιρὸν γέλωτος ἐν εἰρήνῃ, ὥστε μὴ
ἐπὶ τὰ δικαστήρια στρατεύεσθαι ἐν ταῖς γλώτταις
ἔχοντες τὰ ὅπλα, ἀπεστερηκότες χρήματα, γυναῖκας
10 φθείραντες, φίλους φαρμακεύσαντες, ἱεροσυλήσαντες,
προαγωγεύσαντες, ὅρκοις ὀραθέντες ἄπιστοι, τυμπανί-
σαντες, ἄλλος ἄλλου πλήρης κακοῦ. (5) ταῦτα γελάσω
ὁρῶν ἀνθρώπους ποιοῦντας <ἢ> ἐσθῆτα καὶ γένεια καὶ
κεφαλῆς πόνους ἀτημελήτους ἢ γυναῖκα φαρμάκοις ἐπει-
15 λημμένην τέκνου ἢ μειράκια τῆς οὐσίας ἐκβεβρωμένα ἢ
πολίτην γαμετῆς ἀφῃρημένον ἢ κόρην βίᾳ διαπαρθενευ-
θεῖσαν ἐν παννυχίσιν ἢ ἑταίραν οὔπω γυναῖκα γυναικῶν
ἔχουσαν ἤδη πάθη ἢ διὰ ἀσέλγειαν νεανίσκον ἕνα πόλεως
ἐραστὴν ὅλης ἢ τὰς τῶν ἐλαιῶν φθορὰς ἐν μύροις ἢ τοὺς
20 ἐν συνδείπνοις γινομένους διὰ δακτύλων πλείονας ἢ τὰς
δι' ἐδεσμάτων πολυτελείας καὶ γαστέρας ῥεούσας, ἢ
τοὺς ἐπὶ σκηνῆς ἀγωνοθετουμένους δήμους τὰ μεγάλα
δίκαια; ἀφήσει δέ μου τὴν ὄψιν ἀρετὴ διαχυθῆναι
ὑστέρα πονηρίας τεταγμένη; (6) ἢ τοὺς ἀληθινοὺς
25 ὑμῶν πολέμους γελάσω, ὅτε προφάσεις ἀδικημάτων ποιη-
σάμενοι καταμιαιφονεῖσθε δύστηνοι ἐξ ἀνθρώπων θηρία
γεγονότες, αὐλοῖς καὶ σάλπιγξι διὰ μουσικῆς εἰς
ἄμουσα πάθη παροξυνόμενοι, σίδηρος δὲ ἀπότρων καὶ
γεωργίας δικαιότερον ὄργανον σφαγῆς καὶ θανάτων
30 ηὐτρέπισται, ὑβρίζεται δὲ δι' ὑμῶν θεός, Ἀθηνᾶ
πολεμίστρια καὶ Ἄρης ἐνυάλιος καλούμενος, φάλαγγας
δὲ ἀντιστήσαντες ἄνθρωποι κατὰ

made it a desert by your wickedness. Does your marketplace make Heraclitus a good man? No, but Heraclitus can
make you, a city, good. But you do not want that. (4) I,
however, do, and I am a law for others, but being only one
person, I am unable to punish a city. You are amazed that
I never laugh, but I am amazed at those who do laugh, because they delight in wrong-doing while they should be
sullen for not acting justly. Give me an occasion for
laughing in a time of peace when you do not wage war in
court by using your tongues as weapons, and that after you
have committed fraud, seduced women, poisoned friends,
robbed temples, prostituted, been found breaking oaths,
beaten your ritual drums, each one of you filled with a
different evil. (5) Should I laugh when I see men doing
these things, or see them neglect their clothes and beards
and hair, or a woman who attacks her child with drugs, or
youths who have devoured their substance, or a citizen deprived of his wife, or a young woman losing her virginity
by force during nocturnal festivals, or a courtesan who is
not yet a wife but who already has all the misfortunes of
a wife, or a single young man who through licentiousness
is the lover of an entire city, or the ruining of olives
in perfumes, or men at banquets who increase their size
through their fingers, or the extravagance in foods and
diarrhetic bellies, or the important lawsuits for the common people judged on the stage? Will virtue, when ranked
after wickedness, make my face light up? (6) Shall I
laugh at your real wars when you defile yourselves with
bloodshed on the pretext that you are avenging unjust actions? Shall I laugh, you wretched of men, when you have
become beasts, arousing yourselves to gross passions
through the music of flutes and trumpets? Shall I laugh
when an instrument more fitting for ploughing and farming
has been readied for slaughter and death, when your goddess
Athena the warrior, as well as Ares who is called the War-
like, are insulted by you? Shall I laugh when you have
drawn up phalanxes, and, men against men, pray for each

ἀνθρώπων ἀλλήλων σφαγὰς εὔχεσθε, ὡς λειποτάκτας τοὺς
μὴ μιαιφονοῦντας τιμωρούμενοι καὶ ὡς ἀπιστέας τοὺς
ἐμπλεονάσαντας αἵματι τιμῶντες; (7) λέοντες δ' οὐχ
ὁπλίζονται κατ' ἀλλήλων, οὐδὲ ξίφη ἀναλαμβάνουσιν αἱ
5 ἵπποι, οὐδὲ τεθωρακισμένον <ἂν> ἴδοις ἀετὸν ἐπ' ἀετῷ.
οὐδὲν ἄλλο μάχης ἔχει ὄργανον, ἀλλ' ἑκάστῳ τὰ μέρη
καὶ ὅπλα· τοῖς μὲν κέρατα τὰ ὅπλα, τοῖς δὲ ῥύγχη,
τοῖς δὲ πτερά, τοῖς δὲ τάχος, ἄλλοις μέγεθος, ἄλλοις
ὀλιγότης, οἷς δὲ πάχος, οἷς δὲ νῆξις, πολλοῖς δὲ
10 πνεῦμα. οὐδὲν ξίφος ἄλογα ποιεῖ ζῷα χαίρειν
[πολλοῖς] δρῶντα φυλαττόμενον ἐν αὐτοῖς φύσεως νόμον,
ἀλλ' οὐκ ἐν ἀνθρώποις.† μᾶλλον δὲ τοῦτο πλέον ἂν εἴη
παράβασις, ἐν κρείττοσι τὸ ἀβέβαιον.† (8) τέλος δὲ
πολέμων τί ὑμῖν εὐκτέον ἄρα; ἢ δι' ἐκεῖνο παύσετέ
15 με κατηφείας; πόθεν; οὐχὶ δὲ πλέον ὁμοφύλων σφῶν;
καὶ δενδροτομουμένη <γῆ> καὶ ἀναρπαζομένη πόλις καὶ
γῆρας προπηλακιζόμενον καὶ γυναῖκες ἀπαγόμεναι καὶ
τέκνα ἐξ ἀγκαλῶν ἀποσπώμενα καὶ θάλαμοι διαφθειρόμενοι
καὶ παρθένοι παλλακευόμεναι καὶ μειράκια θηλυνόμενα
20 καὶ ἐλεύθεροι σιδηροδετούμενοι καὶ ναοὶ θεῶν κατασπώ-
μενοι καὶ ἡρῷα δαιμόνων ἀνορυττόμενα καὶ παιᾶνες
ἀνοσίων ἔργων καὶ χαριστήρια θεοῖς ἀδικίας; (9) ταῦτα
ἀγελαστῶ. ἐν εἰρήνῃ πολεμεῖτε διὰ λόγων, ἐν πολέμῳ
πολιτεύεσθε διὰ σιδήρου· ἁρπάζετε τὸ δίκαιον ἐν ξίφε-
25 σιν. Ἑρμόδωρος ἐλαύνεται νόμους γράφων, Ἡράκλειτος
ἐλαύνεται ἀσεβείας. αἱ πόλεις ἔρημοι καλοκαγαθίας,
αἱ ἐρημίαι πρὸς τὸ ἀδικεῖν ὄχλοι. τείχη ἔστηκεν
ἀνθρώπων σύμβολα πονηρίας ἀποκλείοντα τὴν βίαν ὑμῶν,
οἰκίαι περιβέβληνται πᾶσιν ἕτερα τείχη πλημμελείας·
30 οἱ ἔνδον πολέμιοι ἀλλὰ πολῖται, οἱ ἐκτὸς πολέμιοι
ἀλλὰ ξένοι. πάντες ἐχθροί, οὐδένες φίλοι. (10) δύναμαι γελάσαι ἐχθροὺς ὁρῶν τοσούτους; τὸν ἀλλότριον
πλοῦτον ἴδιον οἴεσθε, τὰς ἀλλοτρίας γυναῖκας ἰδίας

others' slaughter, and punish as deserters men who do not
murder, and honor as the bravest men who are stained with
blood?   (7) Lions do not arm themselves against each other,
nor do mares take up swords, nor could you see an eagle
armed with a breastplate against another eagle.   They have
no other instrument of battle, but each one's members are
also his weapons.   To some their horns are weapons, to
others beaks, to others wings, to others speed; to some
size, to others smallness; to some stoutness, to some the
ability to swim, to many their breath.   No sword can make
unreasoning animals rejoice, for they see that the law of
nature is preserved in themselves and not in men.   Rather,
and this would be more of a transgression, they see that
there is instability in the superior creatures.   (8) Should
one, then, pray that there be an end to your wars?   Would
you thereby put an end to my dejection?   How could you?
Does it not involve more than your own kinsmen?   A land is
denuded of trees, is sacked, old age is treated with contempt, women are seduced, children are snatched from their
arms, bedrooms are corrupted, virgins are made concubines,
young men become effeminate, free men are clapped into
irons, temples of the gods are pulled to the ground,
shrines of the heroes are dug up, paeans are offered for
profane deeds, and thank offerings are made to the gods
for injustice.   (9) I do not laugh at these things.   In
peacetime you make war with words; during war you govern
by iron.   You snatch away justice with swords.   Hermodorus
is driven away for writing laws, Heraclitus is driven away
for impiety.   The cities are empty of nobility, the deserts
are crowded because injustice is done.   The walls, symbols
of men's wickedness, stand, shutting out your violence.
Houses are enclosed at every point by inferior walls
against transgression.   Those within are hostile, despite
being citizens; those without are hostile despite being
strangers.   All are enemies; none are friends.   (10) Can I
laugh when I see so many enemies?   You consider another's
wealth your own, other men's wives your own, you enslave

νομίζετε, τοὺς ἐλευθέρους ἀνδραποδίζετε, τὰ ζῶντα
κατεσθίετε, τοὺς νόμους παραβαίνετε, παρανομίας
νομοθετεῖτε, πάντα βιάζεσθε ἃ μὴ πεφύκατε. τὰ
μάλιστα δοκοῦντα δικαιοσύνης εἶναι σύμβολα, οἱ νόμοι,
5   ἀδικίας εἰσὶ τεκμήριον. εἰ γὰρ μὴ ἦσαν, ἀνέδην ἂν
ἐπονηρεύεσθε· νῦν δ' εἴ τι καὶ μικρὸν ἐπιστομίζεσθε
φόβῳ κολάσεως, κατέχεσθε εἰς πᾶσαν ἀδικίαν.

8. Τῷ αὐτῷ

Δῆλου μοι, Ἑρμόδωρε, πότε ἀπαίρειν κέκρικας εἰς
10   Ἰταλίαν. δέξαιντό σε οἱ ἐκείνης τῆς χώρας θεοὶ καὶ
δαίμονες ἡδέως. ὄναρ ἐδόκουν τοῖς σοῖς νόμοις τὰ
παρὰ πάσης τῆς οἰκουμένης διαδήματα προσιέναι καὶ
κατὰ τὸ ἔθος τὸ Περσῶν ἐγκλώμενα ἐπὶ στόμα προσκυνεῖν
αὐτούς, οἳ δὲ σεμνῶς πάνυ καθειστήκεσαν. προσκυνή-
15   σουσί σε Ἐφέσιοι μηκέτι ὄντα, ὅταν οἱ σοὶ νόμοι
πᾶσιν ἐπιτάττωσι, καὶ τότε χρήσονται αὐτοῖς ἀναγκαζό-
μενοι. θεὸς γὰρ ἀφείλετο ἐκείνους ἡγεμονίαν καὶ
ἑαυτοὺς ἐνόμισαν ἀξίους δουλεύειν. (2) τοῦτο μεμάθη-
κα καὶ ἐκ πατέρων. ὅλη Ἀσία κτῆμα ἐγένετο βασιλέως
20   καὶ πάντες Ἐφέσιοι λάφυρον. ἀήθεις εἰσὶν ἐλευθερίας
ἀληθοῦς, τοῦ ἄρχειν. καὶ νῦν ὡς εἰκὸς ὑπακούσονται
κελευόμενοι, ἢ μὴ πεισθέντες οἰμώξονται. καὶ μέμφονται θεοὺς ἄνθρωποι ὅτι αὐτοὺς οὐ πλουτίζουσιν ἀγαθά,
οὐ μέμφονται ἴδιον ἦθος ἀφροσύνης. τυφλῶν ἐστι μὴ
25   δέξασθαι ἃ δίδωσι χρηστὰ δαίμων. Σίβυλλα ἐν πολλοῖς
καὶ τοῦτο ἐφράσθη "ἥξειν σοφὸν Ἰταλίησιν ἐξ Ἰάδος
χώρης." εἶδέ σε πρὸ τοσούτου αἰῶνος, Ἑρμόδωρε, ἡ
Σίβυλλα ἐκείνη καὶ τότε ἦσθα, Ἐφέσιοι δὲ οὐδὲ νῦν

free men, you consume living things, you transgress the
laws, you enact illegal laws, you do by force what does
not come to you naturally. What appear to be the greatest
symbols of justice, the laws, are evidence of injustice.
For had they not existed, you would have acted wickedly
without restraint. But now, since you are curbed, even if
only a little, by the fear of punishment, restrain yourself from all injustice.

8. To the Same

Let me know, Hermodorus, when you have planned to
depart for Italy. May the gods and spirits of that land
receive you well. In a dream that I have been having, the
crowns from all over the world approach your laws, and,
according to the custom of the Persians, prostrate themselves and pay homage to them, while the laws, for their
part, stand with great dignity. The Ephesians will pay
homage to you when you are dead, when your laws govern all
men; then they will be forced to live by them. For God
has deprived them of their supremacy and they have considered it proper for themselves to serve as slaves. (2)
I learned this already from our fathers. The whole of
Asia became the King's possession and all the Ephesians
his spoils. They are unaccustomed to true freedom, namely
to ruling. And now, in all likelihood, they will obey
when they are ordered, or, if they do not submit, they
will wail. Men also blame the gods because they do not
enrich them with good things; but they do not blame their
own character for its foolishness. It is characteristic
of the blind not to accept what benefits the spirit gives.
The Sibyl, among many others, has also made this observation: "A wise man will come to Italy from the land of
Ionia." That Sibyl saw you so long ago, Hermodorus, and
even then you existed, but the Ephesians do not even now

βούλονται ὁρᾶν ὃν διὰ θεοφορουμένης γυναικὸς ἀλήθεια
ἔβλεπε. (3) σοφὸς μεμαρτύρησαι, Ἑρμόδωρε, Ἐφέσιοι
δὲ ἀντιλέγουσι θεοῦ μαρτυρίᾳ. ἀποτίσονται ἑαυτῶν
ὕβριν καὶ νῦν ἀποτίνυνται γνώμης ἀναπιμπλάντες σφᾶς
5   κακῆς· οὐκ ἀφαιρούμενος πλοῦτον κολάζει θεός, ἀλλὰ
καὶ μᾶλλον δίδωσι πονηροῖς, ἵν' ἔχοντες δι' ὧν ἁμαρ-
τάνουσιν ἐλέγχωνται καὶ περιουσιάζοντες σκηνοβατῶσιν
αὐτῶν τὴν μοχθηρίαν· ἡ δ' ἀπορία παρακάλυμμά ἐστιν.
μὴ ἐπιλίποι ὑμᾶς τύχη, ἵνα ὀνειδίζησθε πονηρευόμενοι.
10   οὗτοι μὲν χαιρόντων, σὺ δέ μοι δήλου τὸν καιρὸν
τῆς ἐξόδου. πάντως ἐντυχεῖν σοι βούλομαι καὶ περί τε
ἄλλων πάνυ συχνῶν καὶ περὶ αὐτῶν <τῶν> νόμων βραχέα
εἰπεῖν. (4) ἔγραφον δ' ἂν αὐτά, εἰ μὴ περὶ παντὸς
ἐποιούμην ἀπόρρητα μεῖναι. οὐδὲν δὲ οὕτω σιωπᾶται
15 ὡς ἑνὶ λαλῶν εἷς, καὶ ἔτι μᾶλλον Ἡράκλειτος Ἑρμο-
δώρῳ. πολλοὶ οὐ διαφέρουσι κεραμίων σαθρῶν, ὡς μηδὲν
στέγειν δύνασθαι, ἀλλ' ὑπὸ γλωσσαλγίας διαρρεῖν.
Ἀθηναῖοι ὄντες αὐτόχθονες ἔγνωσαν φύσιν ἀνθρώπων,
ὅτι γενόμενοι ἐκ γῆς ἔσθ' ὅτε διερρωγότα ἔχουσι νοῦν.
20 τούτους ἐπαίδευσαν φυλακὴν ἀπορρήτων διὰ μυστηρίων,
ἵν' ὡς φόβῳ σιγῶσιν, ἀλλ' οὐ χρίσει, καὶ μηκέτι
χαλεπὸν ᾖ τὸ μελῆσαν τῇ ψυχῇ σιωπᾶν.

want to see him whom Truth saw through the inspired woman.
(3) You have been attested as wise Hermodorus, but the
Ephesians have contradicted the testimony of God. They
will pay for their insolence and even now they are paying,
since they fill themselves with a wicked judgment. God
punishes, not by taking away wealth, but rather by giving
it to the wicked so that, since they have the means to
err, they might be convicted, and by abounding in wealth,
they might expose their own wickedness. But poverty is
only a disguise. May fortune never forsake you so that
you may be reproached for living wickedly.

Have done with them! But as for you, let me know the
time of your departure. I especially want to meet you and
briefly discuss many other matters as well as the laws
themselves. (4) I would write these things, except that
I must, above all, keep them secret. Nothing preserves
secrecy better than when one person speaks to another, and
all the more when Heraclitus speaks to Hermodorus. Many
people are not different from cracked vessels, since they
cannot retain anything, but let everything leak out
through their endless talking. Athenians, since they were
sprung from the land, know human nature: that men, having
come from the earth, sometimes have a cracked mind. They
educated those men to guard the secrets by means of mysteries, so that they might be silent out of fear, even if
they are not silent out of judgment, and that it might no
longer be difficult to the soul to practice silence.

9. Τῷ αὐτῷ

Ἄχρι τίνος, Ἑρμόδωρε, κακοὶ ἔσονται ἄνθρωποι
καὶ οὐκέτι εἷς ἕκαστος ἰδίᾳ, ἀλλὰ καὶ κοινῇ πόλεις
ὅλαι; Ἐφέσιοί σε ἀνδρῶν ὄντα ἄριστον ἐλαύνουσιν.
5   ἀντὶ τίνος ἢ ὅτι νόμους γράφεις τοῖς ἀπελευθέροις
ἰσοπολιτείας καὶ τοῖς τούτων τέκνοις ἰσοτιμίας;
καίτοιγε ὁ μὲν γνήσιος πολίτης οὐ κριθεὶς ἀγαθὸς
γίνεται, ἀλλὰ γεννηθεὶς ἀναγκάζεται, καὶ οὐδ᾽ ἢν
ἀναγκασθῇ, πολλάκις ἀγαθὸς ἔμεινεν, οἱ δὲ δοικιμασ-
10   θέντες ἀξιοῦνται τοῦ πολιτεύματος μαρτυρήσαντες βίῳ
τὸ ἰσότιμον, πόσῳ κρείττους οἱ δι᾽ ἀρετὴν ἐγγραφό-
μενοι; (2) Λακεδαιμόνιοι δὲ μετ᾽ ἄλλων καὶ τοῦτο
ἀγαθοί, οὐ γράμμασιν ἀποδεικνύντες Σπαρτιάτας ἀλλ᾽
ἀγωγῇ· κἂν ἐλθών τις Σκύθης ἢ Τριβαλλὸς ἢ Παφλαγὼν ἢ
15   μηδὲν ἔχων ὄνομα χώρας ὑποστῇ τὴν Λυκούργειον σκλη-
ραγωγίαν, Λάκων ἐστίν, ὥστε ἕκαστος τῶν πολιτευθέντων
ἐν ἑαυτῷ φέρων τὴν πατρίδα ἔρχεται, πάσης δὲ πόλεως
φυγαδεύει κακία, κἂν ἐν μέσαις ταῖς στήλαις τις οἰκῇ.
οὐδὲ Ἐφέσιον εἶναί τινα πείθομαι, εἰ μὴ ὡς κύνα
20   Ἐφέσιον ἢ βοῦν· ἀνὴρ δὲ Ἐφέσιος, εἰ ἀγαθός, κόσμου
πολίτης. τοῦτο γὰρ κοινὸν πάντων ἐστὶ χωρίον, ἐν
ᾧ νόμος ἐστὶν οὐ γράμμα ἀλλὰ θεός, καὶ ὁ παραβαίνων
ἃ <μὴ> χρὴ ἀσεβήσει· μᾶλλον δὲ οὐδὲ παραβήσεται, εἰ
παραβὰς οὐ λήσεται. (3) πολλαὶ δίκης Ἐρινύες,
25   ἁμαρτημάτων φύλακες. Ἡσίοδος ἐψεύσατο τρεῖς μυριά-
δας εἰπών· ὀλίγαι εἰσίν, οὐκ

9. To the Same

How long, Hermodorus, will men be wicked? Indeed,
it is no longer a matter of each individual being wicked
in his private life, but even of entire cities in their
public life. The Ephesians run you, the most noble of
men, out of town. For what reason, other than that you
wrote civil rights legislation for freedmen and equal
rights laws for their children? And yet, the person of
legitimate birth does not become a citizen only after he
has been judged virtuous, but he is compelled by the simple fact of his birth to be one. Even if he were not compelled, he might frequently remain virtuous! Those, however, who have been tested, are deemed worthy of citizen-
ship, because they have given evidence of their equal rights
by their quality of life. How much superior are those who
are enrolled as citizens because of their virtue! (2) The
Lacedaemonians, as in other matters, are also discrimi-
nating in this, that they proclaim people to be Spartans,
not on the basis of written records, but on the basis of
their conduct. If a Scythian or Triballian or Paphlagonian
or someone bearing the name of no country at all comes and
submits to the hardy training of Lycurgus, he is a Lacon-
ian. So, each person who has been made a citizen goes
bearing his fatherland in himself. Vice, however, lives
in exile from every city even if one should live between
the pillars in the marketplace. I am persuaded that no-
body is an Ephesian except in the sense that a dog or a
cow is an Ephesian. An Ephesian man, if he is good, is a
citizen of the world. For this is the common country of
all men, in which the law is not something written, but is
God, and the one who transgresses against what is not fitting is impious. But, in fact, no one will transgress if
he will not go unnoticed when he has transgressed. (3)
Many are the Furies of justice, guardians against errors.
Hesiod lied when he said that there are thirty thousand of
them. That is too few, and not enough for the wickedness

ἀρκοῦσι κακίᾳ κόσμου· πολὺ ἐστὶ πονηρία. ἐμοὶ δὲ
πολῖται θεοί, θεοῖς ξυνοικῶν δι' ἀρετῆς οἶδα ἥλιον
ὁπόσος ἐστί, πονηροὶ δὲ οὔδ' ὅτι εἰσίν. ἢ αἰσχύνον-
ται Ἐφέσιοι δούλους ἀγαθοὺς εἶναι; εἰκότως· αὐτοὶ
5   γὰρ κακοὶ ἐλεύθεροι, οἳ οὐκ ἐλευθέροις πάθεσιν
εἴκουσι, παυσάσθωσαν οἷοί εἰσι, καὶ ἀγαπήσουσι πάντας
ἰσότητι ἀρετῆς. τί δὲ οἴεσθε, ὦ ἄνθρωποι, εἰ θεὸς
οὐ πεποιηκὼς κύνας οὐδὲ πρόβατα δούλους, οὐδὲ ὄνους
οὐδὲ ἵππους οὐδὲ ὀρεῖς, ἀνθρώπους ἐποίησε;   (4) καὶ
10   ὅτι κρείττονας ἐκάκωσε δουλεία, οὐκ αἰσχύνεσθε καὶ
τοῦτο τῆς ὑμετέρας ἀδικίας καὶ ἔργον καὶ ὄνομα;
πόσῳ κρείσσονες Ἐφεσίων λύκοι καὶ λέοντες. οὐκ
ἐξανδραποδίζονται ἀλλήλους, οὐδὲ ἐπρίατο ἀετὸς ἀετόν,
οὐδὲ λέων λέοντι οἰνοχοεῖ, οὐδὲ ἐξέτεμε κύων κύνα,
15   ὡς ὑμεῖς τὸν τῆς θεοῦ Μεγάβυζον, φοβούμενοι τῇ
παρθενίᾳ αὐτῆς [μὴ] ἄνδρα ἱερᾶσθαι. ἢ πῶς ἀσεβήσαν-
τες εἰς φύσιν εὐσεβεῖτε εἰς ξόανον; ἵνα θεοῖς κατα-
ρᾶται πρῶτον ὁ ἱερεὺς ἀφῃρημένος τὸν ἄνδρα; κατέ-
γνωτε καὶ τῆς θεοῦ ἀκρασίαν, εἰ φοβεῖσθε ὑπ' ἀνδρὸς
20   αὐτὴν θεραπεύεσθαι. (5) "μὴ συγκαθιζέτω μοι δοῦλος
μηδὲ συνδειπνείτω" Ἐφέσιοι λέγουσιν, ἐγὼ δὲ ἐρῶ
δικαιοτέραν φωνήν· συγκαθιζέτω μοι ἀγαθὸς καὶ συνδειπνείτω μοι, μᾶλλον δὲ προκαθιζέτω, προτιμηθήτω·
οὐ γὰρ τύχῃ τὸ ἰσούμενον, ἀλλ' ἀρετή. τί ὑμᾶς
25   ἀδικεῖ Ἑρμόδωρος, Ἐφεσίους ὑπομιμνήσκων πάντας
ἀνθρώπους εἶναι καὶ μηδένα μεγαλαυχεῖν τύχῃ ὑπὲρ
φύσιν; μόνη πονηρία δουλαγωγεῖ, μόνη ἐλευθεροῖ
ἀρετή, ἀνθρώπων δὲ οὐδείς. κἂν ἐπιτάττητε ἄλλοις
διὰ τύχην ἀγαθοῖς οὖσιν, αὐτοὶ δοῦλοί ἐστε δι' ἐπι-
30   θυμίαν, κελευόμενοι ὑπὸ τῶν ἑαυτῶν δεσποτῶν. (6) οὐ
φοβεῖσθε δέ, ὦ ἄνθρωποι, πόλεως ὀλιγανδρίαν; τί οὖν;
ἔπηλυ εἰσάξετε πλῆθος, δέον τοὺς ὑφ' ὑμῶν ἀχθέντας
καὶ τραφέντας

of the world, for its evil is great. But as for me, my
fellow-citizens are the gods. By dwelling with the gods
through virtue I know how great the sun is, but the wicked
do not even know that they exist. Or are the Ephesians
ashamed that slaves are virtuous? They probably are! For
they are wicked freemen, who yield to servile passions.
Let them stop being the kind of persons they are, and they
will love all men with an equal share in virtue. What do
you think, you men? If God did not make dogs or sheep
slaves, nor asses nor horses nor mules, did he then make
men slaves? (4) And given the fact that slavery has
spoiled superior creatures, are you not ashamed of this,
too, that the deed as well as its name are the results of
your injustice? How much superior are the wolves and
lions to the Ephesians? They do not reduce one another to
slavery, nor does one eagle buy another eagle, nor does
one lion pour wine for another lion, nor does one dog cas-
trate another dog, as you did the Megabazus of the goddess,
afraid lest a man as a priest service her virginity! Or
how can you act piously toward a statue, when you have
acted impiously against nature? Is it that he might curse
the gods that the priest is first deprived of his manhood?
You have, in addition, charged the goddess with licentiousness, since you are afraid of her being served by a man.
(5) The Ephesians say "Let not a slave sit with me nor
dine with me." But I shall pronounce a more just dictum:
"Let a good man sit with me and dine with me," rather, let
him take the chief seat, let him receive the greater honor,
for it is not fortune that makes men equal, but virtue.
How does Hermodorus treat you unjustly when he reminds the
Ephesians that they are all but men, and that no one
should boast in the fortune above nature? Evil alone makes
one a slave; virtue alone frees, but no man can do either.
Even if you happen to command others who are virtuous, you
yourselves are slaves on account of your desire, and you
are ordered around by your own masters. (6) Do you men
not fear the depopulation of the city? What then? Will
you import a swarm of foreigners rather than those you

καὶ ἀπειλαῖς καὶ κολάσεσι καὶ φόβοις ἀγαθοὺς γεγονό-
τας; ἔσονται κρείττους, Ἑρμόδωρε, οἱ πεισθησόμενοι
τοῖς σοῖς νόμοις, μὴ χαλέπαινε. μαντεύεται τὸ ἐμὸν
ἦθος, ὅπερ ἑκάστῳ δαίμων. καὶ πεισθήσονται, ὧν ἔσται
5   καὶ τὸ σύμπαν κράτος μιμησαμένων φύσιν. (7) σῶμα
δοῦλον ψυχῆς συμπολιτεύεται ψυχῇ, καὶ οὐ χαλεπαίνει
νοῦς ἰδίοις συνοικῶν ὑπηρέταις, καὶ γῆ, τὸ ἀτιμότατον
ἐν κόσμῳ, οὐρανῷ συνάρχει, καὶ οὐκ ἀναίνεται οὐρανὸς
ἐπίκαιρα ἐδάφη, οὐδὲ καρδία σπλάγχνα, τὸ ἱερώτατον
10   χρῆμα τὰ φαυλότατα ἐν σώματι. ἀλλὰ θεὸς μὲν οὐκ
ἐφθόνησεν ἐπίσης ἅπασιν ὀφθαλμοὺς ἅψαι καὶ ἀκοὰς
ἀναπετάσαι καὶ γεῦσιν καὶ ὄσφρησιν καὶ μνήμην καὶ
ἐλπίδα, καὶ ἡλίου φῶς οὐκ ἀπέκλεισε δούλων, πάντας
ἀνθρώπους κόσμου καταλέξας πολίτας· Ἐφέσιοι δὲ τὴν
15   ἑαυτῶν πόλιν ὑπερκόσμιον οἴονται μηδέποτε τῶν κοινῶν
ἀξιοῦντες. ὁρᾶτε μὴ ἀσεβῆτε θεῷ ἀντιπολιτευόμενοι.
ἀεὶ βούλεσθε μισεῖσθαι ὑπὸ δούλων, καὶ ἐν ᾧ ὑπηρέτουν
πρότερον καὶ ἐν ᾧ ἀτιμοῦνται ὕστερον; (8) τί οὖν
αὐτοὺς ἠλευθεροῦτε, εἰ μὴ ἀξίους ἐνομίζετε; ἢ ὅτι
20   πάθεσιν ὑμῶν ὑπήκουσαν; ἐκείνοις οὖν χαλεπαίνετε οἳ
διὰ τύχην ἐλειτούργουν; ἀλλ᾽ οὐχ ἑαυτοῖς, οἳ διὰ
κακίαν ἐπάσχετε; οἰκτροὶ ἦσαν τὰ κακὰ φόβῳ ἀνεχό-
μενοι, κατάρατοι δ᾽ ὑμεῖς ἐπιτάττοντες τὰ χείρω· καὶ
τότε πικροτέροις ἐδουλεύετε δεσπόταις, καὶ νῦν ἔτι
25   δουλεύετε φοβούμενοι ὧν ἤρξατε. τί οὖν βούλεσθε;
τῆς πόλεως ἀθρόοι πάντες ἐξέλθωσι καὶ ἐξελθόντες
ἰδίαν πόλιν κτίσωσι, καταρώμενοι ὑμῖν καὶ παισὶ
παίδων ἀνεπιβασίαν ψηφισάμενοι; πολεμίους ἑαυτοῖς
τρέφετε, Ἐφέσιοι, καὶ τοῖς μέλλουσι παισὶ πρὸς τοὺς
30   μέλλοντας ἐξ ἐκείνων. ὄψονται, Ἑρμόδωρε, Ἐφέσιοι
τὰ ἑαυτῶν, σὺ δὲ χαῖρε ἀγαθὸς ὤν.

drove out and turned away with threats, punishments, and
fears, in spite of the fact that they were good men?
Those who will obey your laws, Hermodorus, will be better
men. Don't be irritated. My character (each man's character is his own guardian spirit) prophesies this. Yes,
those will obey who have complete power because they have
imitated nature. (7) The body, while a slave to the soul,
is at the same time its fellow citizen, and it does not
irritate the intellect to dwell with its servants. The
earth, the least honored element in the cosmos, reigns
alongside heaven, and heaven does not scorn its mortal
foundation. Nor does the heart, the most sacred organ,
scorn the bowels, the most common parts of the body. God
did not begrudge lighting all men's eyes equally, and
opening their ears, and awakening their taste, smell, memory, and hope. Nor did he shut out the sun's light from
his servants, since he has enrolled all men as citizens of
the cosmos. But the Ephesians think that their city is
above the world and never fit for common men. Watch lest
you act impiously by politically opposing God. Do you
want always to be hated by your servants, both earlier,
when they serve you, and later, when they are dishonored
by you? (8) Why did you free them if you did not consider
them worthy? Or was it because they were obedient to your
passions? Are you, then, angry with those who, because of
fate, served masters, but not with yourselves, who suffered
because of your own wickedness? They were pitiable, because they endured evil through fear, but you were damnable
since you ordered them to ignoble deeds. Then you served
harsher masters, but even now you are still slaves, since
you fear those whom you ruled. What, then, do you want?
Should they all together leave the city and establish their
own city, once they have left yours, and curse you after
voting to ban also your children's children from it? You
foster wars for yourselves, Ephesians, and for your future
children against their progeny. The Ephesians, Hermodorus,
will look after their own affairs but as for you, be of
good cheer, for you are good.

THE EPISTLES OF SOCRATES AND THE SOCRATICS

Translated by

Stanley Stowers (Epistles 1-25)
and
David R. Worley (Epistles 26-35)

1. Σωκράτους

Οὔ μοι δοκεῖς καλῶς τὴν ἐμὴν συνιέναι γνώμην--
οὐ γὰρ ἂν τὸ δεύτερον ἐπέστελλες καὶ πλέονα δώσειν
ὑπισχνοῦ--ἀλλ᾽ ὥσπερ τοὺς σοφιστὰς καὶ Σωκράτην
5 φαίνῃ ὑπονοεῖν παλιμπράτην τινὰ εἶναι παιδείας καὶ
τὰ πρότερον γράψαι οὐχ ἁπλῶς ἀρνούμενον, ἀλλ᾽ ἐπὶ
πλείοσι τῶν τότε δεδομένων ὑπὸ σοῦ. Νῦν δ᾽ οὖν ὑπερ-
βολὰς ὑπισχνῇ καὶ τῷ πλήθει τῶν διδομένων οἴει με
παραστήσεσθαι καταλιπόντα τὴν ᾽Αθήνησι διατριβὴν παρὰ
10 σὲ ἥξειν τὸν οὔθ᾽ ὅλως καλὸν νομίζοντα τοὺς ἐν φιλοσοφίᾳ πιπράσκειν λόγους, ἐμοί τε καὶ σφόδρα ἀηθες.
(2) ᾽Αφ᾽ οὗ γὰρ προσῆλθον αὐτῇ τοῦ θεοῦ κελεύσαντος
φιλοσοφεῖν, παρ᾽ οὐδενὸς οὐδὲν εἰληφὼς εὑρεθήσομαι·
ἀλλὰ τὰς διατριβὰς ἐν κοινῷ ποιούμεθα, ἐπίσης ὁμο-
15 λογήσας ἀκούειν τῷ <πολλὰ> ἔχοντί τε καὶ τῷ μή. Καὶ
οὔτε ἐγκλεισάμενος φιλοσοφῶ καθάπερ Πυθαγόρας ἱστορεῖται οὔτε εἰς τὰ πλήθη παριὼν τοὺς βουλομένους
ἀκούειν ἀργύριον εἰσπράττω, ὅπερ ἄλλοι τέ τινες
πρότερον ἐποίησαν καὶ τῶν καθ᾽ ἡμᾶς ἔνιοι ποιοῦσιν.
20 ῾Ορῶ γὰρ ὅτι τὰ μὲν ἀρκοῦντα καὶ παρ᾽ ἐμαυτοῦ ἔχω, τὰ
δ᾽ εἰς περιουσίαν, πρῶτον μὲν οἷς ἂν λαβὼν παρακατα-
θῶμαι οὐχ εὑρίσκω οὐδένα τῶν δωσόντων μοι πιστότερον.
(3) Οὓς εἰ μὲν φαύλους ὑπολήψομαι, οὐδὲ παρακατατιθέ-
μενος αὐτοῖς ὀρθῶς δόξω φρονεῖν· παρὰ χρηστῶν δέ μοι
25 ἔξεστι καὶ μηδὲν δόντι λαμβάνειν. Οὐ γὰρ ἀργυρίου
μὲν φύλακες πιστοὶ ὑπάρξουσι, χάριτος δὲ ἄπιστοι,
οὐδὲ τὸ μὲν δοθὲν οὐκ ἂν ἀξιώσειαν ἀποστερεῖν, ἐφ᾽
οἷς δὲ καὶ τὸ ἀργύριον ἐδίδοσαν, πρότερον προῖκα

1. Of Socrates

You seem to have misunderstood my intention, for otherwise you would not have written a second letter and even promised to increase your contributions. But you seem to suspect that Socrates, too, is a retailer of education like the Sophists, and that he wrote what he did earlier, not simply to refuse your offer, but to get even more than you had given earlier. But now you make extravagant promises and think you can persuade me through the great number of your gifts to abandon my life in Athens and come to you. But I do not consider it at all right to make money from philosophy, and to do so would be especially out of character for me. (2) For no-one will ever find that I have taken anything from anyone ever since I applied myself to the philosophic life at the command of God. But I give my philosophic instruction in public, and equally allow the one who has much and the one who does not to hear me. But I neither practice philosophy shut up inside, as Pythagoras is said to have done, nor do I go among the masses and demand money from those who want to listen to me, as certain others have done formerly and as some of our contemporaries are still doing. For I see that I already have the necessities from myself, but with regard to superfluous things, in the first place, I find no-one more trustworthy to whom I might entrust them once I have received them, than the very men who would give these things to me. (3) If I suspect that they are worthless men, and yet entrust what I have received to them, I would appear to be insane, but I can get things from good men even though I have not given anything to them. For they will not be faithful guardians of money but unfaithful guardians of a debt of gratitude. If they did not think it right to steal what was given to us, to whom they had also given money because earlier they had freely

εἰληφότες παρ' ἡμῶν, περιόψονται ἡμᾶς ἀπορουμένους.
Ἑνὶ δὲ κεφαλαίῳ· εἰκὸς φίλους μὲν ὄντας πολλὰ καὶ
τῶν ἰδίων ἡμῖν προέσθαι, φίλους δὲ μὴ ὑπάρχοντας ἔνια
καὶ τῶν ἡμετέρων προσαποστερεῖν ζητήσειν. Αὐτὸς δὲ
5 ὥστε τηρεῖν ἀργύριον οὐκ ἄγω σχολήν· (4) θαυμάζω δὲ
[καὶ] τῶν λοιπῶν, οἳ παρασκευάζεσθαι μέν φασιν αὐτῶν
χάριν, φαίνονται δὲ αὐτοὺς διὰ τὰ κέρδη ἀποδόμενοι,
καὶ παιδείας ὀλιγωροῦντες χρηματισμοῦ ἐπιμελοῦνται.
Τοιγαροῦν τῆς μὲν κτήσεως θαυμάζονται, τῆς δὲ ἀπαι-
10 δευσίας καταγελῶνται καὶ τῶν ἄλλων πάντων μακαρίζον-
ται πλὴν ἑαυτῶν. Καίτοι πῶς οὐ δεινὸν ἐπὶ μὲν φίλῳ
δοκεῖν εἶναι αἰσχρὸν ἡγεῖσθαι καὶ μηδ' ἂν βιῶναι
βούλεσθαι ἑτέροις ὄντα πρόσθεμα καὶ ἀλλοτρίων παρα-
σιτοῦντα ἀγαθῶν, ταὐτὸ δὲ τοῦτο πρὸς τὰ χρήματα
15 πεπονθότα μὴ αἰδεῖσθαι; Ἢ οὐκ ἴσμεν, ὅτι καὶ τιμῶνται οὗτοι διὰ τὸν πλοῦτον καὶ μεταπεσούσης τῆς τύχης
ἐν ἀτιμίᾳ διάγουσι τῇ πάσῃ; (5) ὥστε μήτε τιμωμένους
αὐτοὺς χαίρειν (οὐ γὰρ ἐφ' ἑαυτοῖς τιμῶνται) ἀτιμα-
ζομένους τε πολὺ μᾶλλον ἄχθεσθαι· τὸ γὰρ ἀτιμαζόμενον
20 καὶ δι' ὃ παρορῶνται, αὐτοί εἰσι.
     Πρῶτον μὲν οὖν οὐκ ὀρθῶς ὑπέλαβες, εἰ Σωκράτην
οἴει δι' ἀργύριον ποιήσειν, ὃ μὴ καὶ προῖκα αὐτῷ
καλῶς εἶχε πρᾶξαι. Καὶ πρὸς τούτῳ ἐκεῖνο οὐκ ἐλο-
γίσω, ὅτι ἐνταῦθά με πολλὰ κατέχει, καὶ τὸ μέγιστον,
25 αἱ τῆς πατρίδος χρεῖαι. Καὶ μὴ θαυμάσῃς, εἰ καὶ τῇ
πατρίδι χρείας τινὰς φαμὲν ἐκτελεῖν, ὅτι οὔτε ἐν
στρατηγίαις οὔτε ἐπὶ τοῦ βήματος ἐξετάζομαι. (6)
Πρῶτον μὲν γὰρ οἶμαι, καθ' ὃ δύναται ἕκαστος ὠφελεῖν,
ἐξετάζεσθαι. Τὸ δὲ μείζονα ἢ ἐλάττω πράττειν οὐκ ἐπ'
30 αὐτῷ ἐστιν· ἀλλὰ τοῦ μὲν ἕτερα ἔχει τὴν αἰτίαν τοῦ

received from us, then they will not neglect us in our
need.   In sum, it is likely that, if they are genuine
friends, they will freely give us also of their own possessions, but if they are not true friends, they will try
to defraud us also of some of our own possessions.   And I
myself have no time to guard money.   (4) But I am amazed
at the rest, who claim to be making preparations on their
own behalf, but who have manifestly sold themselves for
the sake of profit, and who have little regard for education, but concern themselves with making money.   They are
indeed admired for their possessions, but they are ridi-
culed for their lack of education, and are congratulated
for all other reasons than for themselves.   And yet, is it
not terrible, on the one hand, that we consider it shameful to appear to be dependent on a friend, and would not
wish to be an appendage to others and a parasite on the
goods of strangers, but on the other, that we are not
ashamed when someone is disposed in the very same way
toward money?   Or do we not realize that they are honored
only because of their wealth and that with a change of
fortune they live a life full of disgrace?   (5) As a result, they are not pleased when they are honored (because
they are not honored for themselves), and are even more
disturbed when they are dishonored; for that for which
they are dishonored and disregarded is themselves.

   First, then, you have not understood correctly if you
think that Socrates would do something for money which he
had not already decided to do without charge.   Moreover,
you have not even considered that many things keep me
here, above all, the needs of my country.   And you should
not be amazed, because I am neither holding the office of
a general nor the seat of a judge, if I say that I am
meeting certain needs of my country.   (6) For, first, I
believe that each person should act in that capacity in
which he can render some benefit.   However, to accomplish
greater or lesser things is not in his power; rather, of
the latter, other things are the cause, but of the former

δὲ καθάπαξ αὐτός. Ἔπειτα δὲ οὐ τῶν τοσαύτῃ πόλει
συμβουλευσόντων δεῖ μόνον οὐδὲ τῶν ἡγησομένων κατὰ
γῆν ἢ κατὰ θάλατταν, ἀλλὰ καὶ τῶν ἐπιστησόντων τοὺς
ἐπὶ τὰ τῇ πόλει συμφέροντα ἰόντας. Οὐδὲν γὰρ θαυμασ-
5   τὸν ὑπὸ μεγέθους τῶν ἐπικειμένων οἷον ἀποκοιμίζεσθαι
ἐνίους αὐτῶν, οἷς τοῦ ἐπεγείροντος ὥσπερ μύωπος δεήσει. (7) Πρὸς ἃ δὴ καὶ ἐμὲ ἔταξεν ὁ θεός. Ἐπιεικῶς
μὲν οὖν ἀπεχθάνεσθαί μοι συμβαίνει ἀπ' αὐτοῦ. Ἀλλ'
ἐκεῖνος ἀφίστασθαι οὐκ ἐᾷ, ᾧ πειστέον μᾶλλον. Εἰκὸς
10 γὰρ τό γε ὑγιὲς ἐμοῦ κρεῖττον αὐτὸν εἰδέναι· ἐπεὶ καὶ
πρὸς σὲ βουλευομένῳ ἀπεῖπε μὴ ἰέναι καὶ τὸ δεύτερον
πέμψαντός σου ἀπηγόρευσεν. Ἀπειθεῖν δὲ αὐτῷ ὀκνῶ
καὶ τὸν Πίνδαρον ἡγούμενος εἰς τοῦτο εἶναι σοφόν, ὃς
φησι· "θεοῦ δὲ δείξαντος ἀρχὰν ἕκαστον ἐν πρᾶγος
15 εὐθεῖα δὴ κέλευθος ἀρετὰν ἐλεῖν, τελευταί τε καλλίο-
νες" (= Frgt. 108 Schröder).
        Σχεδὸν γὰρ οὕτω που αὐτῷ ἔχει τὸ ὑπόρχημα.
(8) Πολλὰ δὲ καὶ πολλοῖς τῶν ἄλλων εἴρηται ποιητῶν
περὶ θεῶν καὶ ὅτι τὰ μὲν κατὰ τὴν τούτων βούλησιν
20 πραττόμενα ἐπὶ τὸ λῷον ἐκβαίνει, τὰ δὲ παρὰ θεὸν
ἀλυσιτελῆ ὑπάρχει τοῖς πράξασιν. Ὁρῶ δὲ καὶ τῶν
πόλεων τῶν Ἑλληνίδων τὰς φρονιμωτάτας συμβούλῳ
χρωμένας τῷ ἐν Δελφοῖς θεῷ, καὶ ὅσαι μὲν ἂν τούτῳ
πειθόμεναι πράττωσι, πρὸς ὠφέλειαν αὐταῖς γινομένας,
25 ὅσαι δ' ἂν ἀπειθήσωσιν, ὡς τὸ πολὺ βλαπτομένας. Οὐ
θαυμάσαιμι δ' ἄν, εἴ μοι περὶ τοῦ δαιμονίου ἀπιστή-
σειας λέγοντι. Ἤδη γὰρ πρός με καὶ ἄλλοι οὕτω
διετέθησαν οὐκ ὀλίγοι. (9) πλεῖστοι δέ μοι ἠπίστησαν
ἐν τῇ ἐπὶ Δηλίῳ μάχῃ. Παρῆν γὰρ τότε τῇ στρατείᾳ καὶ
30 συνεμαχόμην πανδημεὶ τῆς πόλεως ἐξεληλυθυίας· ἐν δὲ
τῇ φυγῇ ἅμα πολλοὶ ὑπαπῇειμεν, καὶ ὡς ἐπὶ διαβάσεώς
τινος ἐγενόμεθα, συνέβη μοι τὸ εἰωθὸς σημεῖον.
Ἐνέστην οὖν καὶ εἶπον· "Ἄνδρες, οὔ μοι δοκεῖ ταύτην
πορεύεσθαι· τὸ γὰρ δαιμόνιόν μοι, ἡ φωνή, γέγονεν."

only he himself. Then, again, so great a city needs not
only statesmen or military commanders on land and sea, but
also people who would have charge of men who are concerned
with things profitable for the city. For it is not at all
astonishing if some of them, as it were, fall asleep due
to the magnitude of their responsibilities, and must then
be aroused, so to speak, by a gadfly. (7) And what is
more, God has appointed me to this task. I am then pretty
well hated because of this, but he whom one must rather
obey does not allow me to withdraw. For it is reasonable,
at any rate, that he knows better than I what is sound,
seeing that when I asked about going to you, he forbade me
to go, and when you sent a second letter he warned me.
But I hesitate to disobey him, and I think that in this
regard Pindar was wise, who said, "When God has shown the
beginning for any work, then straight indeed is the path
for pursuing virtue, and more beautiful are its accomplishments" (Fr. 108).

The *Hyporchema* has something very close to this in
it. (8) Many other poets have said a great deal about the
gods, to the effect that the things which are done according to their will turn out well, but that the things which
are done contrary to the will of God prove harmful to
those who do them. And I see that the wisest of the Greek
cities make use of the god at Delphi as their counselor,
and that those who act in obedience to him do so to their
own benefit, but that those who disobey suffer very great
harm. But I would not be surprised if you did not believe
me when I speak of the deity. For already not a few others
have acted this way toward me. (9) A great many did not
believe me in the battle of Delium. For I was present at
that campaign and I fought together with all of the people,
since the city had marched out. But in the retreat many
of us fell back together, and when we came to a crossing,
it fell my lot to give the customary signal. Therefore, I
stood my ground and said, "Men I do not believe that it is
good to go this way, for my deity, the voice, came to me."

Οἱ μὲν οὖν πλείους πρὸς ὀργὴν καὶ ὡσπερεὶ παίζοντος
ἐμοῦ ἐν οὐκ ἐπιτηδείῳ καιρῷ ὁρμήσαντες εὐθεῖαν ἐβά-
διζον· ὀλίγοι δέ τινες ἐπείσθησαν καὶ τὴν ἐναντίαν
ἐμοὶ συναπετράποντο· καὶ οἴκαδε πορευόμενοι διεσώθη-
5   μεν. Τοὺς δ' ἄλλους ἥκων τις ἐξ αὐτῶν πάντας ἔφη
ἀπολωλέναι· εἰς γὰρ τοὺς ἱππέας ἐμπεσεῖν τῶν πολεμίων
ἐπανιόντας ἀπὸ τῆς διώξεως· πρὸς οὓς τὸ μὲν πρῶτον
μάχεσθαι, ὕστερον δὲ περικλειομένους ὑπ' αὐτῶν
πλειόνων ὄντων ἐκκλίναντας καὶ περικαταλήπτους γενο-
10   μένους πάντας ἀπολέσθαι. Αὐτὸς δὲ ὁ ταῦτα ἀπαγγέλλων
τραυματίας ἀφῖκτο καὶ μόνην τὴν ἀσπίδα σῴζων.
(10) Πολλὰ δὲ καὶ ἰδίᾳ προηγόρευσα ἐνίοις τῶν ἀποβη-
σομένων διδάσκοντος τοῦ θεοῦ.
     Σὺ δὲ καὶ τῆς βασιλείας ἔφησας μέρος διδόναι καὶ
15   παρακαλεῖς <με> μὴ ὡς ἀρξόμενον βαδίζειν, ἀλλ' ὡς
τοὐναντίον ἄρξοντα καὶ τῶν ἄλλων καὶ σοῦ αὐτοῦ. Ἐγὼ
δὲ μεμαθηκέναι ἄρχειν οὔ φημι, μὴ εἰδὼς δὲ οὐκ ἂν
δεξαίμην μᾶλλον βασιλεύειν ἢ κυβερνᾶν μὴ ἐπιστάμενος.
Οἶδα δέ, ὅτι εἰ καὶ οἱ ἄλλοι ἄνθρωποι ὁμοίως διέ-
20   κειντο, ἥττονα ἂν ἦν κακὰ ἐν τῷ βίῳ. Νῦν δ' ἡ τῶν
μὴ ἐπισταμένων τόλμα ἐπιχειροῦσα οἷς μὴ ἴσασιν εἰς
τοῦτο ταραχῆς αὐτοὺς προάγει· ὅθεν καὶ τὴν τύχην ἔτι
μείζω πεποίηκε τῇ ἐκείνων ἀνοίᾳ τὴν ταύτης ἐξουσίαν
αὐξάνουσα. (11) Καὶ μέντοι οὐδὲ ἐκεῖνο ἀγνοῶ, ὅτι
25   ἐνδοξότερον εἶναι καὶ περιβλέπεσθαι μᾶλλον εἰκὸς
ἰδιώτου βασιλέα ὄντα. Ἀλλ' ὥσπερ οὐδὲ ἐφ' ἵππον ἂν
εἱλόμην καθίζεσθαι ἄπειρος ὢν ἱππικῆς, ἀλλ' ἐλυσιτέλει
μοι πεζῷ εἶναι, κἂν εἰ ταπεινότερος πολὺ τοῦ ἱππέως
ἦν, οὕτω καὶ περὶ βασιλείας καὶ ἰδιωτείας φρονῶ· καὶ
30   οὐκ ἂν ὑπ' ἐπιθυμίας τῶν μειζόνων ἐξαρθεὶς ἐπιφανεσ-
τέρων ὀρεχθείην συμφορῶν. Ἐοίκασι δὲ καὶ οἱ πρῶτοι
μυθολογήσαντες τὰ περὶ τὸν Βελλεροφόντην τούτῳ τι
παραπλήσιον αἰνίξασθαι. (12) Οὐ γὰρ ὅτι, οἶμαι, τόπου

Most of them then, became angry as if I had told a joke at an inopportune time, and started out on a direct route. But a few were persuaded and turned away with me to the other road, and we came home and were saved. As for the others, a certain person from their number who came back said that they had all died, for they had come upon enemy cavalry returning from the pursuit. At first they fought with them, but then, surrounded by a superior force, they gave ground and were overtaken and were all killed. And the one who told these things came back wounded, saving only his shield. (10) To certain people privately I also predicted many of the things that would happen to them, God all the while instructing me.

You have even said that you would give me a share of your reign, and you urged me not to come as a subject, but on the contrary as a ruler of others and of yourself as well. But I must say that I have never learned how to rule, and not knowing how, I would no more undertake to rule than I would to steer a ship if I did not know how to do it. And I know that if other men, too, felt the same way, there would be less evil in life. But as it is now, the recklessness of those who are ignorant dares them to undertake what they do not understand and leads them into trouble. So through the senselessness of these people it makes fortune still greater by increasing its power over them. (11) At any rate, neither am I ignorant of the fact that you are actually honored and admired more as a king than as a private person. Just as I would prefer not to get on a horse if I were inexperienced in horsemanship, but it would, on the contrary, be much more practical for me to walk, even if it is much more humble than being a rider, so I think the same thing holds true for kingship and the private life. And I would not stretch out to grasp obvious misfortune because I had been excited by a passion for greater things. Indeed, it seems that also the first men who told the myths about Bellerophon hinted at something very similar. (12) For it is not, I think, because

ὑψηλοτέρου ἐπεθύμησεν, ἀλλ' ὅτι πραγμάτων μειζόνων
ἢ καθ' ἑαυτὸν ὠρέχθη, μετὰ ταῦτα αὐτῷ συμφοραὶ ἐγένοντο. Καταπεσὼν γὰρ ἀπὸ τῆς ἐλπίδος αἰσχρῶς καὶ
ἐπονειδίστως. τὸν λοιπὸν ἔζη βίον, διὰ τοὺς ἐφυβρί-
5   ζοντας ἐν τοῖς ἄστεσιν ἐπὶ τὴν ἐρημίαν ἐπεξεληλυθώς,
καὶ τὰς βάσεις ἀπολωλεκώς, οὐχ ἄσπερ ἡμεῖς οἰόμεθα
λέγειν, ἀλλὰ τὴν παρρησίαν, ἐφ' ἧς ὀρθοῦται ὁ ἑκάστου
βίος. Ταῦτα μὲν οὖν ὅπῃ τοῖς ποιηταῖς φίλα, ταύτῃ
ὑπονοείσθω. Τὸ δ' ἐμὸν δεύτερον ἤδη ἀκούεις, ὅτι οὐκ
10   ἀλλάττομαι τῶν ἐκεῖ τἀνθάδε ἀμείνω εἶναι δοκῶν.
'Αλλ' οὐδὲ τῷ θεῷ συναρέσκει, ᾧ μέχρι νῦν συμβούλῳ
τε καὶ ἐπιτρόπῳ ἐμαυτοῦ χρῶμαι.

2. Σωκράτης Ξενοφῶντι

Χαιρεφῶν ὃν τρόπον ὑφ' ἡμῶν σπουδάζεται οὐκ
15   ἀγνοεῖς. 'Ηιρημένος δὲ ὑπὸ τῆς πόλεως πρεσβευτὴς
εἰς Πελοπόννησον τάχ' ἂν καὶ πρὸς ὑμᾶς ἀφίκοιτο. Τὰ
μὲν οὖν τῶν ξενίων εὐπόριστα ἀνδρὶ φιλοσόφῳ· τὰ δὲ
τῆς πορείας ἐπισφαλῆ καὶ μάλιστα διὰ τὰς αὐτόθι νῦν
ταραχὰς ὑπαρχούσας. Ὧν ἐπιμεληθεὶς ἐκεῖνόν τε
20   σώσεις ἄνδρα φίλον καὶ ἡμῖν τὰ μάλιστα χαριῇ.

he desired a higher place, but rather because he tried to do things which were beyond his power, that misfortunes later befell him. For having lost his hope, he lived the rest of his life shamefully and disgracefully, since he had gone out to the wilderness because of those who were insulting him in the towns, and had lost his foundation, which is not speaking as we are accustomed to, but is that boldness of speech upon which each person's life is set upright. Let this, then, be understood in a way dear to the poets. As for me, you have now heard for a second time that I will not exchange my situation here, which I think is better, for a place there. That does not please God, who up to now has been both my counselor and my guardian.

2. Socrates to Xenophon

You are not ignorant of the care I have bestowed on Chaerophon, and now he has been chosen by the city as ambassador to the Peloponnesus, and he will probably also come to you. Hospitality is easily supplied to a philosopher; but travel conditions are unsafe, especially now, because of the troubles which have arisen there. If you take care of him, you will have both saved a friend and also shown the greatest kindness to me.

3. Σωκράτους

Μνήσων ὁ Ἀμφιπολίτης ἐν Ποτιδαίᾳ μοι συνεστάθη.
Οὗτος νῦν Ἀθήναζε ἔρχεται πρὸς τὸν δῆμον ἐκπεσὼν ὑπὸ
τῶν οἴκοι. Τὰ γὰρ ἐκεῖ κεκίνηται μὲν ἤδη, οὔπω δ᾽
5   ἐστὶ φανερά. Οἶμαι μέντοι οὐ πολλοῦ αὐτὰ δηλώσειν
χρόνου. Τούτῳ συλλαβόμενος αὐτόν τε ἄξιον ὄντα
ποιήσεις εὖ καὶ τὰς πόλεις ἀμφοτέρας ὠφελήσεις· τὴν
μὲν τῶν Ἀμφιπολιτῶν, ἵνα μὴ ἀποστᾶσα ἀνήκεστόν τι
κινδυνεύσῃ παθεῖν, τὴν δ᾽ ἡμετέραν, ὅπως μὴ καὶ περὶ
10   ἐκείνης πράγματα ἔχῃ ὡς νῦν γε περὶ Ποτιδαίας μικροῦ
δέομεν ἀπειρηκέναι.

4. Σωκράτους

Κριτοβούλῳ μὲν ἐντυχὼν παρεκάλουν πρὸς φιλοσοφίαν αὐτόν· ὁ δέ μοι δοκεῖ διανενοῆσθαι μᾶλλον ἐξορ-
15   μήσεσθαι πρὸς τὰ πολιτικά. Αἱρήσεται οὖν τὴν πρὸς
ἐκεῖνα ἁρμόττουσαν παιδείαν καὶ τὸν ὑφηγησόμενον
ἐκλέξεται τῶν ὄντων τὸν κράτιστον· σχεδὸν δὲ νῦν
ἐπιδημοῦσιν οἱ δοκιμώτατοι Ἀθήνησι, καὶ πολλοὶ αὐτῶν
καὶ πρὸς ἡμᾶς ἔχουσιν οἰκείως. Τὰ μὲν οὖν ἐκείνου
20   ταῦτα· τῶν δ᾽ ἐμῶν Ξανθίππη μὲν καὶ τὰ παιδάρια
ἔρρωται· αὐτὸς δὲ ὥσπερ καὶ παρόντος σου πράττω.

3. Of Socrates

Mneson of Amphipolis was introduced to me in Potidaea, but he is now coming to Athens to appeal to the people, since he has been exiled by his fellow countrymen. For things there have already been stirred up, but it is not yet public knowledge. However, I do not think that it will be long before it is made known. If you help him, you will be doing a kindness to a man who deserves it, and you will render a benefit to both cities: Amphipolis, that it not revolt and run the risk of inexorable suffering, and ours, that it may not have troubles with that city, as we have just only recently finished having with Potidaea.

4. Of Socrates

When I met Critobulus, I urged him to turn to philosophy, but it seems to me that he has rather set his mind on taking up politics. Therefore, he will choose an education which is suited for that, and as his guide he will select the best person of them all. Right now, I dare say, the most distinguished men are living in Athens, and many of them are on familiar terms with us. So much about him, but concerning myself, Xanthippe and the children are doing well, and I am going about my activities as I did when you were here.

5. Σωκράτης Ξενοφῶντι

Σὲ μὲν ἐν Θήβαις ἡμῖν γενέσθαι ἀπηγγέλλετο,
Πρόξενον δὲ καταλαβεῖν εἰς τὴν Ἀσίαν ὡς Κῦρον
ὡρμηκότα. Εἰ μὲν οὖν εὐτυχῶν ἐφίεσαι πραγμάτων,
5   θεὸς οἶδεν, ὡς ἤδη γέ τινες τῶν ἐνταῦθα καταμέμφεσθαι
αὐτὰ ἐπιχειροῦσιν· οὐ γὰρ ἄξιόν φασιν εἶναι Κύρῳ
βοηθεῖν Ἀθηναίους, δι' ὃν τὴν ἀρχὴν ὑπὸ Λακεδαιμονίων ἀφηρέθησαν, οὐδ' αὐτοὺς ὑπὲρ ἐκείνου πολεμεῖν
καταπολεμηθέντας δι' ἐκεῖνον. Οὐκ ἂν οὖν θαυμάσαιμι,
10   εἰ μεταπεσούσης τῆς πολιτείας συκοφαντεῖν σέ τινες
ἀφ' ἑαυτῶν ἐπιχειρήσουσιν· ἀλλ' ὅσῳ λαμπρότερον τἀκεῖ
χωρήσειν ὑπολαμβάνω, τοσούτῳ σφοδρότερον ἐπικείσεσθαι
τούτους ἡγοῦμαι· τὰς γὰρ ἐνίων φύσεις οὐκ ἀγνοῶ.
(2) Ἡμεῖς δ' ἐπείπερ ἅπαξ εἰς τοῦτο ἑαυτοὺς ἔδομεν,
15   ἄνδρες ἀγαθοὶ γενώμεθα, τῶν τε ἄλλων, ἃ περὶ ἀρετῆς
εἰώθειμεν λέγειν ἀναμιμνησκόμενοι καὶ τὸ "μηδὲ γένος
πατέρων αἰσχυνέμεν" ἐν τοῖς ἄριστα τῷ ποιητῇ εἰρῆσθαι
τιθέντες. Ἴσθι δέ, ὡς δυοῖν τούτοιν μάλιστα προσ-
δεῖται πόλεμος, καρτερίας τε καὶ ἀφιλοχρηματίας· δι'
20   ἐκείνην μὲν γὰρ τοῖς οἰκείοις φίλοι, διὰ καρτερίαν δὲ
φοβεροὶ τοῖς ἀντιπάλοις γινόμεθα· ὧν ἀμφοτέρων οἰκεῖα
ἔχεις τὰ παραδείγματα.

5. Socrates to Xenophon

It was reported to us that you were in Thebes and that you had overtaken Proxenes after he had set out into Asia to meet Cyrus. Whether the undertakings in which you are taking part are fortunate, God knows, since some of those here are already attempting to find fault with them. For they say that it is improper that Athenians help Cyrus, with whose aid the Lacedaemonians robbed them of their sovereignty, or that they fight for him because of whom they had been defeated in war. I would not be surprised, if the political situation worsens, if some will attempt for their own reasons to slander you. But the brighter your fortunes turn out there, the more violently, I do believe, they will set upon you. For I am not ignorant of the nature of some people. (2) Since we once for all committed ourselves to this, let us be better men than others, remembering what we were accustomed to say about virtue, and also "the stock of the father makes no-one a scoundrel," which we consider to be among the best sayings of the poets. And know that both of these virtues are especially necessary for war: both patient endurance and contempt for riches. For through the latter we become dear to our own people and through patient endurance we become formidable to our enemies. You have examples of both of these among your own kin.

6. Σωκράτους

Τοῖν μὲν ξένοιν ἐπεμελήθην ὡς παρεκάλεις, καὶ
τὸν ἐν τῷ δήμῳ συναγορεύσοντα αὐτοῖν ἐσκεψάμην
τῶν ἡμετέρων τινὰ ἑταίρων, ὃς ὑπηρετήσειν ἔφη προθυ-
5   μότερον διὰ τὸ καὶ σοὶ χαρίζεσθαι ἐθέλειν. Περὶ δὲ
τοῦ χρηματισμοῦ καὶ περὶ ὧν προσπαίζων ἔγραφες, τὸ
μὲν ἐπιζητεῖν ἐνίους οὐδὲν ἴσως ἄτοπον, τί πρῶτον μὲν
ἐσπουδακότων τῶν ἄλλων περὶ πλοῦτον ἐγὼ πένης αἱροῦ-
μαι βιοῦν, ἔπειτα ἐξόν μοι παρὰ πολλῶν πολλὰ λαμβά-
10 νειν, οὐ τὰς παρὰ ζώντων μόνον δωρεὰς τῶν φίλων,
ἀλλὰ καὶ ὅσα ἂν τελευτῶντές μοι ἀφῶσιν ἑκὼν παραιτοῦ-
μαι· τὸν δ᾽ οὕτω διακείμενον οὐδὲν θαυμαστὸν μαινό-
μενον παρὰ τοῖς ἄλλοις νομίζεσθαι. (2) Χρὴ δὲ μὴ
τοῦτο μόνον, ἀλλὰ καὶ τὸν ἄλλον ἡμῶν προσεπιθεωρεῖν
15 βίον καὶ εἰ περὶ τὴν χρῆσιν τῶν σωμάτων διαφέροντες
φανούμεθα μὴ θαυμάζειν, ὅτι καὶ περὶ τὸν πορισμὸν
διεστήκαμεν. Ἐμοὶ μὲν τοίνυν ἀπαρκεῖ τροφῇ τε
χρῆσθαι τῇ λιτοτάτῃ καὶ ἐσθῆτι θέρους τε καὶ χειμῶνος
τῇ αὐτῇ, ὑποδήμασι δὲ πάμπαν οὐ χρῶμαι· οὐδὲ πολιτι-
20 κῆς ἐφίεμαι δόξης πλὴν ὅσον ἐκ τοῦ σώφρων εἶναι καὶ
δίκαιος. Ὅσοι δὲ πολυτελείας μὲν τῆς περὶ τὴν
δίαιταν οὐδὲν ἀπολείπουσιν, ἐσθῆτας δὲ διαφόρους οὐχ
ὅτι γε ἔτους τοῦ αὐτοῦ, ἀλλὰ καὶ ἡμέρας τῆς αὐτῆς
ἀμφιέννυσθαι ζητοῦσιν, πολλὰ δὲ χαρίζονται καὶ ταῖς
25 ἀπορρήτοις ἡδοναῖς, (3) καὶ ὃν τρόπον οἱ τὴν κατὰ
φύσιν χρόαν διεφθορότες ἐπακτοῖς χρώμασι κοσμοῦνται,
κἀκεῖνοι τὴν ἐξ ἀρετῆς ἀληθινὴν δόξαν ἀπολωλεκότες--
ἣν εἰκὸς περιγίνεσθαι ἑκάστῳ--, εἰς τὴν ἐκ τῆς ἀρεσ-
κείας καταφεύγουσι, διανομαῖς καὶ ἑστιάσεσι πανδήμοις
30 τὴν παρὰ τῶν πληθῶν εὐφημίαν προκαλούμενοι. Ὅθεν
εἰκότως οἶμαι πολλῶν αὐτοῖς δεῖσθαι συμβαίνει· οὔτε
γὰρ αὐτοὶ ζῆν δύνανται ἀπ᾽ ὀλίγων, οὔτε πλεῖον ἀπο-
δέχεσθαι ἄλλους οὗτοι ἐθέλουσι μὴ μισθὸν τῆς εὐλογίας

6. Of Socrates

I have taken care of the two visitors, as you urged
me to do, and I have sought out one of our companions who
will plead their cause before the people. He said that he
would serve quite readily because he, too, desires to
please you. But concerning the money and the things you
wrote about so mockingly, there is perhaps nothing unusual
about some people inquiring, first of all, why I have
chosen a life of poverty while others zealously pursue
wealth, and then why, although it is possible for me to
get large sums of money from many people, I willingly refuse gifts not only from living friends, but also from
friends who have died and left gifts to me. And it is not
surprising that other people consider one who is thus inclined to be insane. (2) Yet one must consider not only
this feature, but also the rest of our way of life, and if
we appear different from others in regard to bodily practices, one must not be surprised if we also stand apart in
our attitude toward material gain. Therefore, I am satisfied to have the plainest food and the same garment summer
and winter, and I do not wear shoes at all, nor do I desire political fame except to the extent that it comes
from being prudent and just. But those who pursue the
luxurious life forego nothing in their diet, and they seek
to wear different garments not only during the same year,
but even in the same day, and they take great delight in
forbidden pleasures. (3) And in the same manner those who
have destroyed their natural complexion adorn themselves
with artificial colors, and those who have lost the true
fame that derives from virtue (which it is reasonable for
each individual to gain) flee to the fame which results
from flattery, and invite the acclamation of the masses by
means of distributions and public feasts. I believe in
all likelihood that is why they need so much. For neither
are they themselves able to live on a little, nor are
other people any longer willing to grant them approval

φερόμενοι. Ἐμοὶ μὲν πρὸς ἄμφω ταῦτα καλῶς ἔχει ὁ
βίος· καὶ εἰ μέν τί με τῶν ἀληθῶν ἐκφεύγει, οὐκ ἂν
ἰσχυρισαίμην· ὅτι μέντοι ταῦτα μὲν οἱ κρείττους φασὶν
εἶναι βελτίω, ἐκεῖνα δὲ οἱ πολλοί, σαφῶς οἶδα.
5   (4) Πολλάκις δὲ καὶ περὶ τοῦ θεοῦ κατ' ἐμαυτὸν
ἐννοούμενος καθ' ὅ τι εὐδαίμων εἴη καὶ μακάριος, ὁρῶ
τῷ μηδενὸς δεῖσθαι αὐτὸν ὑπερβάλλοντα ἡμᾶς. Φύσεως
γὰρ λαμπροτάτης ἐκεῖνο ἦν οὐ πολλῶν δεόμενον ἑτοίμως
ἔχειν ἀπολαύειν. Καίτοι σοφώτερόν τε εἶναι εἰκός,
10   ὅστις ἑαυτὸν ἀπεικάζει τῷ σοφωτάτῳ, καὶ μακαριώτατον
ὑπάρχειν, ὃς ἂν ὅτι μάλιστα ἐξομοιωθῇ τῷ μακαρίῳ.
Τοῦτο δὲ εἰ μὲν πλοῦτος ποιεῖν ἐδύνατο, πλοῦτόν γ'
ἂν ἐχρῆν αἱρεῖσθαι· ἐπεὶ δὲ ἀρετὴ μόνη φαίνεται
παρασκευάζειν, εὔηθες ἀφέντας τὸ ὂν ἀγαθὸν τὸ δοκοῦν
15   μεταδιώκειν. (5) Ὡς μὲν οὖν τἀμὰ οὐχ οὕτω βέλτιον
ἔχει, οὐκ ἂν μέ τις ῥᾳδίως μεταπείσειε. Περὶ δὲ τῶν
παίδων <καὶ> ὅπερ ἔφησθα δεῖν προνοεῖσθαι, ᾗ διανοοῦ-
μαι περὶ αὐτῶν μαθεῖν ἔξεστι πᾶσιν ἀνθρώποις. Μίαν
ἀρχὴν εὐδαιμονίας ἐγὼ νομίζω φρονεῖν εὖ· τὸν δὲ νοῦ
20   μὲν μὴ μετειληφότα, χρυσίῳ δὲ πιστεύοντα καὶ ἀργυρίῳ,
πρῶτον μὲν ὅπερ οἴεται κεκτῆσθαι ἀγαθὸν οὐκ ἔχειν,
ἔπειτα τοσοῦτον ὑπάρχειν ἀθλιώτερον τῶν ἄλλων, ὅσον
ὁ μὲν ἀναγκασθεὶς ὑπὸ πενίας εἰ καὶ μὴ νῦν, αὖθις
ποτὲ φρονήσει, ὁ δὲ τὰ μὲν ὑπ' οἰήσεως τοῦ εἶναι
25   μακάριος τῆς ἀληθινῆς ὠφελείας ἀμελῶν, τὰ δὲ ὑπὸ
χορηγίας φθειρόμενος πρὸς οἷς ἠτύχει ἤδη, τῶν ὄντως
ἀνθρωπίνων ἀγαθῶν, προσαπεστέρηται <καὶ> τὴν ὑπὲρ τῶν
μελλόντων χρηστὴν ἐλπίδα. (6) Οὐδὲ γὰρ σωθῆναι οἷόν
τέ ἐστι τῷ τοιούτῳ πρὸς ἀρετήν, κατεχομένῳ μὲν ὑπὸ
30   κολακείας ἀνθρώπων ὁμιλῆσαι δεινῶν, κατεχομένῳ δὲ ὑπὸ
γοητείας ἡδονῶν, αἳ κατὰ πᾶν αἰσθητήριον προσβάλλου-
σαι τῇ ψυχῇ πᾶν, εἴ τι καλὸν ἢ σωφρονικὸν ἐν αὐτῇ
ἠρέμα ἐξελαύνουσι. Τίς οὖν ἀνάγκη παισὶν αἰτίαν

unless they are paid for their praise. But as for me, in
regard to both of these things my life is in good condition, and if in some matters the truth should escape me,
I would not be obstinate in my insistence. However, that
the more excellent people say that some things are better,
and the masses other things, I do know very well. (4) And
often when I reflect on why God is happy and blessed, I
perceive that he far surpasses us in that he needs nothing
For that is a characteristic of a most splendid nature,
that by not requiring much it is always ready to have enjoyment. And it is indeed reasonable that he is wise who
copies himself after the wisest, and he is happiest who
assimilates himself as much as possible to one who is
happy. Were wealth able to produce this, he should have
chosen wealth. But since virtue alone seems to provide
this, it is foolish to leave the true good and to follow
after appearance. (5) One could not, then, easily persuade me that my circumstances are not better in this way.
But concerning my children, and your statement that I
should provide for them, all men can learn what I think
about them. I consider the one origin of happiness to be
right thinking. But he who has no understanding, but
trusts in gold and silver, first thinks that he possesses
the good which he does not have, and then becomes much
more wretched than others. It is the same as if one person, although oppressed by poverty, will, even if not now,
then certainly at some later time come to his senses,
while another person, laboring under false notions of what
it is to be truly happy, neglects what is truly beneficial,
and being corrupted by affluence, in addition to the truly
human goods which he has already failed to obtain, is de-
frauded of the hope of future good. (6) For it is not
possible for such a man to come safely to virtue, who is
held captive by the flattery of men who are clever at
speaking, and who is held captive by the sorcery of pleasures, which attack the soul through every sense organ and
gradually drive out every bit of good or moderation that

καταλιπεῖν ἀφροσύνης μᾶλλον ἢ παιδεύσεως οὐ λόγοις
μόνον ἀλλὰ καὶ ἔργοις δηλώσαντας, ὅτι ἐν σφίσιν
αὐτοῖς τὰς ἀπ' αὐτῶν ἔχουσιν ἐλπίδας καὶ μὴ γενομένοις ἀγαθοῖς οὐδὲ ζῆν καταλείπεται, ἀλλὰ λιμῷ
5   φθαρέντες οἰκτρῶς τελευτήσουσι πρέπουσαν ἀργίᾳ δίκην
ἐκτίνοντες; (7) Καίτοιγε ὁ νόμος μέχρι ἥβης κελεύει
παῖδα ἐκτρέφεσθαι ὑπὸ γονέων. "'Υμεῖς δ', ἴσως εἴποι
τις ἂν ἀνὴρ πολιτικὸς ἀγανακτῶν πρὸς τοὺς ἑαυτοῦ
υἱεῖς κληρονομεῖν ἐπιθυμοῦντας, οὐδὲ τελευτῶντος
10 ἀφέξεσθαί μου διανοεῖσθε, ἀλλὰ καὶ τεθνεῶτα τροφὰς
οἱ ζῶντες αἰτήσετε καὶ οὐκ αἰσχυνεῖσθε θανάτου ζωὴν
ἀπρακτοτέραν βιοῦντες; ἀλλὰ τὰ μὲν ἐμὰ περιττεύειν
καὶ μετὰ θάνατον ἀξιοῦτε ἑτέροις, τὰ δ' ὑμέτερα ὑμῖν
οὐδ' εἰς τὸ ζῆν ἐξαρκέσει." (8) Ἐκεῖνος μὲν οὖν
15 σκαιῶς ἴσως πρὸς τοὺς ἑαυτοῦ παῖδας χρήσεται τοῖς
λόγοις πατρικὴν ἅμα πολιτικῇ παρρησίᾳ ἄγων. Τὰ δ'
ἐμὰ λόγων μὲν εἵνεκα ἐπιεικέστερα ὄντα τυγχάνει, ἔργῳ
δὲ οὐ πόρρω φαίνεται πλουτούντων ἀποστατεῖν. Ὅθεν
ἐγὼ χρυσίον μὲν οὐ καταλείψω τοῖς ἐμαυτοῦ παισί, τοῦ
20 δὲ χρυσοῦ κτῆμα τιμιώτερον, φίλους ἐπιεικεῖς· οὓς
φυλάττοντες μὲν οὐδενὸς ἐλλειφθήσονται τῶν ἀναγκαίων,
κακῶς δὲ τὰ περὶ τοὺς φίλους μεταχειρίσαντες εὔδηλον,
ὡς τά γε χρήματα πολὺ κάκιον διοικήσουσιν. (9) Εἰ δέ
σοι τὰς ἐνίων ὀλιγωρίας ὁρῶντι φαύλως δόξω βεβουλεῦ-
25 σθαι, πρῶτον μὲν ἐκεῖνο ὅρα, ὅτι οὐ πάντες ἄνθρωποι
ὁμοίως ἔχουσι πρὸς τοὺς φίλους (εἰσὶ δὲ οἳ καὶ τετε-
λευτηκότων αὐτῶν προνοοῦσιν) ἔπειθ', ὅτι τοὺς ἡμετέ-
ρους τούτων εἰκὸς εἶναι, οὐ φορτικῶς ἡμῖν συνεληλυθό-
τας, οὐδὲ νῦν μόνον, ἀλλὰ καὶ τότε τῆς παρ' ἡμῶν οὐχ
30 ἧττον ὠφελείας ἀπολαύοντας. Τῆς <μὲν> οὖν ὀλιγοχρο-
νίου χάριτος εἰκὸς καὶ τὰς ἀμοιβὰς εἶναι βραχείας, αἱ
πολυχρόνιοι δὲ τῶν εὐεργεσιῶν ἴσην τῇ ὠφελείᾳ τίκτουσι
τὴν ἀμοιβήν. (10) Τὰ δ' ἐμὰ μαντεύομαι προκόπτουσι

might be in it. What, then, compels us to leave the children a cause for folly rather than education? We have
shown them not only in words but also in deeds that their
hopes depend upon themselves, and that, if they do not
become good they cannot truly live, but that, wasted by
hunger, they will die miserably, paying a fitting penalty
for their laziness? (7) Indeed, the law does command that
children be raised by their parents until adulthood. "But
you," perhaps some citizen who is angry at his sons for
setting their hearts on their inheritance might say, "Is
it your intention not to leave me alone when I die? Will
you, the living, even ask the dead for food? And are you
not ashamed of living a life which is more inactive than
the dead? On the contrary, you think that my resources
will, after my death, be more than enough for others, but
yours are not even sufficient for you to live on!" (8) He
does, perhaps, speak with some lack of skill to his sons,
using the paternal prerogative together with civic freedom
of speech. But as for my words, my resources happen to be
rather modest, but in reality they appear to be not far
removed from those of the wealthy. For that reason I will
not leave gold for my sons, but rather something which is
more valuable than gold, namely good friends. If they
keep them, they will lack none of the necessities, but if
they treat their friends badly, it will be evident that
they would be even much worse at managing money. (9) If
it seems to you that I have made a bad decision because
you see the negligence of some, then consider first that
not all men have the same relationship with their friends
(there are some who provide for them even if they have
died); second, that our friends are truly to be classed
with those who did not associate with us in a common way,
but who not only now but also later will enjoy no little
benefit from us. Accordingly, it is clear that for a
favor of short duration the remuneration is of a short
duration, but that long lasting good deeds bring forth a
remuneration equal to the benefit. (10) With respect to

τοῖς ἑταίροις καλλίω φανεῖσθαι· διόπερ οὐδὲ μισθοὺς
αὐτοὺς εἰσπράττομαι, ὅτι οὐδὲν ἔχω πρέπον ἀντικατάλ-
λαγμα φιλοσοφίας ἄλλο πλὴν φιλίαν, καὶ ὅτι οὐχ ὥσπερ
οἱ σοφισταὶ κἀγὼ δέδοικα περὶ τῶν ἰδίων.† Παλαιού-
5   μενα γὰρ ἔννοα? γίνεται καὶ πρὸς <τὸ> γῆρας μᾶλλον
ἀναθεωρεῖσθαι φιλεῖ.† ὅθεν αὐτά τε μάλιστα ὑπὸ τῶν
μαθόντων στέργεται τότε, καὶ ὁ γεννήσας αὐτά† πατὴρ†
ἐπιποθεῖται· περιὼν μὲν οὖν τιμῆς τυγχάνει, τελευτή-
σας δὲ μνήμης ἀξιοῦται· κἂν τῶν οἰκείων τινὰ ἀπολε-
10   λοιπὼς ᾖ, τοῦ δὲ ὡς υἱέως ἢ ἀδελφοῦ κήδονται πᾶσαν
εὔνοιαν εἰς αὐτὸν ἐνδεικνύμενοι, τρόπον τινὰ ἕτερον
συγγενείας τῆς κατὰ φύσιν συνανηρτημένοι αὐτῷ.
     (11) Οὔκουν δύνανται, οὐδ᾽ εἰ βούλοιντο, κακῶς πράτ-
τοντα αὐτὸν παρεξιέναι, ὥσπερ οὐδὲ τοὺς κατὰ γένος
15   προσήκοντας ὑπερορᾶν οἷοί τέ ἐσμεν. Τὸ γὰρ ἐν τῇ
ψυχῇ συγγενές, ἅτε ἐκ τοῦ αὐτοῦ πατρὸς ἀδελφὸν γεγεν-
νημένον, ἀναγκάζει σφᾶς βοηθεῖν τῷ τοῦ τετελευτηκότος
υἱεῖ ὑπομιμνῆσκον τοῦ πατρὸς καὶ τὴν ἐκείνου ὀλιγω-
ρίαν σφετέραν ἀτιμίαν τιθέμενον. Ὅρα οὖν, εἴ σοι
20   δόξω ὅτι ἢ τἀμαυτοῦ κακῶς οἰκονομεῖν ἢ <τὰ> τῶν
παιδίων, ὅπως μηδὲν ὑστερήσωσι τῶν ἀναγκαίων ἐμοῦ
τελευτήσαντος ὀλιγωρεῖν, ὃς οὐδὲ χρήματα αὐτοῖς,
ἀλλὰ καὶ τοὺς τῶν χρημάτων καὶ αὐτῶν ἐκείνων ἐπιμελη-
σομένους καταστησάμενος καταλείπω. (12) Καίτοι ὑπὸ
25   μὲν ἀργυρίου οὐδεὶς βελτίων εἰς τὴν ἡμέραν ταύτην
ἱστορεῖται γενόμενος· ὁ δὲ δόκιμος φίλος καὶ ταύτῃ
αἱρετώτερος τυγχάνει τοῦ δοκίμου χρυσίου, ὅτι οὐ πᾶσι
τοῖς ὀρεγομένοις, ἀλλὰ τοῖς βελτίοσι τῶν φίλων
ὑπηρετεῖ, οὐδὲ τὰς τοῦ βίου χρείας μόνον, ἀλλὰ καὶ
30   τὴν αὐτοῦ τοῦ κεκτημένου ψυχὴν θεραπεύει καὶ εἰς
ἀρετῆς λόγον, ἧς χωρὶς οὐδὲν τῶν ἀνθρωπίνων ὀνίνησι,
πλεῖστα συμβάλλεται. Τὸ μὲν οὖν ἀκριβὲς τούτων πέρι
καὶ κατ᾽ ὄψιν ἐντυχόντες ἀλλήλοις ἐπισκεψόμεθα· πρὸς
ἃ δὲ ἐπιζητεῖς νῦν ἀρκεῖ καὶ διὰ τῶν εἰρημένων ἀπο-
35   κεκρίσθαι μετρίως.

my own deeds, I prophesy that they will appear better to
my friends as time goes on; therefore, I am collecting no
repayment for myself from them, because I know no appropriate remuneration for philosophy except friendship, and
because I have no fear for my own things as the sophists
do. For when they become old, they gain vigor and are esteemed more highly for their age; therefore, they are then
loved especially by students, and the father who produced
them is longed for. So, as long as he lives, he attains
honor and when he is dead, his memory is esteemed, and if
he has left a certain relative behind, he is cared for as
if he were a son or a brother, and they show all good will
to him, since they are bound to him in a way which is different from that of natural kinship. (11) Thus, if he is
doing poorly, they cannot neglect him even if they want
to, just as we could not disregard those who are related
to us by blood. The kinship of the soul, which is like a
brother born from the same father, compels people to help
the son of the deceased when they remember the father, and
it regards their neglect of him as their own dishonor.
Now see if you still think that I am managing either my
own affairs poorly or that I neglect my children, so that
when I have died they will lack none of the necessities!
I do not leave them any money, but rather those who will
take care of them financially and be concerned about them
personally. (12) Indeed, to this day, it is said that no-
one has ever been made better by money. The reason that
the proven friend is more desirable than genuine gold is
that he does not help everyone who reaches out to him, but
he serves only his best friends, nor does he attend only
to the physical necessities of life, but also to the soul
that his friend already possesses, and he contributes most
of all to the reason for virtue, without which nothing human is profitable. We shall examine these things in detail
when we meet face to face. In regard to your inquiries it
now suffices to have answered you briefly through what I
have said.

7. Σωκράτους

Σὲ μὲν οὐ θαυμαστὸν ἐπιστέλλειν ὑπὲρ ὧν
γράφεις· τὴν γὰρ αὐτὴν ὑπολαμβάνεις γνώμην, ἣν
παρόντος σου πρὸς ἡμᾶς εἶχον καὶ νῦν ἀπόντος <σου>
5   φυλάττειν ἔτι τοὺς τριάκοντα. Ἐμοὶ δὲ συνέβη μετὰ
τὴν σὴν ἀποχώρησιν εὐθέως ὑποπτευθῆναι καί τις
λόγος ἐν αὐτοῖς διῆλθεν, ὡς οὐ χωρὶς Σωκράτους
ταῦτ' εἴη πεπραγμένα. Ἡμέραις δ' οὐ πολλαῖς
ὕστερον ἀνακαλεσάμενοί με εἰς τὴν θόλον ἦγον καὶ
10   περὶ τούτων ἐμέμφοντο· καὶ ἐμοῦ ἀπολογουμένου ἰέναι
με ἐκέλευον εἰς Πειραιᾶ καὶ Λέοντα συλλαμβάνειν.
Ἦν δὲ γνώμη αὐτῶν ἐκεῖνον μὲν ἀποκτιννύναι καὶ τὰ
χρήματα αὐτοὺς ἔχειν, ἐμὲ δὲ κοινωνὸν ποιεῖσθαι
τοῦ ἀδικήματος. (2) παραιτουμένου δέ μου καί τι
15   τοιοῦτον εἰπόντος, ὡς οὐκ ἂν ἑκών ποτε ἔργῳ ἐπι-
γραφείην ἀδίκῳ, παρὼν ὁ Χαρικλῆς καὶ ἰδίᾳ ἀγανακτήσας·
"ἦπου οὐδέν, ὦ Σώκρατες," ἔφη, "ἡγῇ κακὸν δύνασθαι
παθεῖν οὕτως αὐθαδῶς διαλεγόμενος;" Κἀγώ, "μυρία μὲν
οὖν νὴ Δί'," εἶπον, "ὦ Χαρίκλεις, οὐ μέντοι τοσοῦτόν
20   γε οὐδέν, ὁπηλίκον εἰ ἀδικήσω." Ἀπεκρίνατο μὲν οὖν
οὐκέτι οὐδὲ εἷς αὐτῶν· δοκοῦσι δέ μοι οὐχ ὁμοίως ἐξ
ἐκείνου τοῦ χρόνου διακεῖσθαι.

(3) Περὶ δὲ ὑμῶν οἱ παρόντες διήγγελλον κατὰ
γνώμην ἄχρι νῦν χωρεῖν τὰ πράγματα. ἔλεγον γάρ,
25   ὅτι οἱ Θηβαῖοι καταφυγόντας ὑμᾶς ἀσμένως ἀπεδέξαντο
καὶ κατιοῦσι πάσῃ προθυμίᾳ συλλαμβάνειν οἷοί τέ
εἰσιν. Ἐταράττοντο δὴ καὶ τῶν ἐνταῦθά τινες τοῖς
λόγοις τούτοις καὶ ὅτι καὶ τὰ ἐκ τῆς Λακεδαίμονος
δυσελπιστότερα ἠγγέλλετο. Ἔλεγον γὰρ οἱ μετὰ τῶν
30   πρέσβεων ἐκεῖθεν ἥκοντες πολέμους τε καταλαβεῖν
τοὺς Λακεδαιμονίους συνεστηκότας μεγάλους καὶ τοὺς
ἐφόρους περὶ τῆς ἐνταῦθα ταραχῆς ἀκούοντας ἀγανακ-
τεῖν οὐκ ἐπ' ὀλέθρῳ λέγοντας αὐτοῖς παραδεδωκέναι
τὴν πόλιν τοὺς Λακεδαιμονίους (τοῦτο μὲν γὰρ ἐξεῖναι
35   καὶ σφίσι κρατήσασι πεποιηκέναι, εἰ ἐβούλοντο τῶν
συμμάχων Κορινθίων

7. Of Socrates

I am not surprised at what you wrote. For you suspect that the Thirty still hold the same opinion, now
while you are away, that they held toward us when you were
present. It happened that I came under suspicion immediately after your departure, and a certain rumor circulated
among them to the effect that these things had not been
done without Socrates. And not many days later they summoned me and brought me to Tholos, where they blamed me
for these things; and when I defended myself, they commanded me to go to Piraeus and to arrest Leon. They intended to kill him, get his money, and make me a party to
the crime. (2) When I refused and said something to the
effect that I would never willingly subscribe to this unjust deed, Charicles, who was present and was already
angry at me for personal reasons, said, "Is it then,
Socrates, that you believe you can suffer no harm, and
thus argue so stubbornly?" And I said, "By Zeus, I can
suffer countless evils, Charicles, but none would be so
great as if I were to act unjustly." After that, none of
them responded again, but it seems to me that from that
time their attitude toward me changed.

(3) Some of those present reported about you that
until now, things were going according to your intention.
They said that the Thebans gladly accepted you when you
fled, and that they would be able to help you with eagerness if you should go back home. What is more, some here
were disturbed by these reports, especially since it was
reported from Lacedaemon that things there were even more
hopeless. For those who came from there with the envoys
said that the Lacedaemonians were involved in great dis-
putes, and that the Ephors were angry when they heard
about the trouble here, saying that the Lacedaemonians had
not handed the city over to them to be destroyed (for had
they wanted to, they could have done so, since they held
the power, for at that time their allies the Corinthians

καὶ Θηβαίων τότε ἐναγόντων), ἀλλ᾽ ὅπως αὐτοί τε
πολιτεύσωνται ἐπιτηδείως ὀλιγαρχούμενοι καὶ τὰ
κοινὰ διοικοῦντες βέλτιον ἢ ἐπὶ τῆς δημοκρατίας.
(4) Εἰ οὖν οὖτοι ἀληθῆ ταῦτα ἀπαγγέλλουσι καὶ τὰ
5   ὑμέτερα οὕτως ὥς φασιν ἔχει, πολλὴ ἐλπὶς ὑμῶν μετὰ
Θηβαίων ἀφικομένων, ἐκείνοις δὲ μὴ βοηθησάντων
Λακεδαιμονίων, ῥᾳδίως καταστήσεσθαι τὰ ἐνθάδε.
Ὁμοῦ δὲ καὶ τῶν ἐπιχωρίων πολλοί, νῦν μὲν διὰ τὸ
δεδοικέναι ἄγουσιν ἡσυχίαν· εἰ δὲ τῶν ὑμετέρων τι
10   ἀλλαχόθεν παραφαίνεται βέβαιον, ἄσμενοι καταλεί-
ψουσι τὰ ἐνταῦθα. Ὅλως γὰρ οὐδὲν ὑγιὲς τῆς
πολιτείας αὐτοῖς καταλείπεται, ἀλλ᾽ ὑπὸ πολλῶν καὶ
συνεχῶν ἀδικημάτων πάντα διέφθαρται, καὶ τὸ μὲν
ἤδη παράπαν, ὡς τὸ καθ᾽ ὑμᾶς μέρος ἀπέρρηκται, τὸ
15   δέ, εἰ μικρᾶς ἔξωθεν ἀφορμῆς ἐπιλάβοιτο, ταὐτὸ
πείσεται τῷ ὑμετέρῳ, ὥστε εἴπερ σοί ποτε ἄλλοτε
καὶ νῦν γέγονε δῆλον, ὅτι πάντων μέγιστον κακὸν
ταῖς πόλεσίν ἐστιν ἡ τῶν ἀρχόντων πονηρία. (5)
Οὗτοι γοῦν οὕτως ἐοίκασιν ἐξηπατῆσθαι περὶ τὸ
20   συμφέρον, ὥστε οὐδὲ διαφθειρόμενα ὁρῶντες τὰ πράγματα παύσασθαι ἐθέλειν· ἀλλ᾽ οἷς ἐταράχθη πρότερον,
τοῖς αὐτοῖς οἴονται καταστήσειν αὐτὰ φυγὰς καὶ
δημεύσεις οὐσιῶν καὶ θανάτους ἀκρίτους ποιούμενοι.
Καὶ οὐχ ὁρῶσιν, ὅτι νοσημάτων πονηρὸς ἂν εἴη ἰατρὸς
25   ὁ τὴν αὐτὴν τῷ συνεστηκότι αἰτίῳ ποιούμενος θερα-
πείαν. Ἀλλὰ τὰ μὲν τούτων ἀνιάτως ἔχει· σὺ δὲ
τῶν σαυτοῦ ἐπιμελούμενος ὀρθῶς ποιήσεις. Μία γὰρ
καὶ τοῖς ἐνθάδε ἐλπὶς ἦν, ἂν ὑμεῖς πράξητε κατὰ
νοῦν, βαρείας πάνυ καὶ χαλεπῆς ἀπηλλάχθαι δεσποτείας.

and Thebans were urging them on), but that they might conduct the government efficiently as an oligarchy and pursue
the common good better than it had been in the time of the
democracy. (4) Therefore, if what they report is true,
and your situation is as they say it is, there is high
hope that when you arrive with the Thebans, things will
readily be restored if the Lacedaemonians do not help the
Thirty. Just now many of the natives are behaving quietly
because of fear. But if any of your expectations are confirmed from some other source, they will gladly abandon
those who are in power here. For there is nothing at all
sound left for them in the state, but everything has been
ruined by many unceasing injustices. Your group has already completely dispersed, while the other group will
suffer the same fate if even a small impulse comes from
the outside. So, if it has been clear to you at any other
time, it has become so especially now that the greatest
evil of all for cities is the wickedness of their rulers.
(5) At any rate, they seem to be so deceived about what is
profitable, that when they see that things are being
ruined, they do not wish to put a stop to it, but they
think they can set things in order by the same means they
used to stir things up in the first place: exile, confis-
cation of property and capital punishment without trial.
And they do not see that that person would be a bad healer
of diseases who attempted to cure the illness with what
caused it in the first place! But while their condition
is incurable, you will do the right thing if you take care
of your own affairs. For those here have one hope, that
if you act sensibly they will be freed from a very oppres-
sive and cruel despotism.

8. Ἀντισθένης Ἀριστίππῳ

Οὐκ ἔστι τοῦ φιλοσόφου τὸ παρὰ τυράννοις
ἀνδράσι εἶναι καὶ Σικελικαῖς προσανέχειν τραπέζαις,
ἀλλὰ μᾶλλον τὸ ἐν τῇ ἰδίᾳ καὶ αὐτάρκων ἐφίεσθαι.
5 Σὺ δὲ οἴει ταύτην εἶναι πλεονεξίαν τοῦ σπουδαίου τὸ
δύνασθαι μὲν κτᾶσθαι χρήματα πολλά, τοὺς δὲ δυνατω-
τάτους ἔχειν φίλους. Οὔτε γὰρ χρήματα ἀναγκαῖά
ἐστιν, οὔτε, εἰ ἀναγκαῖα ἦν, οὕτω ποριζόμενα καλά,
οὔτε φίλοι γένοιντο ἂν οἱ πολλοὶ ἀμαθεῖς ὄντες καὶ
10 ταῦτα τύραννοι· ὥστε σοὶ συμβουλεύσαιμι ἂν ἀπιέναι
Συρακουσῶν τε καὶ Σικελίας. Εἰ δ᾽, ὡς φασί τινες,
ἡδονὴν θαυμάζεις καὶ τούτων ἀντέχῃ ὧν μὴ προσήκει
τοὺς φρονίμους ἀνθρώπους, ἄπιθι εἰς Ἀντίκυραν, καὶ
ὠφελήσει σε ὁ ἐλλέβορος ποθείς· πολὺ κρείσσων γάρ
15 ἐστιν οὗτος τοῦ παρὰ Διονυσίου οἴνου. Ἐκεῖνος μὲν
γὰρ μανίαν ποιεῖ πολλήν, οὗτος δὲ ἀποπαύει. Ὁπόσον
οὖν ὑγίειά τε καὶ φρόνησις νόσου τε καὶ ἀφροσύνης
διαφέρει, τοσοῦτον ἂν καὶ σὺ διενέγκαις πρὸς τὰ νῦν
σοι ὄντα. Ἔρρωσο.

20   9. Ἀρίστιππος Ἀντισθένει

Κακοδαιμονοῦμεν, ὦ Ἀντίσθενες, οὐ μετρίως.
Πῶς γὰρ οὐ μέλλομεν κακοδαιμονεῖν ὄντες παρὰ τυράννῳ
καὶ ὁσημέραι ἐσθίοντες καὶ πίνοντες πολυτελείᾳ καὶ
ἀλειφόμενοί τινι τῶν εὐωδεστάτων μύρων καὶ σύροντες
25 ἐσθῆτας μακρὰς ἐκ Τάραντος; Καὶ οὐδείς με ἐξαιρήσε-
ται τῆς Διονυσίου ὠμότητος, ὃς <με> ὥς τινα ἐνεχύριον
οὐκ ἄγνωτα, ἀλλὰ καὶ λόγων ἐπιμελητὴν τῶν Σωκρατικῶν
κατέχει, ὥσπερ ἔφην, σιτίζων καὶ ἀλείφων καὶ ἀμφιεν-
νὺς τοιαῦτα καὶ οὔτε δίκην φοβεῖται τῶν θεῶν οὔτ᾽
30 ἄνθρωπον αἰδεῖται, ὅστις με τοιαῦτα διατίθεται.

8. Antisthenesto Aristippus

It is not right for a philosopher to associate with
tyrants and to devote himself to Sicilian tables. Rather,
he should live in his own country and strive for self-
sufficiency. But you think that the advantage of the wise
man is the ability to acquire large amounts of money and
to have very powerful friends. Yet money is not necessary,
and even if it were, getting it in this way would not be
good. Nor could the masses ever be your friends, for they
are uneducated, as are tyrants, with respect to these
things. Therefore, I would counsel you to leave both Syracuse and Sicily. But if, as some say, you admire pleasure,
and if you are cleaving to things that are not fitting for
wise men, then go away to Anticyra, and when you have
drunk the hellebore, it will benefit you, for it is much
stronger than the wine of Dionysius. The one produces
great madness and the other cures it. Therefore, to the
degree that health and wisdom differ from sickness and
folly, to that degree you would surpass your present condition. Farewell.

9. Aristippus to Antisthenes

We are wretched beyond measure, Antisthenes. How
could we not be wretched since we live with a tyrant, and
daily eat and drink extravagantly, are anointed with one
of the sweetest-smelling perfumes, and drag about long
Tarentine cloaks? And no one will free me from the cruel-
ty of Dionysius, who holds me as some type of pledge, not
as an obscure person, but rather as one who is a steward
of the Socratic teachings, and as I said, he feeds me,
anoints me and drapes clothing like that around me. And
he neither fears the punishment of the gods nor does he
show respect to any man while he treats me in this way.

Νῦν δ' αὖ καὶ τὸ κακὸν εἰς τὸ δεινότερον οἴχεται,
ὅπου δεδώρηται γυναῖκας Σικελικὰς τρεῖς ἀναλέκτους
τὸ κάλλος καὶ ἀργύρια πάμπολλα. (2) Καὶ πότε παύσε-
ται ἄνθρωπος οὗτος τοιαῦτα ποιῶν, οὐκ οἶδα. Εὖ οὖν
5   ποιεῖς ἀχθόμενος ἐπὶ τῇ κακοδαιμονίᾳ τῶν ἄλλων· κἀγὼ
δὲ ἐπὶ τῇ σῇ εὐδαιμονίᾳ ἥδομαι, ἵνα σοι τὰ αὐτὰ
δόξω ποιεῖν τε καὶ ἀποτίνειν τὰς χάριτας. Ἔρρωσο.

Τῶν τε ἰσχάδων ἀποτίθεσο ἵν' ἔχῃς εἰς τὸ
χεῖμα, καὶ τῶν ἀλφίτων ἔχε τῶν Κρητικῶν· ταῦτα γὰρ
10   δοκεῖ ἀμείνω τοῦ χρήματος εἶναι· καὶ ἀπὸ τῆς Ἐννεακ-
ρούνου λούου τε καὶ πῖνε καὶ τὸν αὐτὸν τρίβωνα θέρους
τε καὶ χειμῶνος ἔχε ῥυπῶντα, ὡς πρέπει τῷ ἐλευθέρῳ
καὶ ζῶντι [ἐν Ἀθήναις] δημοκρατικῶς. (3) Ἐγὼ μὲν
γάρ, ἐξ οὗ εἰς τυραννουμένην ἧκα πόλιν τε καὶ νῆσον,
15   ᾔδειν, ὅτι κακοδαιμονήσω ταῦτα πάσχων, καθάπερ σύ
μοι γράφεις. Νῦν <δὲ> ἐλεοῦντές με περιβλέπονται
Συρακούσιοι καὶ Ἀκραγαντίνων οἱ ἐπιδημοῦντες καὶ
Γελῴων καὶ οἱ ἄλλοι Σικελιῶται. Τῆς δὲ μανίας, ἧς
ἐμάνην εἰς ταῦτα ἐλθὼν ἀβούλως τὰ ἀτοπήματα, ἐπαρῶ-
20   μαι ἀρὰν κατ' ἐμαυτοῦ, ἧς ἄξιός εἰμι, μὴ ἐκλιπεῖν με
τὰ κακὰ ταῦτα, ὁπότε ἐγὼ γεγονὼς ἔτη τοσαῦτα καὶ
φρονεῖν δοκῶν πεινῆν καὶ ῥιγοῦν καὶ ἀδοξεῖν οὐκ
ἠθέλησα οὐδὲ πώγωνα τρέφειν μέγαν. (4) Πέμψω δέ
σοι τῶν θέρμων τοὺς μεγάλους τε καὶ λευκούς, ἵν'
25   ἔχῃς μετὰ τὸ ἐπιδείξασθαι τὸν Ἡρακλέα τοῖς νέοις
ὑποτρώγειν· αἰσχρὸν γὰρ οὔ φασί σοι περὶ τοιούτων
λέγειν ἢ γράφειν. Διονυσίῳ γὰρ ἐάν τις λέγῃ περὶ
θέρμων, αἰσχρόν γε οἶμαι διὰ τοὺς τῶν τυράννων
νόμους. Τὰ λοιπὰ δὲ παρὰ Σίμωνα τὸν σκυτοτόμον
30   βάδιζε διαλεγόμενος, οὗ μεῖζόν σοι ἐν σοφίᾳ οὐδ'
ἔστιν οὐδ' ἂν γένοιτο. Ἐμοὶ μὲν γὰρ ἀπηγόρευται
τοῖς χειροτέχναις προσιέναι, ἐπειδὴ ὑφ' ἑτέρων
ἐξουσίᾳ εἰμί.

Now, moreover, the evil has become more terrible since he
has given me three Sicilian women of exquisite beauty and
a large amount of money. (2) And I do not know when the
man will stop doing such things. Therefore, you are doing
well when you are burdened with the misfortunes of others.
I am delighted at your good fortune, so that I might appear both to be doing the same things for you and also to
be repaying your favors. Farewell.

Put away some dried figs so that you might have some
for the winter, and get some Cretan bread, for these
things seem to be better than money, and both bathe and
drink from the Nine Spouts, and wear the same filthy cloak
summer and winter, as is fitting for a free man living
democratically in Athens. (3) As for me, ever since I
came to a city and an island which are under the rule of a
tyrant, I have known that I would be wretched and suffer
these misfortunes, exactly as you are writing me about.
Now the Syracusans, those from Agrigentum and Gela, and
the other Sicilians who are staying here, are showing
their compassion and coming to see me. For my madness,
which ill advisedly brought me to these absurd circumstances, I have sworn an oath to myself, which I deserve,
that I would not leave these evils; since I have lived for
so many years and I still seem to be reasonable, I have no
desire to suffer hunger or cold, or to be held in ill re-
pute or to grow a long beard. (4) I will send you large
white lupines so that you will have something to eat after
you have produced your *Heracles* for the youths. For they
do not tell you that it is shameful to speak or to write
of such things. But if someone were to speak to Dionysius
about lupines, I think it would be shameful because of the
customs of the tyrants. With regard to the other things,
go to Simon the shoemaker, in whom you have someone who
is greater in wisdom than anyone ever was or will be, and
converse with him. I am forbidden to go to the craftsmen,
since I am under the authority of others.

10. Αἰσχίνης Ἀριστίππῳ

Ἔγραψα μὲν καὶ Πλάτωνι παρακαλῶν, ὅπως διαπρά-
ξησθε σωθῆναι τοὺς Λοκροὺς νεανίσκους, καὶ σοὶ δὲ
τὰ αὐτὰ ἐπιστέλλων οὐχ ἁμαρτάνειν οἶμαι· ποιήσεις
5   γὰρ ἄσμενος. Οἶσθα δὲ τὴν πρὸς αὐτούς μοι ἑταιρίαν
καὶ ὅτι Διονύσιος ἐξηπάτηται ὡς ἀδικούντων αὐτῶν
ἔχων δόξαν. Ἤδη πειρῶ τοῦτο ποιῆσαι θᾶττον.
Ἔρρωσο.

11. Ἀρίστιππος Αἰσχίνῃ

10   Λυθήσονται τῆς φυλακῆς οἱ νεανίσκοι, περὶ ὧν
μοι γράφεις, οἱ Λοκροὶ καὶ οὐ τεθνήξονται· οὐδὲ
ἀπολοῦσι τι τῶν χρημάτων ἥκοντές γε παραυτὰ τοῦ
θανεῖν. Ταῦτα δὲ Ἀντισθένει μὴ λέξῃς, εἰ σέσωκα
τοὺς φίλους. Οὐ γὰρ αὐτῷ ἀρέσκει τυράννοις φίλοις
15   χρῆσθαι, ἀλλὰ τοὺς ἀλφιτοπώλας καὶ τοὺς καπήλους
ἀναζητεῖν, οἵτινες δικαίως τὰ ἄλφιτα καὶ τὸν οἶνον
πωλοῦσιν ἐν Ἀθήναις καὶ τὰς ἐξωμίδας μισθοῦσι τὰς
παχείας, ὁπόταν οἱ σκίρωνες πνέωσι, καὶ τὸν Σίμωνα
θεραπεύειν. Τοῦτο γὰρ οὐκ ἔστι χρῆμα.

10. Aeschines to Aristippus

I also wrote to Plato, urging him that you should strive to save the young Locrian men. And in writing the same thing to you, I do not believe that I am making a mistake, for you will do it gladly. You know of my friendship with them, and that Dionysius is deceived in thinking that they are guilty of wrongdoing. Now try to accomplish this very quickly. Farewell.

11. Aristippus to Aeschines

The young Locrian men about whom you wrote me will be released from prison and will not die, nor will they lose any of their money, though they came close to dying. Do not tell Antisthenes that I have saved the friends. For he does not like to have tyrants for friends, but he rather seeks out the barley meal sellers and tavern keepers who sell barley meal and wine honestly in Athens, and who rent out thick tunics when the winds blow, and he courts Simon. For this is not wealth!

12. Σίμων Ἀριστίππῳ

Ἀκούω σε τωθάζειν ἡμᾶς τῆς σοφίας παρὰ
Διονυσίῳ. Ἐγὼ δὲ ὁμολογῶ εἶναι σκυτοτόμος καὶ
ἐργάζεσθαι τοιαῦτα καὶ ὁμοίως, εἰ δέοι, σκύτη
5   τέμνειν αὖ πάλιν εἰς νουθεσίαν ἀνθρώπων ἀφρόνων καὶ
οὕτω μετὰ πολλῆς χλιδῆς οἰομένων ζῆν παρὰ τὴν
Σωκράτους βουλήν. Ἔσται δὲ ὁ σωφρονιστὴς τῶν
ἀφρόνων ὑμῶν παιδιῶν Ἀντισθένης· γράφεις γὰρ αὐτῷ
κωμῳδῶν ἡμῶν τὰς διατριβάς. Ἀλλὰ τούτων μέν, ὦ
10   θεία φρήν, ἅλις [καὶ] πεπαίχθω πρός σέ μοι. Μέμνησο
μέντοι λιμοῦ καὶ δίψης· ταῦτα γὰρ δύναται μέγα τοῖς
σωφροσύνην διώκουσιν.

13. Ἀρίστιππος Σίμωνι

Οὐκ ἐγώ σε κωμῳδῶ, ἀλλὰ Φαίδων, λέγων γεγο-
15   νέναι σε κρείσσω καὶ σοφώτερον Προδίκου τοῦ Κείου,
ὃς ἔφη ἀπελέγξαι σε αὐτὸν περὶ τὸ ἐγκώμιον τὸ εἰς
τὸν Ἡρακλέα γενόμενον αὐτῷ. Θαυμάζω μέντοι σε καὶ
ἐπαινῶ, εἰ σκυτικὸς ὢν σοφίας ἐμπλησθεὶς καὶ πάλαι
μὲν Σωκράτην ἔπειθες καὶ τοὺς καλλίστους νέους καὶ
20   εὐγενεστάτους παρὰ σὲ καθέζεσθαι, οἷον Ἀλκιβιάδην
τε τὸν Κλεινίου καὶ Φαῖδρον τὸν Μυρρινούσιον καὶ
Εὐθύδημον τὸν Γλαύκωνος καὶ τῶν τὰ κοινὰ πραττόντων
Ἐπικράτεα τὸν Σακεσφόρον καὶ Εὐρυπτόλεμον καὶ τοὺς
ἄλλους· ὡς εἰ καὶ Περικλεῖ γε τῷ Ξανθίππου μὴ αἱ
25   στρατηγίαι ἦσαν καὶ ὁ πόλεμος τότε, κἂν οὗτος, οἶμαι,
ἦν παρὰ σέ. Καὶ νῦν ἴσμεν, ὁποῖος εἶ· Ἀντισθένης
γὰρ παρὰ σὲ φοιτᾷ. Δύνῃ δὲ καὶ ἐν Συρακούσαις φιλο-
σοφεῖν· οἱ γὰρ ἱμάντες τίμιοί εἰσι καὶ τὰ σκύτη.
(2) Καὶ οὐκ οἶσθα, ὡς ἐγὼ μὲν τῶν ὑποδημάτων χρώ-
30   μενος παρέκαστα τὴν τέχνην σου θαυμασίαν τινὰ ποιῶ·
Ἀντισθένης δὲ γυμνοποδῶν τί γὰρ ἄλλο πράττει ἢ σοὶ

12. Simon to Aristippus

I hear that you ridicule our wisdom in the presence
of Dionysius. I admit that I am a shoemaker and that I do
work of that nature, and in like manner I would, if it
were necessary, cut straps once more for the purpose of
admonishing foolish men who think that they are living
according to the teaching of Socrates when they are living
in great luxury. Antisthenes shall be the chastiser of
your foolish jests. For you are writing him letters which
make fun of our way of life. But let what I have said to
you in jest suffice. At any rate, remember hunger and
thirst, for these are worth much to those who pursue self
control.

13. Aristippus to Simon

I do not ridicule you, but rather Phaedo, when he
said that you are more excellent and wiser than Prodicus
of Ceos, who said that you refuted him with regard to his
encomium to Heracles. No, I do admire and praise you,
since, though you are but a shoemaker, you are filled with
wisdom and used to pursuade Socrates and the most handsome
and noble youths to sit with you, youths such as Alcibiades, son of Clinias, Phaedrus the Myrrhinean, and Euthy-
demus, son of Glaucon, and of the men of public affairs,
Epicrates, Sacesphorus, and Euryptolemus and others, I
also think Pericles, son of Xanthippus, was with you when
he did not have to carry out the duties of a general or
there was not a war going on at the time. And now we know
what sort of person you are, for Antisthenes visits you.
And you can also practice philosophy in Syracuse, for
leather thongs and straps are valued here. (2) Don't you
know that I, who wear shoes, will constantly make your
trade into something to be admired? But as for that

ἀργίαν καὶ ἀμισθίαν εἰσάγει πείθων τοὺς νέους καὶ
ἅπαντας 'Αθηναίων γυμνοποδεῖν; Σκόπει οὖν, ὁπόσον
σοι ἐγὼ φίλος ὁ ῥαστώνην καὶ τὴν ἡδονὴν ἀποδεχόμενος.
Σὺ δ' ὁμολογῶν εὐλόγως ἐρωτᾶν Πρόδικον, τὸ ἀκόλουθον
5   οὐκ ἔγνως ἐπὶ σαυτοῦ· οὕτω γὰρ ἂν ἐμὲ μὲν ἐθαύμαζες,
τοὺς δὲ ἔχοντας βαθεῖς πώγωνας καὶ τοὺς σκίπωνας
ἐγέλασας τῆς ἀλαζονείας ῥυπῶντάς τε καὶ φθειριῶντας
καὶ ὄνυχας ὥσπερ τὰ θηρία μακροὺς περικειμένους καὶ
ἐναντίας σου τῆς τέχνης ὑποτιθεμένους ὑποθήκας.

10   14. Αἰσχίνης Ξενοφῶντι

"Ηδη μὲν οἱ περὶ Γρύλλον τὸν παῖδά σου τὸν
Γέταν παρὰ σὲ ἐπεπόμφεσαν ἅπαντα ἀπαγγελοῦντα τὰ
περὶ Σωκράτην, ἃ ἐγένετο ἔν τε τῇ δίκῃ καὶ τῷ θανάτῳ
αὐτοῦ. "Εδει μέντοι καὶ ὧδε τὴν τύχην κωλύμην τινὰ
15   ποιήσασθαι, ὥστε μηδέ σε τυχεῖν 'Αθήνησιν, εἶναι δὲ
περὶ Λακεδαίμονα. Πῶς ἂν οὖν, ὦ Ξενοφῶν, τὴν μιαρίαν
τοῦ βυρσοδέψου 'Ανύτου γράφοιμι τήν τε Μελήτου
τόλμαν καὶ τὸ θράσος αὐτοῖν; Τούτω γὰρ τὼ μιαρωτάτω
ἄνδρε μέχρι τελευτῆς τῶν πραγμάτων παρεμεινάτην
20   πονηρὼ καὶ ἡμῶν οἰομένων αὐτοὺς τὰς τέχνας αὐτοῖν
αἰσχυνθέντας καταθέσθαι ἔτι μᾶλλον ἐχώρησαν τοῦ κακὰ
ἡμῖν παρέχειν. (2) Καὶ εἴπερ Μέλητος ἐν τῷ δικαστηρίῳ οὐδὲν ἴδιον εἶχε†, κακοδαίμων ἦν ἄνθρωπος.
"Ην μὲν γὰρ ἡ ῥίζα τῆς γραφῆς "Ανυτος, δι' ὧν
25   Σωκράτης ἔλεγεν αὐτὸς ἐν τοῖς νέοις ἄρρητα εἶναι τὰ
περὶ βύρσας, ὁπότε διαλέγοιτο καὶ κατασκευάζοι περὶ
τοῦ ἐπιστήμην ἔχοντας προσιέναι <ἐν> τούτοις τοῖς
πράγμασιν, οἷς προσίασιν. †Οὕτως οἱ ἐπαγγελλόμενοι
ὁτιοῦν πράττειν...'Ακουμενὸν τὸν μαθόντα τὰ ἰατρικὰ
30   καὶ τὰ μουσικὰ Δάμονά τε καὶ Κόννον τὸν Μητροβίου.

barefoot Antisthenes, what else has he done than to make
you idle and without an income, since he persuades the
youth and indeed all the Athenians to go barefoot? See,
then, how much of a friend I am, one who is content with
leisure and pleasure. And though you admit that Prodicus
argues reasonably, you do not realize the consequences
for yourself. Otherwise, you would admire me and ridicule those who have long beards and staffs for their
boasting, who are dirty, louse-ridden and have long
fingernails like wild animals and give advice that is
contrary to your craft.

14. Aeschines to Xenophon

    Your son Gryllus has already sent Geta to you, who
told you everything that happened to Socrates during the
trial and at his death. It was necessary that fate also
create a hindrance here, so that you chanced not to be in
Athens, but in Lacedaemon. How then, Xenophon, should I
write to you of the defilement of Anytus the tanner, the
recklessness of Meletus, and the impudence of both of
them? These two most abominable men persisted in wickedness until the end of things, and when we thought that
they were ashamed of their wiles, and had stopped, they
proceeded to inflict still more evils on us. (2) Even if
Meletus did contribute nothing of his own in the law
court, he was still a most wretched man. For the root of
the accusation was Anytus, since Socrates himself, when
he conversed with the youths, said that the tanner's work
was shameful, and since he would discuss and argue about
the need for them to go to those men who have expert
knowledge in these matters to which they would commit
themselves. (In this way, those who profess to do anything at all...Acumenus who had learned medicine and both
Damon and Conon the son of Metrobius music. For I do not

Οὐ γὰρ ᾐδεῖτο, οἶμαι, ὡς μὴ ἐργασάμενος αὐτά, ὁπόταν
οἱ υἱεῖς αὐτοῦ ἀκροασάμενοι Σωκράτους...†ἄχρι νῦν
οὔτε τὸ βῆμα αὐτὸν τρέφειν...οὐ κατατετόλμηται...
καὶ δὴ ἐξηρτήσατο αὐτοῦ ἄλλην τέχνην...κἂν πολλάκις
5   περικρύπτηται περιθέμενος τὴν Ἅιδου κυνῆν ἢ τὸν
Γύγου δακτύλιον καὶ δίκας γράφηται τοῖς ἐν τῇ πόλει·
ζῇ γὰρ ἀπὸ βυρσοδεψικῆς.†   (3) Τὸ μὲν οὖν ὄνομα,
ὥσπερ ἔφην, ἦν Μελήτου τοῦ μαθητοῦ αὐτοῦ καὶ διακόνου
ἅμα· οὗτος γὰρ ὥσπερ ἐν τραγῳδίᾳ ὑπεκρίνετο Μενοικέα
10   τὸν φιλόπολιν, ἀφ' οὗ ἠγανάκτει, ὡς ἡ πόλις ἀδικοῖτο
ὑπὸ τούτων [ἢ] αὐτή.   Ὁ δὲ λόγος ὁ ἄθλιος ἤθελέ σε
εἶναι ἐνθάδε καὶ ἐγέλασας ἂν ἐν ταῖς συμφοραῖς· ἦν
δὲ Πολυκράτους τοῦ λογογράφου· ὃν ἐκεῖνος ὥσπερ ἐν
διδασκάλου παῖδες τὰς ῥήσεις λέγοντες ἀναβὰς ὁπότε
15   κατηγόρει ἐδεδίει τε καὶ ἀπεστρέφετο καὶ ἐπελανθά-
νετο, καὶ ἄλλοι αὐτῷ ὑπέβαλλον, καθότι καὶ Καλλιπίδῃ
τῷ ὑποκριτῇ, καὶ κακὸν κακῶς ἄνω τε καὶ κάτω αὐτόν
τε καὶ τὸ σύγγραμμα ἐπιτρίψας κατέβη.   (4) Σωκράτης
δὲ πάντα μᾶλλον ἐνενοήθη τότε ἢ ἀγῶνα ὅτι ἀγωνίζοιτο
20   τοσοῦτον· καὶ--ὁποῖον γάρ, αὐτὸς οἶδας--μειδιάσας
βλοσυρόν τε καὶ μεμιγμένον γέλωτι ἐκεῖνα εἶπεν, ἅ σοι
οἱ υἱεῖς γράψαντες ἔπεμψαν.   Οἵ τε δικασταὶ τότε μὲν
κρατούμενοι ὑπὸ τοῦ ἐργαστηρίου παντὸς τοῦ ἔξωθεν
περιεστῶτος ὅμως ὑποτιμήσασθαι ἔλεγον· ὁ δὲ μάλα
25   θαρραλέως: "τῆς ἐν Πρυτανείῳ σιτήσεως ὑποτιμῶμαι
ταύτην τὴν δίκην" φησίν.   Οἱ δὲ ἐπέφυσαν τότε δὴ
μᾶλλον· καὶ γὰρ ἀπολογουμένου <αὐτοῦ> δέος ἐποιοῦντο,
μὴ ἀποφύγοι.   Κἂν ἀπέφυγε Σωκράτης· νῦν δὲ οὔτε
κολακείαν οὔτε δέησιν ᾤετο δεῖν προσάγειν τινὰ
30   αὐτοῖς, ἀλλὰ τἀληθῆ καὶ δίκαια λέγειν· οὕτω γὰρ
ἀπολογούμενος εἰ ἑάλω, μὴ αὐτὸς ᾤετο ἀδικήσειν, τοὺς
μέντοι καταψηφισαμένους αὐτοῦ, (5) εἰ μέντοιγε
ποιήσας καὶ εἰπὼν ἀνάξια ἑαυτοῦ καὶ φιλοσοφίας ἀπολυθείη, ἀνδραπόδου βίον ἔφη βιώσειν ἐπαράτου·

think he knew that not having done this work, whenever his
sons attended Socrates' lectures....Up to now the tribunal
where he behaved so boldly does not sustain him, and he
has become dependent on another craft, even if he often
hides himself, putting on the helmet of Hades or the ring
of Gyges, and takes people in the city to court.)   (3) The
name, then, as I said, was that of Meletus, at once his
student and attendant. For he, as though in a tragedy,
played the part of Menoeceus the patriot, according to
whose example he was angry that the city itself was
wronged by these people. But the miserable speech required your presence, and you would have laughed in spite
of your misfortunes. It came from Polycrates the speech-
writer. When he got up to make the accusation, exactly
like children reciting passages in a teacher's classroom,
he got stage fright, became confused and forgot his lines,
and others prompted him as they do Callipides the actor.
And after he had utterly and completely ruined both himself and the speech, he stepped down. (4) But Socrates
had intended anything but that he should make such a
speech--for you know how he spoke--with a seriousness
mixed with laughter he smiled and said the things which
your sons have written down and sent to you. At that time
the judges were being prevailed upon by all the workers
who stood around outside, yet they proposed a lesser
penalty. But he said very boldly, "I propose this punishment: maintenance in the Prytaneum." Then they became
more hostile, for when he was making his defense they were
afraid that he would be acquitted. And Socrates would
have been acquitted, but at the time he believed that he
should not employ either flattery or entreaty with them,
but rather speak truthfully and justly. If he were condemned while defending himself in this way, he thought
that it would not be he who would do anything wrong, but
rather those who had condemned him. (5) If, however, he
were released after he had said or done something unworthy
of himself or of philosophy, he said he would lead the

ἄλλως τε καὶ γῆρας αὐτῷ ἔφη ὑποκεῖσθαι καὶ τὸ ζῆν
μὴ κρεῖττον αὐτῷ ἔσεσθαι τὸ ἔπειτα, ἀλλὰ κάκιον,
κἂν ἀπολυθείη, οὔτε κρεῖττον ἰδεῖν ἢ ἀκοῦσαι ἔτι
δύναιτο, ὥστε κατὰ θεὸν αὐτῷ ἐδόκει ἤδη παρεῖναι ὁ
5   θάνατος. Καὶ καταψηφισθεὶς γελῶν ἐξῄει καὶ τὸν
χρόνον τὸν ἐν τῷ δεσμωτηρίῳ μᾶλλον ἤδετο ἡμῖν διαλεγόμενος ἢ ὁπότε οὐδέπω αὐτὸν ἐγέγραπτο Μέλητος
οὐδὲ ἐνεπεπτώκει εἰς τὸ δεσμωτήριον. Ἔλεγε δὲ
διότι τὸ οἴκημα ἔνθα ἦν καὶ τοὺς δεσμοὺς ἀναγκάζειν
10   αὐτὸν φιλοσοφεῖν· "αἰεὶ μὲν γάρ τοι πρός τινων,
ἔφασκεν, ἐν ἀγορᾷ περιειλκόμην." (6) Καὶ τοιαῦτα
καὶ τοσαῦτα καὶ οὕτως ἡμῖν διελέγετο, ὥστε ἐπιλανθά-
νεσθαι πολλάκις, ὅτι ἐνεπεπτώκει, καὶ προσπίπτειν
λόγοις καὶ φωναῖς τοιαύταις, αἳ οὐκ ἂν λεχθεῖεν ἐν
15   συμφοραῖς· εἶτα δὲ ἀναμιμνησκομένους εἰς αὑτοὺς
ἐπιτιμᾶν ἡμῖν αὐτοῖς τῆς ἀμνημοσύνης ἕκαστον ἑκάστῳ
τῶν παρόντων· τὸν δὲ ὑποτοπάζοντα τὸ γινόμενον ἡμῖν
πάθος διασκοπεῖν καὶ λέγειν, ὡς οὐ μέλει ἡμῖν, εἰ
αὐτίκα τεθνήξοιτο, ὅτι οὕτω γελῶμεν. Καὶ ἐπιλαβό-
20   μενος αὖ Κρίτωνα· "ὦ μῶρε," ἔφη, "νῦν γὰρ θάνε καὶ
Ὀλύμπια καὶ πᾶσα πανήγυρις, ἐπειδὴ ἀποδημεῖν μέλλομεν εἴς τι χωρίον κρεῖττον καὶ τούτου τεθανατωμένοι
ὡς πρὸς τὴν ἀλήθειαν." (7) Ἑτέρους δὲ λόγους καὶ
πολλοὺς καὶ καλοὺς πρὸς Κέβητα καὶ Σιμμίαν τὼ Θηβαίω
25   διελέχθη· ὅτι εἴη ἡ ψυχὴ ἀθάνατος, καὶ ὅτι οἱ τῆς
φρονήσεως ἐπιμεληθέντες εἰς χῶρον τῶν θεῶν ἄπίασι
καὶ οὐδὲν δεινὸν ἐν τῷ λεγομένῳ θανάτῳ πάσχουσιν·
ὥσθ' ἡμᾶς μὴ οἷον κλαίειν Σωκράτην, ὅτι μέλλει ἀποθνήσκειν, ἀλλὰ φθονεῖν αὐτῷ ἡμᾶς δὲ αὑτοὺς κλαίειν,
30   ὅτι ζῶμεν τητώμενοι τοσούτου ἀγαθοῦ τῇ ἀληθείᾳ.
Ἀποδημίαν γὰρ ἔλεγε τὸ χρῆμα τοῦτο καὶ Εὔηνον τὸν
ποιητὴν παρεκάλει δι᾽ ἡμῶν, εἰ εὖ γινώσκοι, ἰέναι
θᾶττον παρ᾽ αὐτόν, ἐπειδὴ φιλόσοφός ἐστι διὰ τὴν
ποίησιν. (8) τὸν γὰρ φιλόσοφον μηδὲν ἄλλο ποιεῖν ἢ
35   θανατᾶν, ἐπειδὴ τῶν τοῦ σώματος αἰτημάτων καταφρονεῖ

life of a cursed slave. Above all, he said that old age
pressed upon him, and that life would not be better for
him afterwards, but worse, and if he were released, he
could no longer see or hear better, with the result that
it seemed to him that according to the will of God, death
was already near. And after he had been condemned, he
went out laughing, and during the time he was in prison,
he enjoyed conversing with us even more than before
Meletus had accused him and he had been thrown into prison. And for that reason, he used to say that the prison
where he found himself and his chains forced him to practice philosophy, "for," he said, "I was always distracted
in the marketplace by certain people." (6) And in this
manner he spoke to us about this and that, so that we
often forgot that he was in prison, and we heard such
words and speeches as would normally not have been spoken
in the midst of misfortunes. And then we would remind
ourselves to reprove one another for forgetting the present circumstances. But, surmising our mood, he looked
around and said that we did not care if he would soon be
dead, since we were laughing so. And seizing Crito, he
said, "Oh you fool, now the Olympian and every other assembly have perished, since when we have died we shall
travel to another country better than even this one, to
truth itself." (7) And he also spoke many other beautiful
words to Cebes and Simmias the Thebans, that the soul is
immortal and that those who cultivate wisdom depart to the
land of God, and that they suffer nothing fearful in so-
called death. As a result, we could no longer weep for
Socrates because he was about to die, but we rather envied
him and wept for ourselves, since we still lived and would
be deprived of what is in truth a great good. For he
called this event a journey, and through us he summoned
the poet Evenus to come to him quickly if he were wise,
since he was a philosopher because of his poetry. (8) For
the philosopher does nothing other than to die, since he
disdains the demands of the body and is not enslaved by

μὴ δουλούμενος ταῖς τοῦ σώματος ἡδοναῖς· τοῦτο δὲ
μηδὲν ἕτερον εἶναι ἢ ψυχῆς ἀπόστασιν ἀπὸ σώματος·
τὸν δὲ θάνατον μηδὲν ἕτερον εἶναι ἢ ψυχῆς αὖ πάλιν
ἀπόστασιν ἀπὸ σώματος. Τούτῳ γὰρ δὴ καὶ μάλα τις
5   πειθήνιος ἐγίνετο· ἐξηπάτα γὰρ ἡμᾶς τούτοις τοῖς
λόγοις, οἶμαι, ἵνα μὴ κλαίωμεν ὡς ἐν κακῷ ἐσομένου
αὐτοῦ· σχεδὸν δέ τι καὶ ἀληθεῖς ἦσαν οἱ λόγοι. Εἶτα
δὴ ἐτελεύτα ποιήσας ἡμέρας τριάκοντα διὰ τὸ πλοῖον
τὸ εἰς Δῆλον πεμπόμενον κατ' ἔτος· οὐ γὰρ ἀφῖκτο
10   ἐπὶ πολλὰς ἡμέρας, καὶ οὐκ ἦν τινα τελευτᾶν δημοσίᾳ
ὥσπερ οἶσθα· ἱεραὶ γὰρ ἦσαν. (9) Τῶν δὲ φίλων
παρῆμεν αὐτῷ τελευτῶντι ἐγὼ καὶ Τερψίων καὶ 'Απολλό-
δωρος καὶ Φαίδων καὶ 'Αντισθένης καὶ 'Ερμογένης καὶ
Κτήσιππος· Πλάτων δὲ καὶ Κλεόμβροτος καὶ 'Αρίστιππος
15   ὑστέρουν· ὁ μὲν γὰρ Πλάτων ἐνόσει, τὼ δὲ ἑτέρω περὶ
Αἴγιναν ἤστην. "Ως δὲ ἔπιε τὸ φάρμακον, ἐπέστελλεν
ἡμῖν τῷ 'Ασκληπίῳ θῦσαι ἀλεκτρυόνα· ὀφείλειν γὰρ
αὐτῷ κατ' εὐχήν τινα, ὁπότε ἠσθένει ἀφικόμενος ἀπὸ
τῆς ἐπὶ Δηλίῳ μάχης. Δακρύσαντες οὖν μετά τινος
20   θαυμασμοῦ ἐκκομίζοντες αὐτὸν κατεθάπτομεν, ὡς τότε ὁ
καιρὸς ἐδίδου καὶ αὐτὸς ἐβούλετο· (10) οὐδὲ γὰρ
πρόνοιάν τινα ἡμῖν ἐπέστειλε ποιήσασθαι τοῦ σώματος·
εἶναι γὰρ αὐτὸ ἄτιμον καὶ μηκέτι χρήσιμον τῆς ψυχῆς
αὐτὸ ἐγκαταλιπούσης. ὅμως δ' οὖν ἡμεῖς εἰς τὸ δυνα-
25   τὸν καὶ τῆς συμφορᾶς ὑπερείδομεν καὶ τῶν λόγων
παρηκούσαμεν καὶ ὡς οἷόν τ' ἦν ἐκαλλωπίσαμεν αὐτὸν
λούσαντες καὶ τοῖς τριβωνίοις ἀμφισχόντες, καὶ
πρεπόντως θάψαντες ἀπῆμεν. Ταῦτ' ἦν τὰ περὶ Σωκράτην
καὶ ἡμᾶς, ὦ Ξενοφῶν. Καὶ σοὶ δὲ ἡ στρατεία ἦν τὸ
30   μέγα ἐμπόδιον, ἐπεὶ ἦσθα ἂν σὺν ἡμῖν θεραπεύων
Σωκράτην ζῶντά τε καὶ τελευτῶντα.

the pleasures of the body; and this is nothing other than
the separation of the soul from the body, and death is
nothing other again than the separation of the soul from
the body. And in this he was very persuasive. For I
think that he was beguiling us with those words so that
we would not lament as though an evil were going to happen
to him. And perhaps the words were also true. Then he
died thirty days later because of the boat sent to Delos
each year. For it did not arrive for many days, and as
you know, state executions were not permitted because
these days were sacred. (9) And the friends who were
present with him when he died were myself, Terpsion,
Apollodorus, Phaedo, Antisthenes, Hermogenes and Ctesip-
pus. But Plato, Cleombrotus and Aristippus did not come;
for Plato was ill and both of the others were in Aegina.
When he had drunk the poison, he commanded us to sacrifice
a cock to Asclepius, for he was in his debt because of a
vow given when he was ill after returning from the battle
at Delium. Then after weeping, but with a certain admira-
tion, we carried him out and buried him, since the time to
do so was opportune and he himself desired it. (10) He
had commanded us beforehand that no care was to be bestowed on the body since it was worthless and no longer
useful after the soul had left it. Nevertheless, as far
as was possible, we disregarded the misfortune and misunderstood his words, and to the degree that we could we
adorned him after we had washed him and put on his garments, and when we had buried him in a fitting manner, we
went away. These are the things which happened to
Socrates and us, Xenophon. But the expedition was a great
hindrance to you, for otherwise you would, with us, have
been attending to Socrates, both when he was alive and
when he was dying.

15. Ξενοφῶν τοῖς Σωκράτους ἑταίροις

Καὶ οἱ περὶ Γρύλλον τὸν υἱέα μου ἐποίουν ὅπερ
ἦν εἰκὸς αὐτοὺς ποιεῖν, καὶ ὑμεῖς εὖ ἐπράττετε,
γράψαντες ἡμῖν τὰ περὶ Σωκράτους. Δεῖ μέντοι γε
5   ἡμᾶς ἄνδρας ἀγαθοὺς γίνεσθαι κἀκεῖνον μὲν ἐπαινεῖν
ὧν ἐβίωσε σωφρόνως καὶ ὁσίως καὶ εὐσεβῶς, αἰτιᾶσθαι
δὲ καὶ ψέγειν τὴν τύχην καὶ τοὺς ἐπισυστάντας αὐτῷ,
οἳ οὐκ εἰς μακρὰν τίσουσι δίκην. Δεινὸν δὲ ποιοῦνται
καὶ Λακεδαιμόνιοι· τὸ γὰρ πάθος ἤδη ἄχρι καὶ δεῦρο
10   ἀφῖκται· καὶ κακίζουσι τὸν δῆμον ἡμῶν λέγοντες, ὡς
πάλιν ἄφραινοι, ἐπεὶ τὸν σοφώτατον καὶ ὑπὸ τῆς
Πυθίας μαρτυρηθέντα σωφρονέστατον ἐπείσθησαν ἀποκτιννύναι. (2) Εἴ του δέοιντο οἱ Σωκράτους ἑταῖροι ὧν
ἔπεμψα, σημαίνετόν μοι. Ἐπικουρήσομεν γάρ, ἐπειδὴ
15   τοῦτο καλὸν καὶ ἀναγκαῖόν ἐστιν. Εὖ ποιεῖτε τὸν
Αἰσχίνην ἔχοντες ἐν αὐτοῖς ὥστε γράφειν μοι. Δοκεῖ
μέντοι χρῆναι ἡμᾶς συγγράφειν, ἅ ποτε εἶπεν ἀνὴρ καὶ
ἔπραξε. Καὶ αὕτη ἀπολογία γένοιτ᾽ ἂν αὐτοῦ βελτίστη
εἰς τὸ νῦν τε καὶ εἰς τὸ ἔπειτα, οὐκ ἐν δικαστηρίῳ
20   ἀγωνιζομένων ἡμῶν, ἀλλ᾽ εἰς ἅπαντα τὸν βίον παρατι-
θέντων τὴν ἀρετὴν τἀνδρός. Καὶ φημι δὴ ἀδικήσειν
τὴν κοινὴν ἑταιρίαν καί, ὡς ἐκεῖνος ἔλεγε, τὴν
ἀλήθειαν, εἰ μὴ ἅσμενοι γράψαιμεν. (3) Ἤδη δέ μοι
καὶ Πλάτωνος περιέπεσε σύγγραμμα τοιοῦτον, ὅπου
25   τοὔνομα ἦν τοῦ Σωκράτους καὶ διάλεξίς τις οὐ φαύλη
πρός τινας. Οἶμαι μέντοι περὶ Μέγαρα ἀνέγνων†....ὡς
λέγεταί τινα τῶν Μεγαρέων τῶν τοιούτων. Ἡμεῖς
μέντοι φαμέν, <οὐχ> ὅτι τοιαῦτα οὐκ ἀκηκόαμεν, ἀλλ᾽
ὅτι τοιαῦτα οὐ δυνάμεθα ἀπομνημονεύειν. Οὐδὲ γὰρ
30   ἐσμὲν ποιηταὶ ὥσπερ καὶ αὐτός, κἂν πάνυ ἀπαρνῆται
ποιητικήν. Θρυπτόμενος γὰρ πρὸς τοὺς καλοὺς φησὶ
μηδὲν εἶναι ποίημα αὐτοῦ, Σωκράτους μέντοι νέου καὶ
καλοῦ ὄντος. Ἔρρωσθόν μοι ὡς ἁρμονιωδεστάτω ἄνδρε.

15. Xenophon to the Friends of Socrates

My son Gryllus did what was fitting for him to do,
and you also did well when you wrote to me what happened
to Socrates. We must truly become good men and praise
him because he lived wisely, devoutly, and piously, but
we must also accuse and blame fortune and those who con-
spired against him. They will soon pay the penalty. And
the Lacedaemonians are also indignant (for word of the
calamity has already reached even there), and they are
blaming our people, saying that they are again acting like
fools, since they allowed themselves to be persuaded to
kill the wisest and, according to the testimony of the
Pythia, also the most temperate of all men. (2) Let me
know if the friends of Socrates should need any of the
things that I sent, for we shall come to their aid since
to do so is proper and necessary. You do well to have
Aeschines among you so that he can write to me. I think
that we certainly need to record what that man said and
did. And this would be the best apology for him, both for
now and the future, if instead of contending in a court of
law, we rather set forth his life and virtue for all time.
And I say that we shall do an injustice to our common
friendship and, as he said, the truth, if we do not willingly write about him. (3) I have already encountered
such a writing from Plato which included the name of
Socrates and a rather significant dialogue with certain
people. At any rate, I believe that I have read in
Megara....Nevertheless, we are not saying that we have not
heard such things, but that we are not able to recount
them. For we are not poets as he indeed is, even if he
does vehemently deny writing poetry. Feigning coyness
toward the fair young men, he said that he had no writings, but that they were the work of the young and fair
Socrates. Farewell my dearest friend.

16. Άριστίππου

Τὰ περὶ τῆς τελευταίας Σωκράτους ἐμάθομεν ἐγώ
τε καὶ Κλεόμβροτος καὶ ὅτι οὐδὲ παριέμενος ὑπὸ τῶν
ἕνδεκα διαδρᾶναι ὑπέμεινε λέγων ὅτι μὴ μέλλοι διδρά-
5   σκειν εἰ μὴ καὶ πρότερον παρὰ τὼς νόμως σωθείη· οὕτω
γὰρ ἂν ἁ πατρὶς αὐτῶ, ὅσον ἐφ' αὐτῷ, καταπροδοθείη.
Ἐμοὶ δὲ ἐδόκει ἀδίκως αὐτὸν ἐμπεσόντα ὅτῳ δή ποτε
τρόπῳ σώζεσθαι. Δοκέω μέντοι πάντα τὰ ἐκείνῳ πρασ-
σόμενα καὶ κακὰ καὶ ἄφρονα δίκαια εἶναι, ὥστε ταῦτα
10 πάλιν μὴ ἐπιμέμφεσθαι ἀμέτρως γεγονέναι. Ἐπέστειλας
δέ μοι, πῶς ἀνεχωρήσατε πάντες ἀπ' Ἀθηνῶν οἱ Σωκράτους ἐρασταί τε καὶ φιλόσοφοι δεδιότες μή τι καὶ ἐφ'
ὑμᾶς ἔλθοι τῶν αὐτῶν [ἂν]· καὶ οὐκ ἐποιεῖτε φλαύρως.
Καὶ ἄμες οὖν ὡς ἐσμέν, ἐν Αἰγίνᾳ διατελέομες ἐπὶ τοῦ
15 παρόντος· εἶτα δὲ παρ' ὑμᾶς ἀφιξόμεθα καὶ εἴ τι
ἔχοιμες βέλτιον ποιέειν, ποιήσομες.

17.

Εἰδὼς ὅπως εἶχες πρὸς Σωκράτην ζῶντα καὶ πρὸς
ἡμᾶς τοὺς ἐκείνου φίλους καὶ ὅτι κατὰ τὸ εἰκὸς
20 ἐθαύμασάς τε καὶ ἐσχετλίασας, εἰ ὁ πρός σέ τε καὶ
τὸν Κεῖον Πρόδικον καὶ Πρωταγόραν τὸν Ἀβδηρίτην
διαμαχόμενος περὶ ἀρετῆς, ᾗ ἂν γένοιτο, καὶ ὅπως ἂν
γένοιτο, καὶ ὅτι χρὴ ταύτης πάντας ἐφίεσθαι, οὗτος
ὡς πονηρότατος καὶ ἀμαθέστατος τοῦ καλοῦ καὶ τοῦ
25 δικαίου πρός τε θεοὺς καὶ πρὸς ἀνθρώπους τοῖς ἕνδεκα
δόξαν ἀνῃρέθη· ἔγραψά σοι πυθόμενος, ὅτι οἴκοι εἴης
ἐν Χίῳ, περὶ τῶν ἔπειτα, ἵνα ἡσθείης. (2) Ἀθηναῖοι
γὰρ ἤδη ποτὲ ἀνύπνωσαν ὑπνώσαντες. Ἄνυτόν τε καὶ
Μέλητον ὡς ἀνοσιουργοὺς προσκαλεσάμενοι ἀπέκτειναν,

16. Of Aristippus

We have learned about the death of Socrates, Cleombrotus and I, and that, in spite of having been given a
chance to escape by the Eleven, he rejected this and remained, saying that he would not go free unless he was
first lawfully acquitted. For thus, his own city, as far
as it concerned him, would be betrayed. But it seemed to
me that since he was unjustly imprisoned he should have
been saved in any way possible. However, I think that
everytyhing he did, even that which was wrong and foolish,
was just, so that I do not blame him for having been immoderate in doing these things. You wrote me about how
all of you, both Socrates' adherents and philosophers,
left Athens, fearing lest something also happen to you.
You were not acting badly. We are presently satying on
in Aegina, but next we will come to you, and if we can do
anything to make things better, we shall do so.

17.

I know about your relationship with Socrates when he
was alive, and also with us, his friends, and that you
were rightly amazed and complained bitterly when he argued
with you, Prodicus of Ceos and Protagoras of Abdera, concerning virtue, where it comes into being, and how it
comes to be, and that everyone should aim at it--that man
was killed when it was so decreed by the Eleven as if he
were the most evil and the most ignorant of men concerning
what is good and just with God and men. Therefore, since
I learned that you are living in Chios, I am writing you
about the things which happened afterwards, so that you
may be gladdened. (2) For already the Athenians, who had
fallen asleep, have awakened. Both Anytus and Meletus
were called into court and executed for acting impiously,

ὅτι αἴτιοι τῇ πόλει ἐγένοντο τοσούτου κακοῦ. Προφάσεις δὲ αὗται κατ' αὐτοῖν εὑρέθησαν· ἀληθεῖς μὲν γὰρ
<αὗται αἱ αἰτίαι, ὅτι οἱ> Ἀθηναῖοι περιῄεσαν μετὰ
τὸν θάνατον αὐτοῦ παρὰ πάντων εὐθυνόμενοι τῶν γενο-
μένων, ὅτι γε οὐκ ἐχρῆν οὐκ ἀδικοῦντα αὐτὸν κατη-
γορηθῆναι, μὴ <ὅτι> ἀποκτιννύναι. Τί γὰρ εἰ τὴν
πλάτανον ἢ τὸν κύνα ὤμνυε; τί δὲ εἰ ἀνηρώτα ἰδίᾳ καὶ
κοινῇ πάντας ἀνθρώπους, ὅτι οὐδὲν εἰδεῖεν οὔτε
δίκαιον οὔτε καλόν; εἶτα δὲ οἱ νέοι πάντες εἰς
ἀκρασίαν καὶ ἀκοσμίαν ἐτρέποντο ἐν τῇ πόλει· αἰεὶ
γὰρ τοῦτον καθόσον οὖν ᾐσχύνοντο. (3) Ἐκίνησε δὲ
αὐτοὺς μάλιστα καὶ τὸ τοῦ νεανίσκου τοῦ Λακεδαιμονίου
πάθος. Ἧκε γάρ τις κατ' ἔρωτα Σωκράτους συγγενέσθαι
αὐτῷ, μὴ προειδὼς Σωκράτην, ἀλλ' ἀκούων περὶ αὐτοῦ.
Ὡς δὲ ἡδομένῳ αὐτῷ τῆς ἀφίξεως ὄντι ἤδη περὶ τὰς
πύλας τοῦ ἄστεος προσηγγέλθη, ὅτι Σωκράτης, πρὸς ὃν
ἐληλύθοι, τεθνήκοι, ἐς μὲν τὴν πύλην οὐκέτι εἰσῆλθε,
διαπυθόμενος δέ, ὅπου εἴη ὁ τάφος, προσελθὼν διελέγετο τῇ στήλῃ καὶ ἐδάκρυε, καὶ ἐπειδὴ νὺξ κατέλαβεν
αὐτόν, κοιμηθεὶς ἐπὶ τοῦ τάφου ὄρθρου πολλοῦ φιλήσας
τὴν ἐπικειμένην αὐτῷ κόνιν πολλὰ καὶ τεριασπασάμενος
πάσῃ φιλότητι ᾤχετο ἀπιὼν Μέγαράδε. (4) Ἤισθοντο
οὖν καὶ τοῦτο Ἀθηναῖοι καὶ ὅτι μέλλοιεν Λακεδαιμο-
νίοις διαβάλλεσθαι ἐπὶ τοῖς δεινοτάτοις, εἰ ἐκείνων
μὲν οἱ υἱεῖς τοὺς παρ' αὐτοῖς σοφοὺς δι' ἔρωτος
ποιοῦνται, αὐτοὶ δὲ ἀποκτιννύασι, καὶ οἱ μὲν τοσοῦτον
διάστημα ἀφικνοῦνται ἰδεῖν Σωκράτην, οἱ δ' οὐχ ὑπο-
μένουσι παρ' αὐτοῖς ἔχοντες αὐτὸν φυλάξαι. Χαλεπη-
νάμενοι οὖν μόνον οὐ διέφαγον τὼ πονηρὼ ἄνδρε ἐκείνω,
ὥστε τὴν μὲν πόλιν ἀπολελογῆσθαι, ὅτι αὐτὴ τούτων
οὐδὲν δρᾷ, τοὺς δ' αἰτίους τεθνάναι. Ἐκριφέντες
οὖν οἷόν τι κοινὸν ἄγος τῶν Ἑλλήνων, μᾶλλον δὲ
πάντων ἀνθρώπων, ὤνησαν μὲν ἡμᾶς, ὤνησαν δὲ καὶ τοὺς
ἄλλους ταῦτα παθόντες. Πάλιν οὖν συνελευσόμεθα
Ἀθήναζε οἱ ἀναξίως ἀνασεσοβημένοι ὡς τὸ πρόσθεν.

since they caused so great an evil to the city. And these
allegations were found against both of them. For the
charges were true, because after his death the Athenians
were called to account by all for the things which had
happened, since they should not have accused him, for he
had done nothing wrong, much less kill him. So what if
he swore by the Plane tree or the Hound? And what if he
did convince all men through his questioning, both privately and publicly, that they know nothing, either right
or good? And afterwards all the young men of the city
turned to self-indulgence and unruliness, for they had
always felt ashamed before him to some degree. (3) And it
was especially the misfortune of the Lacedaemonian youth
that moved them. For out of love for Socrates he came to
be with him, although he had not seen him before, but had
only heard of him. Full of gladness at his arrival at the
city gate, he was told that Socrates, to whom he had come,
was dead. So he did not go through the gate, but after
enquiring where the tomb was, he went to it and spoke to
the gravestone and wept. And when night came upon him, he
slept on the grave, and very early in the morning he re-
peatedly kissed the dust lying over it, saluted it with
great affection, and then returned to Megara. (4) Consequently, the Athenians learned of this and that they would
be accused of the most terrible things by the Lacedaemonians if their sons adopted the Athenians' wise men out of
love, but the Athenians kill them, and that they came such
a great distance to see Socrates, but that the Athenians
could not continue to guard him although they had him with
them. Being embittered, they all but consumed those two
evil men, with the result that the city made a defense to
the effect that it had done none of these things, but that
the culprits were dead. Thus driven out like a common
curse from the Greeks, or rather from all men, they benefited both us and also others by experiencing these things.
Once again, then, those of us who have unjustly been driven
away shall be united in Athens as before.

18. Ξενοφῶν τοῖς Σωκράτους ἑταίροις

"Αγοντες τὴν ἔτειον ἑορτὴν τῇ 'Αρτέμιδι τῇ
ὑφ' ἡμῶν καθιδρυμένῃ περὶ τὴν Λακωνικὴν ἐπέμψαμεν
παρ' ὑμᾶς, ἵνα ἵκοισθε· καλὸν μὲν εἰ πάντες· εἰ δὲ
5   μὴ οἷόν <τε>, συνθύτας τινὰς ἐξ ὑμῶν πέμψοιτε· τοῦτο
γὰρ κεχαρισμένον ἡμῖν ἐστιν. 'Εγένετο δὲ 'Αρίστιππος
ἐνταῦθα καὶ ἔτι πρότερον Φαίδων, καὶ ἐγανύσκοντο
τοῦ τόπου καὶ τῆς ἄλλης δημιουργίας τῶν οἰκοδομιῶν
καὶ [ἔτι πρότερον] τῶν φυτῶν, ἅτινα αὐτὸς ταῖς
10   ἐμαυτοῦ χερσὶν ἐφυτευσάμην. "Εχει γὰρ ὁ τόπος καὶ
θήραν, ὥστε ἔνι ὑμῖν καὶ κυνηγετεῖν, ἵνα μετ' ἀνδρίας
(ὅπερ καὶ φίλον τῇ θεῷ) θαλίας ἄγωμεν καὶ χάριν
εἰδείημεν αὐτῇ, ὅτι με ἀνεσώσατο ἄρα ἀπὸ βασιλέως
τοῦ βαρβάρου καὶ τῶν ἔπειτα περί τε τὸν Πόντον καὶ
15   τὴν Θρᾴκην κακῶν σχεδόν τι μειζόνων, ὅτε δὴ ἐδοκοῦ-
μεν ἤδη σεσῶσθαι ἀπὸ τῆς τοσαύτης πολεμίας γῆς.
(2) Εἰ δὲ μὴ ἵητε, ἡμῖν μὲν ἦν ἀναγκαῖον γράφειν
ὑμῖν. Πεποίημαι δέ τινα ἀπομνημονεύματα Σωκράτους.
"Οταν οὖν μοι δόξῃ εὖ ἔχειν παντελῶς, διαπέμψομαι
20   αὐτὰ καὶ ὑμῖν. 'Αριστίππῳ μὲν γὰρ καὶ Φαίδωνι ἐδόκει
ἁρμόδιά τινα εἶναι. Προσαγορεύσατε <δὲ> Σίμωνα τὸν
σκυτοτόμον καὶ ἐπαινέσατε αὐτόν, ὅτι διατελεῖ
προσέχων τοῖς Σωκράτους λόγοις καὶ οὔτε πενίαν οὔτε
[τὴν] τέχνην πρόφασιν αἰνίττεται τοῦ μὴ φιλοσοφεῖν
25   καθάπερ τινὲς τῶν ἄλλων μὴ βουλόμενοι λόγους τε καὶ
τὰ ἐν λόγοις ἐξειδέναι τε καὶ θαυμάζειν.

18. Xenophon to the Friends of Socrates

Since we are celebrating the yearly feast of Artemis, whose temple we built in Laconia, we are writing to you so that you might come. It would be good if you could all come, but if that is not possible, you might send some from among you to join in the sacrificing, for that would please us. Aristippus was here, and still earlier, Phaedo, and they were pleased with the place, and also the workmanship of the buildings, and with the plants which I planted with my own hands. For the place also has a hunting ground, so that you can also hunt in order that we may celebrate the feast with a show of bravery (which is dear to the god) and thank her, since she rescued me from the barbarian king and later from much greater evils in both Pontus and Thrace when we thought that we had already been rescued from this very hostile land. (2) But if you do not come, then you must write to us. I have written down some memoirs about Socrates. When I am fully satisfied with them I shall send them to you also. For Aristippus and Phaedo think that they are well written. Greet Simon the shoemaker and commend him, because he continues to devote himself to the teachings of Socrates and uses neither his poverty nor his trade as a pretext for not doing philosophy, as certain others do who do not want to understand fully or to admire Socrates' teachings and their contents.

19. Τοῦ αὐτοῦ (scil. Ξενοφῶντος)

῏Ηκε, θαυμασιώτατε, παρ' ἡμᾶς· πεποίηται γὰρ
ἡμῖν τὸ ἱερὸν τῆς ᾽Αρτέμιδος μάλα ἀριπρεπές τι καὶ
περίφυτος ὁ χῶρος καὶ ἀνεῖται ἱερὸς εἶναι καὶ τὰ
5   ὄντα ἡμᾶς διαβοσκήσει· ῾Ως γὰρ Σωκράτης ἔλεγεν, "εἰ
μὴ ἀρκέσει ἡμῖν ταῦτα, ἡμεῖς αὐτοῖς ἀρκέσομεν."
῎Εγραψα δὲ καὶ Γρύλλῳ τῷ υἱῷ καὶ τῷ ἑταίρῳ, εἴ του
δέοι, παρέχειν σοι. Γρύλλῳ δ' ἔγραψα, ἐπειδὴ ἀπὸ
νέου ἔτι κομιδῇ εἰς αὐτὸν ἐβάλλου καὶ φιλεῖν ἔλεγες.
10 ῎Ερρωσο.

20.

Τὴν μὲν σὴν καρτερίαν καὶ πάλαι ᾔδειν καὶ
σφόδρα θαυμάζω, διότι διατελεῖς παντὸς ὧν ἐπάνω
πλούτου καὶ δόξης καὶ οἷον ἐξ ὧν βιοῖς ἀπεικόνισμά
15 τι Σωκράτους περίει ᾽Αθήνησιν. ῾Ημεῖς δὲ καὶ αὐτοὶ
ἐπιμελούμεθα νέων ἐν Θήβαις παραδιδόντες αὐτοῖς οὓς
ἠκούσαμεν λόγους παρὰ Σωκράτους. ῎Εστι τε τοῦτο
καὶ ἡμῖν καὶ τοῖς συνοῦσι κεχαρισμένον.

19. Of the Same Person (Xenophon)

Come to us, most excellent sir. We have built a very splendid temple to Artemis, and the place is planted about with trees and it has been consecrated to sacred use, and what is there will sustain us. For as Socrates used to say, "If these things will not be sufficient for us, we shall be sufficient for them." And I have written to both my son Gryllus and to my friend to help you if you need anything. I wrote to Gryllus, seeing that already during your childhood you used to attach yourself to him, and used to express your love for him. Farewell.

20.

I have known your patient endurance in the past, and I admire it greatly since you continue to be above all wealth and fame, and you live beyond them, as it were, a kind of copy of Socrates, as you go around Athens. But as for ourselves, we are attending to the youths in Thebes, handing on to them the teachings which we heard from Socrates. This has been very rewarding, both for us and for those who are with us.

21. [Αἰσχίνης] Ξανθίππῃ τῇ Σωκράτους

Εὔφρονι τῷ Μεγαρεῖ ἔδωκα ἀλφίτων χοίνικας ἓξ
καὶ δραχμὰς ὀκτὼ καὶ ἐξωμίδα καινὴν τὸ χεῖμά σοι
διαγεγεῖν. Ταῦτα οὖν λάβε καὶ ἴσθι Εὐκλείδην καὶ
5   Τερψίωνα πάνυ καλώ τε καὶ ἀγαθὼ ἄνδρε καὶ σοί τε καὶ
Σωκράτει εὔνω. Ἡνίκα δ' ἂν οἱ παῖδες ἐθέλοιεν παρ'
ἡμᾶς ἰέναι, μὴ κώλυε· οὐ γὰρ πόρρω ἐστὶν ἰέναι εἰς
Μέγαρα. Τῶν δὲ πολλῶν σοὶ δακρύων, ὦ ἀγαθή, ἅλις.
Ὀνήσει γὰρ οὐδέν, σχεδὸν δέ τι καὶ βλάψει. Ἀνα-
10   μιμνήσκου γὰρ ὧν ἔλεγε Σωκράτης καὶ τοῖς ἤθεσιν αὐτοῦ
καὶ τοῖς λόγοις πειρῶ ἀκολουθεῖν, ἐπεὶ λυπουμένη παρ'
ἕκαστα καὶ σεαυτὴν ἀδικήσεις ὅτι μάλιστα καὶ τοὺς
παῖδας. (2) Οὗτοι γὰρ οἱονεὶ νεοττοί εἰσι Σωκράτους,
οὓς δεῖ οὐ μόνον τρέφειν ἡμᾶς, ἀλλὰ καὶ ἡμᾶς αὐτοὺς
15   αὐτοῖς πειρᾶσθαι παραμένειν· ὡς εἰ σὺ ἢ ἐγὼ ἢ ἄλλος
τις, ὅτῳ μέλει τελευτήσαντος Σωκράτους τῶν παίδων,
ἀποθάνοι, ἀδικήσονται οὗτοι, ἔρημοι γενόμενοι τοῦ
βοηθήσοντος καὶ θρέψοντος ὁμολογουμένως· ὅθεν πειρῶ
ζῆν αὐτοῖς. Τοῦτο δὲ οὐκ ἂν ἄλλως γένοιτο, εἰ μὴ τὰ
20   πρὸς τὸ ζῆν αὐτὴ <αὐτῇ> παρέχοις. Λύπη δὲ δοκεῖ τῶν
ἐναντίων ζωῇ εἶναι, ὅπου βλάπτονται ὑπ' αὐτῆς οἱ
ζῶντες. (3) Ἀπολλόδωρος ὁ μανικὸς ἐπικαλούμενος
καὶ Δίων ἐπαινοῦσί σε, διότι παρ' οὐδενὸς οὐδὲν
λαμβάνεις, φὴς δὲ πλουτεῖν. Καὶ εὖ ποιεῖς. Εἰς
25   ὅσον γὰρ ἐγώ τε καὶ οἱ ἄλλοι φίλοι ἰσχύομεν ἐπικου-
ρεῖν σοι, δεήσει οὐδενός. Θάρρει οὖν, ὦ Ξανθίππη,
καὶ μηδὲν καταβάλῃς τῶν Σωκράτους καλῶν εἰδυῖα, ὡς
μέγα τι ἡμῖν ἐγένετο οὗτος ὁ ἄνθρωπος· καὶ ἐπινόει
αὐτὸν ὁποῖα ἔζησε καὶ ὁποῖα ἐτελεύτησε. Ἐγὼ μὲν
30   γὰρ οἶμαι καὶ τὸν θάνατον αὐτοῦ μέγα τε καὶ καλὸν
γεγονέναι, εἰ δή τις καθ' ὃ χρὴ σκοπεῖν σκοποίη.
Ἔρρωσο.

21. Aeschines to Xanthippe, the Wife of Socrates

I gave Euphron of Megara six measures of barley meal
and eight drachma and a new coat for you so that you can
make it through the winter. Therefore, accept these
things and know that Eucleides and Terpsion are very good
and noble men who have good will toward both you and
Socrates. When the children should want to come to us, do
not stop them, for the trip to Megara is not long. And
let the abundance of the tears that you have shed suffice.
For they will do no good, but rather harm. Remember what
Socrates used to say and try to follow his customs and
advice, for by grieving constantly you will harm both
yourself and especially your children. (2) For they are,
as it were, the nestlings of Socrates, and we must not
only feed them, but we ourselves must also try to remain
alive with them. Since if you or I or anyone else who
cares about the children of the dead Socrates should die,
they will suffer harm, for they would clearly be deprived
of anyone who would help or maintain them. Therefore, try
to stay alive for them. But you cannot do this if you do
not provide yourself with the necessities of your own
life. Grief seems to be among the enemies of life, since
the living are harmed by it. (3) Apollodorus, who is
called the mad-man, and Dio praise you, because you are
not receiving anything from anyone and yet you say that
you are rich. In that, you are right. For as long as I
and the other friends have the power to help you, you will
lack nothing. So, take courage, Xanthippe, and do not
discard any of the good instructions of Socrates, since
you know how important that man was to us, and meditate on
how he lived and how he died. On my part, I think that
even his death was great and noble, if one views it in
the way one should. Farewell.

22. Σιμμία καὶ Κέβητι

Ἦν λόγος, ὅτι πένητος πλουσιώτερον οὐδὲν
εἴη. Κινδυνεύω γὰρ ὡς ὁρῶ μὴ πολλὰ ἔχων πολλὰ
κεκτῆσθαι δι᾽ ὑμᾶς τοὺς φίλους, οἵτινες ἐπιμελεῖσθε
5   ἡμῶν. Ποιοῖτε δ᾽ ἂν εὖ, εἰ, ὅταν ὑμῖν περί του
γράψω, πέμποιτέ μοι. Τῶν δὲ συγγραμμάτων οὔπω τι
εἶχον τοιοῦτο ὥστε καὶ ἄλλοις θαρρεῖν δεικνύναι δίχα
ἐμοῦ ὡς παροῦσιν ὑμῖν ἔνδον ἐν τῷ οἴκῳ, ἔνθα
Εὐκλείδης κατέκειτο, ἀσμένως ἐλέσχαινον. Οἴδατον
10   δὲ δή, ὦ φίλοι, ὡς οὐχ οἷόν τε ἀναλαβεῖν ἐστι τὸ
ἅπαξ ἐλθὸν εἰς τοὺς πολλοὺς γράμμα. (2) Πλάτων μὲν
γὰρ δύναταί τι μέγα καὶ ἀπὼν τοῖς λόγοις· ὅθεν ἤδη
καὶ περὶ Ἰταλίαν θαυμάζεται καὶ περὶ Σικελίαν πᾶσαν.
Ἡμεῖς δὲ μόλις οἶμαι καὶ ἑαυτοὺς πείθομεν ὡς ἄξια
15   εἶναι ταῦτα σπουδῆς τινος. Καὶ οὐχ ὅτι ἐμοὶ μέλει
μὴ διαπίπτειν περὶ τῆς δόξης τῆς περὶ τὴν σοφίαν,
ἀλλὰ περὶ Σωκράτους φροντιστέον, μὴ ἐν ἐμοὶ κινδυ-
νευθῇ τὴν ἐκείνου ἀρετὴν κακῶς εἰπόντι ἐν τοῖς ἀπο-
μνημονεύμασιν. Οὐδὲν δὲ οἶμαι διαφέρειν ἢ βλασφη-
20   μεῖν τινα ἢ μὴ ἄξια δοκεῖν συγγράφειν τῆς ἀρετῆς,
περὶ ὅτου συγγράφει τις. Τὸ δέος οὖν τοῦτό ἐστιν,
ὅγε νῦν ἡμᾶς ἔχει, ὦ Κέβης τε καὶ Σιμμία, εἰ μή τι
ἕτερον δόξει ὑμῖν αὖ πάλιν περὶ τούτων. Ἔρρωσθον.

22. To Simmias and Cebes

Word has it that there is nothing wealthier than a
poor man. Yes, I run a risk when I see that, though I own
very little, I possess a great deal, through you my
friends, who are taking care of us. And you would be doing a good thing if you would send me something when I
write to you for it. But as to my writings, I do not yet
have anything of the sort that I would have the confidence
to show to others without being there myself, as when I
readily chatted with you when you were present in the
house where Eucleides was lying ill. And you must know,
friends, that it is impossible to take back a writing once
it has reached the hands of the public. (2) Truly, Plato
is able to have a great influence through his writings,
even though he is away, and because of them he is already
admired in Italy and all of Sicily. But I scarcely think
that we ourselves are convinced that these things are
worth any serious consideration. It is not that I am concerned lest the glory of wisdom be diminished, but I must
think about Socrates, that he not be endangered by my doing a poor job of describing his virtue in the *Memorabilia*.
And I believe that it makes no difference whether one de-
fames someone directly or writes things which seem to be
unworthy of the virtue of the one he is writing about.
This, then, is the fear of which we are now possessed,
Cebes and Simmias, that you might hold a still different
opinion about these matters. Farewell.

23. Αἰσχίνης Φαίδωνι

Ὁπότε ἐγενόμην ἐν Συρακούσαις εὐθέως κατὰ τὴν
ἀγορὰν Ἀριστίππῳ ἐνέτυχον· ὁ δὲ λαβόμενός μου τῆς
δεξιᾶς παραχρῆμα μηδὲν μελλήσας εἰσάγει παρὰ Διονύσι-
5   ον καί φησιν· "Ὦ Διονύσιε, εἴ τις ἀφίκοιτο παρὰ σέ,
ἵνα σε ἄφρονα ποιήσειε, ἆρ' οὗτος οὐχὶ κακά σε ἐργάζεται;" Εὐθέως ὡμολόγει ὁ Διονύσιος. "Τί οὖν," ἔφη
ὁ Ἀρίστιππος, "σὺ τοῦτον ἂν ἐργάσαιο;" "Τὰ κάκιστά
γε," ἔφη. "Τί δ', εἴ τις," ἔφη, "ἀφίκοιτό σε φρόνι-
10   μον ποιῆσαι, ἆρά γε οὐχὶ οὗτος ἂν ἀγαθά σε ἐργάζοιτο;"
Πάλιν οὖν ὁμολογήσαντος τοῦ Διονυσίου, "καὶ μήν," ἔφη,
"οὗτος Αἰσχίνης τῶν Σωκράτους γνωρίμων ἥκει φρόνιμόν
σε ποιῆσαι ὥστε καὶ ἀγαθά σε ἐργάζοιτο ἄν· εἰ δὲ
ταῦτα δικαιοῖς, ἅτινα ὡμολόγησάς μοι ἐν τῷ λόγῳ,
15   Αἰσχίνην εὖ ποίει." (2) Κἀγὼ ὑπολαβὼν ἔφην· "Ὦ Διονύσιε, ἑταιρικόν τι καὶ θαυμαστὸν ποιεῖ Ἀρίστιππος
οὗτος οὕτω συλλαμβάνων μοι· ἡμῖν δὲ οὐ τοσαύτη ἐστὶ
σοφία, ἀλλ' ὁπόση μὴ ἀδικῆσαί τινας ἐν τῇ συνουσίᾳ."
Ἀγάμενος δὲ τοῦ εἰρημένου ἔφη ὁ Διονύσιος καὶ
20   Ἀρίστιππον ἐπαινεῖν τῶν εἰρημένων καὶ ἐμὲ εὖ
ποιήσειν, ἅτινα ὡμολόγησεν ἐν τῷ πρὸς Ἀρίστιππον
λόγῳ. Οὗτος οὖν ἤκουσεν ἡμῶν τοῦ Ἀλκιβιάδου καὶ
ἡσθεὶς ὡς ἐφαίνετο παρεκάλει καὶ εἴ τινες ἄλλοι
εἰσὶν ἡμῖν τῶν διαλόγων ἀναπέμψαι. Ὑπισχνούμεθα
25   οὖν ταῦτα ἡμεῖς, ὦ ἄνδρε φίλω τε καὶ ἑταίρω, ἀφιξό-
μεθά τε διὰ ταχέων. Ἀναγινώσκοντος δέ μου παρῆν
Πλάτων--ὀλίγου δέω ἔλαθον γράψαι ὑμῖν--καὶ ἐδόκει
αὐτῷ ἰδίᾳ περὶ ἐμοῦ διαλέγεσθαι διὰ τὸν Ἀρίστιππον.
(3) Ἔφη γάρ μοι ὡς τοῦ Διονυσίου ἀπηλλάγη· "Ὦ
30   Αἰσχίνη, τούτου παρόντος τοῦ ἀνθρώπου--ἔλεγε τὸν
Ἀρίστιππον--οὐδὲν οὐδαμῇ ἔγωγε ῥᾳδίως ἐθέλω λαλεῖν.
Διονύσιος μέντοι μαρτυρήσει μοι, ἅτινα ἐγὼ εἶπον περὶ
σοῦ." Καὶ ὁ Διονύσιος τῇ ὑστεραίᾳ ἐν τῷ κήπῳ πόλλ'
ἄττα ἐμαρτύρει τῷ Πλάτωνι ὡς εἰρηκότι περὶ ἐμοῦ.
35   Τῆς μέντοι παιδιᾶς τῆς πρὸς ἀλλήλους--παιδιὰν γὰρ
αὐτὸ χρὴ λέγειν--παρεκάλουν αὐτοὺς παύσασθαι τόν τε
Ἀρίστιππον καὶ τὸν Πλάτωνα διὰ τὴν πρὸς τοὺς

23. Aeschines to Phaedon

When I got to Syracuse, right away I met Aristippus
in the market. And having taken my right hand, without
delay he led me to Dionysius and said, "Dionysius, if
someone were to come to you in order to make you a fool,
would he not be doing evil to you?" Immediately, Dionysius agreed. "What then," said Aristippus, "would you do
to him?" "The most evil things," he answered. "And what
if someone were to come to you to make you wise, would he
not indeed be doing something good to you?" And when
Dionysius again agreed, he said, "This Aeschines, a disciple of Socrates, comes to make you wise so that he can
also do some good to you. If you hold the things on which
you have agreed with me to be right, then treat Aeschines
well." (2) Then I broke in and said, "Dionysius, Aristippus is doing a friendly and admirable thing by helping me
in this way, but we do not have such great wisdom, but
only enough that we do not harm people when we associate
with them." And Dionysius, pleased with what I had said,
answered that he approved of Aristippus' statements and
that he would treat me well, as he had agreed to when he
spoke to Aristippus. Then he heard my *Alcibiades* read and
he seemed to be pleased, and asked that if we had any
other dialogues, to send them to him. We promised to do
so, dear friends and comrades, and so we shall soon come.
While I was reading, Plato was present (I almost forgot to
write this to you), and it seemed good to him to speak
privately about me because of Aristippus. (3) For when he
had left Dionysius, he said to me, "Aeschines, when this
man is there--he means Aristippus--I never want to speak
freely. However, Dionysius will be my witness for the
things I said about you." And the next day in the garden,
Dionysius did give abundant testimony to what Plato had
said about me. But I urged Aristippus as well as Plato to
stop their jesting with each other (for one should call it
jesting), because of the reputation they had with the

πολλοὺς δόξαν. Οὐ γὰρ καταγελαστότερα ἔτι ἔχοιμεν
ἄν, ἀλλ' ἄττα πράττοντες [ἢ] τοιαῦτα ἐπιδεικνύμενοι.

24. Πλάτωνος

Οὔπω μὲν εἶχον τούτων τι πέμπειν εἰς Συρακούσας
5   ὧν ἔφης 'Αρχύταν δεηθῆναι λαβεῖν παρὰ σοῦ· θᾶττον
δὲ καὶ οὐ διὰ μακροῦ πέμψομέν σοι. 'Εμοὶ δὲ φιλοσοφία οὐκ οἶδ' ὅ τι ποτὲ χρῆμα γέγονεν ἆρά γε
φλαῦρον ἢ καλόν, ὁπότε ἐγὼ μισῶ νῦν συνεῖναι τοῖς
πολλοῖς. Οἶμαι μὲν οὖν ὡς δικαίως διάκειμαι,
10 ἀμαθαίνουσι δὲ κατ' ἰδέαν πᾶσαν ἀφροσύνης οἵ τε
ἰδίᾳ τι ποιοῦντες καὶ οἱ τὰ κοινὰ πράττοντες. Εἰ
δὲ ἀλόγως τοῦτο πάσχω, οὕτω γε ἴσθι, ὅτι μόλις ἂν
τοῦτο ἐγένετό μοι ζῆν· ἄλλως δὲ <καὶ> οὐκ ἔνι μοι
ψυχῆς λαμβάνειν· (2) διὸ δὴ ἐκ τοῦ ἄστεος ἀπηλλάγην
15 ὥσπερ εἱρκτῆς θηρίων. Διατρίβω μέντοι οὐ μακρὰν
'Ηφαιστιαδῶν καὶ τούτων τῶν χωρίων καὶ συνέγνων,
ὅτι Τίμων οὐκ ἦν ἄρα μισάνθρωπος· μὴ εὑρίσκων μέντοι
ἀνθρώπους οὐκ ἠδύνατο θηρία φιλεῖν· ὅθεν καθ'
ἑαυτὸν καὶ μόνος διεβίου κινδυνεύων δὲ τυχὸν ἴσως
20 μηδὲ ἐκείνως εὖ λογίζεσθαι. Σὺ δὲ ἐκδέχου ὅπως
βούλει· ἐμοὶ γὰρ ὧδε τὰ τῆς γνώμης ἔχει ἄποθεν εἶναι
τοῦ ἄστεος εἴς τε νῦν καὶ τὸν ἄλλον ἅπαντα χρόνον,
ὅντινα ἂν ζῆν ὁ θεὸς ἡμῖν διδῷ.

masses. For we make ourselves ridiculous in nothing so
much as when we do such things or when we make a display
of ourselves in such things.

24. Of Plato

I do not yet have any of the things to send to Syracuse which you said that Archytas wanted to receive from
you. But we shall send them to you very soon. I do not
know whether philosophy has become something good or bad
for me since I now hate to associate with the masses.
Yet I think that my inclination is right, since both those
who live private lives and those who engage in public affairs are ignorant with every sort of foolishness. And
if I do suffer this contrary to reason, know that while
this to me is scarcely living, I cannot live in any other
way. (2) Therefore, I left the city as if it were a cage
for animals. Still, I live not far from Hephaestia and
these districts of it, and I have come to agree that Timon
was not a misanthrope. Since he found no men he could not
befriend animals, and therefore he lived alone and to himself, but since he was in constant danger, perhaps his
calculations in that case did not turn out well. Take
that as you will. My decision is to be far away from the
city, both for the present and for as long as God might
grant me life.

25. Φαῖδρος Πλάτωνι

Γράφεις μοι ὡς λυπεῖν με μὴ θέλων ἀπεκρύψω,
ὅτι μέλλεις ἄρα πόρρωτέρω ἀποδημεῖν, καὶ αὐτὸς δὲ
ἄρχομαι ποθεῖν σε νὴ τὸν Δία τὸν Ὀλύμπιον. Ἀλλὰ
5   πρὸς Διὸς φιλίου τε καὶ ἑταιρείου, ὦ Πλάτων, καὶ
τοῦ εἴτε κατὰ γῆν ἐν εὐσεβῶν χώρῳ ὄντος εἴτε κατὰ
ἄστρα, ὅπερ καὶ μάλα πείθομαι, Σωκράτους, μὴ περιίδῃς
ἡμᾶς ἀπαιδεύτους εἰς τέλεον γενομένους, ἀλλ' ἵνα, ἥν
τινα προκοπὴν ἔσχομεν ἐπ' ἐκείνου τοῦ δαιμονίου
10 ἀνθρώπου, ταύτην σὺ σώσῃς καὶ ἐπί τι ἀγάγῃς τέλος.
(2) Ἐμοὶ γὰρ ἥδιον φιλοσοφίας οὐδὲν καὶ τῶν ἐν
φιλοσοφίᾳ λόγων· ἐτιθηνήθην γὰρ ἐκ νέου ἔτι πάλαι
Σωκρατικοῖς ὡς ἄν τις εἴποι βαυκαλήμασιν ἐν παντὶ
ἁρμοδίῳ καὶ ἱερῷ τόπῳ, τοῦτο μὲν Ἀκαδημίᾳ, τοῦτο
15 δὲ Λυκείῳ τε καὶ Ἰλισσῷ ὑπὸ τῇ θείᾳ πλατάνῳ ἱστα-
μένης μεσημβρίας, ἵνα Λυσίας ὁ Κεφάλου τὰ περὶ
ἔρωτος διωρθοῦτο. Ἐν οὖν τοῖς πιστοῖς χωρίοις
περιάγων τε καὶ περιαγόμενος ἀρετῆς τῆς ἀφ' ὑμῶν
ἐπιμπλάμην καὶ ἦν ἐπίφθονος Ἀλκιβιάδῃ τε τῷ
20 Κλεινίου καί τισιν ἄλλοις τῶν νέων, οἳ μᾶλλον
ἐβούλοντό μου προεδρίας ἀξιοῦσθαι παρ' ὑμῖν τοῖς
σοφοῖς, καὶ οὐδέποτέ με καταπροέδοτε τῷ ὄντι ἐμπλή-
σαντες? φιλοσοφίας <ἧς> ἐδίψων εἰς τὸ πάμπαν.

25. Phaedrus to Plato

You wrote to me that since you did not wish to cause me grief, you concealed that you are about to move farther away, but by Zeus the Olympian, I am beginning to miss you. Yet by Zeus the Guardian of Friendship and Fellowship, Plato, and by Socrates, whether he is on the earth in a land of the godly or whether among the stars, of which I am fully persuaded, do not allow us to be completely uneducated, but if we made any progress in the presence of that divine man, on your part, preserve it and lead us to some goal. (2) For there is nothing dearer to me than philosophy and the discourses that deal with philosophy. I was nurtured from my youth up, as one might say, on the Socratic lullabies in every appropriate and holy place, partly in the Academy, and partly in the Lyceum and by the Ilissus under the divine plane tree at high noon, where Lysias the son of Cephalus was set right about love. So, as I walked and as I was led around secure places I filled myself with your virtue and I was envied by Alcibiades the son of Clinias, and by certain other youths who wanted more than I to be considered worthy of the first place in the company of wise men. You never abandoned me, but, in truth, filled me with philosophy which I so greatly thirsted after.

26. Πλάτωνι

Οἱ ἀπ' Αἰγύπτου ἀφικόμενοι ἀγαθοὶ ἄνδρες ἀπήγ-
γελλον ἡμῖν, ὅτι τὴν πᾶσαν Αἴγυπτον περισκεψάμενος
νῦν διατρίβεις περὶ τὸν Σαϊτικὸν νομὸν λεγόμενον
5   ἐκπυνθανόμενος τῶν κεῖθι σοφῶν, ὅ τι αὐτοῖς φαίνοιτο
[τὰ] περὶ τοῦ σύμπαντος, ὅπως ἐγένετο, καὶ ᾧ λόγῳ
νῦν τὴν πᾶσαν κίνησιν ἔχει κατὰ μέρος καὶ κατὰ τὸ
ὅλον. Δυσκόλως δέ φασιν αὐτοὺς τοῖς Ἕλλησι διαλέγεσθαι, ὅτῳ δήποτε οὖν παθήματι χρωμένους, εἰ μὴ
10   ὅσον Πυθαγόρᾳ ἐκοινώνησαν τοὺς λόγους τοὺς περὶ
φύσεως καὶ γεωμετρίας καὶ ἀριθμοῦ <οἱ> περὶ Ἡλίου
πόλιν, καὶ τούτῳ γε οἶμαι στρατηγησαμένῳ αὐτούς, ὥς
τινες ἱστοροῦσι, (μέμνηνται γὰρ τῶν μύθων τῶν περὶ
Πυθαγόραν, ἡνίκα τὰ περὶ Αἴγυπτον διηγοῦνται ἡμῖν,
15   Τίμαιός? τε καὶ Θεόδωρος ὁ Κυρηναῖος) εἴτε καὶ ἄλλως
ἐπελθεῖν αὐτοῖς οἰκειωθέντι. (2) Εὖ δὲ καί σοι νῦν
καὶ τὰ οἴκοι Ἀθήνησι πάντα κατὰ θεὸν ἔχει. Ἐπίστελλε δὲ ἡμῖν καὶ πάλιν σύ, ὅπως διάκεισαι τοῦ
σώματος, ὡς τά γε τῆς ψυχῆς [τότε] ἴσμεν ὑγιᾶ διά
20   τε φρόνησιν καὶ ἀρετήν. Καὶ εἴ του δέοιο τῶν σῶν,
γράφε ἡμῖν· τὰ γὰρ ἐμά, ὦ Πλάτων, σά φημι εἶναι δίκη
ἀπάσῃ, ὥσπερ καὶ Σωκράτους ἦν. Σημαίνοις δὲ ἡμῖν
περὶ τῶν ἐγχωρίων θεαμάτων καὶ τῆς περὶ ταῦτα μεγα-
λουργίας, τομάς τε λίθων εἰς ἄπλετόν τι μέγεθος
25   ἐπηγερμένας καὶ ἐργασίας αὐτῶν ἀνδρεικέλους τε καὶ
εἰς τὰ ἄλλα ζῷα ἀπεσχηματισμένας τέχνῃ παλαιᾷ καὶ
οὐκ εἰς τὸν τρόπον τὸν Ἑλληνικόν, καὶ ἃ τῶν ἄλλων
πάλιν τεχνημάτων πολυμόρφων ζῳδίων ἐπιδείκνυται τὴν
ἰδίαν φύσιν, καὶ ἄσκησιν † <πα>ντολαν τῆς ἐπινοίας
30   ἐν τοῖς γενομένοις.† (3) Ἄσμενος δ' ἂν καὶ αὐτὸς
τῶν Πυραμίδων κατεῖδον τὸ μέγεθος καὶ τὴν Μέμφιν καὶ
αὐτήκοος ἐγενόμην τοῦ ἱεροῦ λόγου καὶ τῆς παγκάλης
τοῦ Νείλου θέας διερχομένου τε τὴν Αἴγυπτον καὶ
ἐπισχομένου τῇ πλημμυρίδι κατὰ τὴν ἑτέραν ὥραν καὶ
35   τὴν εἰς τὸ πάλιν ἀπόρροιαν αὐτοῦ. Ταῦτα γὰρ πάντα
εἰς τὸ ἄπιστον λεχθῆναι νομίζω, ἃ παρὰ τοῖς πολλοῖς
οὕτω μεγάλα ἐστὶ καὶ ἀξιέραστα τῆς ὄψεως.

26. To Plato

Those who returned from Egypt, good men, reported to
us that after carefully looking around all of Egypt you
are now spending time in the so-called Saitic district,
inquiring of the wise men there what they think about the
universe, how it came into being, and by what principle it
moves throughout its individual parts and the whole. It
is said that, on the basis of some experience or other,
they are reluctant to speak with the Greeks, except that
those in Heliopolis did share with Pythagoras their teachings about nature, geometry, and arithmetic. He, I think,
tricked them, as some report (Timaeus and Theodoros of
Cyrene mention some of the stories about Pythagoras when
they tell us about Egypt), or he otherwise became familiar
enough with them to attack them. (2) As things are now
well with you, your family affairs in Athens, too, are according to God's will. Write us again about your bodily
health, for we know that because of your understanding and
virtue you are healthy in soul. And if you need anything
that is yours, write us, for my possessions, Plato, are by
all rights yours, even as they were Socrates'. You might
tell us about the sights of the country and their magnif-
icence: the blocks of hewn stone erected into some immense
structure, their works of art shaped in human as well as
other forms by an ancient technique and in a style unlike
the Greek, and other works of art which in turn display
the individual nature of polymorphic statuettes and the
varied art of design represented in them. (3) Gladly
would I myself gaze at the grandeur of the Pyramids and
see Memphis, hear the holy teaching, and see the beauty of
the divine Nile as it flows through Egypt, stopped in flood
in one season, then returning again to its flow. I frankly
find that all these things, which to the masses are impres-
sive and worth seeing, are told to the point of unbelief.

27. Ἀρίστιππος Ἀρήτῃ τῇ θυγατρί

Ἐκομισάμην παρα σοῦ γράμματά μοι πεμφθέντα
διὰ Τελέα, ἐν οἷς ἐδέου με παραγενέσθαι ὡς τάχιστα
εἰς Κυρήνην λέγουσα οὐκ εὖ σοι ἀπαντᾶσθαι οὔτε παρὰ
5 τῶν ἐπισκόπων οὔτε ἱκανὸν εἶναι οἰκονομῆσαι τὸν ἄνδρα
αἰδώ τε ἔχοντα καὶ θορύβων πολιτικῶν ζῆν μακρὰν εἰθισ-
μένον. Ἐγὼ δὲ πειρώμενος ὡς ἂν ἀφεθείην ὑπὸ Διονυσίου πλεῦσαι πρὸς σέ, ἐμποδών μοι τοῦ χρεῶν στάντος
ἐν Λιπάραις μαλακῶς ἔσχον· ὅτε δὴ καὶ τοὺς περὶ
10 Σώνικον ἀριστά μοι προσφερομένους ἐνόησα τημελοῦντάς
με γνησίως†, καὶ ὡς ἂν εἰ ἀρκεῖταί τις ζῆν τῶν διάθεσιν φιλικήν†. (2) Περὶ ὧν δὲ ἔκρινας τίνα ἕξεις
τιμὴν ὑπ' ἐμοῦ ἠλευθερωμένοις, οἳ καὶ ἔλεγον Ἀριστίππου μὴ ἀποχωρήσειν, ἕως ἂν αὐτοῖς ᾖ δύναμις ἀρέσ-
15 κειν ἐκείνῳ τε καὶ σοί, πάντ' οὖν αὐτοῖς πίστευε·
περιέσται γὰρ αὐτοῖς ἐκ τῆς ἐμῆς βιοτῆς μὴ εἶναι
κακοῖς. Ὑποτίθεμαι δέ σοι τὰ πρὸς ἄρχοντας οἰκονομεῖν ὥστε τὸ ἐμὸν συμβούλευμα τοῦτο συμφέρον. Τοῦτο
δὲ ἦν μὴ τοῦ πλείονος ὀριγνᾶσθαι. Ἄριστα γὰρ οὕτως
20 ἐξάγεις τὰ κατὰ τὸν βίον ὑπεροπτικὴ παντὸς οὖσα τοῦ
πλέονος. Οὐ γὰρ δὴ ἐκεῖνοι τοσοῦτόν σε ἀδικήσαιεν
<ἂν>, ὥστε <σε> ἐνδεᾶ γενέσθαι. Οἱ δύο μὲν γάρ σοι
κῆποι μένουσιν ἱκανοὶ ὄντες καὶ πολυτελεῖ βίῳ. Τὸ
δ' ἐν τῇ Βερενίκῃ κτῆμα καὶ μόνον καταλειφθὲν πρὸς
25 ἀρίστην διαγωγὴν οὐχ ὑπολείψει. (3) Τῶν μικρῶν ὑμᾶς
οὐ παρακελεύομαι καταφρονεῖσθαι, ἀλλὰ μὴ ἐπὶ μικροῖς
ταράττεσθαι, ἔνθα οὐδὲ ἐπὶ μεγάλοις καλὸν ἡ ὀργή.
Εἰ δέ μου διαλυθέντος ὑπὸ τῆς φύσεως ποιῆσαι ἐμὸν
βούλημα ζητεῖς, [ὡς] ὅτι κράτιστα παιδεύσασα τὸν
30 Ἀρίστιππον Ἀθήναζε χώρει Ξανθίππην τε καὶ Μυρτὼ πρὸ
παντὸς ποιουμένη, αἵ με πολλάκις ἐλιπάρουν ἐπὶ μυστή-
ριά σε ἄγειν. Τὸ οὖν ἡδὺ βιότευμα μετὰ τούτων ἔχουσα
κατάλιπε τοῖς ἐν Κυρήνῃ ἐπισκόποις ὅ τι ποτ' ἂν ἐθέ-
λωσιν ἀδικεῖν (σὲ γὰρ οὐκ εἰς τὸ φυσικὸν τέλος ἀδική-
35 σουσι) πειρῶ δὲ μετὰ Ξανθίππης καὶ Μυρτοῦς ζῆν, ὡς
ἐμοὶ φίλον μετὰ Σωκράτους, πλέον <διὰ> τῆς ἐκείνων
φιλίας σεαυτὴν στέλλουσα· κεῖθι <γὰρ> τὸ σοβαρὸν οὐκ

27. Aristippus to his Daughter Arete

I have received the letters you sent to me by Telea, in which you request me to come as quickly as possible to Cyrene. You say that you are not well received by the municipal officials, and that your husband cannot adminis- ter your affairs because he is shy and used to live far removed from the clamor of political life. But as I tried to gain my release from Dionysius and sail to you, fate hindered me and in Lipara I became ill. When I saw that the family of Sonicus treated me most kindly and that they were genuinely interested in my welfare.... (2) Concern- ing your questions as to how you should regard the men I set free, who kept on saying that they would not leave Aristippus so long as it was in their power to please him and you, trust them in everything. As a result of my way of life they will not be bad. I advise you to settle your affairs with the officials so that this advice of mine may be beneficial. And it would be this: do not desire too much. For you are living your life in the very best way when you disdain all excess. For they would not wrong you to the point that you would be in need. You still have two gardens, enough for a luxurious life. The property in Berenice, even if it alone were left, would not fail to supply you with a very high standard of living. (3) I do not bid you to despise minor matters, but not to be dis- turbed by them, since even in major matters anger is not good. If, after I have departed this life, you wish to do my will, go to Athens, after you have given Aristippus the best possible education, and hold in the highest esteem Xanthippe and Myrto who often urged me to bring you to the mysteries. If you then live a pleasant life with them, let the officials in Cyrene commit any wrong they wish (for they will not wrong you to the point that you die), and try to live with Xanthippe and Myrto as I was pleased to do with Socrates; you are arraying yourself all the more through your friendship with them. For there, inso- lence is not at home. (4) But if Lamprocles the son of

ἐπιχώριον. (4) Εἰ δ' ἔλθοι θᾶττον ἅμα Λαμπροκλῆς
εἰς Κυρήνην ὁ Σωκράτους, ὃς ἐν Μεγάροις ὡμίλει μοι,
ποιήσεις ἄριστα κοινουμένη τὸν βίον αὐτῷ καὶ μηδὲν
διαφορώτερον τοῦ τέκνου τιμῶσα. Θῆλυ δὲ τέκνον εἰ
5   μηκέτι τρέφειν βούλει διὰ τὸ πολλὰ ἀνιᾶσθαι ἐπὶ παι-
δοτροφίᾳ, τὸ τῆς Εὐβοΐδος θυγάτριον, ὃ δὴ ἐλευθέρως
ἦγες † ἐμοί τε χαρίζεσθαι βουλομένη ἐπὶ τῷ τῆς ἐμῆς
μητρὸς ὀνόματι <ὠνόμασας> Μίκαν· καὶ γὰρ ἐγὼ πολλάκις
Μίκαν αὐτὸ προσηγόρευσα.† Πρὸ παντὸς δὲ ἐπισκήπτω
10   <σοι> τοῦ μικροῦ Ἀριστίππου ἐπιμελεῖσθαι, ὅπως ἄξιος
ἡμῶν καὶ φιλοσοφίας· ταύτην γὰρ αὐτῷ καταλείπω τὴν
ὄντως κληρονομίαν, τἆλλα μὲν γὰρ τοῦ βίου καὶ τοὺς ἐν
Κυρήνῃ ἄρχοντας ἔχει πολεμίους. (5) Περὶ φιλοσοφίας
δὲ οὐδέν μοι γέγραφας, ὅτι ταύτην σοῦ τις ἀφῄρηται.
15   Μέγα οὖν, ὦ ἀγαθὴ γύναι, χαῖρε ἐπὶ τῷ πλουτεῖν πλοῦτον
τὸν ὑπὸ σοὶ κείμενον καὶ κτηματίτην ποίει τούτου τὸν
υἱόν, ὃν ἐβουλόμην μὲν αὐτὸς ἤδη ἐμὸν υἱὸν εἶναι.
Ἐπειδὴ δὲ ἀναλύω μὴ ἐμπλησθείς? αὐτοῦ, πέποιθα καί
σοι, διότι τὴν αὐτὴν ἄξεις πορείαν τὴν συνήθη ἀγαθοῖς
20   ἀνδράσιν. Ἔρρωσο καὶ περὶ ἡμῶν <μὴ> ἀγανάκτει.

28. Φιλίππῳ

Ἀντίπατρος ὁ φέρων τὴν ἐπιστολὴν τὸ μὲν
γένος ἐστὶ Μάγνης, γράφει δὲ Ἀθήνησι πάλαι τὰς
Ἑλληνικὰς πράξεις· ἀδικεῖσθαι δέ φησιν ὑπό τινος ἐν
25   Μαγνησίᾳ. Διάκουσον οὖν αὐτοῦ τὸ πρᾶγμα καὶ βοήθησον
ὡς ἂν δύνῃ προθυμότατα. Δικαίως δ' ἂν αὐτῷ βοηθοίης
διὰ πολλὰ καὶ διότι παρ' ἡμῖν ἀναγνωσθέντος ἐν δια-
τριβῇ τοῦ σοὶ πεμφθέντος ὑπὸ Ἰσοκράτους λόγου τότε
τὴν μὲν ὑπόθεσιν ἐπήνεσε, τὸ δὲ παραλιπεῖν τὰς εἰς
30   τὴν Ἑλλάδα γενομένας εὐεργεσίας ὑμῶν ἐνεκάλεσεν.
Πειράσομαι δ' αὐτῶν εἰπεῖν ὀλίγας. (2) Ἰσοκράτης
μὲν γὰρ οὔτε τὰς εἰς τὴν Ἑλλάδα γενομένας εὐεργεσίας

Socrates, who was my companion in Megara, should rather
come to Cyrene, you will do well to share your livelihood
with him and regard him no differently than your own
child. If you no longer want to rear a young girl because
you are very disheartened at the prospect of rearing children, adopt the daughter of Eubois whom you used to treat
as though she were free, and whom you called by my
mother's name, Mika, when you wanted to please me; indeed,
I too, often called her Mika. But above all I urge you to
care for little Aristippus so that he may be worthy of us
and of philosophy. That is the real inheritance I leave
him, for in the other aspects of his life he will have the
officials in Cyrene as his enemies. (5) But concerning
philosophy you have not written me that anyone has robbed
you of it. So, my good woman, rejoice greatly in the
wealth which you have accumulated and make your son, whom
I would like to have as my own, its possessor. Since I
shall die without enjoying him, I trust you will guide him
on a course of life that is customary for good men. Farewell, and do not be distressed about us.

28. To Philip

   Antipater who brings this letter is a native of Magnesia, but he has for some time in Athens been writing a
Greek history. He says that he has been unjustly treated
by someone in Magnesia. Therefore listen carefully to his
story and help him as actively as you can. It is right
for you to help him for many reasons, and especially because, when the speech sent to you by Isocrates was read
to us in our company, he commended the argument of the
speech but criticized the absence of an account of the
benefits you conferred on Greece. I shall attempt to mention a few of them. (2) For Isocrates did not reveal the
benefits that you and your ancestors conferred on Greece,

ὑπὸ σοῦ καὶ τῶν <σῶν> προγόνων δεδήλωκεν οὔτε τὰς
ὑπό τινων κατὰ σοῦ γεγενημένας διαβολὰς λέλυκεν οὔτε
Πλάτωνος ἐν τοῖς πρὸς σὲ πεμφθεῖσι λόγοις ἀπέσχηται.
Καίτοι χρῆν πρῶτον μὲν τὴν ὑπάρχουσαν οἰκειότητα πρὸς
5   τὴν ἡμετέραν πόλιν αὐτὸν μὴ λαθεῖν, ἀλλὰ ποιῆσαι καὶ
τοῖς ἀπὸ σοῦ γενομένοις φανεράν. Ἡρακλῆς γὰρ ὄντος
νόμου τὸ παλαιὸν ἡμῖν μηδένα ξένον μυεῖσθαι βουληθεὶς
μυεῖσθαι γίνεται Πυλίου θετὸς υἱός. (3) Τούτου δὲ
ὄντος τοιούτου τοὺς λόγους ἐξῆν Ἰσοκράτει λέγειν ὡς
10   πρὸς πολίτην, ἐπειδὴ τὸ γένος ὑμῶν ἐστιν ἀφ' Ἡρακλέους, μετὰ δὲ ταῦτα τὰς Ἀλεξάνδρου τοῦ σοῦ προγόνου
καὶ τῶν ἄλλων τὰς εἰς τὴν Ἑλλάδα γενομένας εὐεργεσίας ἐξαγγέλλειν. Νυνὶ δὲ ὥσπερ ἀπορρήτους συμφορὰς
αὐτῶν κατασεσιώπηκε. Ξέρξου γὰρ πρέσβεις ἐπὶ τὴν
15   Ἑλλάδα πέμψαντος γῆν καὶ ὕδωρ αἰτήσοντας Ἀλέξανδρος
τοὺς μὲν πρέσβεις ἀπέκτεινεν· ὕστερον δὲ στασιαζόντων
τῶν βαρβάρων οἱ Ἕλληνες ἐπὶ τὸ ἡμέτερον Ἡράκλειον
ἀπήντησαν· Ἀλεξάνδρου δὲ τὴν Ἀλεύου καὶ Θετταλῶν
προδοσίαν τοῖς Ἕλλησι μηνύσαντος ἀναζεύξαντες οἱ
20   Ἕλληνες δι' Ἀλέξανδρον ἐσώθησαν. (4) Καίτοι τούτων
χρὴ μὴ μόνον Ἡρόδοτον καὶ Δαμάστην μεμνῆσθαι τῶν
εὐεργεσιῶν, ἀλλὰ καὶ τὸν ἐν ταῖς τέχναις ἀποφαινόμε-
νον <ἐκ τοῦ τῶν προγόνων ἐπαίνου> εὔνους δεῖν προσεῖ-
ναι τοὺς ἀκροατάς. Προσῆκε δὲ καὶ τὴν ἐν Πλαταιαῖς
25   ἐπὶ Μαρδονίου γεγενημένην δηλῶσαι καὶ τὰς ἐξῆς τοσαύ-
τας τῶν <σῶν> προγόνων εὐεργεσίας. Οὕτω γὰρ ἂν ὁ
περὶ σοῦ γραφεὶς λόγος τῆς παρὰ τῶν Ἑλλήνων εὐνοίας
ἔτυχε μᾶλλον ἢ μηδὲν ἀγαθὸν περὶ τῆς ὑμετέρας βασιλείας εἰπόντος. Ἦν δὲ καὶ τὰ παλαιὰ διαλεχθῆναι τῆς
30   Ἰσοκράτους ἡλικίας, τὸ δὲ εὐθαλῶς, ὥς φησιν αὐτός,
ἀνθούσης τῆς διανοίας. Ἀλλὰ μὴν καὶ τὰς διαβολὰς
ἐνῆν λῦσαι τὰς τὸ πλεῖστον ὑπ' Ὀλυνθίων γινομένας.
(5) Τίς γὰρ ἂν οὕτως εὐήθη σε νομίσειεν, ὥστε σοι
πολεμούντων Ἰλλυριῶν καὶ Θρᾳκῶν ἔτι τε Ἀθηναίων καὶ
35   Λακεδαιμονίων καὶ ἄλλων Ἑλλήνων καὶ βαρβάρων πόλεμον

nor did he refute the slanders against you which had been
spread by certain people, nor did he refrain from speaking
of Plato in the speeches sent to you. Indeed, in the
first place he had not to overlook the existing friendship
between you and our city, but had to make it clear to your
successors. For formerly, when it was the law that no
foreigner could be initiated, Heracles, wanting to be
initiated into the mysteries, became an adopted son of
Pylos. (3) Since this was so, Isocrates could have spoken
to you as to a fellow citizen since your family stems from
Heracles, and he could afterwards have proclaimed the
benefits that accrued to Greece from Alexander your ances-
tor and others. But now he has kept silent about them as
though they were something to be kept secret. For when
Xerxes sent ambassadors into Greece to ask for land and
water, Alexander killed them. Later when the Barbarians
were seditious, the Greeks met in our temple of Heracles.
When Alexander revealed the betrayal of Aleuas and the
Thessalians to the Greeks they broke camp and were saved
by Alexander. (4) Furthermore, it was not only Herodotus
and Damaster who had to mention these benefits, but also
the man who declares in his *Rhetoric* that a speaker should
make his listeners well disposed to what he has to say by
praising their forefathers. It would also have been fitting to tell what had happened in Plataea in the time of
Mardonius and to speak of the good deeds of your fathers
that followed. For a speech composed about you in this
way would meet with greater favor among the Greeks than
one which says nothing good about your kingdom. These
time-honored stories were being discussed vigorously during Isocrates' old age at a time, as he himself says, when
his own intellectual ability was still strong. He could
also have refuted the slanders spread for the most part by
the people of Olynthus. (5) Who would consider you so
foolish that while the Illyrians, Thracians, and further
the Athenians, Laconians, and other Greeks and Barbarians
are waging war against you, you would begin a war with the

πρὸς Ὀλυνθίους ἐξενεγκεῖν; Ἀλλὰ περὶ μὲν τούτων οὐκ
ἐν ἐπιστολῇ πρὸς σὲ μηκυντέον. Ἃ δέ ἐστιν οὐκ ἐμπο-
δῶν τοῖς τυχοῦσιν εἰπεῖν ἐκ πολλοῦ τε χρόνου τοῖς πᾶσι
κατασεσιώπηται, συμφέρει δέ σοι πυθέσθαι, ταῦτά μοι
5   δοκεῖ φράσειν καὶ τούτων ἀξιώσειν εὐαγγελίᾳ δικαίαν
χάριν Ἀντιπάτρῳ <παρὰ σοῦ> δοθῆναι. Περὶ γὰρ τῆς
γινομένης Ὀλυνθίοις χώρας, ὡς ἔστι τὸ παλαιὸν Ἡρακλειδῶν, [ἀλλ' οὐ Χαλκιδέων], ὁ φέρων τὴν ἐπιστολὴν
μόνος καὶ πρῶτος ἀξιοπίστους μύθους εἴρηκε. (6) Τὸν
10   αὐτὸν γάρ φησι τρόπον Νηλέα μὲν ἐν Μεσσήνῃ, Συλέα δὲ
περὶ τὸν Ἀμφιπολιτικὸν τόπον ὑφ' Ἡρακλέους ὑβριστὰς
ὄντας ἀπολέσθαι καὶ δοθῆναι παρακαταθήκην φυλάττειν
Νέστορι μὲν τῷ Νηλέως Μεσσήνην, Δικαίῳ δὲ τῷ Νηλέως
ἀδελφῷ τὴν Φυλλίδα χώραν· καὶ Μεσσήνην μὲν ὕστερον
15   πολλαῖς γενεαῖς Κρεσφόντην κομίσασθαι, τὴν δὲ Ἀμφι-
πολῖτιν Ἡρακλειδῶν οὖσαν Ἀθηναίους καὶ Χαλκιδεῖς
λαβεῖν· ὡς δ' αὕτως ὑφ' Ἡρακλέους ἀναιρεθῆναι κα-
κούργους καὶ παρανόμους Ἱπποκόωντα μὲν ἐν Σπάρτῃ
τύραννον, Ἀλκυονέα δὲ ἐν Παλλήνῃ, καὶ Σπάρτην μὲν
20   Τυνδάρεῳ, Ποτίδαιαν δὲ καὶ τὴν ἄλλην Παλλήνην Σιθῶνι
τῷ Ποσειδῶνος παρακαταθέσθαι, καὶ τὴν μὲν Λακωνικὴν
τοὺς Ἀριστοδήμου παῖδας ἐν ταῖς Ἡρακλειδῶν καθόδοις
ἀπολαβεῖν, Παλλήνην δὲ Ἐρετριεῖς καὶ Κορινθίους καὶ
τοὺς ἀπὸ Τροίας Ἀχαιοὺς Ἡρακλειδῶν οὖσαν κατασχεῖν.
25   (7) Τὸν αὐτὸν δὲ τρόπον ἐξαγγέλλει περὶ τὴν Τορωναίαν
τοὺς Πρωτίδας τυράννους Τμῶλον καὶ Τηλέγονον ὡς
Ἡρακλῆς ἀνέλοι, καὶ περὶ Ἀμβρακίαν Κλείδην καὶ τοὺς
Κλείδου παῖδας ἀποκτείνας Ἀριστομάχῳ μὲν τῷ Σιθῶνος
τὴν Τορωναίαν τηρεῖν προστάξειεν, ἣν Χαλκιδεῖς ὑμετέ-
30   ραν οὖσαν κατῴκισαν, Λαδίκῃ δὲ καὶ Χαράττῃ τὴν Ἀμβρα-
κικὴν χώραν ἐγχειρήσειεν, ἀξιῶν ἀποδοῦναι τὰς παρα-
καταθήκας τοῖς ἀπ' αὐτοῦ γινομένοις. Ἀλλὰ μὴν καὶ
τὰς ὑπογυίους Ἀλεξάνδρου τῆς Ἡδωνῶν χώρας κτήσεις
Μακεδόνες πάντες ἴσασι. (8) καὶ ταῦτά ἐστιν οὐ προφά-
35   σεις [Ἰσοκράτους] οὐδ' ὀνομάτων ψόφος, ἀλλὰ λόγοι
δυνάμενοι τὴν σὴν ἀρχὴν ὠφελεῖν.

people of Olynthus? Yet I should not speak at length about
these things in a letter to you. But what one cannot say to
people who are far away is, after a long time, not spoken of
by anyone. Yet it is fitting that you know about them. I
therefore think it proper to speak of them, and believe
that because of them Antipater will receive well-earned
thanks from you for his news. The bearer of this letter
was the only person who first gave credible accounts about
the land of the Olynthians, namely that of old it belonged
to the Dorians, not to the people of the Chalcidice. (6)
He says that Heracles in the same manner killed Neleus in
Messenia but Syleus in the area of Amphipolis because they
were insolent men, and that Messenia was given to Nestor,
the son of Neleus as a trust, and the land of Pylos was
given to Dikaios the brother of Neleus. Many generations
later Cresphontes acquired Messenia but Amphipolis, which
had belonged to the Dorians, was taken over by the Athenians and the people of the Chalcidice. Hippocoon, the
tyrant of Sparta and Alcyoneus of Pallene were killed in
the same way by Heracles as wicked and lawless men. Sparta was entrusted to Tyndareus and Potidaea and the rest of
Pallene to Sithon the son of Poseidon. Laconia took back
the sons of Aristodemus with the return of the Dorians,
and Pallene, while belonging to the Dorians, took possession of the Eretrians, the Corinthians and the Achaeans
from Troy. (7) In the same way he recounts that in the
region of Torone, Heracles killed the tyrants Tmolus and
Telegonus, the sons of Proteus, and that after he had
killed Cleides and his sons in the neighborhood of Ambracia, he ordered Aristomachus the son of Sithon to guard
Torone which, since it belonged to you, the people of the
Chalcidice settled, but that he handed over the region of
Ambracia to Ladike and Charatte having in mind that they
would return to his progeny the land that had been entrusted to them. Indeed, all of Macedonia knows the recent acquisitions of Alexander in the land of Edoni.
(8) And these are not pretenses of Isocrates or mere idle
sounds; rather they are words able to benefit your rule.

Ἐπειδὴ δὲ καὶ περὶ τῶν Ἀμφικτυονικῶν πραγμάτων δῆλος
εἶ σπουδάζων, ἐβουλήθην σοὶ φράσαι μῦθον παρὰ Ἀντιπάτρου, τίνα τρόπον πρῶτον οἱ Ἀμφικτύονες συνέστησαν,
καὶ πῶς ὄντες Ἀμφικτύονες Φλεγύαι μὲν ὑπὸ Ἀπόλλωνος,
5   Δρύοπες δὲ ὑπὸ Ἡρακλέους, Κρισαῖοι δὲ ὑπὸ τῶν Ἀμφικτυόνων ἀνηρέθησαν· οὗτοι γὰρ πάντες Ἀμφικτύονες γενόμενοι τῶν ψήφων ἀφῃρέθησαν, ἕτεροι δὲ τὰς τούτων
ψήφους λαβόντες τῆς τῶν Ἀμφικτυόνων συντελείας μετέ-
σχον, ὧν ἐνίους σέ φησι μεμιμῆσθαι καὶ λαβεῖν ἆθλον
10   Πυθίοις τῆς εἰς Δελφοὺς στρατείας παρὰ τῶν Ἀμφικτυόνων τὰς δύο Φωκέων ψήφους· (9) ὧν ὁ τὰ παλαιὰ καινῶς
καὶ τὰ καινὰ παλαιῶς ἐπαγγελλόμενος διδάσκειν λέγει
νῦν οὔτε τὰς ἀρχαίας πράξεις οὔτε τὰς ὑπὸ σοῦ νεωστὶ
διαγωνισθείσας οὔτε τὰς τοῖς μεταξὺ χρόνοις γενομένας
15   μεμύθευκε. Καίτοι δοκεῖ τὰς μὲν οὐκ ἀκηκοέναι, τὰς
δ' οὐκ εἰδέναι, τῶν δὲ ἐπιλελῆσθαι. Πρὸς δὲ τούτοις
ἐπὶ πράξεις σε δικαίας παρακαλῶν ὁ σοφιστὴς τὴν <μὲν>
Ἀλκιβιάδου φυγὴν καὶ κάθοδον ἐπαινῶν ἐν παραδείγματι
δεδήλωκε, τὰ δὲ μείζω καὶ καλλίω πράγματα <τὰ> τῷ
20   πατρί σου πραχθέντα παρέλιπεν. (10) Ἀλκιβιάδης μὲν
γὰρ ἐπ' ἀσεβείᾳ φυγὼν καὶ πλεῖστα τὴν πατρίδα τὴν
αὐτοῦ κακῶς ποιήσας εἰς αὐτὴν κατῆλθεν· Ἀμύντας δὲ
ὑπὲρ βασιλείας στάσει νικηθεὶς βραχὺν χρόνον ὑποχωρή-
σας μετὰ ταῦτα πάλιν Μακεδονίας ἦρξεν. Εἶθ' ὁ μὲν
25   πάλιν φυγὼν αἰσχρῶς τὸν βίον ἐτελεύτησεν, ὁ δὲ σὸς
πατὴρ βασιλεύων κατεγήρασεν. Παρήνεγκε δέ σοι καὶ
τὴν Διονυσίου μοναρχίαν, ὥσπερ προσῆκόν σοι τοὺς
ἀσεβεστάτους, ἀλλ' οὐ τοὺς σπουδαιοτάτους μιμήσασθαι,
καὶ ζηλωτὴν τῶν κακίστων, ἀλλ' οὐ τῶν δικαιοτάτων
30   γενέσθαι. Καὶ φησι μὲν ἐν ταῖς τέχναις προσήκειν
οἰκεῖα καὶ γνώριμα τὰ παραδείγματα φέρειν· ὀλιγωρήσας
δὲ τῆς τέχνης ἀλλοτρίοις καὶ τοῖς αἰσχίστοις καὶ τοῖς
πρὸς τὸν λόγον ὡς ἐναντιωτάτοις παραδείγμασι χρῆται.

Since you give serious attention to the circumstances of
the Amphictionies, I would like to tell you Antipater's
story: how the Amphictionies were first organized, and how
the members of the Amphictiony were done away with, the
Phlegyae by Apollo, the Dryops by Heracles, and the Cris-
aeans by the Amphictionies. All these, though members of
the Amphictionies, were excluded from voting; others took
over their votes and shared in the assembly of the Amphictionies. He says you imitated some of the latter and during the Pythian games received the five votes of the Pho-
cians from the Amphictionies as a reward for your campaign
against Delphi. (9) Now, this man who professes to be
teaching old things in new ways and new things in old ways
has, in fact, failed to record both your early and recent
accomplishments, not to speak of those which fall in between! Indeed, he appears not to have heard of some, to
be ignorant of others, and to have forgotten still others.
Furthermore, this sophist, in exhorting you to the right
courses of action, praised and used the exile and return
of Alcibiades as an example, but he neglected the much
more important and noble deeds, namely those of your
father. (10) Alcibiades was exiled for impiety, and after
he had greatly harmed his own fatherland, he returned to
it. But Amyntas was overthrown during a sedition aimed at
his sovereignty, and went abroad for a short time, but
soon returned to rule over Macedonia again. Alcibiades
had to leave the country again and died a shameful death;
your father, however, ruled to his old age. He also set
before you the monarchy of Dionysius as though the proper
thing for you to do was to imitate the most impious rather
than the most excellent men, and to become an emulator of
the most wicked rather than the most just men. Indeed, he
says in his *Rhetoric* that one should present family members and well known persons as examples, but then he neglects the rule and uses strangers and the most wicked men
as examples, and even ones that are as contrary to the
subject as they can possibly be. (11) And further,

(11) Καίτοι πάντων καταγελαστότατα τοιαῦτα γράφων
χαριέντως ἀμύνασθαί φησι τῶν μαθητῶν τοὺς ἐπιτιμῶν-
τας. Οἱ δὲ χειρωθέντες [τῶν αὐτῷ πλησιαζόντων ἀκμά-
ζοντες] τῆς ῥητορικῆς τῇ δυνάμει καὶ παρὰ ταῦτα οὐδὲν
5   ἔχοντες εἰπεῖν οὕτως ἐπήνεσαν τὸν λόγον, ὥστε τὸ πρω-
τεῖον τῶν λόγων τῷ λόγῳ τούτῳ δεδώκασι. Καταμάθοις
δ' ἂν ἐν βραχεῖ τὴν ᾽Ισοκράτους ἱστορίαν καὶ τὴν παιδείαν ἐξ ὧν Κυρηναίους μὲν ποιεῖ τοὺς Βάττου ὄντας
ἀποίκους τῶν Λακεδαιμονίων, τὸν δὲ Ποντικὸν μαθητὴν
10 ἀπέδειξε τῆς αὐτοῦ σοφίας διάδοχον, οὗ σὺ πολλοὺς
τεθεαμένος σοφιστὰς βδελυρώτερον οὐχ ἑώρακας. (12)
Πυνθάνομαι δὲ καὶ Θεόπομπον παρ' ὑμῖν μὲν εἶναι πάνυ
ψυχρόν, περὶ δὲ Πλάτωνος βλασφημεῖν καὶ ταῦτα ὥσπερ
οὐ Πλάτωνος τὴν ἀρχὴν τῆς ἀρχῆς ἐπὶ Περδίκκᾳ κατα-
15 σκευάσαντος καὶ διὰ τέλους χαλεπῶς φέροντος, εἴ τι
γίνοιτο παρ' ὑμῖν ἀνήμερον ἢ μὴ φιλάδελφον. ῞Ινα οὖν
Θεόπομπος παύσηται τραχὺς ὢν κέλευσον ᾽Αντίπατρον
παραναγνῶναι τῶν ῾Ελληνικῶν πράξεων αὐτῷ, καὶ γνώσε-
ται Θεόπομπος δικαίως <μὲν> ὑπὸ πάντων ἐξαλειφόμενος,
20 ἀδίκως δὲ τῆς παρὰ σοῦ χορηγίας τυγχάνων. (13) ῾Ομο-
οίως δὲ καὶ ᾽Ισοκράτης, ἐπειδὴ νέος μὲν ὢν εἰς τὸν
δῆμον μετὰ Τιμοθέου καθ' ὑμῶν ἐπιστολὰς αἰσχρὰς
ἔγραψεν, νυνὶ δὲ πρεσβύτης ὢν ὥσπερ ἔχθων? ἢ φθονῶν
τὰ πλεῖστα τῶν ὑμῖν ὑπαρχόντων ἀγαθῶν παραλέλοιπεν·
25 ἀπέσταλκε δέ σοι λόγον, ὃν τὸ μὲν πρῶτον ἔγραψεν
᾽Αγησιλάῳ, μικρὰ <δὲ> διασκευάσας ὕστερον ἐπώλει τῷ
Σικελίας τυράννῳ Διονυσίῳ· τὸ δὲ τρίτον τὰ μὲν
ἀφελὼν τὰ δὲ προσθεὶς ἐμνήστευσεν ᾽Αλεξάνδρῳ τῷ
Θετταλῷ· τὸ δὲ τελευταῖον νῦν πρὸς σὲ γλίσχρως αὐτὸν
30 ἀπηκόντισεν. Βουλοίμην δ' ἂν χωρῆσαι τὸ βιβλίον ἀνα-
μνῆσαι τὰς ἐν τῷ λόγῳ πρὸς σὲ πεμφθείσας ὑπ' αὐτοῦ
προφάσεις. (14) ᾽Επὶ μὲν γὰρ ᾽Αμφιπόλεώς φησι κωλῦσαι τὴν γενομένην εἰρήνην γράψαι λόγον ὑπὲρ τῆς
῾Ηρακλέους ἀθανασίας, ὕστερον δὲ αὐτῷ σοι φράσειν.
35 ῾Υπὲρ ἐνίων δὲ διὰ τὴν ἡλικίαν ὁμολογῶν μαλακώτερον

although he wrote such extremely absurd things, he says
that he charmingly deflected the attack of those of his
students who reproached him. Those disciples of his, however, who were given to high oratory and had fallen under
the power of rhetoric and had nothing else to say, praised
the speech to such an extent that they granted it the
first place among his speeches. You might briefly observe
the level of Isocrates' historical knowledge and learning
from the fact that he makes the Cyreneans, who were set-
tlers under Battus, to be colonists of the Lacedaemonians,
and that he presents as the successor to his own wisdom
the disciple from Pontus, who is the most loathsome of the
many sophists you have seen. (12) I learn that Theopompus,
too, is very cold in your presence, and that he is slandering Plato to the effect that Plato did not bring about the
beginning of your rule during the time of Perdiccas, and
that Plato does not behave angrily throughout if something
not quite gentle or humane should transpire in your presence. So that Theopompus might stop being bitter, bid
Antipater to read from his Greek history to him, and Theopompus will understand that on the one hand he was justly
wiped from everyone's mind, and that on the other he unjustly shares in your bounty. (13) Likewise Isocrates
also, when he was young, together with Timothy wrote disgraceful letters against you to the people and now that he
is old has, out of envy or hate, left most of your good
deeds untold. And he sent you a speech which he first
wrote for Agesilaus, and then, slightly revising it, he
later sold it to Dionysius the tyrant of Sicily. A third
time he hawked it to Alexander the Thessalian after making
some omissions and additions. Now at last he has carefully fired it off at you. Would that this paper had room
to recall his false pretences in the speech he sent to
you. (14) For he says that the peace that came over Amphipolis prevented him from writing a speech about the im-
mortality of Heracles but that he would give it to you
later. For some things which he admits to have written

γράφειν συγγνώμης ἀξιοῖ τυχεῖν· μὴ θαυμάζειν δέ, εἰ
καί πως ἀναγνοὺς ὁ Ποντικὸς ἀμβλύτερον καὶ φαυλότερον
ποιεῖ φαίνεσθαι τὸν λόγον· τὸν Πέρσην δὲ ὡς κατα-
στρατηγήσεις αὐτὸν εἰδέναι σέ φησιν. Ἀλλὰ γὰρ τὰς
5   λοιπὰς σκήψεις γράφοντα ἐπιλείπει με τὸ βιβλίον·
τοσαύτην ἡμῖν σπάνιν βιβλίων βασιλεὺς Αἴγυπτον λαβὼν
πεποίηκεν. Ἔρρωσο καὶ Ἀντιπάτρου διὰ ταχέων ἐπιμεληθεὶς πρὸς ἡμᾶς αὐτὸν ἀπόστειλον.

29. Φιλίππῳ

10   Περδίκκας μὲν ἐνδεδεῖχθαί μοι δοκεῖ περὶ πολλοῦ
ποιούμενος κατὰ τὸν Ἡσίοδον τὰ ἡμίσεα πάντων κεκτῆσθαι νομίζων τὰ μὲν χρήματα καὶ διὰ τύχην ἄν τινα
πολλὰ κτήσασθαι <οὐ> τῶν βελτίστων εἶναι. Σοὶ δὲ
ὅσιόν ἐστιν ἀδελφὰ τοῖς παρ' ἐκείνου ὑπηργμένοις
15   πράττειν, ὅπως ἂν δοκῇς καὶ τὸ ἦθος ἀδελφὸς εἶναι
τοῦ περὶ σοῦ διανοηθέντος τοιαῦτα. Νόμιζε δὲ πάντας
προσέχειν σοι τὸν νοῦν καὶ σκοπεῖν ποῖός τε ἔσῃ πρὸς
τὸν ἀδελφὸν καὶ τοὺς μὲν βελτίστους ἀγωνιᾶν βουλομένους καὶ ἐξισοῦσθαί σε τῇ τοῦ ἀδελφοῦ ἐπιεικείᾳ καὶ
20   ὑπερβάλλειν, τοὺς δὲ φαύλους φθονοῦντας ἡδέως ἄν τι
ἰδεῖν περὶ ὑμᾶς γινόμενον πλημμελές. Οὓς δεῖ νομί-
σαντα πολεμίους εἶναι μετὰ τῶν βελτίστων ἀγωνίζεσθαι
αὐτὸν ὄντα ἕνα τούτων. Δοκεῖ γάρ μοι οὐ μόνον σοι
ἁμιλλητέον εἶναι πρὸς τὰ τοῦ ἀδελφοῦ ἔργα, ἃ ἐκείνῳ
25   ὑπὲρ τοῦ κοινοῦ πέπρακται, ἀλλὰ καὶ πρὸς τὰς σὰς
εὐεργεσίας, ὅπως μὴ καταδεέστεραι αἱ παρὰ σοῦ πρὸς
ἐκεῖνον γίνωνται. Περὶ πλείστου δὲ δεῖ σε ποιεῖσθαι
σώφρονά τε εἶναι καὶ κατήκοον τοῦ ἀδελφοῦ ὄντος περὶ
σὲ οἷός περ νῦν ἐστιν. Ἔρρωσο.

rather feebly because of his advanced age, he begs your
indulgence, and he says that he would not be surprised if
the Pontian should somehow make the speech appear duller
and meaner when he reads it, and that you yourself know
how you outgeneralled the Persian. But I do not have
enough paper to write down the rest of his excuses, such
a scarcity of paper did the king create for us by taking
Egypt. Farewell. Take care of Antipater quickly and
send him back to us.

29. To Philip

Perdiccas seems to me to have demonstrated amply that
he places a high value on possessing, in the words of
Hesiod, "half of everything" (*Works* 40). He thinks that
to acquire vast sums of money through some act of fortune
is not characteristic of the most noble men. It behooves
you to act in a way befitting the resources you have received from him so that you may appear also in your character to be a brother of the man who was so disposed toward you. Recognize that everyone is watching you to see
what your relationship is with your brother, and that the
most noble men anxiously desire that you equal your brother's gentleness and even surpass it, but that the worst
of men would, out of envy, like to see anything in your
life that is amiss. Such men you must regard as enemies,
but you must join in the struggle in the company of noble
men as one of them. I think that you must not only compete with the deeds your brother performed for the common
good, but with your own benefactions as well, so that they
may not be inferior in comparison with his. Above all,
you should strive to be wise and to obey your brother
while he is disposed to you as he now is. Farewell.

30.

(1) Ἐνόμιζον ἐπιτήδειον εἶναί μοι μηδὲν τῶν
καλῶς ἐχόντων παραλιπεῖν καὶ διὰ τὴν Πλάτωνος ἐντολὴν
καὶ διὰ τὴν ὑπάρχουσαν ἐμοὶ καὶ σοὶ φιλίαν. Καὶ ᾤμην
5 δεῖν γράψαι πρὸς σὲ πῶς διακείμενος τυγχάνω τὸ σωμάτιον καὶ διότι νομίζω παραγενόμενόν σε εἰς Ἀκαδημίαν
συνέχειν τὸν περίπατον. Ταῦτα δὲ ὡς δίκαιά ἐστι καὶ
καλῶς ἔχοντα πειράσομαί σοι φράζειν. Πλάτων, καθάπερ
καὶ σὺ οἶσθα, καὶ ἐν τῇ οὐ τυχούσῃ τιμῇ τὴν ἐν Ἀκα-
10 δημίᾳ διατριβὴν ἦγε νομίζων εἶναί τι καὶ πρὸς δόξαν
ὀρθὴν καὶ πρὸς τὸν αὐτοῦ βίον καὶ τὴν ὕστερον παρ'
ἀνθρώποις μνείαν ἐσομένην. (2) Καὶ τούτων οὕτως
ἐχόντων διότι σε περὶ πλείονος ποιούμενος ἐτύγχανε,
τελευτῶν τὸν βίον ἐμαρτύρησε. Ἐπέσκηψε γὰρ πᾶσιν
15 ἡμῖν τοῖς οἰκείοις, ἄν τι πάθῃς, πρὸς ἑαυτὸν θεῖναί
σε, νομίσας οὐκ ἀπαλλαγήσεσθαί σε τὸ παράπαν τῆς
Ἀκαδημίας. Διὸ δὴ καὶ μάλιστά μοι φαίνεταί σοι
προσῆκον εἶναι καὶ ζῶντα καὶ τεθνηκότα Πλάτωνα τιμᾶν.
θεῶν γὰρ δὴ καὶ γονέων καὶ εὐεργετῶν ποιητέον ἐπι-
20 μέλειαν τὸν χαρίεντα. Οἰκειοτάτη δὲ τοῖς εἰρημένοις
εὑρίσκοιτ' ἂν οὖσα ἡ Πλάτωνος συνουσία πρὸς τοὺς
συνόντας. Τῶν μὲν γὰρ ὡς γεννήσας, τῶν δὲ ὡς εὐερ-
γέτης ἐπεμελεῖτο, κοινῇ δὲ πρὸς ἅπαντας θεοῦ τάξιν
εἶχε. (3) Συμβουλεύω δὲ καλὸν ἡγούμενος καὶ δίκαιον
25 εἶναι χάριν ἀποδιδόναι σε Πλάτωνι πασῶν μεγίστην
κἀκείνῳ μάλιστα ἀρμόζουσαν· ἀποδοίης δ' ἂν εἰ παρα-
γενόμενος <εἰς> τὴν Ἀκαδημίαν <τὸν περίπατον
συνέχοις>· σοφία γὰρ ἀληθὴς λέγοιτ' ἂν ἐνδίκως
βεβαιότης καὶ πίστις. Προσήκει δὲ ἡμᾶς ἐν τούτοις
30 πολὺ τῶν ἀνθρώπων διαφέρειν. Σὺ δὲ καὶ δοκεῖς πλέον
τοῦ προσήκοντος ἐπιμελὴς εἶναι.

30. (Speusippus to Xenocrates)

I considered it my duty not to overlook any of the things that are good, both because of Plato's command and because of the friendship which exists between you and me. I thought I should write you about my physical condition, and also because I think that if you come to the Academy you will keep the School together. I shall try to show you that this is right and proper. Plato, as you also know, held the School in the Academy in no ordinary esteem, thinking it to be something which leads to the right kind of reputation, and which contributed to his own life and to the later preservation of his memory among men. (2) This being so, he confirmed at his death that he held you in high regard. He enjoined all of us who belong to his household, if something should happen to you, to bury you next to him, for he thought that you would not at all separate yourself from the Academy. It therefore appears to me especially fitting that you should honor both the living and the dead Plato, for it becomes an accomplished gentleman to pay careful attention to his gods, ancestors, and benefactors. One would find that Plato's association with his friends agrees most closely with what has been said. He cared for some as a father, for others as a benefactor; and in general in the opinion of everyone he held the place of a god. (3) Considering it to be good and proper, I advise you to show the greatest gratitude to Plato, and to do so especially in a way appropriate to him. You would do so by returning to the Academy and keeping the School together. One might fairly call relia-bility and faithfulness true wisdom. We should in these things be very different from the majority of men. But you appear to be more diligent than duty requires.

31.

Ἔδοξέ μοι γράψαι πρὸς σὲ ἐπιστολὴν περὶ τῶν
συμβεβηκότων μοι κατὰ τὸ σωμάτιον. Οὐ γὰρ μετρίως
ἐκλελοίπασιν αἱ δυνάμεις τῶν μερῶν ἁπάντων, ὥστε
5 μηδὲν αὐτοῖς ἐνεργεῖν δύνασθαι· κατὰ τύχην δέ τινα
ἡ γλῶττα καὶ τὰ περὶ τὴν κεφαλὴν μεμένηκε, εἰ μὴ καὶ
διὰ τὸ κεχαρισμένον καὶ διὰ τὸ θειότατον εἶναι.
Πάλαι μὲν οὖν ἐβουλόμην παρεῖναί σε· εὖ δὲ ποιήσεις
καὶ νῦν παραγινόμενος. Καὶ γὰρ τῶν περὶ ἐμὲ προστήσῃ
10 κατὰ τρόπον, ὡς ἐγὼ εὖ οἶδα, καὶ τῶν ἐν τῷ περιπάτῳ
ἐπιμελήσῃ προσηκόντως.

32.

Οἶμαι φανερὰν εἶναι διὰ παντὸς τοῦ χρόνου τὴν
ἐμὴν προθυμίαν καὶ ὅτι πολλὴν πρόνοιαν εἶχον περὶ
15 ὑμῶν οὐκ ἄλλου <δέ> τινος ἕνεκεν μᾶλλον ἢ τῆς ἐπὶ
τοῖς καλοῖς φιλοτιμίας. Νομίζω γὰρ δίκαιον εἶναι
τοὺς ὄντας τῇ ἀληθείᾳ ἐπιεικεῖς καὶ πράττοντας
τοιαῦτα τυγχάνειν δόξης τῆς προσηκούσης. Ὅτι δὲ τὰ
κυριώτατα τοῦ σώματος καὶ τῷ ὄντι ἡ κεφαλὴ καὶ τὰ ἐν
20 αὐτῇ περίεστιν, εὖ ἔχει. Τῶν δὲ λοιπῶν τὴν προσήκου-
σαν ἐπιμέλειαν ποιοῦ μετά τε ἰατρῶν καὶ αὐτὸς ἐπι-
βλέπων τὸ χρήσιμον. Ἀνδρίᾳ γὰρ καὶ ῥώμῃ καὶ τάχει
διενεγκεῖν δόξειεν ἂν χαρίεντος εἶναι. (2) Ἐγὼ δέ,
καθάπερ καὶ σὺ οἶσθα, Πλάτωνα θαυμάσας δι᾽ ἐκεῖνον
25 καὶ τὴν πόλιν ὑμῶν καὶ τὴν ἐν Ἀκαδημίᾳ διατριβὴν
ἡδούμην καὶ διέμεινα πάντα τὸν χρόνον ἀνέγκλητον
ἐμαυτὸν ἐφ᾽ ὅσον ἠδυνήθην πρὸς τὸ ἐκείνου ἦθος
διατηρήσας. Ἐπεὶ δὲ κατὰ τὰ συμβαίνοντα ἐκεῖνος μὲν
ἐχωρίσθη τῆς ἐν ταὐτῷ ἡμῖν συνουσίας, τὰ δὲ νομιζό-
30 μενα συνετελέσαμεν καὶ κοινῇ καὶ ἰδίᾳ τιμῶντες ἐκεῖνον, ἐχωριζόμεθα κατὰ τὰς αἱρέσεις, ἃς ἕκαστος ἡμῶν
ἐδοκίμαζεν. (3) Ἐγὼ μὲν οὖν ἀεί ποτε καὶ τῇ φύσει
παντελῶς οἰκεῖος ὢν ἡσυχίας καὶ σχολῆς ὑπῆρχον,

31. (Speusippus to Xenocrates)

I decided to write you a letter about my health, for
my strength has completely failed me in all parts of my
body so that I cannot do anything with them. Fortunately
my tongue and the faculties of my head are intact, perhaps
because they are most favored and most god-like. For a
long time I have wished that you were here, and you will
do well if you come now. For you will indeed manage my
affairs properly, as I well know, and you will care for
the interests of the School in an appropriate way.

32. (Xenocrates to Speusippus)

I think that my eagerness has throughout been clearly
evident, and that I showed great care for you for no other
reason than my desire to be distinguished in what is noble,
for I consider it just that those who are truly reasonable
and act accordingly should achieve the reputation they deserve. That the most important parts of your body, especially your head and its faculties, are healthy, is good.
Take care, with the help of physicians, of the remaining
parts, but you yourself must observe what is useful. For
it might appear to be characteristic of an accomplished
man to be distinguished in courage, strength, and speed.
(2) As you yourself know, I admired Plato, and it was because of him that I respected your city and the school in
the Academy, and kept myself as blameless as I could
throughout the entire time, while I closely observed his
character. But when chance had removed him from our company in the Academy, and we had observed the customary
rites by honoring him publicly and privately, we divided
according to those principles which each of us had judged
appropriate to himself. (3) So, since I was by constitu-
tion always drawn to quiet and leisure, I chose, insofar

ἀνυπεύθυνός τε ὢν ἄνθρωπος εἰς τὸ δυνατὸν ἠρούμην
διαγενέσθαι. Καὶ γὰρ ἐφιλοσόφουν, ὅπως ἐμαυτοῦ τε
<ὡς> οἷόν <τε> ἦν καὶ τῶν ἄλλων ἀνθρώπων διάφορος
γίνωμαι. Δεῖ οὖν φανερὸν γενέσθαι, διότι εἰμί, οἷός
5   πέρ φημι, ἄλλως τε <καὶ> ἐπεί γε σὺν θεῷ εἰπεῖν
ῥᾴδιόν ἐστιν. Ἔρρωσο.

33.

      Ἔδοξέ μοι γράψαι ἐπιστολὰς τὴν μὲν ἑτέραν
μᾶλλόν τι σεμνυνομένην τὴν δὲ τῶν κατ᾽ οἶκον εἰθισ-
10 μένων λέγεσθαι τρόπῳ. Καὶ γὰρ ἐνεθυμήθην ὅτι δοκοῦσιν ἐνίοτε συμβαίνειν ἀκαιρίαι τοῦ λαμβάνειν τὰ
ἐπεσταλμένα. Ὀτὲ μὲν γὰρ τυγχάνει ἕκαστος ἡμῶν
σπουδάζων, ἔστι δ᾽ ὅτε πρὸς παιδιὰν ἀνιέμενος καὶ
ἱλαρώτερον ἔχων τῷ δὲ παρρησίαν ἄγειν ἁπλῶς ἡδόμενος.
15 (2) Πρῶτον μὲν οὖν συγχαίρω Συρακουσίοις, ὅτι πέπαυν-
ται τὸν χοῖρον ἴακχον καλοῦντες καὶ τὸν βοῦν γαρόταν
καὶ τὰ ἄλλα τὰ ἡδέα <καὶ> κομψὰ ταῦτα, καρποτόκον τε
μῆνα, ὅτι καρπὸς ἐν αὐτῷ γίνεται, καὶ τὰ εἰς Δελφοὺς
πεμφθέντα ἀναγράψαι τὰ σοφά, ἐφ᾽ οἷς ἔοικε ὁ Ἀπόλλων
20 οὐχ ὡς πατὴρ διατεθῆναι ἀκούσας καὶ τὸ ἀμάξιον ἰδὼν
τὸ ἐν τῷ ἱπποδρόμῳ περιτρέχον αὐτόματον· ἀλλά μοι
δοκεῖ βουληθῆναι παῦσαι ἀφικνούμενον αὐτὸν τοιαῦτα
θεωρήματα. Ὀρθῶς <οὖν> ἔχει ἴσως τοὺς καλοὺς γενομένους θεοφιλήτους νομίζειν. Ἐγὼ δὲ οὔπω σε μιμνή-
25 σκω τῆς ἐπιστολῆς, ἣν ἔγραψας πρὸς ἐμὲ ὅτι αἴτιος
εἴην ἐγὼ τοῦ ἐπιμεληθῆναι τὴν πρᾶξιν ταύτην καὶ μὴ
ἀνεθῆναι, καὶ ἔφης καλῶς ποιεῖν, εἰ καὶ αὐτὸς ἀνε-
χοίμην ἀπορίας καὶ πραγματείας. (3) Ἕτερος μὲν οὖν
ἄν τις εὐθέως μεμνημένος ἐπιστολὰς ἔπεμπε πρὸς σὲ νῦν
30 κελεύων ἐκείνων μεμνῆσθαι· ἐγὼ δὲ καιρὸν τηρήσας ποτὲ
ἐπιστελῶ. Πάνυ δὲ πολλοῦ ἐτιμησάμην ἂν ἀπὸ μηχανῆς

as it was possible, to be accountable to no-one. For
truly, I used to reflect on how I might become, to the
degree that it was possible, a more excellent person than
I myself was or other men were. It should, then, be clear
that I am what I say, especially since, with God's help
it is easy. Farewell.

33.

I decided to write two letters to you, the one more
solemn, the other in the familiar style in which we are
accustomed to speak. I truly felt that there are sometimes inappropriate moments for receiving written instructions, for each of us happens at one time to be in a serious mood, and at another to be amused and cheerful and
simply to delight in bold speaking. (2) First, then, I
congratulate the people of Syracuse, because they have
stopped calling the swine "iacchus" and the ox "garotas,"
and other pleasant things by such subtleties (and the moon
"fruit-bearer" because fruit is produced by it). I do not
think that Apollo had a fatherly disposition when he heard
of the clever words that the Delphians had been sent to
engrave and set up publicly, and when he saw the wagon
circling around in the hippodrome under its own power!
I believe that when he arrived he wished such spectacles
to cease. It is, then, perhaps accurate to think that
those men who have become good are loved by the gods. I
am not reminding you of the letter you wrote me, to the
effect that I was responsible for the management of this
undertaking. And you said that I was doing well since I
indeed endured difficulties and troubles. (3) If someone
else remembered those things, he would quickly write you
and bid you to remember now, but I shall reserve an opportunity to write about them. I would like very much to
see, apart from any contrivance, whether you maintain that

θεωρεῖν, πότερον ἐκεῖνο τὸ σχῆμα διατελεῖς ἔχων ἢ
γέγονας ἡμῖν σεμνός τε καὶ αὐθάδης, ὅτι διαλέγεται
περὶ σοῦ τὰ παιδία ἐν ταῖς ὁδοῖς καὶ Πολύξενος ἐν
τοῖς πορθμείοις καθήμενος καὶ οἱ ποιμένες ἐν τοῖς
5   ὄρεσι. Τουτὶ τὸ νεανικόν ἐστι καὶ ἀγαπητόν; Οὐ
δήπου. Ἀλλὰ νῦν δείξεις, οἷοι καὶ Δαναοῖσι μετέασιν
ἀριστῆες εὐδικίας ἀνέχοντες ὅθεν δὴ γίνεται πάντα τὰ
καλά. Καὶ τὴν ἀκαδημίαν κοσμήσεις ὥστε κλέος αὐτῆς
εἶναι ὅσόν τ᾽ ἐπικίδναται ἠώς.
10   Ἐμοὶ δὲ σκέλη μὲν καὶ πόδες φύσονται πλείονα ἢ
τῷ Γηρυόνῃ. Τόν τε γὰρ Φιλιστίωνα ἀποπέμψετε καὶ
ἄλλον ὄντινα τρόπον δυνατόν ἐστι τὴν δύναμίν μου
αὐξήσετε. (4) Ἀπόπεμψον δέ μοι μίαν † Μοίριδος καὶ
Ἐχεκράτους πυθόμενος τὰς περὶ Διονυσίου συνουσίας·
15   πάνυ γὰρ ἀξιηκόους αὐτὰς οἴομαι εἶναι ἀνδρὸς Φοίβου
κοινώμασι βλαστόντος.† Ἐπίστελλε δὲ καὶ εἴ που δεῖ
ἐπιμελεῖσθαι τῶν ἐνθάδε ἢ ἰδίᾳ πρὸς τὴν πόλιν ἢ καὶ
εἴ ποθεν ἄλλοθεν συμπαρασκευασάμενος, ὡς ἕτοιμοί
εἰσιν, οἵπερ συναπέστελλον ὑμᾶς. Γίνωσκε δὲ ὅτι
20   πολλοὺς οἶμαι φανεῖσθαι τοὺς ἑτοίμους ὄντας συνεπιμε-
λεῖσθαι τῶν ὑπαρχόντων, ἐάν σοι φαίνηται τὰ παρ᾽ ἡμῶν
κατὰ τὸ προσῆκον ὑφηγούμενα· τὰ δὲ παρ᾽ ἡμῖν ἔχει
παραπλησίως ὥσπερ καὶ ὑμῶν ἐπιδημούντων. Ἔρρωσο.

character or whether you have become pompous and self-willed in your relationship with us because the children in the streets talk about you, as do Polyxenus while sitting on the ferry-boat and the shepherds in the mountains. Is this the character that is youthful and to be desired? Certainly not! But now you must demonstrate that the best men among the Greeks strive to maintain justice from which all good things come. And you will adorn the Academy so that its fame spreads as far as the morning light reaches.

My legs and feet have grown larger than those of Geryon. Send Philistion and strengthen me in whatever other manner you can. (4) Send me one...inquiring from Moeris and Echecrates about their association with Dionysius, for I certainly think that they are worth hearing on it--a man springing from a union with Phoebus! When those men who joined in sending you are ready, write whether I should take care of matters here privately or whether you have helped in providing for the city from some other quarter. You should know that in my view many will show themselves prepared to join in caring for your possessions if the precepts we laid down should appear appropriate to you. Conditions here are in much the same state as when you were home. Farewell.

34.

(1) Βούλομαί σοι μετὰ παιδιᾶς παρρησιάσασθαι,
ἐπειδὴ καὶ σὺ περὶ ἐμοῦ προεισβέβληκας τῷ τρόπῳ τούτῳ.
λέγω δή σοι εὖ πράττειν, εἰ ἄρα τοῦτό ἐστι τοῦ χαί-
5   ρειν ἄμεινον, ὡς οὐκ ἔστιν, ἀλλὰ τοῦ μὲν ἥδεσθαι ᾧ
Λασθενία καὶ Σπεύσιππος χρῆται, αἴτιος τοῦ εἰς Σικελίαν στόλου ὁμολογῶν εἶναι καὶ πλείονας τοῦ Γηρυόνου
χεῖρας καὶ πόδας ἔξων, μᾶλλον δὲ τοῦ Βριάρεω, ἐάν σοι
Φιλιστίων ὁ ἰατρὸς ἀφίκηταί τε καὶ τὰ ἄλλα ὅσα ἐπὶ τῷ
10   γαρότᾳ, περὶ οὗ σὺ εὐμαρῶς ἅτε σοφὸς ὢν ἐξηπατήθης
ὡς ἔγωγε ὠνόμασα, ἅτε γὰρ οἶμαι ἐν τῷ ἥπατι τῆς
Ἑλλάδος κατοικοῦντά σε οὐδὲν λεληθέναι.   (2) Συνήδο-
μαι δὲ τοῖς Ἀθηναίοις, εἰ μὴ ἀνάγκη αὐτοῖς ἔσται τὸν
σοφιστὴν σοφὸν καλεῖν μηδὲ τοὺς θεοῖσιν ἐχθροὺς νεκ-
15   ροῖσι δὲ φίλους τιμᾶν μηδὲ τὰ περὶ τοῦ ἀγαθοῦ φενα-
κίσματα θαυμάζειν μηδὲ τὸ ἁμάξιον θεωρεῖν, ἐφ' οὗ σὺ
ἐκπορεύῃ, καὶ εἰ μὴ ἀποπορεύῃ, ὅπως μὴ τὰς θύρας
ἐμπίπρῃς τῶν γειτόνων μηδὲ καταδείξῃς τὴν τῶν σατύρων
σοφίαν, ἣν πρὸς ἐμέ ποτε συμπίνων ἐν Ἰταλίᾳ ἐπηγγέλ-
20   λου, μηδὲ ὅτι δένδρα μὲν ἅπαντά ἐστιν ἕτερον δὲ συκῆ
καὶ μυρρίνη καὶ δάφνη, ἐφ' οἷς μέγα φρονοῦσιν οἱ
τρισάθλιοι.   (3) Ἤδη γὰρ ἐνθουσιάζω τε καὶ ἐπισκοπῶ
τὸ θεῖον ὡς δίκαιον κακὸν ἐπράξατο.   Κέλευσον δέ μοι
Πολύξενόν τε καὶ τοὺς ἑταίρους καὶ τὰ γραΐδια καὶ
25   τοὺς νομεῖς γράψαι τὰς παρ' ἡμῖν συνουσίας· πάνυ γὰρ
οἴομαι αὐτὰς ἀξιηκόους εἶναι ἀνδρὸς Κέκροπος κοινώμασι βλαστόντος ᾧ σὺ οὐχ ὡς πάτριον ἐχαρίσω, ἀλλ' ὡς
μὴ χραίνῃς τὰ ἱερεῖα, παναπόπληκτος ἐγένου νόσων τε
...ἵνα δὲ ἐπίσχῃς τὰ κατ' οἶκον ἐπιστόλια εὐτραπέλως
30   γράφων, οὕνεκεν τοῦ εὐκαταφρονήτου ἀργυριδίου, διόπερ
καὶ ὑμεῖς Ἑρμείαν κολακεύοντες τολμᾶτε θεραπεύειν.
Ἐπὶ δὲ ταῖς παροιμίαις τε καὶ ταῖς παραβολαῖς, αἷς
χαίρετε, τοιοῦτόν τι βούλομαι εἰπεῖν.   Φασὶ γὰρ
Ἴωνάς τινας εἰς Λακεδαίμονα ἀφικομένους ἀσχημονῆσαι

34. (Dionysius to Speusippus)

I want to speak to you boldly in sport, since you
have already made remarks about me in this manner. I use
"Do well" in greeting you, if indeed it is better than
"Joy to you" (which it is not). But it is better than
"Enjoy yourself," which Lasthenia and Speusippus use. He
admits to being responsible for the expedition to Sicily,
and he has larger hands and feet than Geryon, and much
more than Briareus. If Philistion the physician should
come to you...and whatever else in addition to the "garotas," about which you were easily deceived, since you are
a philosopher, to the effect that I was responsible for
the name, for I think that you have not overlooked a
single thing that has settled in the liver of Greece!
(2) I rejoice with the people of Athens, since they no
longer need to call a sophist a philosopher or honor the
enemies of the gods and the friends of the dead or admire
trickery in connection with the good or watch the wagon on
which you go out, and since you do not return lest you
burn down the doors of your neighbors or teach the wisdom
of the satyrs which you proclaimed while drinking with me
in Italy or that all the trees are different, a fig, a
myrtle, a bay-wood, things on which thrice-cursed men have
high thoughts! (3) For already I am inspired and look
upon the divine after it had made an evil man just. But
bid my Polyxenus, the comrades, old women and legislators
to write about their association with us, for I certainly
think that they are worth hearing on it--a man springing
from a union with Cecrops, whom you did not please as your
father. But, that you might not defile the offerings,
completely astounded you became ill...and that you might
stop writing familiar letters so wittily for the sake of
contemptible money, which is also the reason why you so
boldly flatter and pay court to Hermes. I have decided to
say the following in the proverbs and parables in which
you delight. They say that some Ionians came to Sparta

τι τῶν οὐκ ἐννόμων, τοὺς ἐφόρους δὲ καὶ γέροντας
δεινῶς φιλοτιμηθῆναι καὶ ἐξευρεῖν αὐτούς· φοβεῖσθαι
οὖν σφόδρα τοὺς ἁλόντας, ἐπεὶ ἤγοντο εἰς τὴν ἀγοράν,
τοὺς δὲ Λακεδαιμονίους ἀνακηρύξαι ὡδί πως αὐτοῦ·
5   "κέλονται τοὶ ἔφοροι καὶ τοὺς μὲν...ἰατροὺς? ἔτι
πονηροτέρους ἦμεν, καὶ μέχρι μὲν τούτων ἴσασι † τί
ἴσον ἔχοιμεν." Ἐὰν δὲ τὰ ἄλλα σωφρονῇς κἀγώ σοι
συσσωφρονήσω.

35.

10   Ταῦτά ἐστιν ἃ Ἄδραστος παρὰ Κλεινία ἔλαβεν.
ἐμὶν δὲ δοκέει ταῦτα οὐκ ἄξια εἶμεν ὑφ' ἀμέων ὅτῳ
κα τύχῃ ῥιπτεῖσθαι, τοσοῦτον χρόνον φυλαχθέντα ἀμῶν
ἕνεκα. οὐδὲ τῷ ἀλαζόνι εἴκω· ἀλλ' ἐμὶν δοκέει ἐν
δέοντι τυχόντα μὲν ἀνδρὸς νέω καὶ φυλακτικῶ..., ὑπε-
15   ροφθέντα <δὲ> κακὸν ῥάψαι τὸν ὑπεροπτεύσαντα, ὡς διὰ
τὰν δύναμιν μὲν φιλοσοφοῦντα, τῷ πάθει δὲ <μὴ>, μηδὲ
τῷ ἤθει. καὶ ὅστις ἄγαν φαμᾶν καὶ ὀργανικῶν (?) καὶ
ἐνυπνίων, τῶν πάντα πέπτηεν, μεστὸς εἴη, καὶ οὗτος
πραγματωδέστερός κα γένοιτο αὐτὸς αὐτῳ. ὅστις δὲ
20   ποτὶ πάντα φέρεται κοσμηθεὶς ὑπὸ τάξιός τινος τῶν
τοιούτων, ἐννοώτερός κα εἴη τῶ θείω. συνοδὸς δὲ μοι
ἐσσὶ κατὰ φιλοσοφίαν, ὡς οὐκ ἄλλο τι οὐδὲν δεῖ
λέγειν <ἢ> ὅτι ἀσπάζομαί τυ. ἀλλ' ἔρρωσο.

and behaved disgracefully and broke the law. But the
ephors and elders showed remarkable patriotic zeal and
found them out. They were exceedingly afraid as they were
led into the assembly, but the Spartans made the following
proclamation: "The ephors advised that they...are still
worthless physicians, and that until they understand these
matters, we should be somewhat equable." But if you act
with moderation in the other matters, I shall join you in
doing so.

35.

These are the things that Adrastus received from
Clinias. But I do not think that they deserve to be
thrown to whoever happens to be present, for they have
been preserved for our sakes for a long time. I am not
succumbing to arrogance when I say this, but I do think
that at the proper time they could benefit a cautious
young man, but that when they are looked down upon, they
can harm the sorry person who disdains them. Such a man
engages in philosophy because of his intellectual ability,
but does not do so with his emotions and character. And
the person who is overly full of oracles and devices and
dreams, before which everything cowers in fear, will himself become overwrought. But the person who conducts himself in everything by ordering his life to what is pre-
scribed by these teachings, will to a greater degree have
the divine in his mind. But you are my companion in
philosophy, and therefore I need say nothing more than
that I greet you. Farewell.

INDEX OF NAMES

Complete index. Names are given in the form in which they appear in the English translation. References are to page and line of the Greek except when writer and addressee have been conjectured by previous editors.

GREEK INDEX

Select index.　References are to page and line.

ἀβασίλευτος, 116,4

ἀβέβαιος, 114,13; 204,13

ἀγαθός, 62,20.21; 80,15; 86, 1; 156,31; 188,11; 190, 30.31

ἀγαθῶς, 38,13

ἄγαμαι, 94,2; 102,6.10; 136,21

ἀγανακτέω, 240,16.32; 254,10; 284,20

ἀγαπάω, 200,26; 212,6

ἀγελαστέω, 200,14; 204,23

ἀγέλαστος, 200,21

ἀγνοέω, 88,17; 124,14; 138, 18; 196,10; 224,24; 226, 15; 230,13

ἄγνοια, 120,17; 196,24

ἀγορά, 36,12; 96,24; 100,3. 9; 104,9; 122,12; 144,9. 18; 150,3.5; 154,6; 160, 5.26; 202,1; 274,3; 306,3

ἀγοραῖος, 148,16

ἀγράμματος, 120,32

ἀγρός, 62,19.22

ἀγωγή, 186,18; 210,14

ἀγών, 60,11; 132,18; 154,3; 160,2; 192,5; 254,19

ἀγωνίζομαι, 134,19; 254,19; 260,20; 294,22

ἀγωνιστής, 50,3; 82,17

ἀδιαφέρω, 78,10

ἀδικέω, 56,7.12; 122,9; 196, 23; 200,24.31; 248,6; 254,31; 260,21

ἀδικία, 64,18; 206,5.7

ἄδικος, 122,2.4

ἀδοξέω, 246,22

ἀδοξία, 66,11; 136,10

ἄδοξος, 64,2; 66,18.20

ἀδύνατος, 88,6

ἀθάνατος, 256,25

ἄθλιος, 132,23; 234,22; 254,11

ἆθλος, 190,28; 192,1

αἰδέομαι, 220,15; 244,30

αἰδώς, 146,10.14; 282,6

αἵρεσις, 94,3; 298,31

αἱρετός, 56,2.14; 144,3; 152,8; 238,27

αἱρέω, 130,17; 144,9; 232, 8; 234,13; 300,1

αἴσχιστος, 290,32

αἰσχρός, 40,9; 78,6; 102,17; 106,15; 142,17; 144,2; 154,14; 246,28; 292,22

αἰσχρῶς, 106,11; 226,3

αἰσχύνη, 106,20

αἰσχύνω, 112,15.16; 174,17; 212,3.10; 236,11; 252,21; 264,11

αἰτέω, 54,8.12; 66,18.20.21; 68,17; 72,2; 76,3.20; 88, 25.28; 102,16.25; 104,3. 7.9; 174,9

αἰτιάομαι, 120,16; 260,6

ἀκαίριος, 300,11

ἄκαιρος, 88,7

ἀκολουθέω, 92,30; 270,11

ἀκόλουθος, 108,14

ἀκόσμητος, 162,22

ἀκοσμία, 264,10

315

διατρίβω, 70,16; 96,25;
    160,5; 280,4
διαφέρω, 60,3; 140,18.20.29;
    146,18; 168,4; 208,16;
    232,15; 244,18; 272,19;
    296,30
διαφεύγω, 144,9
διαφθείρω, 84,33; 126,24;
    242,13.20
διαφθορά, 128,18
διάφορος, 284,4; 300,3
διαφυλάττω, 170,15
διδάσκω, 56,11; 70,17; 100,
    5.12; 106,19; 130,3; 144,
    20.23; 170,23; 174,3;
    176,16; 190,11; 196,16;
    224,13; 290,12
διδασκαλεῖον, 100,3
διδάσκαλος, 96,20; 144,19;
    254,14
διήγησις, 186,13
δικαιοπραγέω, 56,11; 202,6
δικαιοπραγία, 188,4
δίκαιος, 44,20; 122,4; 200,
    20; 262,25
δικαιοσύνη, 152,26.29; 206,4
δικαίως, 62,4
διορθόω, 278,17
δίψη, 250,11
δοκέω, 54,12; 80,6; 118,
    15.19
δοκιμάζω, 36,25
δόλος, 68,24
δόξα, 48,5; 58,13; 66,10;
    78,12; 96,2; 98,6.10;
    102,11.29; 142,19; 144,8;
    154,26; 168,9; 232,20.27;
    248,7; 268,14; 272,16;
    276,1; 296,10; 298,18
δοξοκοπία, 188,4
δορυφόρος, 126,9
δουλαγωγέω, 212,27
δουλεία, 58,13; 126,16;
    212,10

δουλεύω, 66,11; 78,17; 84,
    29; 98,6; 106,11; 206,
    18; 214,24.25; 258,1
δοῦλος, 42,11; 48,11; 84,
    30; 212,4
δυσάρεστος, 120,21
δυσγένεια, 136,10
δυσελπιστός, 240,29
δυσεξήγητος, 186,4
δυσνόητος, 186,3
δυστυχέω, 88,5
δυσφημός, 152,19
δωρεά, 162,5; 232,10
δωρέομαι, 162,5
δῶρον, 42,6; 46,15; 62,1
ἐγγράφω, 210,11
ἐγκαλέω, 284,30
ἔγκλημα, 192,8
ἐγκρατής, 60,26
ἐγκράτεια, 62,3; 64,22;
    86,1
ἐγκρατῶς, 62,9
ἐθίζομαι, 68,2; 70,24;
    282,6; 300,9
ἔθος, 104,1; 126,28; 158,
    8; 206,13
εἰκάζω, 98,10
εἰκότος, 120,15
εἰρήνη, 58,6; 120,9.24;
    202,7; 204,23
ἐκθεραπεύω, 168,8
ἐκκαθαίρω, 176,14
ἐκκόπτω, 200,26
ἐκουσίως, 56,8
ἐκπονέω, 168,27
ἐκτιμάω, 46,24
ἐκτός, 54,16.17
ἑκών, 108,3; 240,15
ἐλαύνω, 204,25.26; 210,4
ἔλεγχος, 158,16

θεός, 208,3.5; 210,22; 212,
    2.7.17.19; 214,10.16;
    218,12; 222,7.14.19.20.
    23; 224,13; 226,11; 230,
    5; 234,5; 244,29; 256,4.
    26; 262,25; 276,23; 280,
    17; 296,19.23; 304,14

θεοφίλητος, 300,24

θεοφορέομαι, 208,1

θεραπεία, 162,9; 198,19;
    242,5

θεραπεύω, 138,18; 196,11.21;
    212,20; 238,30; 248,19;
    304,31

θεωρία, 186,6

θηρίον, 168,15; 202,26;
    276,18

θλίβομαι, 88,10

θράσος, 252,18

θρασύς, 192,21

θρεπτέον, 178,2

θυμός, 44,20

θύω, 76,6.7

ἰάομαι, 180,26; 194,11;
    196,16.20

ἰατρεύω, 180,26; 198,8

ἰατρικός, 184,7

ἰατρός, 36,11; 48,2; 66,15.
    18; 124,6.11.12; 168,8;
    180,4; 196,7; 198,2;
    242,24; 298,21; 306,5

ἰδιοπραγία, 46,5

ἴδιος, 44,8; 46,13; 54,11;
    104,7; 148,25; 210,3;
    240,16; 244,4; 264,7;
    274,28; 276,11; 302,17

ἰδιωτεία, 224,29

ἰδιωτεύω, 82,5

ἰδιώτης, 44,5; 174,12;
    224,26

ἱερόν, 268,3

ἱεροσυλέω, 202,10

ἱλαρός, 300,14

ἵππος, 74,2.3.4.7.8.9

καθαρπίζω, 140,22

καθήκω, 40,3

καιρίως, 188,12

καιρός, 224,2; 300,30

καίω, 124,8

κακία, 62,24; 66,24; 68,28;
    78,17; 120,9; 180,23;
    194,24; 200,15.16.19;
    202,1

κακίζω, 136,22

κακοδαιμονέω, 244,21.22;
    246,15

κακοδαιμονία, 246,5

κακοδαιμονίζω, 118,5

κακοδαίμων, 252,23

κακός, 46,6.17.26; 58,7;
    62,20.21; 86,10; 148,28;
    150,28; 156,32; 170,16.
    17; 176,15

κακουργός, 168,6

καλοκαγαθία, 204,26

καλός, 38,10.12; 48,10; 56,
    6; 60,2.3.4; 62,23; 96,
    20; 106,16; 116,10; 144,
    2; 262,24

καλῶς, 38,24; 40,5.20

καρηκομόω, 112,6

καρτερέω, 136,9

καρτερία, 64,22; 70,17; 80,
    3; 84,33; 160,29; 174,3;
    230,19.20; 268,12

καρτερικός, 68,25

καταβλάπτω, 148,24.32.33;
    150,9

καταγελαστός, 276,1; 292,1

καταγελάω, 220,10

καταγινώσκω, 88,9; 168,22

καταγράφω, 186,12

καταγωνίζομαι, 72,17; 136,1

καταμανθάνω, 292,6

καταμέμφομαι, 36,18; 230,5

χρηματισμός, 232,6

χρήσιμος, 44,6; 258,23;
    298,22

χρῆσις, 232,15

χρησμός, 88,3

χρυσίον, 48,4.5.6

χρυσός, 50,15; 174,18;
    236,20

ψέγω, 36,8; 260,6

ψευδής, 144,8

ψεύδομαι, 190,26; 196,25.
    27; 210,25

ψεῦδος, 176,17

ψυχή, 40,13.18; 44,21; 45,
    16; 48,3; 54,14; 62,9.24;
    80,14; 84,18; 108,12.17;
    118,20.24; 120,4; 126,13;
    136,9; 164,3.13.19.25;
    166,2.3.8; 176,6.15;
    180,3; 188,15; 194,6.17.
    27; 208,22; 214,6; 234,
    32; 238,16.30; 256,25;
    258,2.3.23; 276,14; 280,
    19

ψῦχος, 150,29.33

ὦ, 126,22; 128,4.28; 132,23;
    136,21; 140,14; 148,9;
    150,16; 152,23; 190,29;
    256,20; 272,10; 274,25

ὠμότης, 244,26

ὠφέλεια, 62,2; 82,9; 222,24;
    234,25; 236,30.32

ὠφελέω, 80,11; 122,25; 128,
    15; 148,20; 154,33; 162,
    6; 176,3.10; 220,28; 228,
    7; 244,14; 288,36

CORRIGENDA

p. 5, l. 12: III > II.26.1

    H. Temporini > Wolfgang Haase and Hildegard Temporini

    1977 > 1992

p. 17, l. 26: : > ;

p. 27, l. 4: 1969 > 1269

p. 60, l. 6: Πηνελόπη > Πηνελόπη

p. 61, last line: God > the god

p. 69. l. 11: effiminate > effeminate

p. 82, l. 29: ἀνφρώπους > ἀνθρώπους

p. 245, l. 1: Antisthenesto > Antisthenes to

www.ingramcontent.com/pod-product-compliance
Lightning Source LLC
Chambersburg PA
CBHW030638270326
41929CB00007B/119